THE
BIG
BASICS
BOOK OF
THE INTERNET
Second Edition

by Joe Habraken

A Division of Macmillan Computer Publishing
201 W. 103rd Street, Indianapolis, Indiana 46290 USA

International Standard Book Number: 0-7897-1259-8

Library of Congress Catalog Card Number: 97-66491

99 98   8 7 6 5 4 3

Interpretation of the printing code: the rightmost double-digit number is the year of the book's first printing; the rightmost single-digit number is the number of the book's printing. For example, a printing code of 97-1 shows that this copy of the book was printed during the first printing of the book in 1997.

Screen reproductions in this book were created by means of the program Collage Complete from Inner Media, Inc, Hollis, NH.

Printed in the United States of America

Publisher
Roland Elgey

Publishing Manager
Joe Wikert

Editorial Services Director
Elizabeth Keaffaber

Managing Editor
Tom Hayes

Acquisitions Editor
Martha O'Sullivan

Acquisitions Coordinator
Michelle Newcomb

Product Development Specialist
Henly Wolin

Production Editor
Tom Lamoureux

Technical Editors
Coletta Witherspoon
Tony Schafer

Book Designer
Barbara Kordesh

Cover Designer
Jay Corpus

Production Team
Trey Frank
Bill Hartman
Kay Hoskin
Heather Howell
Tony McDonald
Tim Neville
Angela Perry

Indexer
Craig Small

Contents

Part 1 How To...

Connect to Your Service Provider   **63**

Configure Your TCP/IP Software   **81**

Find and Install a Web Browser   **97**

Explore the World Wide Web   **111**

Play Sound and Video Clips with Helper Applications   **129**

Chat with People on the Internet   241

Use Internet Video Conferencing   261

Secure Your System and Practice Proper Netiquette   271

Part 2   Do it Yourself

Part 3   Quick Fixes

Part 4   Handy References

Introduction

You can't avoid the Internet. Every way you turn you are bombarded with information regarding the Net. An ad pops up on your TV screen promising that you can find information about the live-action remake of the Disney classic film *101 Dalmations* at **www.disney.com/101/** (pronounced dubayou-dubayou-dubayou-dot-diznee-dot-kahm-slash-101-slash); the next commercial may even be an advertisement for WebTV, a service that can connect you to the Internet via your television You flip to a page in *Time* magazine and find out that you can write to the editor at **talktotime@time.timeinc.com**. At work, you need additional information about the new copier your company just purchased and the manufacturer's customer service rep tells you to download the information you need from their FTP site. What do these odd bits of text, periods, and strange acronyms stand for? Where can you find out about all this hip '90s technology that's taking the country by storm? Once you find out about it, how can you tap into it and reap its benefits?

Welcome to *The Big Basics Book of the Internet, Second Edition*. This book doesn't assume that you're a computer wiz, a software maven, or even a seasoned programmer. It provides instructions that tell and show you (the average computer user) how to connect to the Internet and make full use of its resources. In this book, you won't find a bunch of cryptic commands you need to memorize. And you won't find long-winded discussions about how the Internet was built and why.

Instead, *The Big Basics Book of the Internet, Second Edition* gives you complete and concise information about the most commonly-used Internet features. It weeds out all the high-tech fluff and offers you the practical instructions you need to survive and succeed on the Internet. Like those illustrated books that teach you how to fix your plumbing or create a quilt, this book provides step-by-step instructions and is thoughtfully illustrated, to both tell and show you how to perform such tasks as:

- Setting up your modem (or using a network connection) to connect to the Internet from Windows 95.

- Using an online service (such as The Microsoft Network or CompuServe) as an easy way into the Internet.

- Finding and setting up a Web browser to make it easy to move around the Internet. (You'll even learn what the Web and Web browsers are.)

- Sending and receiving mail electronically.

- Sharing common interests with other people in newsgroups (using electronic bulletin boards where you can post and read messages).

- Playing movie clips, animations, sound recordings, and other snippets that you will find as you wander the Internet.

- Navigating great interactive content as you peruse sites on the World Wide Web.

- Chatting with other users live using a number of different software venues.

- Finding specific information on the Internet.

- ...and much, much more.

How Can I Find What I Need in this Book?

This *Big Basics Book* has four easy-to-use, distinct parts. Each part focuses on a particular type of information and presents that information in the best format for beginners. You don't need to read the book from cover to cover; you can just skip to the section you need.

Part 1: How To   covers all the tasks that a new or casual Internet-user needs. A brief introduction leads into each task, and complete step-by-step instructions show you just what to do. A clear illustration accompanies almost every step, and cross-references tell you where to look in the book for even more information.

Part 2: Do It Yourself   also offers illustrated steps that explain how to perform specific tasks. However, this part covers practical projects you can use to hone your skills and become more productive on the Internet.

Part 3: Quick Fixes   anticipates the inevitable: It identifies the problems that every Internet user will encounter and offers the simplest solutions for those problems. Scan the Quick Finder Table at the beginning of this section to quickly locate your problem.

Part 4: Handy Reference   is a list of lists, including lists of Internet sites where you can obtain files, chat with complete strangers, and write letters to famous people. You'll also find lists of commands that are just too boring to include anywhere else in the book.

Even if you think using a computer is as fun as having your toenails pulled out, you can learn something from this book. This book makes the computer learning curve as painless as possible, so you can become as confident as the next person (or your kid) when you use your computer. And so, on to the action!

How This Book Is Set Up

This book was specially designed to make it easy to use. Each task has a title that tells you what you'll be doing. Immediately following the title is a Guided Tour, which shows you step-by-step how to perform the task. Additional text tells you why you might want to perform the task and provides details on what to do. The following figure shows you how the pages are layed out.

Running heads help you find what you want to learn (and skip what you don't).

Additional information answers questions you might have.

Tips provide shortcuts or reference other useful material.

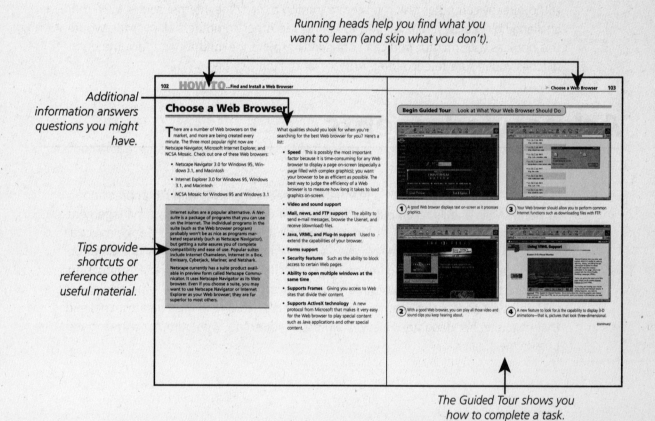

The Guided Tour shows you how to complete a task.

To help you quickly figure out which buttons to press and which commands to enter, this book uses the following standard conventions:

Text you are supposed to type and keyboard keys you have to press appear in bold. For example, if the step says, type **http://www.whitehouse.com** and press **Enter**, you type the text "http://www.whitehouse.com" and press the Enter key on your keyboard.

If you have to press two keys at the same time to execute a command, the key combination appears as **Key1+Key2**, which means you hold down the first key and press the second key. For example, if you're told to press **Ctrl+B**, hold down the Ctrl key while pressing the B key.

Menu names and commands are also bold, so if you're told to open the **File** menu and select **Save**, click File in the menu bar at the top of the window, and then click the Save command.

> Look to these sidebars for tips, hints, references to other sections of the book, and additional information about how to perform a task.

...And Away We Go

Although any computer task can seem daunting at first, the Internet seems even more challenging because it requires you to connect to other computers all over the world. With this book as your mentor, you can confidently explore the Internet and face the minor glitches you're sure to encounter. And so, let the journey begin.

Acknowledgments

Big Books like this are certainly a team effort. Special thanks and much appreciation to Henly Wolin and Tom Lamoureux at Que; their editorial skills, project management abilities, and willingness to burn the midnight oil have truly made this book project a success. Another extremely key player was Coletta Witherspoon, our technical editor. She is incredibly insightful and her breadth of technical knowledge is truly staggering. A sincere thanks also goes out to Martha O'Sullivan, formerly of Que, who selected me to take this wild ride on the Internet; she has moved on to one of life's greatest challenges, that of raising her daughter. Finally, a big thank you to my wife, Kim, for allowing me to pursue my dreams.

Trademarks

Terms suspected of being trademarks or service marks have been appropriately capitalized throughout this book. Que Corporation cannot attest to the accuracy of this information. Use of a term in this book should not be regarded as affecting the validity of any trademark or service mark.

PART 1

How To...

The Internet has been touted as the ultimate tool of the information age—the pinnacle of "let your fingers do the walking." From a computer in your cozy home or office, you can connect to other computers all over the world, shop at electronic malls, view video clips of yet-to-be-released films, listen to music clips, research topics of interest, invest your money, send and receive mail electronically, talk with other people, and even conduct video conference with people most anywhere on the planet.

Before you can take advantage of the Internet and all that it has to offer, you need to acquire and set up the tools required to tap its resources. In this part, you'll learn all you need to know to start: how to set up a modem, subscribe to an Internet service, and set up Windows to establish your Internet connection. You'll also learn how to set up and use the programs you need in order to take full advantage of all the Internet features like a seasoned Internet user.

What You Will Find in This Part

HOW TO...

What Is the Internet?

The Internet is a global collection of high-powered computers that are connected to each other with network cables, telephone cables, microwave dishes, satellites, and every other kind of electronic wizardry currently available. Think of it as an enormous phone system for computers.

As awesome as all this sounds, it really doesn't mean much, until you look at what these interconnected computers can do for you. Each computer on the Internet stores resources, including documents, sound and video clips, program files, electronic shopping centers, animations, pictures, interactive content and anything else that can be stored and presented electronically. When you connect to the Internet, all these resources are available to *you*.

And because any person who is connected to the Internet is connected to you, you can communicate with anyone on the Internet by sending e-mail, posting messages in newsgroups (electronic bulletin boards), chatting in real time in various chat areas, and even telephoning and video-conferencing over the Net.

This section provides an overview of what's available on the Internet and what you can expect when you connect. Simply follow the Guided Tours throughout this section to take a glance at what the Internet has to offer.

What You Will Find in This Section

Find an Entrance Ramp to the Internet

How do you connect to the Internet? That depends a great deal on whether your computer is already connected to a network. If your computer is connected to a network (say, at the place where you work), and if this network is on the Internet, you can usually connect for free by having the person who acts as network administrator set up the connection. Often a business will have its own Internet server—a computer that is charged with the business of connecting to the Internet and holding all of the company's or institution's Internet information, such as a Web page. This means that a connection to the Internet via a business network can provide you with a very fast link (because of high-speed phone lines) to the Net and all its resources.

If you're at home or you work at a place where the computers are not networked, you have to connect via a modem to an Internet Service Provider's computer (ISP). An ISP is a company that allows you to connect to and use its computer to connect to the Internet. First, call an ISP in your area and start an account, which will probably cost about $15 to $25 per month. These providers offer accounts that vary—some may limit the number of hours you can spend on the Internet without paying additional (usually hourly) charges, or they may offer you unlimited access to the Internet (in terms of time) for a flat rate.

The ISP usually gives you the software and instructions you need to connect. This software enables your computer and modem to dial the phone number of the service provider's computer to establish a connection. Once you establish a connection, you can run other programs that make it easy to navigate the Internet.

The next three sections provide detailed instructions on how to find a reliable service provider, set up your modem, and establish your Internet connection for the first time. The following Guided Tour provides an overview of these operations so you'll know what to expect.

Begin Guided Tour Establish an Internet Connection

1 If your computer is on a network that is already connected to the Internet, ask the person who acts as your network administrator to help you establish a connection.

Guided Tour   Establish an Internet Connection

Modem

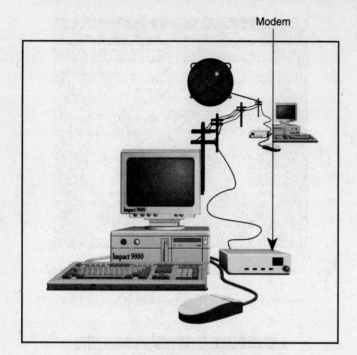

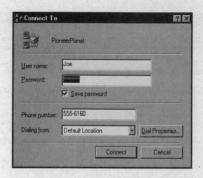

(4) A special computer program tells the modem which phone number to dial and how to establish the connection between your computer and the service provider's computer. "Configure Your TCP/IP Software" on page 81 explains how to connect to the Internet using Windows.

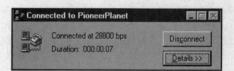

(2) If your computer is not on a network, you need a modem. The modem will dial the phone number and transfer the data between your computer and the Internet. See "Set Up Your Modem in Windows 95" on page 56 to learn how to install a modem.

(5) This specialized program dials and connects to the Internet but does not allow you to do much else. You need additional programs to use the Internet features.

(3) You also need to subscribe to an Internet service provider. The service provider's computer acts as your gateway or onramp to the Internet. Information moves to and from your computer via the provider's computer, which serves as a middleman. The tasks in "Connect to the Internet" (page 27) tell you how to shop for an ISP.

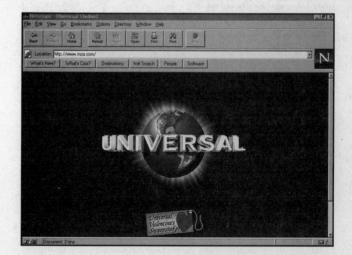

(6) Once you connect your computer to the Internet, you use other programs that bring the Internet to your computer. The Web browser shown here allows you to access the World Wide Web, a graphical part of the Internet. You'll learn all about Web browsers later in this book.

(continues)

Guided Tour   Establish an Internet Connection   *(continued)*

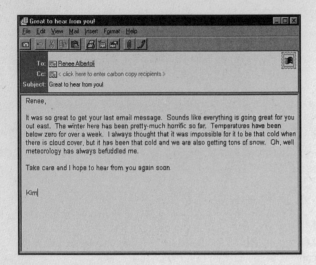

7 E-mail programs such as Microsoft Internet Mail (shown here) allow you to send and receive messages electronically. You can correspond to anyone in the world who is connected to the Internet. To send and receive e-mail, see "Send and Receive Electronic Mail," which begins on page 193.

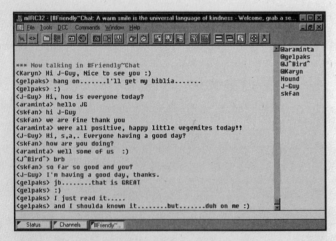

8 Chat programs such as mIRC, an Internet Relay Chat client, (shown here) allow you to carry on conversations with other users. Any message you type appears on the screens of all the other users on the chat channel (often referred to as a "chat room") that you're on. "Chat with People on the Internet" (page 214) tells you how to start.

9 Additional programs, such as the File Transfer Protocol (or FTP) software shown here, help you find the files that you need and copy them from the Internet to your computer.

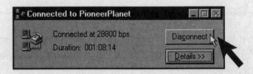

10 When you finish working or playing on the Internet, you hang up, which disconnects your modem and computer from the ISP's computer.

The Graphical World of the World Wide Web

In the early days of the Internet, accessing its numerous resources required the understanding of a command line-oriented computer operating system known as UNIX (pronounced "You-nicks"). You had to memorize a ton of commands to navigate the Net. Although UNIX is still around and you may still run into it if you connect to the Internet via a terminal at a college or university (for more about UNIX see page 25), programmers have developed more user-friendly software avenues to the Internet.

The most popular of these offerings is the World Wide Web (or *Web*, for short). The Web is a collection of interconnected documents stored on computers all over the world. Each Web document might contain text, pictures, animated graphics, and maybe even video and sound. Many sites now include interactive multimedia content ranging from games to educational presentations. You can watch videos on the Web, listen to music, read a book, even shop. The Web offers nearly everything that you could want. It's a flea market of services, goods, ideas, sounds, and images.

In addition, Web documents contain links to other Web documents; it's the links that tie together all the sites that hold these documents. Suppose, for example, that you are reading an article that mentions Oprah Winfrey, and her name appears in blue or is underlined (both of which are common ways to indicate that the text acts as a link to another document). You click the highlighted text, and a page specially devoted to Oprah Winfrey pops up on your screen. This link to a new Web site where the Oprah Winfrey content is held is handled seamlessly by your Web browser.

Links make it easy to wander the Web without really knowing what you're doing or where you're going. You simply click link after link to aimlessly peruse all the documents you find interesting. The following Guided Tour gives you a brief overview of the World Wide Web and shows you what to expect. See "Find and Install a Web Browser" on page 97 to learn how to begin your own wanderings.

> Web browsers have recently become so sophisticated that they enable you to use most Internet features. Netscape Navigator and Microsoft Internet Explorer, two popular Web Browsers, enable you to send and receive mail, download files from the Internet, and even read and post messages in newsgroups (electronic bulletin boards).

Begin Guided Tour   Wander the World Wide Web

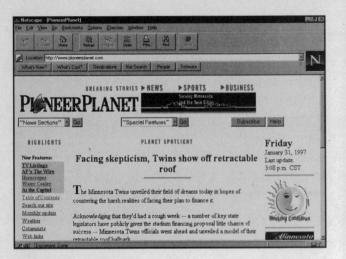

1 To tap into the Web, you need a special program called a Web browser. This program gives the Internet a pretty face and allows you to easily move around the Internet. Netscape Navigator (shown here) is one of the more popular Web browsers.

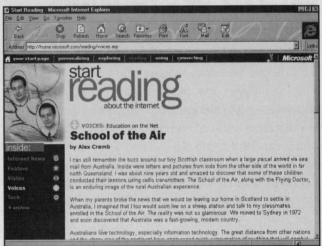

3 In most cases, when you click a link, the Web browser automatically opens and displays the Web page to which the link points.

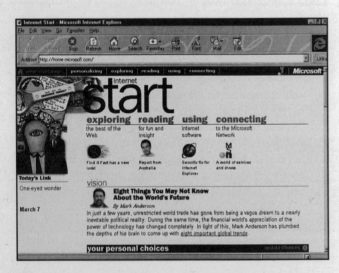

2 When you start the Web browser, it automatically loads a home page (a start page that takes you to a particular site). Often these sites are determined by the service provider that you use. Internet Explorer (shown here) takes you to a start page that you can customize, making your Web browsing easy and efficient. You can click links that bring up other Web documents or help you perform a variety of tasks.

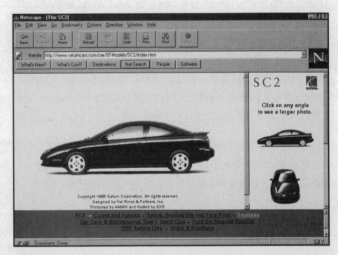

4 Some links point to Web content such as pictures, video and sound clips, or files that the Web browser can "play." Netscape Navigator can display common graphic files like the one shown here (Internet Explorer from Microsoft also has this ability).

Guided Tour   Wander the World Wide Web

5 For files that the Web browser cannot open, you can use special applications that open the files. In this figure, Internet Explorer used ActiveMovie to play a selected video clip. For more information on playing special file types, see "Play Sound and Video Clips with Helper Applications" on page 129 and "Find and Install Browser Plug-ins and Active X Controls" on page 145 for details.

6 Every Web document has a unique address called a *URL* (pronounced "yew-are-ell" and which stands for Uniform Resource Locator). If you know a document's URL, you can type it in the **Location** text box in Netscape (or the Address box in Internet Explorer), press the **Enter** key, and your Web browser opens the document. "Explore the World Wide Web" on page 111 explains how to use URLs to load Web documents.

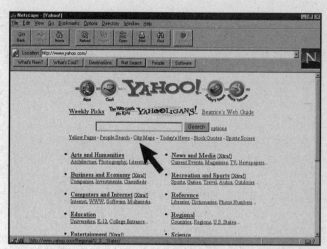

7 The Web has many sites where you can find the link you're looking for. The Yahoo Home Page (shown here) contains links to thousands of documents, grouped by category. "Search for Information on the Web" on page 170 explains this and other available search tools.

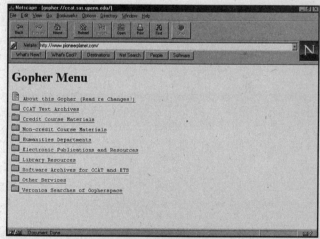

8 Web browsers also enable you to go beyond the Web and use other Internet resources, such as the Gopher menu system shown here.

Search for Information

Sociologists commonly refer to the current era as the "Information Age." When you first hit the Internet, you may find yourself thinking that it's more like the Information Overload Age. You'll find sites that have electronic versions of classic literature, teasers for just about any magazine you can find in print, pages and pages of movie facts and trivia, stock quotes, collections of music, gobs of computer graphics, tons of games and other interactive content, and mountains of additional information. At first, the enormity of the offerings will overwhelm you. And if you need specific information for a project you're working on, you may have trouble finding a place to start.

Fortunately, some companies and institutions on the Internet have built search tools (or *search engines*) that can ferret out the information you need and tell you where to find it. Most of these search tools (Web

Crawler, Lycos, Yahoo!, and Alta Vista) search the Internet on a regular basis to find information that has been added to the Internet since the last search. The tool then creates an index of all the information it finds.

When you connect to an Internet site that is the home of a search tool, you usually will be greeted by a form that asks what you want to search for. You type one or two words in a search box, and then press Enter or click a button to start the search. The search engine displays a list of locations that match your search parameters.

The following Guided Tour shows you some of the more useful search tools in action. In addition, "Explore the World Wide Web" (page 111) provides the locations of popular search tools and gives detailed instructions on how to use them.

Begin Guided Tour   Use Internet Search Tools

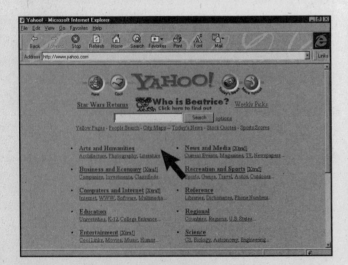

1 The best search tools are available on the World Wide Web. Yahoo!, shown here, provides you with two ways to find information. One way is to click a category to find information by topic.

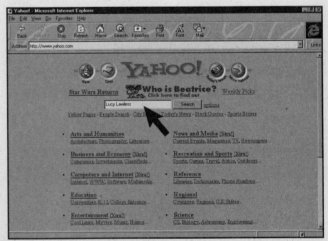

2 At Yahoo!, you can also search for specific information by typing a topic in the text box and clicking the **Search** button.

Guided Tour   Use Internet Search Tools

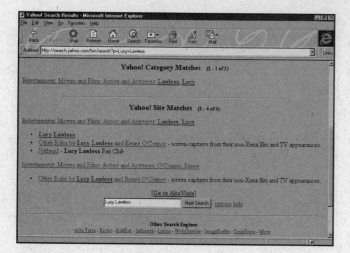

③ When Yahoo! completes its search, it displays a list of Internet sites that might have the information you're looking for. Simply click a link to go to the desired site.

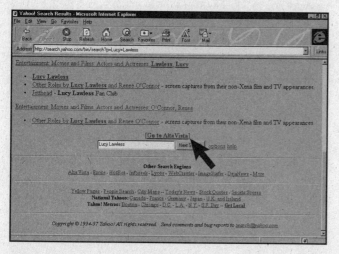

④ Yahoo! also contains links to other Internet search tools. If Yahoo! doesn't find what you're looking for, you can use another search tool by clicking its link. In particular, Yahoo! enables you to redo the search via Alta Vista—a search engine that indexes over 30 million Web pages.

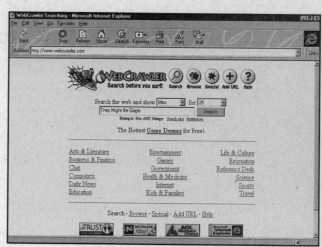

⑤ The popular WebCrawler is a *form-based* search tool. You complete the form by typing one or two words of the topic in which you're interested. Then you click the **Search** button.

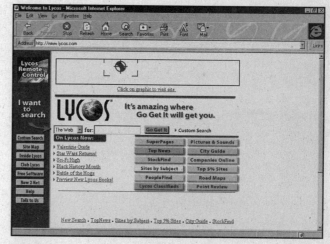

⑥ Lycos is also a form-based search tool. Again, you type a unique word or two, and then send Lycos off on the search. Lycos completes a typical search in seconds.

(continues)

Guided Tour   Use Internet Search Tools

(continued)

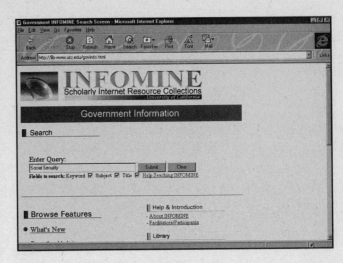

7 HotBot, shown here in Netscape Navigator, is one of the newest Web search engines. This search tool is highly customizable and uses a menu system to aid you in your search.

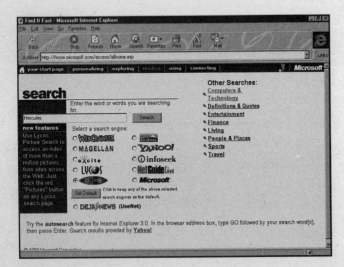

8 Many World Wide Web start pages, such as those provided by Internet Explorer (shown here) and Netscape Navigator, supply you with a search page that allows you to select from a list of search engines as you prepare to search.

You can also run a quick search from most Web browsers by clicking the Search button on the browser toolbar.

9 In some cases, one of the more general search engines such as Web Crawler or Alta Vista may not be able to pinpoint the information that you want. Search tools that maintain databases and information about particular topics make it easy for you to find information on a certain subject. An example is the Infomine at the University of California. It makes it easy for you to search for information on law and the government.

Use Electronic Mail

One of the most often-used features on the Internet is electronic mail (e-mail for short). With e-mail, you can type a message, address it, and send it without ever leaving your keyboard. The mail arrives in the recipient's electronic mailbox usually within seconds (although it can take several minutes). Depending on the reliability of your friend, you can expect a response in a matter of minutes or hours rather than days. The speed at which e-mail reaches the recipient has lead to the creation of a new nickname for the regular mail that we send through the post office—*snail mail*.

When someone sends you an e-mail message, it's stored in your e-mail mailbox (on your service provider's computer). Using a special e-mail program, you connect to your service provider's computer, download your messages, and then read your mail. You can then answer, copy, or foward to the message if necessary.

As you can see, e-mail eliminates the need for postage stamps, and greatly reduces the time it takes to send and receive messages. As long as both you and your fellow correspondent check your mail several times a day, e-mail conversations can eliminate the need to use a mail carrier.

To see how easy it is to send and receive e-mail, take the following Guided Tour. To learn more about e-mail and how to address your e-mail messages, see "Send and Receive Electronic Mail" on page 193.

Begin Guided Tour   Send and Receive Mail

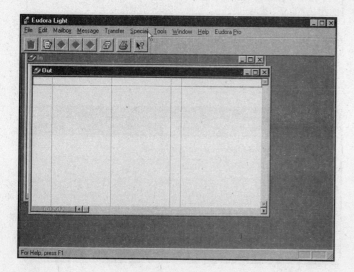

1 One of the most widely-used Internet e-mail programs is Eudora, shown here. A number of other e-mail software packages are in use—such as Microsoft Internet Mail and Netscape Mail.

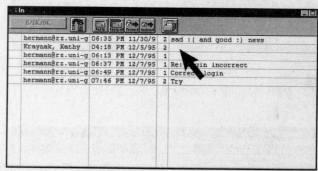

2 After you connect to your service provider's computer, you check your mail. Your e-mail downloads from the provider's mail server to your computer. Eudora displays a list of messages. Double-click the description to read the message's contents.

(continues)

Guided Tour Send and Receive Mail *(continued)*

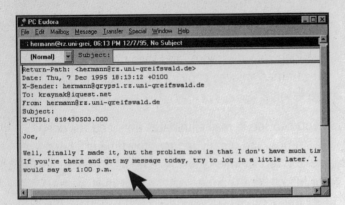

3 The contents of the selected message appear in a separate window, where you can read them.

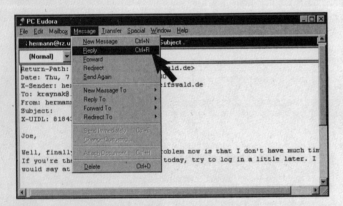

4 You can reply to an e-mail message by selecting the **Message**, **Reply** command.

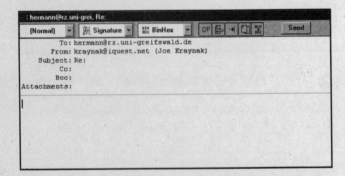

5 When you click **Reply**, a new window appears for your response. Eudora automatically enters the message description and the recipient's e-mail address for you.

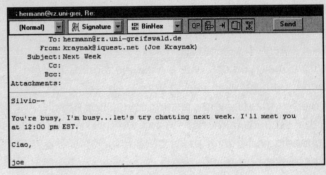

6 You type your message in the area at the bottom of the window.

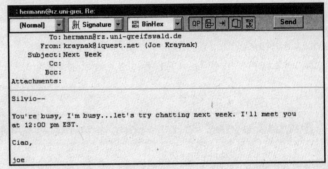

7 You then click the **Send** button to dispatch your missive. Your response should reach the recipient's mailbox in a matter of seconds (although it might take longer).

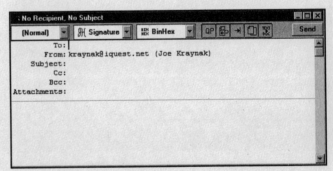

8 When you enter the command to send a new message, a window appears for the message (just as it did for your response). Eudora does not address the message for you.

Guided Tour Send and Receive Mail

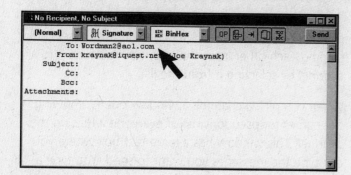

9 You type the person's e-mail address next to **To:**. An e-mail address usually consists of an abbreviated form of the person's name, followed by the at sign (@), followed by the address of the person's service provider.

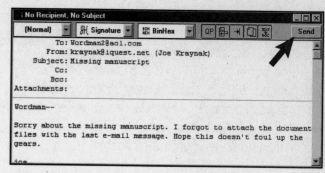

11 You type your message in the blank area at the bottom of the window, and then click the **Send** button.

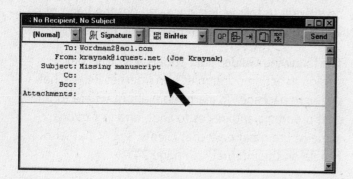

10 You must type a description of the message in the **Subject** line. This description will appear on the recipient's screen when he checks for mail.

Chat with Other People

If you like to talk to complete strangers (commonly known as "netizens") and make new friends, there's no better place to do it than on the Internet. With a chat program, you can carry on conversations with groups of people (or just one or two others) by typing messages back and forth. You even have the option of using an anonymous nickname.

Some chat programs also allow you to represent yourself as a picture or graphic in the chat area. This picture, or *avatar* as it's known, can be of you, your favorite movie star, or any other image. Avatars add a visual aspect to chatting on the Internet.

Here's how it works. You connect to your service provider's computer and fire up your chat program. In the case of Internet Relay Chat, you select an IRC server to connect to. These chat servers usually have more than one hundred channels, each devoted to a different topic of conversation. For example, you might find a channel called Friends where people are talking about the latest episode of *Friends*, or a

channel called Newbies, where new Internet users are helping each other learn the Internet. You tune into a channel by selecting it from the list.

When you pick a channel, a window opens, showing the names (or pseudonyms) of everyone who's on the channel. This window has a large text box where you can type the messages you want to send. You type a message and click the **Send** button or press **Enter**, and your message pops up on your screen and on the screen of everyone on the channel. Likewise, the messages that other people type pop up on your screen. As you can guess, a running conversation can be difficult to follow. But once you get the hang of it, you'll become addicted to the frenetic banter.

The following Guided Tour shows a typical chat session in action using mIRC, an Internet Relay Chat software package. To learn more about where to find chat programs and places to chat, and to explore some of the great new chat clients, see "Chat with People on the Internet" on page 241.

Begin Guided Tour   Chat on the Internet

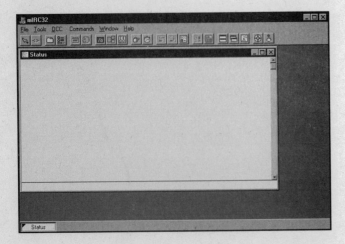

1 The easiest way to chat is to use a special chat program, such as mIRC (Internet Relay Chat).

Guided Tour Chat on the Internet

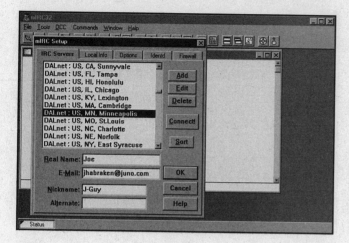

2 First, you select the name of the chat server you want to use. You must also enter information about yourself, such as your name, the nickname you want to use, and (optionally) your e-mail address.

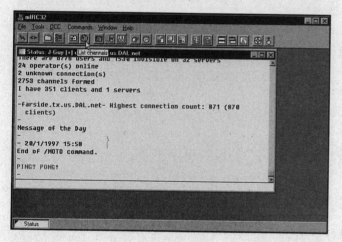

3 Once you enter the appropriate information, you can connect to the chat server. As you can see, not much is going on at this stage, although you are connected to the chat server.

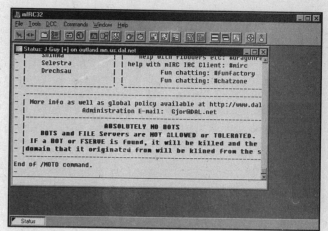

4 In some programs, you must enter a command to access the chat channels, which are the discussion areas for various topics. In mIRC there is a button that lists all the available channels on the server.

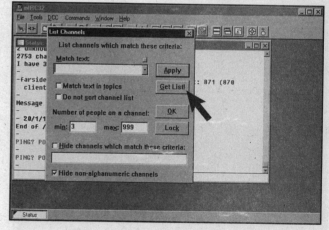

5 A List Channels box appears in mIRC. This allows you to list all the available channels or to search for a channel on a particular subject.

(continues)

Guided Tour Chat on the Internet *(continued)*

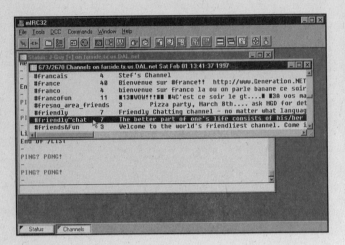

6 Once the list of channels appears, you can scroll through the list and pick the channel you wish to chat on. Each channel represents a different conversation. The channel list usually tells how many people are currently on each channel. Double-click the desired channel to join.

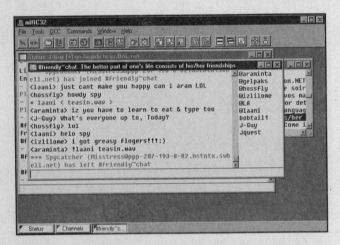

7 In the next window, you can join in the chat discussion. Usually, this window contains the names of all the users on the chat channel and has a place to enter and read messages.

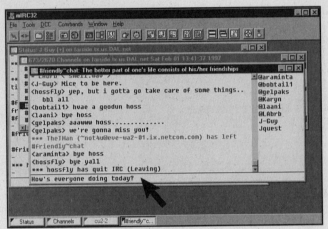

8 You enter your messages in a text box in this window. Type your message into the text box, and then press **Enter** or click a particular button.

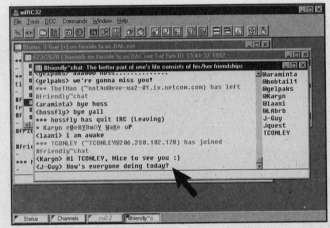

9 The message you enter appears in the discussion window and on the screen of each user who is on the channel.

Transfer Files from the Internet

As you've learned, you need a Web browser to wander the World Wide Web. Similarly, you need an e-mail program to send and receive messages, a Gopher program to display Gopher menus, a chat program to talk with people, perhaps even a video conferencing program to set up that big meeting. Knowing all that, you're probably beginning to wonder where you can purchase all these programs and how much this Internet thing is going to cost. While today's Web browsers can handle many of the tasks you may be involved in on the Net, you still may have the need for additional software.

Fortunately, you can get all of the Internet programs you need from the Internet itself. Freeware or shareware (try before you buy) versions of these programs are stored on computers all across the Internet. You simply connect to a computer that has the program you want, and then you copy it. The program file is copied from the Internet to your hard drive, from which you can then install the program.

You can also copy other types of files from the Internet. For example, you can copy a file that has a list of current chat servers. Or, you can copy sound files, video clips, pictures, games, and many other types of files.

Web browsers have the ability to download files to your computer. You simply go to the home page that has a link to the file you need, click the link, and the file is copied to your computer. A huge number of files can be copied in this way; there is, however, another avenue for the transfer of files called FTP.

FTP stands for File Transfer Protocol, a set of rules and regulations that govern how files are transferred from special repositories of files called FTP servers or sites. With an FTP program, you can connect to an FTP site (a computer on the Internet where files are stored). Many FTP sites allow anonymous file transfers, which means that anyone can connect to the site and copy files. Other FTP sites are for "members only" and require a password to connect.

When you connect to an FTP site, a list of the available directories and files appears. You can move through the directory tree and display lists of files in much the same way you do in the Windows Explorer. You can then copy the file to your computer simply by clicking its name or by copying it from one window to another using your FTP program.

This Guided Tour shows how easy it is to copy files from the Internet using your Web browser and FTP. For more information about how to use your Web browser to transfer files and connect to FTP sites, see "Find and Copy Files from the Internet" on page 179.

Begin Guided Tour   Copy Files Using Your Web Browser and FTP

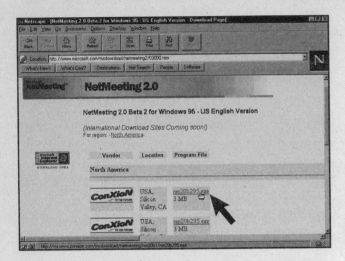

1 The easiest way to copy files from the Internet is to use a Web browser like the one shown here. Click the file that you want to download and the Web browser will start the process. A dialog box will appear and let you know that the file is being downloaded. Just sit back and relax.

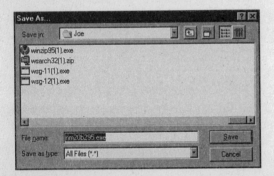

2 You will be asked to either open the file or save it to your hard drive or other storage device on your computer.

To use the Save As dialog box you need to designate a name for the file that you are downloading, as well as a location on your computer, probably a particular folder. The file name is usually provided for you, and since many of these files are executable you should not change the name. To designate a folder on your computer, click the Save In drop-down box and select a location.

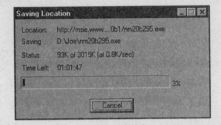

3 Once you designate the place to save the file, the download process begins.

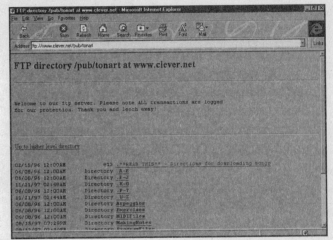

4 Web browsers also have the ability to connect to FTP sites, allowing you to download files using the Transfer File Protocol. When you connect to an FTP site, you see a list of directories and files.

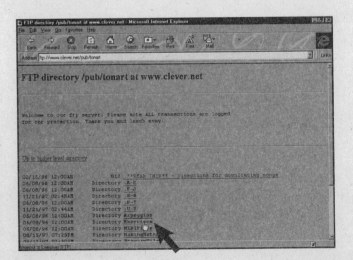

5 To access a particular directory, you click its link.

Guided Tour   Copy Files Using Your Web Browser and FTP

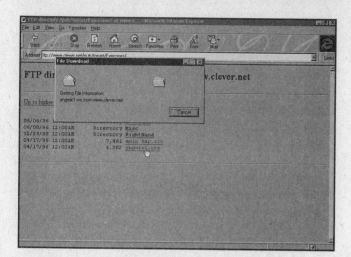

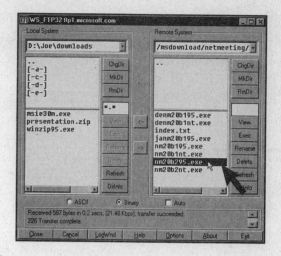

6 To copy a file from the directory to your computer, you click the name of the desired file. Your Web browser will download the file and display a dialog box that asks you where you would like to save the file.

8 To copy a file (or files) to your computer, you first select the file you want to copy from the list of files and directories at the FTP site.

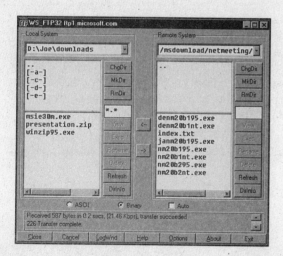

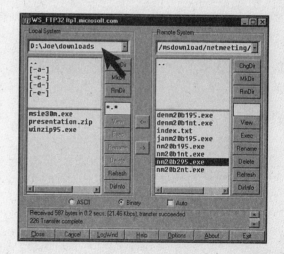

7 Another way to download files is to use a special FTP program. This figure shows the program WS_FTP, which displays two lists: one that shows the contents of your computer, and one that shows the directories and files at the FTP site.

9 Then, in the list that shows the contents of your computer, change to the drive and directory where you want the copies stored.

(continues)

Guided Tour   Copy Files Using Your Web Browser and FTP   *(continued)*

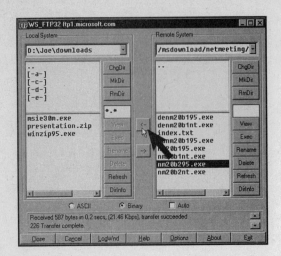

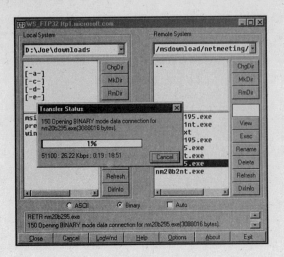

10 Click the **<-** button (the arrow that's pointing toward the contents of your hard drive) to copy the names of the files from the Internet site to the selected folder or directory on your computer.

11 As your FTP program copies the selected file(s) to your computer, it displays a dialog box showing you the progress of the operation.

Many files are stored on the Internet in a compressed form so they take up less storage space and travel more quickly through the phone lines. Before you can use these files, you have to decompress them using a special program. For instructions on how to decompress files, see "Find and Copy Files from the Internet" on page 179.

Telnet to Other Computers

One of the most complex operations you can perform on the Internet is *telnetting* (short for "networking over the telephone"). With a Telnet program, you connect to another computer and use it as if you were sitting at its keyboard. For example, you can connect to the Washington University library's computerized card catalog and use its resources just as if you were sitting in front of a PC at that library.

> If you have Windows 95, you already have a Telnet program. It's called Telnet.exe, and it is in your Windows folder. You can run this program simply by changing to the Windows folder and then double-clicking the **Telnet** icon. However, you must first establish your Internet connection.

Almost every Telnet site greets you with a rudimentary menu system and a set of onscreen instructions that explain how to use the system. Most of the menus you encounter require you to select a menu option by typing the number that appears next to the option. You select a series of options until you find what you need—or until you reach a dead end. The following Guided Tour leads you through a typical Telnet session, giving you a brief introduction to telnetting.

Begin Guided Tour   Use Another Computer with Telnet

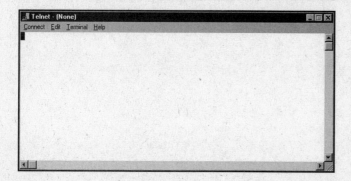

1 A Telnet program allows you to connect to another remote computer and use it just as if you were sitting at its keyboard.

2 When the Telnet program connects your computer to the remote computer, the remote computer usually asks you to enter a username and a password. At Telnet sites that allow anonymous access, you can type **anonymous** as your username and your e-mail address as the password.

(continues)

Guided Tour   Use Another Computer with Telnet *(continued)*

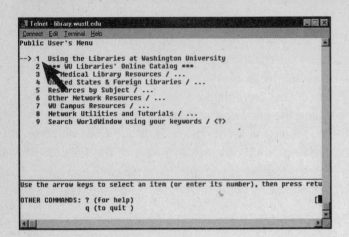

3 The remote computer usually displays a menu system at the top of the window. In most cases, you can select an option from the menu by typing the number that appears next to the option. Some systems have other ways of marking menu options, such as underlining one of the characters in the option's name.

4 Some Telnet sites require that you type commands at a prompt. In such cases, instructions usually appear at the bottom of the screen telling you what to type. If no instructions appear, you can often view a list of commands or instructions by typing **help** or **?** at the prompt and pressing **Enter**.

5 When you first connect, look for the command to exit or quit the Telnet session. If you can't find a command, you can usually exit by typing **q** or **exit** and pressing **Enter**. You should exit the remote computer before you shut down your Telnet program.

Take a Quick Look at UNIX

UNIX (pronounced "You-nicks") comes from the words UNI (single user) and MULTICS (the multi-user operating system on which UNIX is based). Because UNIX enables many users to use one computer and perform several tasks at the same time, it is the primary operating system on many of the computers you will encounter on the Internet. Think of it as the "DOS of networks:" It's the ugly face that stands behind many parts of the Internet and performs the basic operations that enable computers on the Internet to function.

Many colleges and universities still use UNIX to run their large mainframe computers. If you are a student, alumnus, or employee who gets your Internet access through an educational institution, you may have to learn some UNIX to navigate the Net.

Fortunately, you can usually avoid UNIX, just as you can avoid DOS by using Windows. However, you should be aware that UNIX does exist, and you should be able to recognize its ugly countenance when you see it. This information will help keep you from going into shock if you happen upon a UNIX prompt (a bit of confusing text on the screen that signals you to type something). The following Guided Tour gives you a brief glimpse of UNIX, and intends to prepare you for the off-chance that you encounter it.

Begin Guided Tour   Work at a UNIX Prompt

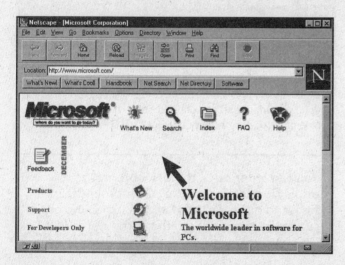

1 As you *surf* (move around) the Internet, you usually encounter screens something like this one. These screens provide a graphical way of touring the Internet.

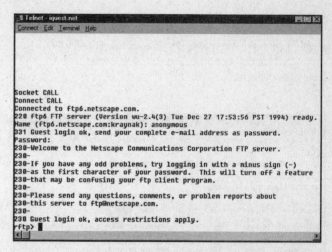

2 On rare occasions, you will happen across a UNIX prompt like the one shown here. In such a case, you have to know which commands to type and how to type them.

(continues)

Guided Tour　Work at a UNIX Prompt

(continued)

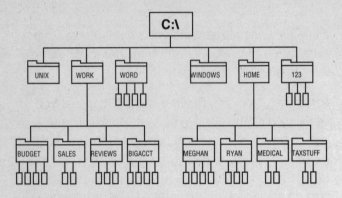

```
C:\
```

UNIX · WORK · WORD · WINDOWS · HOME · 123

BUDGET · SALES · REVIEWS · BIGACCT · MEGHAN · RYAN · MEDICAL · TAXSTUFF

3 UNIX organizes files in directories and subdirectories. So to use UNIX, you need to know how to display directory and subdirectory names, change to a directory, and display the names of the files in the current directory.

```
rftp> ls
```

4 The first command you usually enter is **ls**, which tells UNIX to display a list of the files and directories on the current drive. To enter the command, type **ls** and press **Enter**. (UNIX commands are case-sensitive, and you usually enter them in lowercase characters.)

```
Telnet - iquest.net
Connect  Edit  Terminal  Help
230-Please send any questions, comments, or problem reports about
230-this server to ftp@netscape.com.
230-
230 Guest login ok, access restrictions apply.
rftp> ls
Socket CALL
200 PORT command successful.
150 Opening ASCII mode data connection for /bin/ls.
total 14
dr-xr-xr-x  14 root    sys       512 Dec     :11 .
dr-xr-xr-x  14 root    sys       512 Dec   7  :11 ..
drwxr-xr-x   6 root    sys       512 Nov 23 05:   4 2.0b3
drwxr-xr-x   5 root    sys       512 Nov 23 05:14 2.0beta
drwxr-xr-x   5 root    sys       512 Sep 29 03:04 betas.obsolete
d--x--x--x   2 root    sys       512 Sep 29 03:04 bin
drwxr-xr-x   4 root    sys       512 Sep 29 03:04 collabra
dr-xr-xr-x   2 root    sys       512 Sep 29 03:04 dev
d--x--x--x   2 root    sys       512 Sep 29 03:04 etc
dr-xr-xr-x   2 root    sys       512 Sep 29 03:04 lib
drwxr-xr-x   5 root    sys       512 Sep 29 03:04 netscape
d--xrwx--x   8 root    893       512 Sep 29 03:05 private
dr-xr-xr-x   5 root    sys       512 Dec  5 04:55 pub
dr-xrwxr-x   3 root    893       512 Sep 29 03:05 unsupported
226 Transfer complete.
rftp>
```

5 The list that appears shows both directory and file names. A directory name is preceded by a forward slash (/) instead of the backward slash used in DOS.

```
drwxr-xr-x   5 root    sys       512 Sep 29 03:04 netscape
d--xrwx--x   8 root    893       512 Sep 29 03:05 private
dr-xr-xr-x   5 root    sys       512 Dec  5 04:55 pub
dr-xrwxr-x   3 r       893       512 Sep 29 03:05 unsupported
226 Transfer complete.
rftp> cd /pub
```

6 To change to a directory, type **cd *directory name*** (where *directory name* is the name of the directory you want to change to) and press **Enter**. You can then enter the ls command to view a list of files and subdirectories in that directory.

```
rftp> cd /pub
250 CWD command successful.
rftp> cd ..
250 CWD command successful.
rftp>
```

7 To move back up to the previous directory in the directory tree, type **cd ..** and press **Enter**.

```
250 CWD command successful.
rftp> cd ..
250 CWD command successful.
rftp> exit
```

8 The most important UNIX command you'll learn is the command to exit the system. At the UNIX prompt, try entering **q**, **quit**, or **exit** and pressing **Enter**. If none of those commands work, try pressing **Ctrl+C** or **Ctrl+D**.

You can enter **cal** at the UNIX prompt to display a calendar for the current month. Enter **finger** to display a list of all the users who are currently using UNIX on this computer.

HOW TO...

Prepare to Connect to the Internet

A s with any new adventure, you have to prepare for your Internet journey. You must have the right equipment, a service provider you can dial to connect to the Internet, and the software you need to make the most of your journey.

In this section, you'll find out what you need to venture into the Internet. In case you don't have a modem yet, this section tells you how to shop for a modem that's fast enough to handle Internet connections. And for those of you who have older computers, this section tells what additional equipment you'll need in order to take advantage of all the Internet's features.

You will also learn how to locate an Internet service provider or use your existing online service (such as CompuServe or Prodigy) to connect to the Internet. Using the list of service providers in the Handy Reference section on page 441, you can contact a service provider in your area today and be up and running immediately.

What You Will Find in This Section

Find a Fast Modem

Before you can connect to the Internet, you should make sure you have all the right equipment. Obviously, the first thing you need is a fast modem (or a network connection). If you are going to connect to the Internet through a network at your school or business, you don't need (or want) a modem. The network connection transfers data to your computer more quickly than any modem is capable of.

Those of you who are less fortunate will need the fastest modem you can get your hands on (or afford). As you surf the Internet, you will encounter thousands of multimedia files, including computer graphics, sounds, video clips, and animations. All these files are large, and they take a long time to travel through the phone lines. Therefore, the faster the modem you have, the less time you'll be twiddling your thumbs waiting for data to reach your computer.

Modem speeds are commonly expressed in *bits per second* (bps), where the more bits per second, the faster the modem. Just a couple of years ago 2,400-bps modems were a common commodity among computer users. These modems were used to download files from local bulletin boards and send e-mail. However, a 2,400-bps modem is too slow to handle Internet data transfers, or satisfactorily interface with the highly graphical environment of the World Wide Web. Today, a 2,400-bps modem would be useful only for e-mail.

Modem technology has improved a great deal and most new computers now come with at least a 28.8 bps modem (that's 28,800 bps compared to 2,400-bps—a huge improvement). A 28.8 modem will allow you to surf the Web in style and download files from the Internet without running your connection time into astronomical figures.

New modems that run at a speed of 36.6 bps are now available and modems will soon be available that run at an amazing 56,000 bps. The limiting factor as far as speed is concerned, however, is your phone line. Most current lines can handle transfer rates of only 28.8 even under ideal conditions. Some Internet Service Providers and phone companies are working on boosting their line speeds, which will eventually make the faster 36.6 and 56K modems worth having.

There is a way to greatly increase your speed over a modem by having a special phone line installed in your home called an *ISDN* line. ISDN stands for Integrated Services Digital Network. This type of line can provide connection of 128,000 bps but requires a special ISDN modem. The fee for this type of line can also be high.

The Guided Tour shows you the type of modem you need, provides brief instructions on how to set up a modem in Windows 95, and shows you how to check the speed of your modem.

Speed is the major concern when you're shopping for a modem, but you should also consider other modem features such as whether the modem can handle voice calls, (so you can use your computer as an answering machine), whether the modem can send and receive faxes, and whether the modem is internal or external (whether it sits inside your PC or connects to your PC with a cable).

Begin Guided Tour   Install a Fast Modem

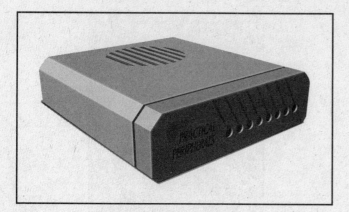

1 If you don't have a modem or a network cable connection, buy a modem that is 28,800 bps or faster. Modems are fairly inexpensive in terms of computer hardware and a good, fast modem will pay for itself in the long run.

2 Follow the instructions that came with the modem to connect it to your computer, or see "Install a Modem" on page 52. Then open the Windows Control Panel.

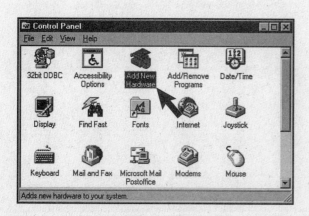

3 Double-click the **Add New Hardware** icon.

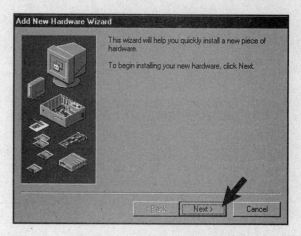

4 The Add New Hardware Wizard leads you step-by-step through the modem installation. Respond to the dialog boxes that appear. See "Set Up Your Modem in Windows 95" (page 56) for details.

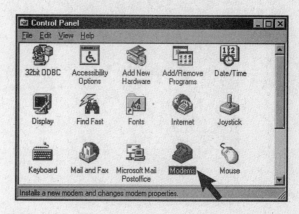

5 If you already have a modem installed but you're not sure how fast it is, open the Windows Control Panel and double-click the **Modems** icon.

(continues)

Guided Tour Install a Fast Modem *(continued)*

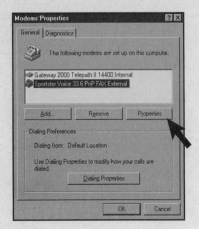

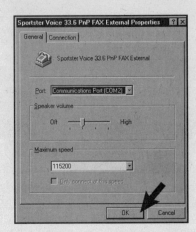

6 A dialog box appears, showing information about your modem. Click the **Properties** button to see how fast your modem is.

8 Click the **OK** button to close the Properties dialog box, and then click the **Close** button to close the Modems Properties dialog box.

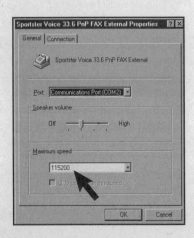

Your modem speed in Windows 3.1 is handled by the software that comes packaged with the modem. When you configure the software and the modem, follow the manufacturer's guidelines for bps settings. Unfortunately, Windows 3.1 does not provide the hardware control for modems that Windows 95 does.

7 The Properties dialog box appears. At the bottom of the dialog box is the maximum speed at which the modem can transfer data. Because most modems use data compression, the speed you see is typically higher than the modem's speed rating.

While you might think that having the modem set at the highest possible speed is the best way to go, there are times when you may want to fine-tune your settings. If you're experiencing a lot of file transfer errors during downloading, you may want to lower the maximum speed to around 57,600. This reduces possible transfer errors by taking into account noise and interference in your phone lines.

Acquire Additional Equipment

Although a network or modem connection is the essential element for connecting to the Internet, you need some high-powered equipment to get the most out of the Internet. For example, if you have anything less than an SVGA (Super Video Graphics Adapter) monitor, you will be sorely disappointed when you try to view pictures on the Internet. And if you want to hear the sounds of the Internet, you'll need a sound card and speakers. You might also need more memory, more disk space and…well, you get the idea.

The Guided Tour leads you through a checklist of things you need in order to take full advantage of the Internet. In addition, the following sections go into more detail about the various types of hardware you'll need.

Make Sure You Have Enough Memory

Most new computers come with 8 or 16 megabytes of RAM (random-access memory), which your programs use to store data while your computer is using that data. Most Internet programs run sufficiently with 8 megabytes. However, if you plan to work with other programs while you're on the Internet, you probably will want to upgrade to 16 megabytes. The general rule in computing is: the more memory the better. The Guided Tour shows how to check your system's memory.

Check the Free Space on Your Hard Disk

Your computer is going to need some free disk space for the Internet. The Internet software you will use can take up several megabytes of disk space. In addition, Windows will undoubtedly use some of your disk space for memory, and some of the graphics and movie clips you will want to copy from the Internet can demand more than a megabyte of disk space apiece.

You should have at least 50 megabytes of free disk space before you begin. (You can find out how much free space your hard disk has by using the Windows Explorer.) Simply run Explorer and then right-click your hard drive. Clicking **Properties** will display a pie-chart that shows how much disk space is still free.

If you're low on disk space, you might consider installing a bigger hard disk or removing some of the programs and files that you no longer use. Whatever you do, be sure to back up all the files on your hard disk before you clean house—just in case you delete something by mistake.

In Windows 95, you can usually reclaim a great deal of hard disk space by emptying the Windows Recycle Bin. Before you do this, however, make sure you won't need any of the files it contains. To empty the Bin, double-click the **Recycle Bin** icon, open the **File** menu, and select **Empty Recycle Bin**. Another place where you may end up with files that you don't need is your Windows/temp directory. Old Windows temporary files (.tmp) can build up there and waste disk space. Some programs that you install also leave items in the temp directory. Check this directory periodically and delete old .tmp and unneeded files.

Wire Your Computer for Sound

The Internet has become alive with sound via the World Wide Web. Sound files can be found and played in a variety of formats that provide you everything from an audio clip of a popular song, to a sound bite from the evening news, to a real-time sound link that allows you to listen to an entire radio broadcast. For instance, the Real Player from RealAudio allows you to listen to recorded and live audio broadcasts that can be accessed on a number of Web pages. National Public Radio maintains a page that allows you to listen to excerpts from such popular radio programs as *Morning Edition* and *All Things Considered*. The MSNBC news site (a cooperative effort between Microsoft and NBC news) provides access to sound clips from current news stories.

The Internet has become sound-intensive. Video conferencing and phone calls over the Internet have also become a reality. You can now listen to the Internet as well as look at it.

To take advantage of the use of sound on the Internet, you must equip your computer with a sound card and speakers—and don't go cheap. Purchase a 16-bit sound card with a couple of good speakers. A 16-bit sound card can play stereo recordings; an 8-bit sound card can't. You may also want to invest in a sound card that provides full duplex. This makes it

easier to send and receive voice information over the Internet. An inexpensive microphone (which comes standard with some computers and sound cards) will also broaden your capabilities in relation to voice communication on the Net.

Video on Your Computer

You can also go one step beyond sound and set your computer to send and receive video. This technology is really starting to take off, and there are some good bargains as far as hardware is concerned. You can follow one of two routes: You can install a video capture board in your computer and then attach a digital camera or a video camera that you already own; or you can buy a digital camera that hooks to the parallel port of your computer, making it unnecessary to add another internal device to your computer. Image quality varies greatly among the different cameras. However, the less expensive parallel port cameras that come in color and black and white offer a surprisingly clear image.

Begin Guided Tour Make Sure Your Computer Is Internet-Ready

 To view graphics on the Internet, you need an SVGA monitor and video adapter that can display at least 256 colors.

Guided Tour Make Sure Your Computer Is Internet-Ready

2 Even if you have an SVGA monitor, it might not be set to a high-resolution. In Windows 95, you can find out about resolution by checking your monitor's properties. Right-click a blank area of the Windows desktop, and a shortcut menu appears. Click **Properties**.

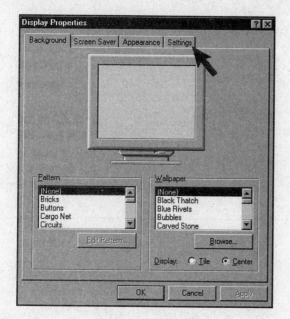

3 You can use the options in the Display Properties dialog box to turn the screen saver on or off, change the Windows colors, and check your monitor setup. Click the Settings tab.

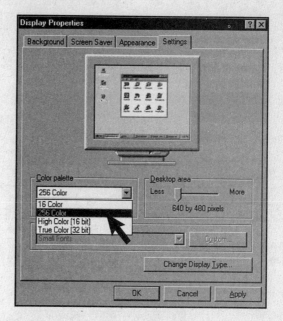

4 The Color palette setting should be 256 or more. If the setting is lower than that, click the button to the right of the text box, and then click **256**. If there isn't a setting of 256 or higher, check your monitor's documentation to learn how to change the setting.

In Windows 3.1, you can check your monitor settings by opening the **Main** group window and double-clicking the **Windows Setup** icon. The Windows Setup dialog box shows whether your monitor is set to VGA or SVGA. If the monitor is set to SVGA, open the **Options** menu and select **Change System Settings**. Open the **Display** drop-down list, and click the correct display type for your monitor. Then, click **OK**.

(continues)

Guided Tour Make Sure Your Computer Is Internet-Ready *(continued)*

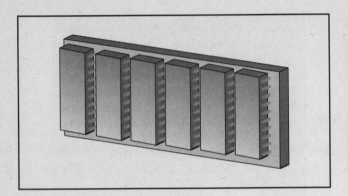

5 Your computer uses RAM to temporarily store the data it is processing. RAM consists of electronic chips like the one shown in this figure. Your computer should have at least 8 megabytes of RAM. If you have 16 megabytes of RAM, you are even further ahead of the game.

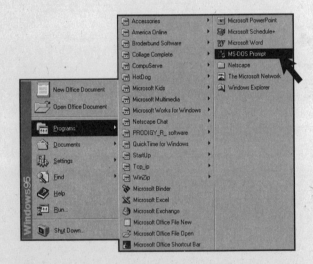

6 You can check the amount of memory from the DOS prompt. To go to the DOS prompt in Windows 95, open the **Start** menu, point to **Programs**, and click **MS-DOS Prompt**. In Windows 3.1, double-click the **MS-DOS Prompt** icon in the **Main** program group window.

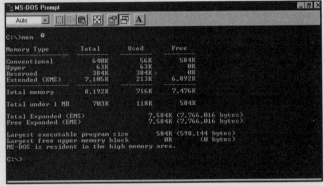

7 At the DOS prompt, type **mem** and press **Enter**. DOS displays your computer's total amount of memory.

Another option to check the memory in Windows 95 is to go to the Control Panel and choose **System**. Then click the **Performance** tab. Or right-click the **My Computer** icon, select **Properties** from the menu, then click the **Performance** tab.

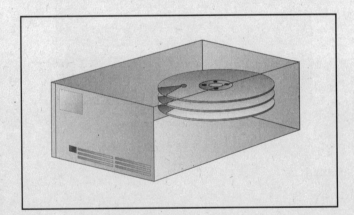

8 Your hard disk stores program files and data files. If your hard disk has fewer than 50 megabytes of free space, you might run into problems when you install an Internet program or copy *(download)* files from the Internet.

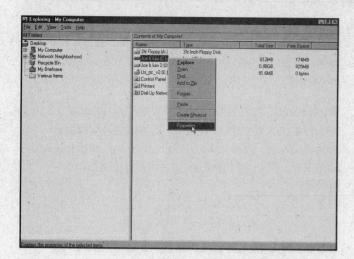

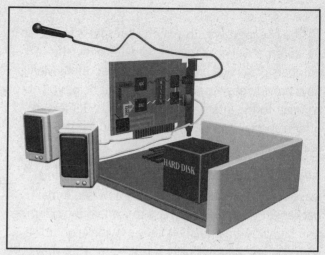

9 In Windows 95, you can check the amount of free disk space in the Windows Explorer; right-click the drive you want to check for free space and select **Properties** on the shortcut menu.

11 Many Internet sites have sound recordings that you can play. Although you can enjoy the Internet without listening to sounds, a stereo sound card, speakers, and a microphone will greatly enhance your Internet experience.

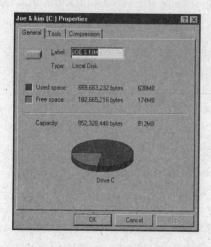

10 A graph appears showing how much free space is still available on the drive.

Find a Service Provider

The cheapest way to surf the Internet is to use an Internet Service Provider (ISP). Recently, the numbers of service providers has skyrocketed. Many now provide easy-to-use software that helps you connect to the Internet via their service. Some also offer a special start page that links you to special features and information.

ISPs get you on the Internet and then pretty much leave it up to you as to what Web browser, e-mail package, or FTP client you use to explore the information highway. In a nutshell, they provide economical connect time and flexibility for the user. They may leave the novice user a little confused, however. The alternative to ISPs are online services such as America Online and CompuServe. These services provide the user an interface that is extremely easy to negotiate. Online services also offer special features that you cannot normally get on the Internet.

The rates charged by Internet service providers and Online services used to vary greatly; now, however, you will find flat rate deals from both of these Internet connection sources. Whether you use an Internet Service Provider or Online service really depends on your own personal preference. Each gives you access to the World Wide Web, e-mail, and the ability to download files.

In addition, a good service provider supplies generic software that's designed to make establishing a connection easy. The sections titled "Connect to Your Service Provider" and "Configure Your TCP/IP Software" outline the steps you need to follow to copy these files from your service provider, to install the files, and to connect to your service provider.

To find a local service provider, you can look in your local Yellow Pages. There will certainly be some listed there. There are also a number of magazines dedicated to the Internet that you can pick up at any newsstand. They will often list service providers in the back of the magazine. You can also flip to the Handy References section on page 441 that lists a number of providers.

Windows 95 also supplies a way to find a local Internet provider. The Internet Connection Wizard provided with Windows 95 software will provide you with a list of local numbers that can get you connected.

What to Look for in a Service Provider

Because there are so many service providers from which to choose, you should do some comparison shopping. Ideally, the service provider you choose will offer the following features:

- **Local access number**   If you have to dial long distance to connect, you're going to end up with a steep long-distance bill in addition to your Internet bill. Of course, if you live in the boonies, you may not be able to avoid long-distance charges.

- **Internet software and instructions** Connecting to the Internet Service Provider for the first time is difficult. The Internet Service Provider should help you set up the connection for free.

- **PPP or SLIP service (preferably PPP)**   PPP stands for Point-to-Point Protocol; SLIP stands for Serial Line Internet Protocol. Both PPP and SLIP enable you to connect directly to the Internet so that you can use programs on your own computer (instead of on the service provider's computer). PPP is the preferred connection type. Avoid anything called "terminal" or "dial-up" service, which gives you an indirect Internet connection.

- **Reasonable startup fee**   Most service providers will not levy a startup fee. They want you to try their service in the hopes that you will become a regular user (and pay your monthly fee on time).

- **Unlimited connect time**   Many service providers charge a flat monthly rate for using the service. Beware of providers who charge by the hour or minute. Some service providers limit you to 100 or 200 hours of use per month, which is plenty.

- **A technical support number**   Occasionally, you might have to call for help. Make sure that the service provider is willing (and able) to give you the support for which you are paying.

Local service providers such as city newspapers and other institutions often offer a glossy connection to the Internet via a special home page. When you connect to the provider's Web site, you are given access to items that normally would be found only on a commercial online service. Choosing the right provider can help you get a real value out of your connection to the Internet.

You'll Need Some Information in Order To Connect

When you call your Internet service provider for the first time, make sure you have the answers to the following questions:

What is your computer type (PC- or Macintosh-compatible)?

What is your operating system (Windows 95, Windows 3.1, or Mac OS)?

What is your modem's speed (in bps)?

What is the COM port used by your modem (COM1, COM2, and so on)? Macs do not have COM ports.

What username and password would you like to use to log on to the service?

COM stands for Communications, and a port is an outlet into which you plug a cable. Modems on most new computers are connected to COM1. Check the documentation that came with your computer or refer to "Install a Modem" on page 52 to determine which COM port your modem uses. Mac users, make sure your modem is plugged into the modem port of your computer.

When you call, have pen and paper handy. The service provider will give you the information you need to connect: the phone number that your modem must dial, the modem speed setting, and your username and password. (A username is the name assigned to you by your service provider. It usually consists of the first letter of your first name, followed by your last name—such as jsmith.)

The service provider may give you additional information over the phone or may offer to send it to you as e-mail. If you choose to receive the information electronically, you will have to connect to your service provider (using Windows Terminal or HyperTerminal as explained in "Connect to Your Service Provider" on page 63) and check your mail. If you choose to take the information over the phone, work through the following Guided Tour to learn what to write down.

Get the Information You Need to Connect

- **Connection type: SLIP and PPP**   To connect directly to the Internet, you need a SLIP or PPP connection. Circle the type of connection you have.

- **Internet phone number**   The most important piece of information is the number your modem must dial to connect to the service provider's computer. Write the phone number in this blank.

- **Username or User ID**   Although you might get to pick your username or user ID, often the service provider assigns it to you. Whenever you dial into the service, you will be asked to identify yourself. Write this information down so you will have it later.

- **Password**   Don't write down your password here. Instead, write it down on a piece of scrap paper and stick it in your sock drawer (or somewhere else where nobody dares to look). You'll need to enter this password whenever you connect to the service provider's computer.

- **E-mail address**   You'll use your e-mail address to tell other people how to address e-mail to you. You'll also need to enter your e-mail address in your Internet programs. This address consists of your username, followed by the at sign (@), followed by your Internet post office address (for example, **jsmith@pop.iquest.net**).

- **Domain Name Server**   This "address" consists of four numbers separated by periods (such as **012.345.678.9111**). A domain name server is a tool that the service provider's computer uses to locate other computers on the Internet.

- **Domain Name**   A domain name identifies each computer on the Internet. Each service provider's computer has a domain name, which might look something like **iquest.com**. Write down the domain name of your service provider's computer.

- **IP address**   IP stands for *Internet Protocol*, a system that governs the transfer of data over the Internet. If your service provider assigns your computer a specific IP address, write it down. Some service providers automatically assign an IP address when you connect to the service.

- **News server**   In the section titled, "Read and Post Messages in Newsgroups" on page 219, you will learn how to read and post messages in newsgroups (Internet bulletin boards). To do this, you need to know the name of your service provider's news server. This name usually looks something like **news.iquest.com**.

- **Mail server**   In the section titled, "Send and Receive Electronic Mail" on page 193, you will learn how to send and receive e-mail. All mail must pass through your service provider's mail server. Write down the mail server's name for future reference. Mail server names usually look like **mailhost.PioneerPlanet.infi.net or pop.mcp.com**.

Use Your Office or School Network Connection

Most people connect to the Internet using a modem. However, if you are a college student, or if you work at a company where the computers are networked, it's likely that the network is already connected to the Internet. In fact, the computer you use at work or school may already be set up to connect to the Internet.

In some school settings, you may have to deal with UNIX to connect to the Internet. See "Use a UNIX Menu System" on page 68 for more information on dealing with UNIX.

This type of connection (a direct network connection) is the best type of Internet connection you can have. Instead of using a modem to transfer data across the Internet, a network uses high-speed cables. Because of this, you get an almost immediate response to any request for data. Web pages pop up on your screen almost immediately, and your computer is rarely disconnected by a glitch in the phone lines.

If the network you're on is not connected to the Internet, there's not much you can do about it.

A *network administrator* is in charge of setting up and maintaining the network. You have to go through that person in order to establish your Internet connection. The network administrator takes care of signing you up, setting up your software, and teaching you the one or two steps you need to take to connect to the Internet.

> Don't attempt to set up a direct network connection by yourself. The network administrator has special training and knows the network settings you must enter to connect. If you enter the wrong settings, you risk fouling up the network and making the administrator's job more difficult.

Because the steps you take depend on how your network administrator has set up your system, no Guided Tour can show you how to do it. Check with your network administrator to determine how your system is set up, and be sure to ask which software you need to use to access the Internet.

Use America Online's Internet Connection

In the past, the simplest way to get on the Internet was through the use of commercial online services such as Prodigy, America Online, the Microsoft Network, or CompuServe. For a monthly charge (and usually some connect time charges that are levied per hour-of-use), the online service provides you with all you need to start, including the following:

- **The program you need to connect to the service**   This program will dial into the service, connect, and provide a screen that lets you explore the service and access the Internet.

- **Easy setup**   The online service provides a disk that comes with a setup program. You simply run the setup program and follow the on-screen instructions. The program sets up your modem, helps you pick a local number to dial, and gets you up and running in no time.

- **A local service number**   If you live in or near a major city, you can dial a local number to connect, thereby avoiding long-distance charges.

- **A free trial membership**   All of the online services mentioned here provide a trial period of free membership (up to 50 free hours!). If you want to stop using the service, you simply call them and cancel your account.

However, the influx of new, "customer-oriented" service providers has blurred the lines about the best way to connect to the Internet. Online services provide a great deal of hand-holding, but many of the larger service providers also provide good customer service. Commercial sites can charge a monthly fee and additional connect time, which would cost more than a flat fee offered by a service provider.

Some questions that you may want to ask yourself and your potential Online service or Internet Service Provider as you choose your connection to the Internet are as follows:

☐ Yes ☐ No   Do I want to take the Internet connection for a test-drive during a free trial period?

☐ Yes ☐ No   Do I want an easy-to-use interface that gives me a great deal of assistance in finding information, sending e-mail, and interacting with other users?

☐ Yes ☐ No   Do I want access to special content areas that are not provided with a regular Internet connection?

☐ Yes ☐ No   Do I want a connection that is easy to apply parental controls to?

☐ Yes ☐ No   Do I want to download my own software such as Web browsers and e-mail clients from the Internet and have greater flexibility in choosing the software that I use?

☐ Yes ☐ No   Do I want a service that provides local news and information?

☐ Yes ☐ No   Do I want easy access to local phone numbers for my connection?

☐ Yes ☐ No   Do I want a flat rate that provides me with unlimited connect time to the Internet?

If you answer "yes" to the first four questions, an Online service may be best for you. A "yes" to the last four questions probably makes you a good candidate for a local service provider.

However, the flat rate connection can now be found with some of the Online services. You will find that the strengths of Online services are the ease-of-use and additional content that they provide. The Strengths of a local Internet Service Provider can include good pricing, no problem connecting at peak hours, and access to local news and information. Whichever route you go, you will find that the Internet is really an incredible avenue to a virtual world of facts and fun.

You can find free offers for most online services in computer magazines. Or, call one of the following toll-free numbers:
Prodigy: 1-800-PRODIGY
CompuServe: 1-800-487-0588
America Online: 1-800-827-6364
Microsoft Network: 1-800-FREE-MSN
Take as many free offers as you can find, and try out the different services. You'll learn a great deal for free. Just be sure to cancel the service at the end of the trial period.

Begin Guided Tour   Connect to the Internet with America Online

America Online has recently released updates of their interface software. Version 3.0 is the current version and exists in a special Windows 95 edition. The Windows 95 version of the America Online software allows you to use Microsoft's Internet Explorer 3.0 as your Web browser.

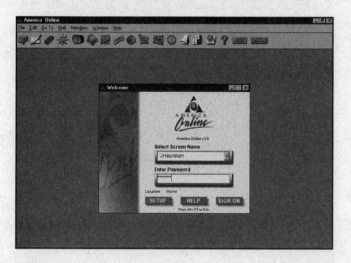

1 Connect to America Online as you normally do.

2 Minimize the Welcome screen, so that you can see the Channels screen.

3 The Channels screen has a button called Internet Connection. Click the **Internet Connection** button to view a list of Internet features.

(continues)

Guided Tour   Connect to the Internet with America Online   *(continued)*

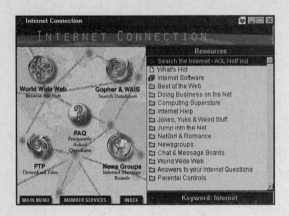

4 The Internet Connection appears, displaying links to the various Internet features. To wander the World Wide Web (as an example), click the **World Wide Web** icon.

You can also go directly to the Web via the AOL toolbar. Click the Internet button (the globe) to open the Web browser.

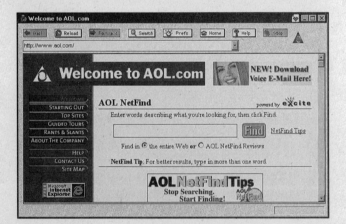

5 America Online has its own Web browser, which allows you to navigate the World Wide Web. Click any available links (buttons or highlighted text) to move around the Web. For more information on how to navigate the Web, see "Explore the World Wide Web" on page 111.

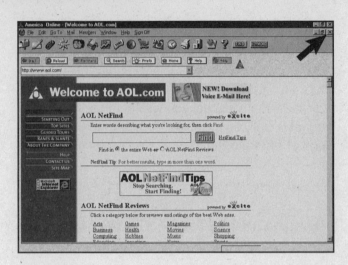

6 When you finish using the Web browser, click its **Close** button.

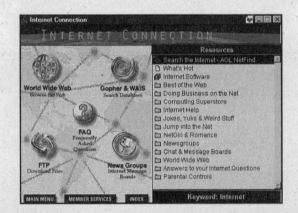

7 America Online closes the browser window and returns you to the Internet Connection window. You can use other icons in this window to explore Gopher, WAIS, or Newsgroups, or to use FTP to copy files from the Internet.

Guided Tour   Connect to the Internet with America Online

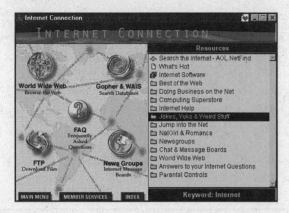

8 The panel on the right provides links to specific, commonly-used Internet features.

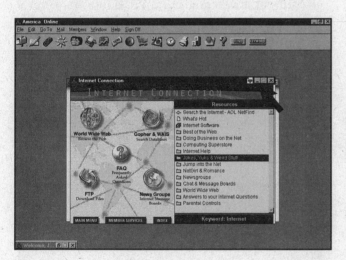

10 Double-click the Internet Explorer icon on the Windows Desktop to start the Web browser.

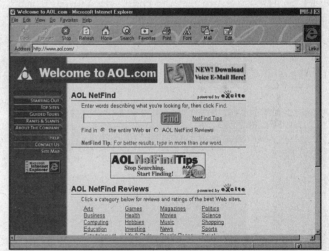

9 You can also use Microsoft Internet Explorer as your Web browser when you use America Online. It comes with the Windows 95 version of the AOL software. Minimize the America Online window by clicking the **Minimize** button.

11 The Web browser opens and goes to the America Online Home Page.

12 When you have completed browsing the Web, close the Internet Explorer software. Make sure that you exit from America Online to close the connection.

Once you log onto the Internet via the America Online software, you can actually use any browser you care to. Minimize the AOL window as you did in the Guided Tour above and then start your favorite Web browser.

Use CompuServe's Internet Connection

Unlike America Online, which requires you to access the Internet just as if you were using an America Online service, CompuServe provides a more direct and faster, Internet connection.

CompuServe has recently streamlined their look and feel and it now sports a simple-to-use interface that offers you several quick ways to access the Internet. When you log onto the CompuServe service, you can start their Web browser (a modified version of Microsoft Internet Explorer) with a quick click a prominent Internet button. You will also find that CompuServe has moved some of its content to Web pages, which you can access once you've opened the CompuServe Web browser.

CompuServe offers all the typical Internet features such as FTP, newsgroups, and chats; you launch these from a special menu that you find on the Start page when you access the Web. CompuServe still bills you for excess hours, and it has not adopted a flat-rate approach like American Online and Prodigy. Make sure that you get version 3.02 of the CompuServe software to take advantage of the new interface and easy Net connectability.

The following Guided Tour shows just how easy it is to connect to the Internet through CompuServe.

> Local Internet service providers have proven to be a real bargain for offering unlimited hours of Internet access at around $20 a month. Online services are now jumping on the bandwagon as well, and America Online, Prodigy, and the Microsoft Network all offer flat rates for unlimited connect time.

Begin Guided Tour Connect to the Internet with CompuServe

1 CompuServe is one of the few online services that requires you to select a feature before you connect. To wander the World Wide Web with CompuServe, click the Internet button.

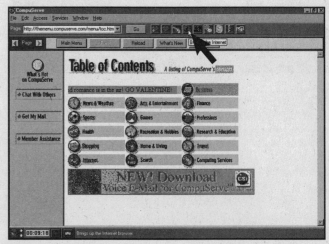

2 You can also go to CompuServe's version of Microsoft Internet Explorer by clicking the **Internet** button on CompuServe's toolbar.

Guided Tour   Connect to the Internet with CompuServe

3 CompuServe's start page provides you with easy access to other Internet features such as Newsgroups and FTP via a series of buttons.

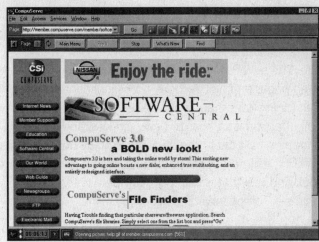

5 CompuServe has also placed some of its own content on the Web and you can use your start page to access their private file library.

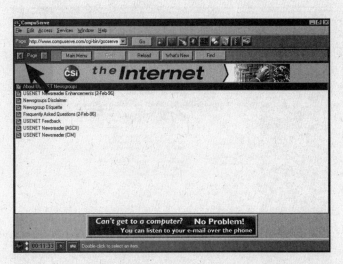

4 After clicking one of the Internet tool buttons such as Newsgroups, you are taken to another page that gives you access to the particular feature you chose. To return to the Start page, click the **Back** button.

6 CompuServe also offers their members a unique opportunity to design their own home page. You can place your own content on the page and even design the way it looks.

Use Prodigy's Internet Connection

Prodigy was originally a typical online service providing a large amount of content on its own site. The new Prodigy has moved all of its content to Web pages and has become more like an Internet Service Provider than an online service. Sure, Prodigy still offers bulletin boards, news services, and online shopping as it did in the past, but Prodigy now prides itself on its Internet access. Prodigy also has a new look and feel that is helping it compete with the giants—CompuServe and America Online.

Prodigy provides you with two choices for viewing its Web content and the rest of the Internet: Netscape Navigator or Microsoft Internet Explorer. Prodigy will mail you a disk that sets you up with an Internet connection and gives you the browser of your choice. If you already have a service provider and want to switch, you can download the Prodigy start-up software directly from Prodigy's Web page **http://www.prodigy.com**.

Accessing the Internet with Prodigy is very simple: Double-click the **Prodigy Internet** icon on the Windows desktop. Once the dial-in procedure is completed, you are taken directly to the World Wide Web and a personalized start page on the Prodigy Web network. From that starting point, you can access Prodigy features on various pages or you can branch out and explore other Web pages by using your browser.

Begin Guided Tour   Connect to the Internet with Prodigy

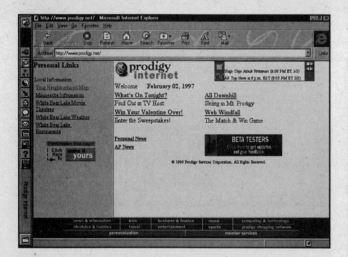

1 After the dial-in is complete (Prodigy remembers your user-name and password, so you do not have to enter these), your Web browser is activated (Internet Explorer is shown here) and you are taken to a special personalized Prodigy start page.

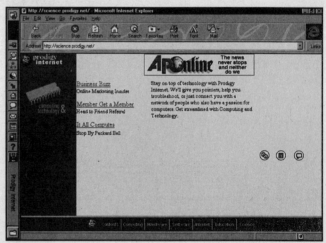

2 You can access Prodigy content from your start page by clicking the appropriate link. Subject areas are listed at the bottom of the page. Computing and Technology is just one of the special content areas that Prodigy offers.

Guided Tour   Connect to the Internet with Prodigy

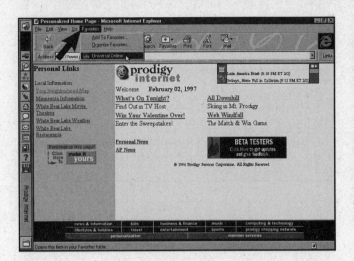

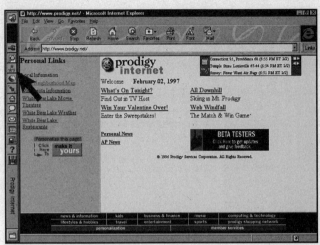

3 Since you are on the World Wide Web, you need only enter an URL in the Browser address box or click one of the favorite sites that you've added to your favorites list to move to a non-Prodigy Internet site.

5 E-mail, newsgroups, and other regular Internet features and some special Prodigy content areas are handled by a special Prodigy Internet toolbar.

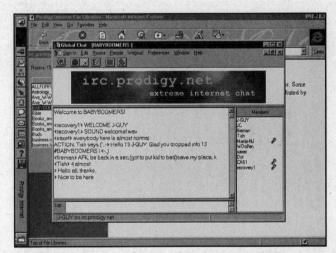

4 When you want to return to your Prodigy start page, click the **Home** button on the Web browser.

6 Prodigy connects you to Internet Chat with a click of the Chat button.

(continues)

Guided Tour Connect to the Internet with Prodigy *(continued)*

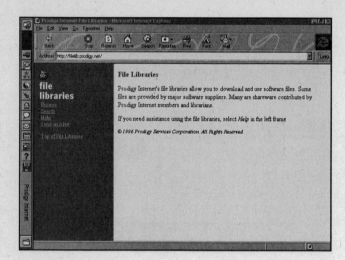

 Click the **File Libraries** button to access Prodigy's file library.

Prodigy uses its Web browser as the sole tool for using the Internet. For example, instead of using a special Gopher or FTP program, Prodigy requires you to access Gopher menus and to download files by using the Web browser.

Use the Microsoft Network's Internet Connection

The Microsoft Network (or MSN for short) is Microsoft's offering in the realm of the online service. With Windows 95, you have the software you need to connect to MSN, along with a free one-month membership. To sign on and start your MSN account, simply double-click the **MSN** icon on your Windows desktop. Then follow the onscreen instructions (and have your credit card handy) to sign on and start using the service.

You can also request a CD-ROM from Microsoft that makes the installation process even easier. It is auto-loading, and it provides you with all the applications you will need to take advantage of MSN's special content.

MSN has followed Prodigy's lead and has all its special content on various Web pages that you can access if you are a member. You also get other standard services such as e-mail, newsgroups, and online chat forums. MSN uses Internet Explorer as its Web browser for accessing MSN content and the rest of the WWW.

Since you are always on the Web when you log on to the MSN as a member, it is very easy to move to your favorite Web sites outside of the MSN pages. Type in the appropriate URL or select one of your non-MSN favorites from your Favorites list.

As with all of the online services, MSN supplies you with a start page on the Web that gives you access to the MSN content. You can also customize this page to include links to other home pages on the Web.

This Guided Tour shows you how to sign on to the Microsoft Network and establish your Internet connection through this new online service. However, the steps may vary slightly depending on the direction that MSN takes by the time you sign on.

Begin Guided Tour   Connect to the Internet Through MSN

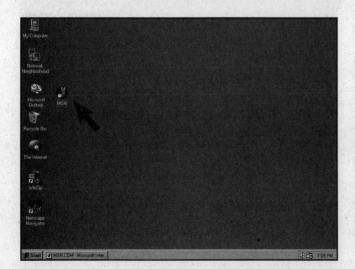

1 After you set up your MSN account, you can sign on at any time by double-clicking the **MSN** icon on your Windows desktop.

2 A dialog box asks you to enter your Member ID and password. Enter the requested information and click the **OK** button.

(continues)

Guided Tour Connect to the Internet Through MSN *(continued)*

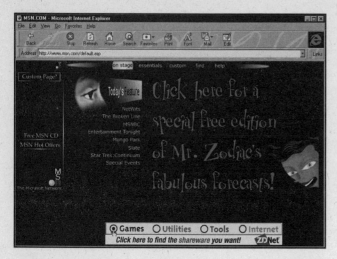

3 When you connect, you are taken to the MSN start page. Microsoft has moved all its content to Web pages, which you can access with Internet Explorer.

4 MSN offers tons of special content such as Expedia, a service that helps you to plan a trip and even lets you book your own airfares over the Web.

As you can see from these Guided Tours of Online services, the general trend is toward moving the service's content onto Web pages, making their operation seamless with the rest of the World Wide Web. This drastic change by the large Online services shows the impact that the Web and the Internet is having on the movement of information around the world.

5 Other special Web sites on the MSN include Microsoft Cinemania Online.

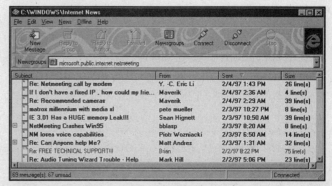

6 MSN offers additional Internet Features such as Newsgroups.

7 MSN also supports Internet e-mail. Microsoft Exchange, a mail and fax package that is installed with Windows 95, can be used as your e-mail client.

HOW TO...

Set Up Your Modem

A modem is a device that changes digital information into analog beeps and buzzes that can be sent over a phone line. At the other end, a receiving modem converts the beeps and buzzes back into digital computer data. A communications program at each end controls the whole exchange.

Some modems directly relay digital information, providing the user with a very fast connection. ISDN modems can transfer digital and analog information over high-speed ISDN lines. However, the expense of ISDN lines and modems makes the connection to the Internet over normal phone lines the only choice for most home computer users.

As you learned in "Prepare to Connect to the Internet" on page 27, you need a modem in order to connect to an Internet site. With your modem, you can travel to the Internet cyberspace where you can jump from one location on the Net to another via various interconnected modems. And with the proper program, you can use your modem to receive (download) files from various Internet sites, called FTP (file transfer protocol) sites.

In this section, you'll learn how to install your modem under Windows 95. If you're a Windows 3.1 user, don't feel left out—there's just not a lot you have to do under Windows 3.1 (after you get the modem physically installed, that is) to get your modem to work. But, not to worry; along the way, you'll see tips for you Windows 3.1 users.

What You Will Find in This Section

Install a Modem

There are two types of modems: internal (which are inside the PC) and external (which connect by a cable to the back of the PC). Of the two, external modems are the easier to install.

Regardless of the type of modem you buy, before you can install it, you have to select the *COM port* the modem will use. You can think of a port in the same way the captain of a ship does—as a place to drop off and pick up supplies. In the case of a PC, a port is where a device such as a modem can drop off or pick up data. In other words, a port is a route through which a device such as a modem communicates with your PC.

Your PC has two kinds of ports: COM ports, also known as serial ports, and parallel ports, which are generally used for printers. When connecting a modem, you'll use one of the COM (serial) ports. Your PC has up to four of these COM ports, but it can use only two of them at any one time.

Your modem uses a COM port. Other devices that might use COM ports (and therefore cause a conflict by using the port your modem wants to use) include a mouse, scanner, or serial printer. (Most printers, however, are parallel, not serial, so this is usually not a problem.)

The COM port setting that a modem uses depends on whether it's an external or internal modem. If your modem is external, its COM port number is based on the external port to which it is connected. For example, if you connect your external modem to the port marked COM1 on the back of your PC, the modem uses the COM port setting "COM1." If you connect the modem to the COM2 port instead (if there is one), the modem uses COM2.

If your modem is internal, its COM port setting is set either with a set of jumpers or DIP switches on the modem card itself, or through special software that came with your modem when you bought it. If your modem uses jumpers, the settings for the various

COM ports are probably printed on the card—so you shouldn't have to hunt down your manual just to set your jumpers.

When selecting a COM port for your modem, keep in mind that even an unused COM port can cause a conflict. How so? Well, most PCs come with at least one, if not two, COM port connectors accessible through the back of the PC. You can identify a COM port by looking at it: A COM (serial) port has pins— exactly 9 or 25 of them—instead of holes. If your PC has a COM1 connector and you insert an internal modem, you must set the modem's COM port to COM2 because even though nothing is cabled to the COM1 connector, the PC considers it "in use." If you want to use two internal serial devices, you can usually disable the COM1 connector (check your PC's manual for details).

> If you use Windows 95, you'll need to perform some extra steps after you install your modem. Be sure to read "Set Up Your Modem in Windows 95" on page 56 for more information.

Before You Install an Internal Modem

Before you can insert your internal modem, you need to make sure that you set it to use the appropriate COM port. Usually you set the COM port by changing some DIP switches or jumpers on the modem card. DIP switches are kind of like light switches: They're either set on or off. By setting these switches to certain positions, you can select the COM port you want to use. Check the manual that came with the modem for details on which switch to change in order to select the COM port you want. If you want to use COM1, you usually don't have to do anything because your modem was probably preset for COM1 when it was shipped. Then, before you touch the modem itself, make sure that you've discharged any static by touching something metal (but do not touch your PC's case—that's not where you want the static to go).

> You can change the COM port settings for some modems using a software program included with the modem instead of a bunch of switches. Check the modem's manual for help.

Setting Communications Parameters

After you install your modem, you'll need to install a communications program, which you use to control each telecommunications session. For general use of your modem, you'll use a program such as Windows 95's HyperTerminal (or Terminal, if you use Windows 3.1), or others such as ProComm Plus or CrossTalk. To connect to the Internet, you'll use TCP/IP software such as Trumpet Winsock or Dial Up Networking. In any case, you'll need to use your particular program to set up your communications parameters before you're ready for business.

> If you plan to connect to the Internet directly through your network, you can forget this nonsense; the network itself handles everything. However, setting up the TCP/IP information in the Networking dialog box of Windows 95 should be configured by your network administrator.

Every telecommunications session has particular parameters under which it operates. There are four basic parameters involved: the speed of the transmission, the number of data bits, the number of stop bits, and the parity. The speed of the transmission is measured by bits per second or *bps* (sometimes called the "baud rate"). Most modems today transmit at a rate of either 28,800 or 14,400 bits per second. The speed of the transmission is determined by the speed of the slowest of the two modems in the connection. For example, if you use a 28,800 bps modem and you connect to the Internet at 14,400 bps, 14,400 bps will be the speed of the transmission.

> The number of data bits and stop bits and the parity of the transmission are used to determine whether the data being sent over the phone line is received correctly. In the past it was necessary that you configured your connection software to the appropriate stop bits and parity. Now online services check the modem as you dial in and set these parameters accordingly.

Begin Guided Tour   Install an Internal Modem

1 Turn off your PC and unplug it from the wall. Then disconnect anything else that plugs into your PC—such as your monitor, modem, or printer. (You'll probably have to unscrew them first.)

Before you touch anything inside your PC, touch a doorknob or something metal to eliminate static electricity. Do not touch the PC's metal case.

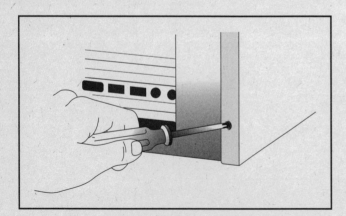

2 Unscrew the PC's cover. Remove the cover by sliding it forward or backward (depending on the cover's design) and then lifting it straight up.

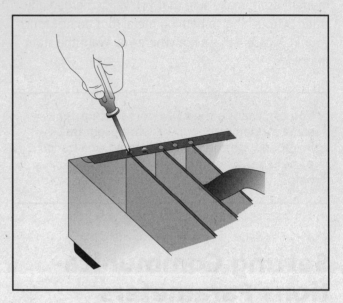

3 Locate an open slot and unscrew the retaining screw holding the slot cover in place. Remove the slot cover. (Don't throw the cover away; if you ever take the modem out, you'll need it.)

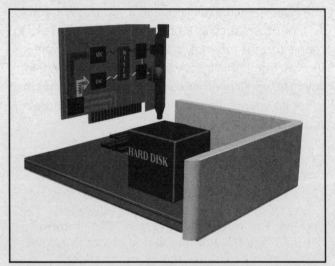

4 Hold the modem at the top with both hands and gently position the edge connectors on the bottom of the card over their slots. Gently rock the card until it slips into place.

Leave the PC open while you test the modem. You can correct problems more easily if you still have access to the modem.

Guided Tour   Install an Internal Modem

(continued)

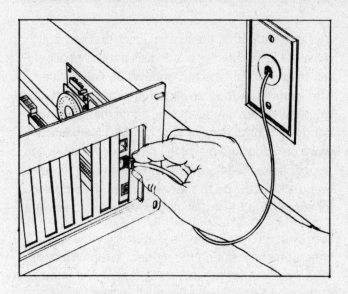

5 On the back of the modem, you'll see two connections. Plug the phone cord into the one marked "To Line" or "To Wall." Plug the other end of the phone cord into a regular telephone jack.

> If you have only one phone line, you must disconnect your phone from the wall and plug it into the connector on the modem marked "To Phone." Then follow step five to connect the modem's phone cord. However, with only one phone line, you can't use the modem and the phone at the same time.

Begin Guided Tour   Install an External Modem

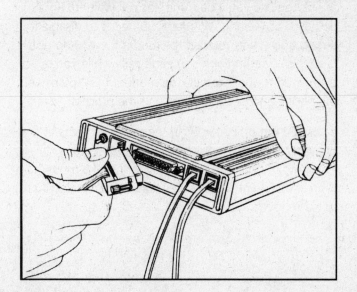

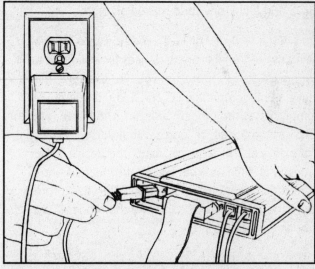

1 Connect the serial cable to the back of the modem. Connect the other end to a serial (COM) port on your PC.

2 Next, plug in the power cable.

3 On the back of the modem, you'll see two telephone jacks. Connect a phone cord to the one marked "To Line" or "To Wall." Then plug the other end of the phone line into a phone jack and turn on your modem.

> If you have only one phone line, you must disconnect your phone from the wall and plug it into the other phone jack on the modem (the one marked "To Phone"). If you do this, you cannot use your phone and the modem at the same time.

Set Up Your Modem in Windows 95

After you install your modem, you need to configure it in order for the modem to work correctly under Windows 95. Thankfully, Windows 95 includes Plug and Play technology that makes this process fairly painless.

Exactly how much Plug and Play (PnP) will do for you depends partly on the type of PC you own. If you bought your PC in 1995 or later, chances are pretty good that it came equipped with a PnP-compatible *BIOS*. The BIOS is a series of chips inside your PC that handle all the input and output of your computer (things such as getting data off the hard disk, sending a document to the printer, and saving a file on a floppy diskette). If your BIOS supports PnP, you're halfway there. The other key to using PnP is that the new device you're installing—in this case, the modem—must be PnP-compatible. You need both a PnP BIOS and a PnP device to make PnP work.

So what exactly is PnP? It's a method through which Windows 95 enables new devices to work in your PC, without a lot of input from you. For example, if you have a PnP-compatible PC and a PnP modem, you simply install the modem and turn the PC on, and the BIOS automatically recognizes that you've installed a new device. The PC then "asks" the device some questions, such as what brand of modem it is and which COM port it's attached to. With this information, the PC can easily configure the modem for use under Windows 95.

Also make sure that the new modem that you purchased is designated as a PnP device; this will allow you to take advantage of Windows 95 PnP abilities. After you install your new internal modem or attach your new external modem, you can either go to the Windows control panel and select **Add New Hardware** or reboot the machine and allow Windows to identify the added hardware. Either of these routes eventually takes you to the same set of dialog boxes for completing the installation of your new hardware.

Even with PnP, you will have to answer some questions. Sometime during the modem setup, Windows 95 will ask you for the area code and phone number of the telephone line your modem will be using. Windows 95 also asks if you need to dial something such as a 9 to get an outside line, and whether or not the phone line you'll be using has call waiting. If you do have call waiting, Windows 95 needs to disable it temporarily when you use the modem; if you do not disable call waiting and someone calls while you're connected to the Internet, the modem tries to answer the phone and disconnects you in the process.

If you did not buy your PC in the past two years, it probably is not PnP-compatible. But don't worry. Windows 95 makes it super-easy to install a modem, even without PnP. Follow the steps in the Guided Tour to learn how.

Begin Guided Tour   Configure Your Modem for Windows 95

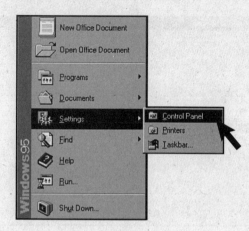

1 Open the **Start** menu, select **Settings**, and select **Control Panel**.

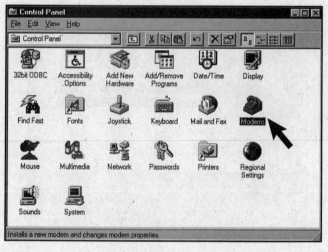

2 Double-click the **Modems** icon. The Modems Properties dialog box appears.

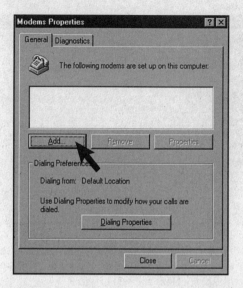

3 Click **Add**.

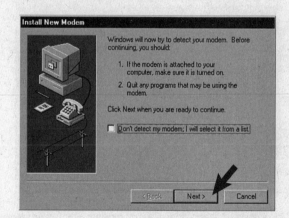

4 Even if you don't have Plug and Play, you should let Windows 95 try to detect your modem. Turn your modem on and click **Next**.

(continues)

Guided Tour Configure Your Modem for Windows 95 *(continued)*

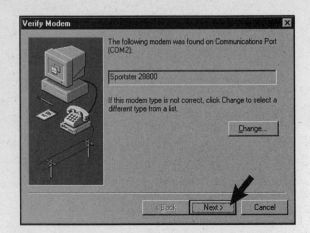

5 In the Verify Modem dialog box, Windows 95 tells you what kind of modem it found. If it identified your modem correctly, click **Next** and skip to step 9.

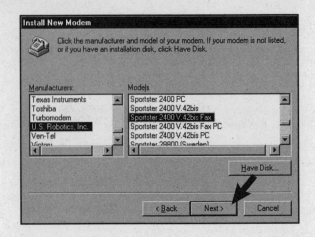

7 Click the brand and model names of your modem. (If the modem came with an installation diskette, insert it and click **Have Disk** instead.) Click **Next**.

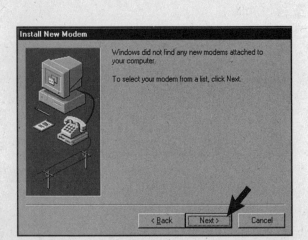

6 If Windows cannot identify your modem, you'll see this message. Click **Next**.

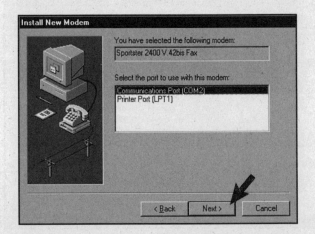

8 Select the COM port you want to use and click **Next**.

Guided Tour   Configure Your Modem for Windows 95

(continued)

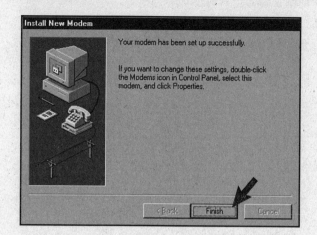

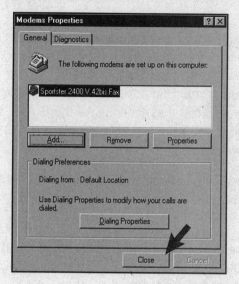

9 In the Install New Modem dialog box, click **Finish**.

10 Click **Close** to return to Windows.

If you want to change any of your choices later (if, for example, you want to change your modem's phone number), just repeat the process and make any necessary changes in the Modems Properties dialog box.

Find Out If Your Modem Works

Now that you've installed your modem, you're probably anxious to see if the thing is working. Some modems come with software you can use to test them. If yours did not and you don't have any other way to test the modem, take this Guided Tour to test it. If you're in Windows, you'll start a DOS window first.

If the test fails, consider each of these problems and try the possible solutions.

- If nothing seems to happen, first make sure that the modem is turned on and plugged in. If you're using an internal modem, try taking it out and reseating it.

- If you know it's on but it still doesn't work, make sure that your modem is connected to a phone jack. If it's a new phone jack and you haven't used it before, you need to make sure that it's working. To test a phone jack, plug a regular phone (not one of those digital read-out things) into it and see if you can hear a dial tone.

> If you can get a digital-only phone to work in the phone jack, don't try to use that particular phone line for your modem. The phone line carries extra digital "stuff" that can interfere with modem communications.

- If you can't hear the modem dialing, check the preferences for your communications program to see if it is turning off your modem's internal speaker (or turning it down so low that you can't hear it).

- If you receive a write fault error when you test the modem using the Guided Tour, your computer is having trouble locating the modem. This usually happens when you select the wrong COM port during installation. Select a different one and try the modem again.

- If you have an older modem and it has a switch that sets the COM port, make sure that switch matches the setting you chose during installation. Check the modem's manual for help. Also, the communications program that you want to use (in this case, the TCP/IP software) needs to use the same COM port that the modem is on or they won't find each other.

- If your modem appears to be working but stops suddenly in the middle of transmission, you probably have a COM port conflict. Try setting the modem to another COM port.

- If the modem doesn't answer at the other end, make sure that the number you're trying to use is a valid one. Dial it using a regular phone to make sure the number is correct. Be sure that the modem is dialing a 9 if necessary to get an outside line. When typing the number, you can enter the 9 followed by a comma, as in "9,5551212"; this tells the modem to pause a second to access the outside line.

- Make sure you've disabled call waiting. The modem will disconnect you if you have call waiting turned on and another call comes in. The best solution is to have separate phone and modem lines. If that's not possible, enter ***70** in front of the phone number you want to call (*70,355-9089). If you use an old-fashioned rotary (pulse) system, enter **1170** instead (1170,355-9089).

- If you're typing a message and you can't see what you're typing on-screen, you need to turn on local echo. To do so, stop your Internet session and choose the appropriate menu command in your TCP/IP program (such as Trumpet Winsock) to turn on local echo.

- If you're seeing double (two of everything you type), change to full duplex and turn off local echo in your TCP/IP program.

- If you can't get the modem to hang up after exiting your TCP/IP program, try turning off your modem if it's external. You can also try unplugging the phone line. As a final resort, restart your PC.

For further help with modem problems, check out the Quick Finder table in Part 3 to quickly locate your problem and find its solution.

Begin Guided Tour   Testing Your Modem

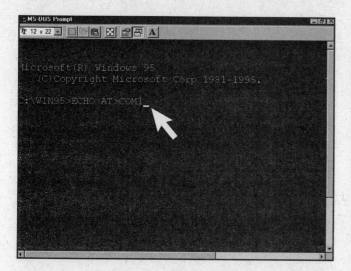

1 Power up the PC. If you have an external modem, turn it on. Open a DOS window and type **ECHO AT>COM1** if your modem is connected to COM1. If you connected your modem to COM2 instead, type **ECHO AT>COM2**. Press **Enter**.

To open a DOS window in Windows 95, click the **Start** button, select **Programs**, then select **MS-DOS** Prompt. To open a DOS window in Windows 3.1, open the **Main** window and double-click the **MS-DOS Prompt** icon.

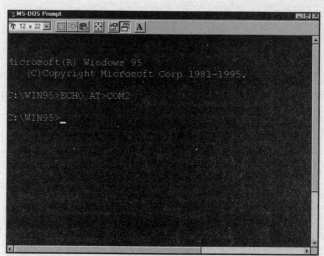

2 If everything works right, you will be returned to a DOS prompt without incident. If you left the PC's case open during the testing phase, go ahead and close it up. You're done.

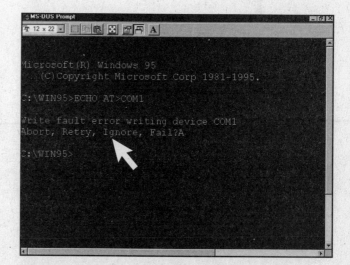

3 If something's not right (if the modem is connected—assigned—to the same COM port as another device, for example), you'll get the error message **Write fault error writing device COM1. Abort, Retry, Ignore, Fail?** Press **A** for abort and check out the text discussion for help determining what's wrong.

HOW TO...

Connect to Your Service Provider

In some cases, your service provider will place the files and instructions you need to start on the provider's computer (called a *server*). You can then use your modem and a telecommunications program (which controls the modem) to connect to the server and copy the files to your computer. This section explains how to do that. After you have the files, you can then go through the steps to become a well-connected citizen of the Internet.

If you've never used a telecommunications program (or you don't even know that you have one), this procedure can be a bit challenging. But don't panic. You'll learn how to use the telecommunications program that comes with Windows 95 to connect to your service provider's computer and get your files.

If your service provider mailed the files and instructions to you, you can skip this section. You can also skip this section if you purchased a special Internet program (such as Internet in a Box) at your local computer store. Such programs usually contain all the tools you need to establish a direct Internet connection without the help of your service provider.

What You Will Find in This Section

Use a Windows Telecommunications Program

If your service provider told you that you have to *download* (copy) the files and instructions from the service provider's computer, you have to connect to the service provider's computer to fetch the files you need. You do this by using a *telecommunications* program. This program tells your modem how to dial and how to transfer data between your computer and the service provider's computer. If you don't have a telecommunications program that you are accustomed to using, you can use HyperTerminal, which comes with Windows 95.

Direct and Indirect Connections

When you connect to the service provider's computer using HyperTerminal, your computer acts as a *terminal* of the service provider's computer and is said to be connected *indirectly* to the Internet. With an indirect (terminal) connection, you type at your keyboard, but your service provider's computer carries out your commands.

With a direct connection, you use programs on your computer to steer your way around the Internet. To use any of the nifty Internet programs you've previewed earlier in this book, you eventually need to establish a direct connection.

So why are you bothering with this indirect connection? Because you'll need some files from your service provider (and possibly from the Internet itself), and the only way to get these files is to use an archaic indirect connection. Be patient—you have to do this only once.

> With a *direct Internet connection*, you run programs on your computer. These programs give the Internet a graphical look and make it easy to navigate. With an *indirect connection*, you use a menu system on the service provider's computer to access the Internet. This menu system can be awkward to use.

Pick a Telecommunications Program

Fortunately, Windows 95 comes with a telecommunications program you can use; it's called HyperTerminal. The Guided Tour shows you how to connect to your service provider's computer with HyperTerminal.

You may also have received a Windows telecommunications program with your modem. It may be better than HyperTerminal, so feel free to use it instead. Note, however, that the steps for using your program will vary from the steps in the Guided Tour.

Begin Guided Tour   Connect Using Windows HyperTerminal

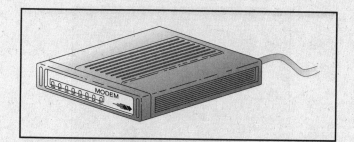

1 If you have an external modem, turn it on. (Internal modems receive power from the power supply in the system unit.)

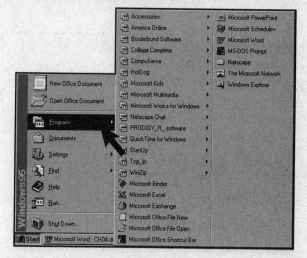

2 In Windows 95, you use the Start button to start all your programs. Click the **Start** button, and then point to **Programs**.

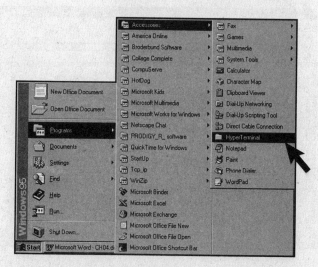

3 The Programs submenu appears, showing icons for programs and program groups. Point to **Accessories**, and then click **HyperTerminal**.

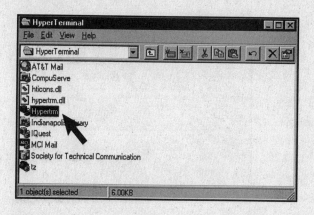

4 The HyperTerminal window appears. You will use this window to create an icon for dialing and connecting to your service provider. Double-click the **Hypertrm** icon.

5 The Connection Description dialog box appears, asking you to type a description for the new connection. This description will appear below the icon you create. Type a name for the connection in the **Name** text box.

6 In the **Icon** box, click the icon you want to use to represent the connection. Then click **OK**.

(continues)

Guided Tour Connect Using Windows HyperTerminal *(continued)*

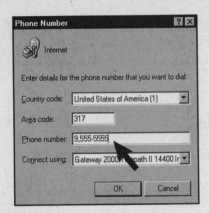

7 Click inside the **Phone number** text box and type the phone number of the service provider's computer. If you must dial a 9 to get an outside line, type **9** and a comma (,) before the phone number (the comma tells the program to pause before dialing the phone number). Don't forget to add 1-800 or an area code (respectively) for toll-free and long-distance calls.

Windows allows you to set dialing preferences for all your modem calls. Open the Control Panel, click **Modems**, and then click the **Dialing Properties** button. Enter the requested information, such as the number to dial for an outside line, before a long distance call, or to disable call waiting.

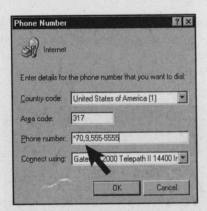

8 If you have call waiting and you get an incoming call while connected, it will automatically disconnect you from your service provider. You should disable it by typing a code in front of the phone number (or before 9,). In most areas, the code is ***70,**. Click **OK**.

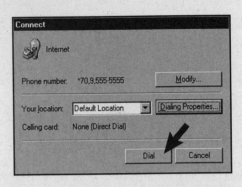

9 The Connect dialog box appears when you're ready to dial your service provider's computer. Click the **Dial** button.

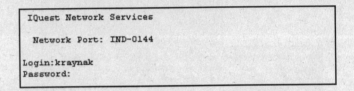

```
IQuest Network Services

  Network Port: IND-0144

Login:kraynak
Password:
```

10 HyperTerminal dials the phone number you entered and connects with your service provider's computer. This computer is set up to ask for your login name (username) and password. Type your login name exactly as your service provider told you to type it (usually in lowercase letters) and press **Enter**.

11 After you enter your login name, the service provider prompts you for your password. Type your password and press **Enter**. When you type, your password may not appear at all, or it may appear as a series of asterisks (********).

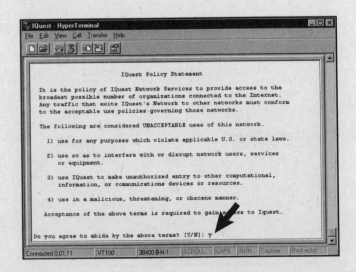

12 Your service provider's computer may display an opening screen asking you to agree to the terms of service. You can move on by typing **Y** for Yes.

Guided Tour Connect Using Windows HyperTerminal

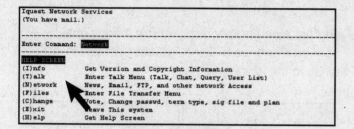

```
Iquest Network Services
(You have mail.)

--------------------------------------------------------
Enter Command: Network
--------------------------------------------------------
HELP SCREEN
(I)nfo          Get Version and Copyright Information
(T)alk          Enter Talk Menu (Talk, Chat, Query, User List)
(N)etwork       News, Email, FTP, and other network Access
(F)iles         Enter File Transfer Menu
(C)hange        Vote, Change passwd, term type, sig file and plan
(E)xit          Leave This system
(H)elp          Get Help Screen
```

13 You should eventually see a menu like the one shown here. If you see a prompt instead, try typing **menu** at the prompt and pressing **Enter**. Skip ahead to the section, "Use a UNIX Menu System," for details on how to proceed.

Use a UNIX Menu System

In certain situations, you may have to navigate a UNIX menu system to connect to your service provider's computer and log in. This menu system allows you to run programs on your service provider's computer to access your e-mail, copy files, and even wander the Web. Compared to other tools you will use to navigate the Internet, this menu is fairly archaic; however, it does give you the basic access you need to start.

All menu systems sport a different look, provide different options, and have their own ways of asking you to select an option. Most menus have a high-lighted or underlined letter that you press (on your keyboard) to select the option. Other menus place a number next to each option, and you press a number to select one. Once you select a command, you press Enter to execute it. Most commands you select open another menu from which you select additional options. Continue to select options until you find what you're looking for.

> When you first encounter the menu, look at the bottom of the screen for instructions that explain how to select and enter commands. In many cases **Ctrl + h** or the command **help** will bring up a help menu that explains some of the Unix commands.

The following Guided Tour takes you on an Internet excursion with a typical UNIX menu. Later in this section, you will use this menu to check your e-mail (for instructions from your service provider) and to copy files from your service provider's computer.

Begin Guided Tour Select Options from a UNIX Menu

1 When you connect to your service provider, you meet a UNIX menu system. In this case, you select an option from the menu by pressing the letter in parentheses. For example, press **N** for (N)etwork.

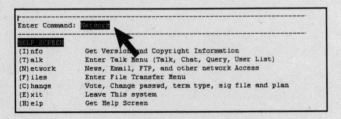

2 Notice that the command line above the menu displays the selected command. To enter the selected command, press **Enter**.

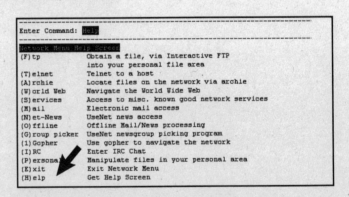

3 Entering the Network command brings up another menu displaying the network options. In this case, most of the network options provide access to the Internet. If your UNIX menu system offers a Help command, execute it now.

Guided Tour   Select Options from a UNIX Menu

```
(F)tp           Obtain a file, via Interactive FTP

This command will allow you to get files from remote systems, via
Unix FTP (File Transfer Protocol).  The files will then be stored in you
personal files area.  You can then download them to your local system by
using the (P)ersonal option below.  FTP is very easy to use, you will be
asked for a hostname.  You can either enter the full domain name or the
address of the site you wish to access.  A domain name looks like
"ftp.iquest.net", and an IP address would be 198.70.36.70.  You will the
be asked for a username and password.  On some systems, you can enter a
name of 'anonymous' and a password of 'username@iquest.net'.  On most
systems, you can abbreviate the password to 'username@' dropping off the
of your local system.  Once your connected, type 'help' and the system w
give you a list of commands.

(T)elnet        Telnet to a host

The Telnet command will allow you to login to a remote system on the
Internet.  Unlike FTP, Telnet allows you to connect to the remote system
a user, and run programs.  Some of the uses are to access other Archie a
--More-- (18%)
```

4 In this case, the Help command brings up a list of the other commands on the menu with a description of each command. If all of the help text does not fit on the screen, an indicator such as "--More--" appears at the bottom of the screen. You can usually move down the page by pressing the **Spacebar**.

```
the file.

(P)ersonal      Manipulate files in your personal area

This is your personal file area.  From this area, you can download
files you FTP'ed or saved from WWW or Gopher.  This is different then th
(F)iles option on the main menu, although it is possible to access your
area from the (F)iles option on the main menu.  You can save NewsGroup e
and Personal mail, and download them from this option.

(E)xit          Exit Network Menu

This option will take you back to the Main Menu.

(H)elp          Get Help Screen

        If you need further assistance, please feel free to send e-mail
        support@iquest.net or call IQuest Network Services at 722-4600.

Press [RETURN] to continue
```

5 When you reach the end of the file, you can go back to the menu by pressing **Enter** (Return).

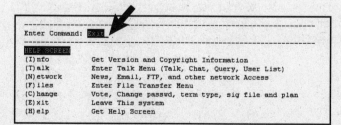

```
--------------------------------------------------
Enter Command: Exit
--------------------------------------------------
HELP SCREEN
(I)nfo          Get Version and Copyright Information
(T)alk          Enter Talk Menu (Talk, Chat, Query, User List)
(N)etwork       News, Email, FTP, and other network Access
(F)iles         Enter File Transfer Menu
(C)hange        Vote, Change passwd, term type, sig file and plan
(E)xit          Leave This system
(H)elp          Get Help Screen
```

6 As you select commands, you move from one menu to another. To back up to a previous menu, enter the Exit command. For example, in the menu system shown here, you would press **E** to select Exit and then press **Enter**.

```
Galaxy Mall The Scene SuperSearcher NanoLinks WWW Services

[IMAGE]

WELCOME TO IQUEST NETWORK SERVICES

 Please select from the icons above or the following menu of choices:

WWW SERVICES AND HOME PAGES - EVERYTHING YOU WANTED TO KNOW ABOUT INTE
AND WWW SERVICES HERE AT IQUEST

GALAXY MALL - BROWSE AND PURCHASE SERVICES AND PRODUCTS AT OUR VARIOUS
CLIENTS SITES

THE SCENE - RELAX AT THE SCENE, THE COOLEST SPOT ON THE WEB FOR ART AN
-- press space for more, use arrow keys to move, '?' for help, 'q' to qu
Arrow keys: Up and Down to move. Right to follow a link; Left to go ba
H)elp O)ptions P)rint G)o M)ain screen Q)uit /=search [delete]=history
```

7 Eventually, a command you enter will take you to a specific service screen. In this figure, the service provider has connected to the World Wide Web. (Notice how different the Web looks when you use a terminal connection; you get no fancy text or pictures.)

8 At the bottom of the screen, there is usually some text that explains the available commands and tells you how to proceed. In this case, you can see more of this Web page by pressing the **Spacebar**.

```
Commands: Use arrow keys to move, '?' for help, 'q' to quit, '<-' to go
Arrow keys: Up and Down to move. Right to follow a link; Left to go ba
```

9 Here's another type of instruction you might find at the bottom of a screen.

```
--------------------------------------------------
Enter Command: Exit
--------------------------------------------------
HELP SCREEN
(I)nfo          Get Version and Copyright Information
(T)alk          Enter Talk Menu (Talk, Chat, Query, User List)
(N)etwork       News, Email, FTP, and other network Access
(F)iles         Enter File Transfer Menu
(C)hange        Vote, Change passwd, term type, sig file and plan
(E)xit          Leave This system
(H)elp          Get Help Screen
```

10 For now, remain connected to your service provider so you can check your e-mail and get your files. However, when you do finish an Internet session, you enter the **Quit** or **Exit** command to return to the opening menu. Then select **Quit** or **Exit** and press **Enter** to log out and disconnect.

Check Your E-Mail

Because connecting to the Internet the first time is somewhat complicated, your Internet service provider will usually send you instructions on how to copy the files you need and install them on your computer. These instructions are probably sitting in your e-mail box.

Your job is to use the service provider's UNIX menu to open and display the e-mail message on screen. The *Guided Tour* shows you how to use a UNIX menu to check for incoming e-mail messages (and how to use Terminal or HyperTerminal to save the messages).

Remember, however, that your UNIX menu might have different e-mail commands and ways of entering those commands.

> Your service provider may send you instructions in a file (usually called README.TXT) instead of by e-mail. To copy this file to your computer, skip ahead to "Retrieve Files from Your Service Provider" on page 72.

Begin Guided Tour   Use Your E-Mail

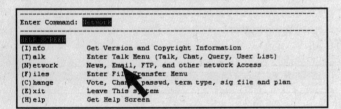

```
Enter Command: Network
-----------------------------------------------------------
HELP SCREEN
(I)nfo          Get Version and Copyright Information
(T)alk          Enter Talk Menu (Talk, Chat, Query, User List)
(N)etwork       News, Email, FTP, and other network Access
(F)iles         Enter File Transfer Menu
(C)hange        Vote, Change passwd, term type, sig file and plan
(E)xit          Leave This system
(H)elp          Get Help Screen
```

1 Connect to your service provider as explained earlier. Then display the opening UNIX menu and look for the E-Mail command. In this example, you must enter the **Network** command to get to the e-mail command.

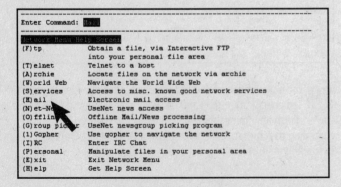

```
Enter Command: Mail
Network Menu Help Screen
(F)tp           Obtain a file, via Interactive FTP
                into your personal file area
(T)elnet        Telnet to a host
(A)rchie        Locate files on the network via archie
(W)orld Web     Navigate the World Wide Web
(S)ervices      Access to misc. known good network services
(M)ail          Electronic mail access
(N)et-News      UseNet news access
(O)ffline       Offline Mail/News processing
(G)roup picker  UseNet newsgroup picking program
(1)Gopher       Use gopher to navigate the network
(I)RC           Enter IRC Chat
(P)ersonal      Manipulate files in your personal area
(E)xit          Exit Network Menu
(H)elp          Get Help Screen
```

2 The Network submenu appears, and you can see the Mail command. Select the **Mail** command and press **Enter**.

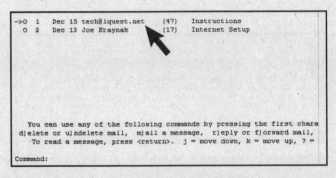

```
->O  1    Dec 15  tech@iquest.net    (47)    Instructions
  O  2    Dec 13  Joe Kraynak        (17)    Internet Setup




   You can use any of the following commands by pressing the first chara
 d)elete or u)ndelete mail,  m)ail a message,  r)eply or f)orward mail,
   To read a message, press <return>.  j = move down, k = move up, ? =
Command:
```

3 The Mail command displays a list of messages you've received. Hopefully, it contains an e-mail message from your service provider. Look at the bottom of the screen for instructions on how to select and display a message.

4 Follow the on-screen instructions to select and display the contents of the e-mail message from your service provider. In the system shown here, you would press **j** to move down to the next message or **k** to move to the previous message, and then press **Enter**.

Guided Tour   Use Your E-Mail

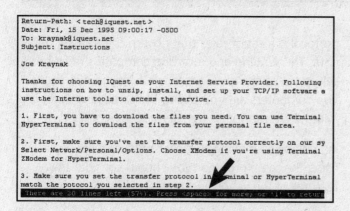

```
Return-Path: <tech@iquest.net>
Date: Fri, 15 Dec 1995 09:00:17 -0500
To: kraynak@iquest.net
Subject: Instructions

Joe Kraynak

Thanks for choosing IQuest as your Internet Service Provider. Following
instructions on how to unzip, install, and set up your TCP/IP software a
use the Internet tools to access the service.

1. First, you have to download the files you need. You can use Terminal
HyperTerminal to download the files from your personal file area.

2. First, make sure you've set the transfer protocol correctly on our sy
Select Network/Personal/Options. Choose XModem if you're using Terminal
ZModem for HyperTerminal.

3. Make sure you set the transfer protocol in  minal or HyperTerminal
match the potocol you selected in step 2.
There are 20 lines left (57%). Press <space> for more, or 'i' to return
```

5 The selected message appears on your screen. If it is long, you may have to press **Spacebar** or **Enter** to display more of the message.

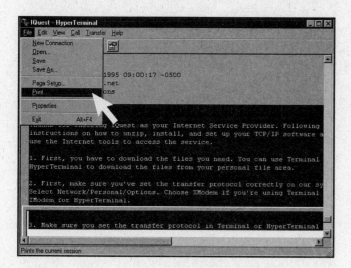

6 After the entire message appears, you can print it. First, drag over the text to select it (otherwise, you'll end up printing all the menus and other text displayed during the session). Then open the **File** menu and select **Print**.

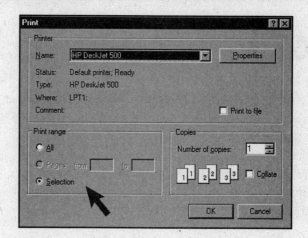

7 Click the **Selection** option button only the text you dragged over. Click **OK**.

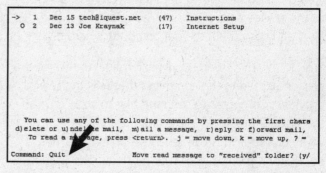

```
->  1   Dec 15 tech@iquest.net    (47)    Instructions
O   2   Dec 13 Joe Kraynak        (17)    Internet Setup




    You can use any of the following commands by pressing the first chara
d)elete or u)ndel  e mail,  m)ail a message,  r)eply or f)orward mail,
    To read a m  age, press <return>.  j = move down, k = move up, ? =

Command: Quit                      Move read message to "received" folder? (y/
```

8 After you print the message, enter the command to quit or exit the e-mail area.

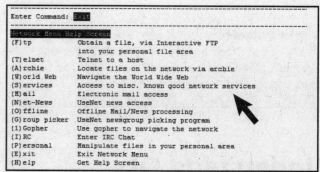

```
Enter Command: Exit

Network Menu Help Screen
(F)tp           Obtain a file, via Interactive FTP
                into your personal file area
(T)elnet        Telnet to a host
(A)rchie        Locate files on the network via archie
(W)orld Web     Navigate the World Wide Web
(S)ervices      Access to misc. known good network services
(M)ail          Electronic mail access
(N)et-News      UseNet news access
(O)ffline       Offline Mail/News processing
(G)roup picker  UseNet newsgroup picking program
(1)Gopher       Use gopher to navigate the network
(I)RC           Enter IRC Chat
(P)ersonal      Manipulate files in your personal area
(E)xit          Exit Network Menu
(H)elp          Get Help Screen
```

9 You return to the menu you were at before you selected the Mail command. For now, stay connected to your Internet service provider so you can copy the files you need (as explained in "Retrieve Files from Your Service Provider," coming up next).

Retrieve Files from Your Service Provider

A good service provider supplies the files you need to connect to the Internet. These files are set up specifically to allow *your* computer and modem to connect to the service provider. The service provider enters such settings as your modem speed, the COM port your modem is plugged into, your username, and your password, so you don't have to configure the programs yourself. Most service providers also give you a Web browser, an e-mail program, and other programs for accessing the Internet.

In most cases, the service provider mails you a disk with the essentials. In some cases, however, the service provider places the files in a special storage area on its computer. To get them, you must connect to the service provider (using HyperTerminal), find the files, and copy them to your computer's hard disk.

You do this by setting up HyperTerminal to receive the files and entering the command that tells the service provider's computer to send the files to you. You can then take a break while the files are transferred to your computer (this can take several minutes, depending on the speed of your modem). The Guided Tour walks you through the process of a typical file transfer.

> Because all service providers do not use the same system for storing files, you must ask where your files are stored. The service provider shown in the Guided Tour places the files in a special file area for each user.

Understand File Transfer Protocols

To ensure that the file is transferred reliably over the phone lines, you must pick a *file transfer protocol*. A protocol is a set of rules that govern the transfer of data. The sending and receiving computers must be set up to use the same protocol. If they're not, the two computers are not talking the same language, and the file cannot be transferred successfully.

In addition to making sure that both systems are using the same protocol, you should consider the features of the various protocols:

- **Xmodem** is an early protocol that is slow by today's standards. It can handle file transfers okay, but it can transfer only one file at a time. If you're using Terminal (Windows 3.1), this is the best protocol available.

- **Ymodem** is a step up from Xmodem. It is slightly faster and slightly better at detecting errors in the transfer, and it allows you to transfer more than one file at a time.

- **Zmodem** is two steps up from Xmodem. It is faster than Ymodem, allows you to transfer more than one file at a time, and recovers well when telephone line noise interrupts a transmission. If you're using HyperTerminal (with Windows 95), this is the protocol to use.

- **Kermit** is an old, slow protocol that's still in use in some educational institutions. Its claim to fame is that it is good at detecting transmission errors.

> The transfer protocol that you use will depend on what your terminal program offers, no matter whether you are using Windows 3.1 or 95 as your operating system. Most terminal software offers Xmodem, Ymodem, and Zmodem. Zmodem is the fastest of these protocols.

Binary or Text File Transfer?

In some cases, you might have to specify the type of file transfer you want to do: binary or text. Binary file transfers are for program files, graphic files, and any other file that's NOT a text file. Text file transfers are for text files only.

For more information about copying files from a remote computer to your computer, see "Find and Copy Files from the Internet," on page 179.

see "Find and Copy Files from the Internet," on page 179.

Begin Guided Tour Download Files with HyperTerminal

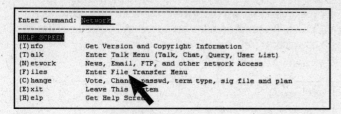

1 Connect to your service provider as explained earlier. Then display the opening UNIX menu and look for the command to access the file transfer area.

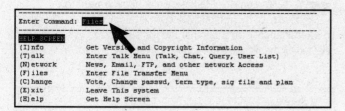

2 When you find the command you're looking for, select it. For example, in this system you would select the **Files** command and press **Enter**. This usually opens another menu that provides more specific options.

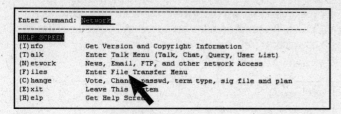

3 Continue to enter menu commands until you reach the file and you see a command that allows you to enter file transfer options or pick a protocol. Select that command (**Options**, for example) and press **Enter**.

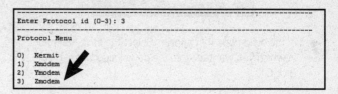

4 A list of available file transfer protocols appears. Select **Zmodem** and press **Enter**. This tells the service provider's computer which protocol to use when communicating with your computer.

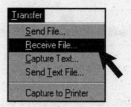

5 Next you must tell HyperTerminal how to receive files. Open the **Transfer** menu and select **Receive File**.

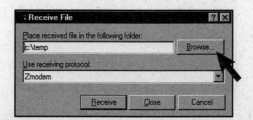

6 The Receive File dialog box asks you where you want the files stored and which protocol to use. Click the **Browse** button to pick a folder in which to save the files.

(continues)

Guided Tour Download Files with HyperTerminal *(continued)*

7 In the dialog box that appears, select the drive and folder in which you want to store the downloaded files. Then click **OK**.

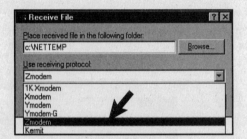

8 Back in the Receive File dialog box, you're ready to pick a protocol (which must be the same protocol you selected in step 4). Open the **Use receiving protocol** drop-down list and click **ZModem**.

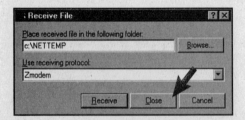

9 Click the **Close** button to close the dialog box and put the settings into effect.

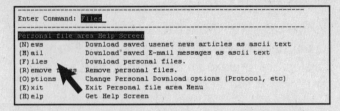

10 Use the service provider's menu to go to the area that contains the startup files your service provider set aside for you. In the example shown here, I selected **Files**, **WIN** (for Windows), **Personal area** (for my "directory"), and then **Files** (to download a file).

11 A file list appears. Mark each file that you want to download by typing its selection letter or number. (Usually an asterisk appears to show that the file is selected.) When you've selected all the files you want, press **Enter**.

12 You may have to answer a couple of questions to confirm your request and specify whether you want the files deleted from the server after downloading. Answer the questions as instructed. (It's a good idea not to delete the files until you're sure they're on your computer.)

Although you should leave the startup files on the server until you're sure you have them safely on your computer, you should go back later and remove the files from the server. Most service providers charge you for the storage you use on the server.

Guided Tour   Download Files with HyperTerminal

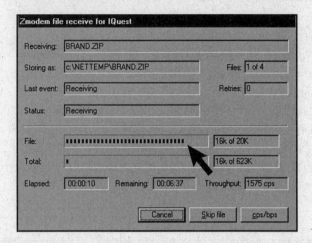

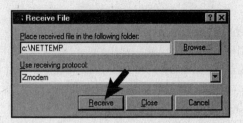

13 After you answer the questions, the service provider should start sending the files, and HyperTerminal should start receiving them. If that happens, a dialog box appears, showing the progress of the transfer.

14 If the transfer does not start, you may have to tell HyperTerminal to start receiving the files. To do so, open the **Transfer** menu and select **Receive File**. In the Receive File dialog box, click the **Receive** button. HyperTerminal should start receiving the files, and then you should see the dialog box shown in step 13.

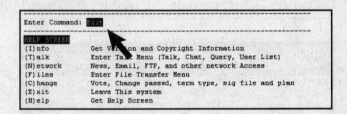

15 When you finish transferring files, back out of the UNIX menu system and exit. Then exit HyperTerminal.

Copy Files from the Internet

After you have secured a way to connect to the Internet either by the Windows 95 dial-in software or Trumpet Winsock and have either a FTP program or a Web browser, you will be able to download and install various files. To download files with FTP or your Web browser you will need to know the address of an FTP site or a Web site that offers the files. For more information on downloading files from the Internet see "Find and Copy Files from the Internet" on page 179.

One of the most useful files you can download is Winzip. Winzip is a shareware program that allows you to decompress files that have zipped for downloading. A zipped file is actually a group of files that have been compressed together. When you unzip a compressed file, you will find that it usually consists of a number of files. This Guided Tour will show you how to download Winzip with either an FTP program or a Web browser.

Begin Guided Tour   Download Winzip with WSFTP and Netscape Navigator

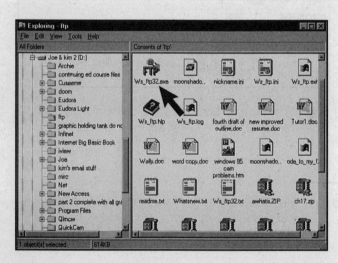

1 Use your Dial-Up networking icon or Trumpet Winsock to connect to your Internet service provider. Open the Windows Explorer and open the FTP directory; Double click the Ws_ftp32 icon to start the FTP software.

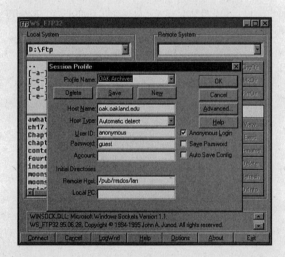

2 Connect to the **oak.oakland.edu** FTP site. This is one of the many FTP software repositories available on the Net.

Guided Tour   Download Winzip with WSFTP and Netscape Navigator

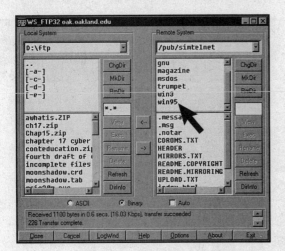

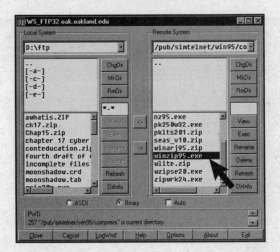

3 After you're connected, double-click the **Pub** directory to open it, and then double-click the **simtelnet** directory to open it. This directory contains a number of subdirectories listed by types of files. Double-click the **win95** directory.

5 Several different file compression utilities are listed in this directory. Click **winzip95.exe**. This file is the compressed Winzip software program. Click the **download** button (the right-pointing arrow) to download the software program to your computer.

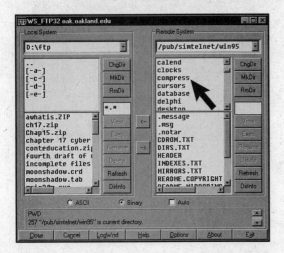

4 This site lists the Windows 95 files in various categories. Scroll down and double-click the **compress** directory to open it.

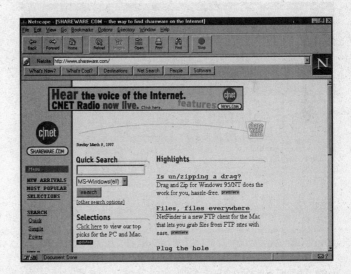

6 You can also download Winzip using your Web browser. Connect to your Internet service provider and then start your Web browser. Type **http://www.shareware.com** and press **Enter**.

(continues)

Guided Tour   Download Winzip with WSFTP and Netscape Navigator

(continued)

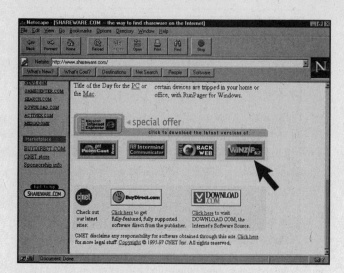

7 Scroll down the shareware.com page. There is a Winzip icon that you can use to download the current version of Winzip. Click the icon.

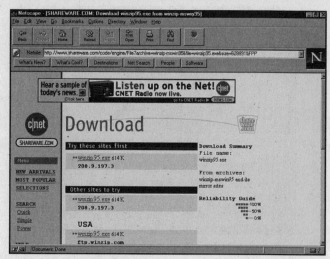

9 Select a site to download the file from by clicking the link.

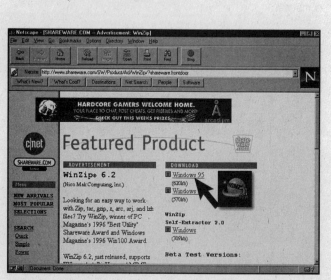

8 Select the **Windows 95** link to download the Winzip software.

10 When the download box opens, select an appropriate directory on your computer for the file, and then click **Save**.

Install Your Files

After downloading the files to your computer, you can install the software. Most software that you download will come in two flavors: zipped files and auto-executables. The zip files are compressed using a compression scheme called zip. You can decompress the zipped file and then install the resulting software by unzipping the program using Winzip—the software that you downloaded above. Auto-executable files are also compressed; double-clicking the file will decompress the software providing the files necessary for installation.

Begin Guided Tour   Install Your Files

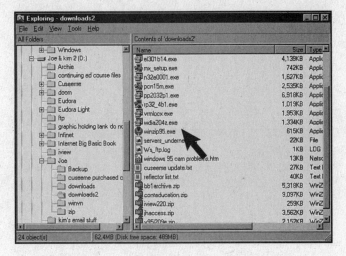

1 Use the Windows Explorer to open the directory that you downloaded the Winzip95.exe file to. Double-click the **Winzip95** file.

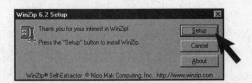

2 The files needed for the installation will automatically extract. Click **Setup** to continue the installation.

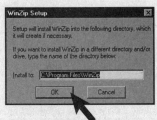

3 A directory will be created automatically for the Winzip software. Click **OK** to continue.

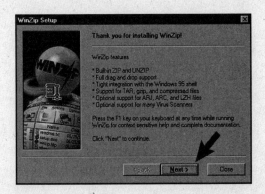

4 Follow the prompts on the various screens to complete the installation. Click **Next**.

5 After the software installation is complete, the Winzip software will start. Now you are ready to unzip any files that you may download from the Internet. You will typically start the software via the Windows 95 start menu.

HOW TO...

Configure Your TCP/IP Software

The language of the Internet is TCP/IP (Transmission Control Protocol/Internet Protocol). *TCP/IP* is a set of rules that control how data passes between computers on the Internet. Whether you connect to the Internet via modem or through a direct network connection, you need some kind of TCP/IP program.

If you use a direct network connection, you're ready to use the Internet. You can skip this section and jump to "Find and Install a Web Browser" on page 97.

> If you have a direct network connection to the Internet *and* you use Windows 95, you may still have to configure a program called the Direct Network Connection. See "Install TCP/IP Software for Windows 95" on page 82.

If you plan to connect to the Internet through a modem, you'll need a TCP/IP program. Windows 95 includes a built-in TCP/IP program, but you'll need to install it.

> If you use Windows 3.1, a TCP/IP program called Trumpet Winsock was probably included with the files you received from your Internet Service Provider.

What You Will Find in This Section

Install TCP/IP Software for Windows 95

A *protocol* is a set of rules that govern the exchange of information. TCP/IP defines how information is exchanged on the Internet in particular. Therefore, you must install the TCP/IP protocol for your modem to know how to "talk" on the Internet when you connect.

Windows 95 provides its own TCP/IP software for your use. However, it is not usually installed when Windows 95 is set up, so you will probably have to install it. The Guided Tour in this section shows you how to do just that.

Depending on the type of Internet connection you have, installing the TCP/IP program can be a two-step process. No matter what, you'll need to install the TCP/IP protocol. In addition, if you're using a SLIP dial-up Internet account, you'll need to install the SLIP/CSLIP protocol. That's where you might run into a snag: To install the SLIP or CSLIP protocol, you need the CD-ROM version of Windows 95.

There are also two routes to configuring the TCP/IP protocol on your computer. You can manually configure the protocol; or you can use the Internet Connection Wizard provided with Windows 95 to assist you. Both of these possibilities are discussed in this chapter's Guided Tour.

> Even if you've used Trumpet Winsock in the past, don't use it with Windows 95. Windows 95 prefers its own TCP/IP program; therefore, I suggest you use it instead.

In addition to installing the TCP/IP software, you must configure the Dial-Up Networking program so it can function as your Internet Connector. You need to do this whether you connect to the Internet through a modem or through a direct network connection. You learn how to configure the Windows 95 TCP/IP software in "Configure the Dial-Up Networking Program in Windows 95" (page 90).

Begin Guided Tour   Add TCP/IP Protocol

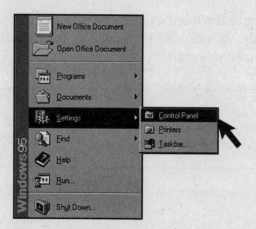

1 Click the **Start** button, select **Settings**, and click **Control Panel**.

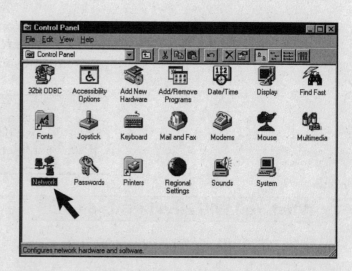

2 In the Control Panel window, double-click the **Network** icon.

Guided Tour   Add TCP/IP Protocol

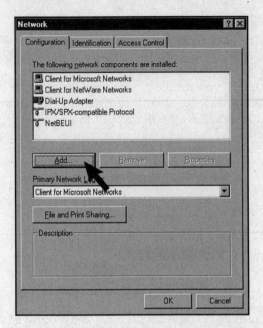

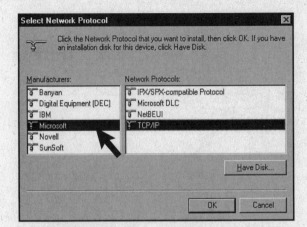

5 In the Select Network Protocol dialog box, select **Microsoft** from the Manufacturers list. Under Network Protocols, select **TCP/IP**. Click **OK**.

3 The Network dialog box appears. If you have already installed the TCP/IP protocol, skip to step 6. If not, click the **Add** button.

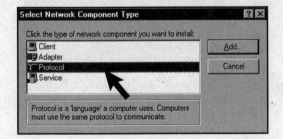

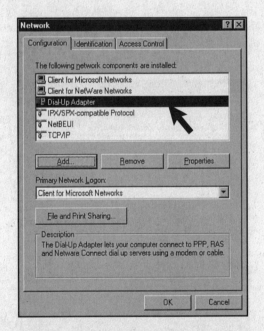

4 Select **Protocol** from the list and click **Add**.

6 If you plan to use a dial-up connection (if you will use your modem to dial into your Internet service provider), select **Dial-Up Adapter** from the network components list. To use a direct network connection (if you will connect through your company's network), select your network adapter instead. Click **Properties**.

(continues)

Guided Tour   Add TCP/IP Protocol

(continued)

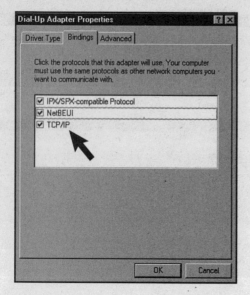

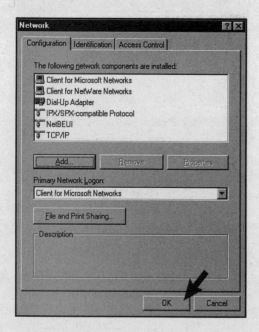

7 The Dial-Up Adapter Properties dialog box appears. Click the **Bindings** tab and select the **TCP/IP** option if it's not already checked. Click **OK**.

8 Click **OK** to close the Network dialog box.

If you have a network card installed and you are not connecting through your network (but through a modem and a service provider instead), you should change the Properties settings of the network card so that TCP/IP is not selected on the Bindings tab (see Step 7).

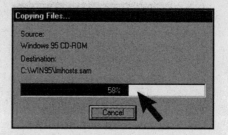

9 Insert the Windows diskette or CD, and Windows 95 starts copying the appropriate files.

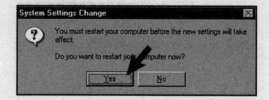

10 When it finishes, you'll need to restart the PC to put your changes into effect. Shut down your programs and click **Yes**.

Begin Guided Tour   Add SLIP or CSLIP Protocol

1 Insert the Windows 95 CD, and the Windows 95 CD-ROM dialog box appears. Click **Add/Remove Software**.

> To install SLIP or CSLIP protocol, you must use the Windows 95 CD-ROM. If you purchased Windows on floppy disk, you won't be able to complete this task.

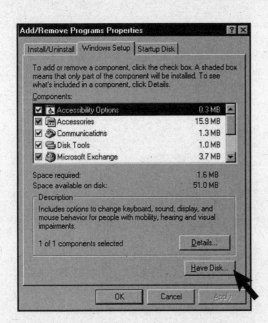

2 In the Add/Remove Programs Properties dialog box, click the **Windows Setup** tab, if necessary. Then click **Have Disk**.

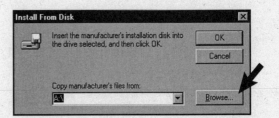

3 The Install From Disk dialog box appears. Click **Browse**.

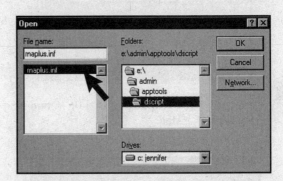

4 Change to the **admin\apptools\dscript** folder, select the **rnaplus.inf** file, and click **OK**.

5 In the Install From Disk dialog box, click **OK**.

(continues)

Guided Tour   Add SLIP or CSLIP Protocol

(continued)

6 Select the **SLIP and Scripting for Dial-Up Networking** option and click **Install**.

8 Close the Windows 95 CD-ROM dialog box by clicking the **Close** button.

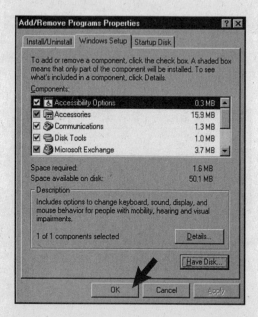

7 In the Add/Remove Programs Properties dialog box, click **OK**. Windows copies the appropriate files to your computer.

Enter Your Internet Account Information in Windows 95

After you install the TCP/IP protocol, you have to configure it. To do so, you enter your Internet account information, which you get from your Internet service provider. If you're connecting to the Internet through your office network, ask your network administrator to give you this information. You need to know these things:

- The IP and subnet mask (if applicable) of your connection. Depending on the type of service you get, your provider will probably assign you an address *dynamically* (each time you dial in). This allows a single provider to service a large number of users using a small number of actual

Internet connections. If you're willing to pay for it, you can have a permanent address assigned to you. An IP address consists of a series of numbers such as 198.70.144.66. Most subnet masks are 255.255.255.0, but yours may be different. Ask your service provider to be sure.

- Your host and domain name
- The DNS address and search order of the Internet server (if applicable)
- The gateway address

When you have the information you need, you're ready to configure the TCP/IP protocol.

Begin Guided Tour   Enter Your Internet Information

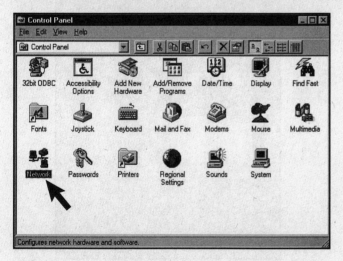

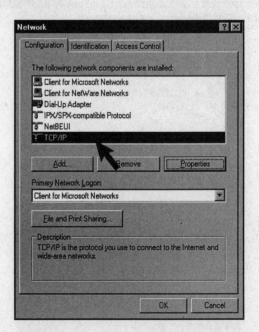

1 Click the **Start** button, select **Settings**, and click **Control Panel**.

2 Double-click the **Network** icon.

3 Select **TCP/IP** from the network components list and click **Properties**.

(continues)

Guided Tour Enter Your Internet Information *(continued)*

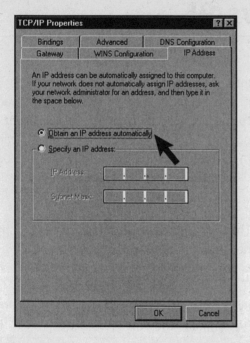

If you are connecting through your network, you may not need to configure DNS. Check with your system administrator.

6 Enter the **Host** and **Domain** names you were given. (This is probably your Internet address. For example, in the Internet address jfulton@mcp.com, the host name is jfulton, and the domain name is mcp.com.)

7 Under **DNS Server Search Order**, enter the DNS server address. If you're not sure what it is, try 128.95.1.4, which is common. Click **Add** to add it. Repeat for additional DNS servers.

8 Under **Domain Suffix Search Order**, enter the domain name again (such as mcp.com). Click **Add** to add it. Repeat for additional domains.

4 In the TCP/IP Properties dialog box, click the **IP Address** tab. If your service provider assigns the address dynamically, click **Obtain an IP address automatically**. If your service provider gave you an actual address, click **Specify an IP address** and fill in the **IP Address** and **Subnet Mask** boxes.

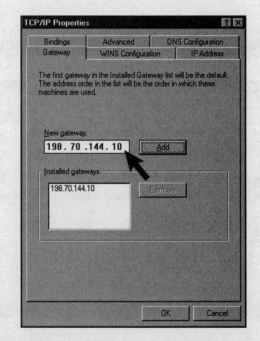

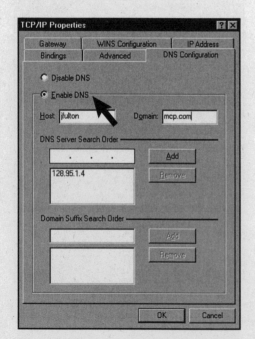

9 Click the **Gateway** tab.

10 Enter the gateway address and click **Add**.

5 Click the **DNS Configuration** tab and select **Enable DNS**.

Guided Tour   Enter Your Internet Information

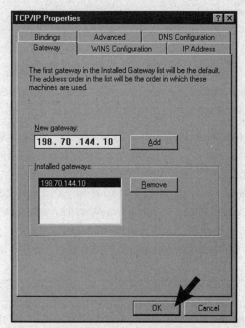

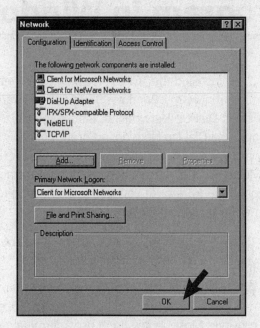

11 Click **OK** to close the TCP/IP Properties dialog box.

12 Click **OK** to close the Network dialog box. Then restart the PC to put your changes into effect.

Configure the Dial-Up Networking Program in Windows 95

Having installed the TCP/IP protocol, you're ready to configure the Windows 95 TCP/IP program that uses it: Dial-Up Networking. Before you start to configure the Dial-Up Networking program, get the following information from your service provider (if you will be using an Internet connection) or from your network administrator (if you will be connecting to the Internet through your office network).

- The phone number you will call to connect to your service provider (if applicable).

- Whether or not you will log in through a terminal window after you connect to your service provider. Most people don't use a terminal window. However, if for any reason, the way you log in to your Internet provider changes from day to day or week to week, and, therefore, you can't automate your login with a script, you'll want Windows 95 to display a terminal window so you can type your login manually.

- If you have a SLIP account (as opposed to PPP), you need to know whether or not your service provider uses compressed SLIP (known as CSLIP).

- Whether or not your service provider has written a *script* you can use to connect to the Internet quickly and simply. This script is usually saved to a file that you download from your service provider in the same way you downloaded your original Internet programs. See "Find and Copy Files from the Internet" on page 179 for help.

> If necessary, install the Dial-Up Networking program before proceeding. Double-click the **Add/Remove Programs** icon in the Control Panel, click the **Windows Setup** tab, and then select **Dial-Up Networking** from the Communications options. If it's already installed, you'll find it on the Accessories menu.

Begin Guided Tour   Configure Dial-Up Networking

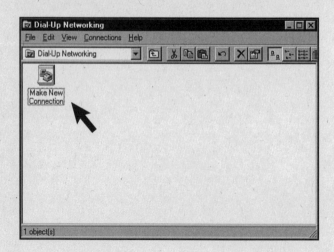

1 Double-click the **Dial-Up Networking** icon in the My Computer folder, or click the **Start** button, select **Programs**, select **Accessories**, and click **Dial-Up Networking**.

> You can also access Dial-Up Networking by double-clicking the **Dial-Up Networking** icon in the My Computer folder.

2 The Dial-Up Networking screen appears. Click **Next** or, if necessary, double-click the **Make New Connection** icon.

Guided Tour Configure Dial-Up Networking

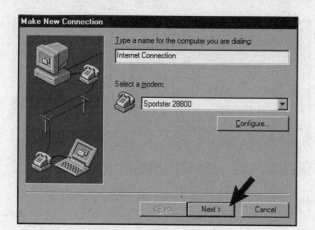

3 Enter a name, such as **Internet Connection,** for your new connection. Click **Next**.

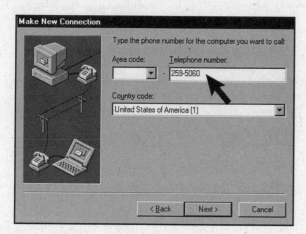

4 Enter the phone number of your service provider. If you're connecting through your network, enter any number—it will be ignored anyway. Click **Next**.

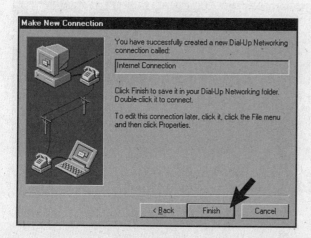

5 Click **Finish**, and Windows adds an icon for the new connection to the Dial-Up Networking folder.

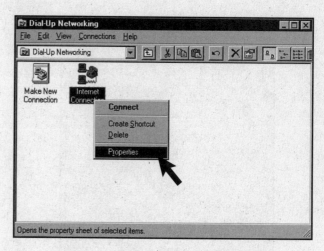

6 Right-click your new icon and select **Properties** from the shortcut menu that appears.

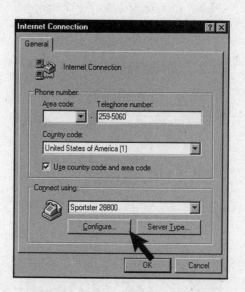

7 If your service provider told you that you will need a terminal window displayed after you connect, click **Configure**. If not, skip to step 9.

(continues)

Guided Tour Configure Dial-Up Networking *(continued)*

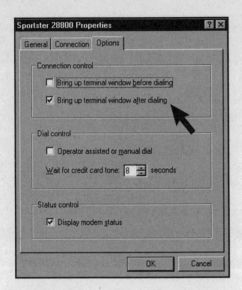

8 In the Properties dialog box, click the **Options** tab. Select **Bring up terminal window after dialing** and click **OK**.

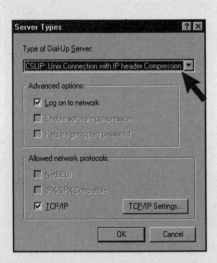

9 In the Internet Connection dialog box, click **Server Type**. The Server Types dialog box appears.

10 In the Type of Dial-Up Server list, select the appropriate option: **PPP**, **SLIP**, or **CSLIP** (if your service provider told you to use SLIP compression). If you're connecting through your network, select **NRN: NetWare Connect**. Click **OK**.

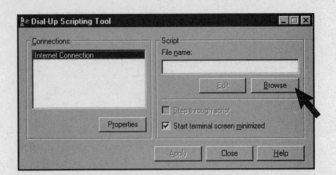

11 If your service provider gave you a dial-up script that you can use to easily configure your connection, open the **Start** menu, select **Programs**, select **Accessories**, and click **Dial-Up Scripting Tool**.

12 In the Dial-Up Scripting Tool dialog box, select your connection from the list and click **Browse**.

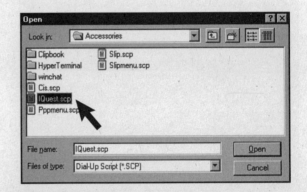

13 Select the script file from the list and click **Open**.

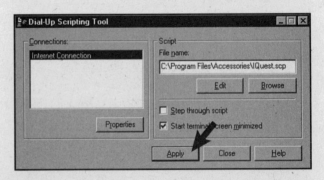

14 Click **Apply**, and then click **Close**.

Use the Internet Connection Wizard

Manually configuring your TCP/IP connection parameters may seem a little daunting. But, as the guided tour shows you, it is really a very straight-forward process. Some service providers now provide setup software that automatically configures your computer's connection to their network (taking care of the dial-in setup and the TCP/IP protocol). Windows 95 has also automated some of the process with a tool called the Internet Connection Wizard. The Internet Connection Wizard (or the *ICW* as it is called) is found on recent releases of the Windows 95 CD-ROM. The ICW is also available with another Microsoft product called Microsoft Plus, which is an add-on enhancement program for Microsoft Windows 95.

To see if you have the ICW installed on your computer all you have to do is click the **Start** button and point at **Programs**, then **Accessories** on the Start menu. A menu choice called Internet Tools will open in the Accessories group. Point at the Internet Tools group and a menu choice of Get On the Internet will appear. If you see that choice you have the ICW installed and can use it to help set up your Internet connection.

To use the ICW you will have to record the same information that you did for manually configuring the TCP/IP protocol. Consult the list under the "Configure the Dial-Up Networking Program in Windows 95" on page 90 to get ready to use the ICW.

The ICW can be used to configure both the dial-in and the TCP/IP or you can manually configure either of these before you invoke the ICW. For instance, if you already have configured the dial-in based on information from your service provider, you can have the ICW just configure the TCP/IP protocol.

One incredible aspect of the ICW is that it can actually help you find a local service provider. If you allow the ICW to have complete control over the connection process, it will connect your modem to an 800 number that provides a list of service providers in your area code and 3-digit exchange. Once it configures your computer for a particular provide, you will of course have to make arrangements to sign on with the provider before you will be able to directly connect to the Internet via their service.

Begin Guided Tour   Use the Internet Connection Wizard

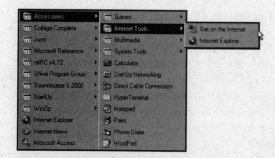

1 Click the **Start** button, then point at **Programs**, then **Accessories**. To invoke the ICW, point at **Internet Tools** and then click **Get on the Internet** (in some versions of Windows 95 the choice may be *Internet Setup Wizard*).

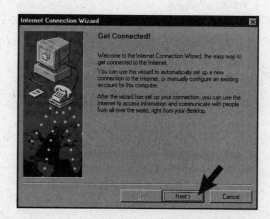

2 The ICW opens with a screen that tells you that you can either automate the entire Internet connection process or use settings that you have already configured. Click **Next**.

(continues)

> **Guided Tour**   Use the Internet Connection Wizard   *(continued)*

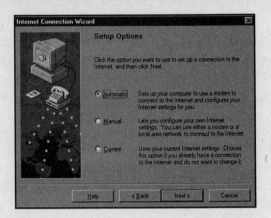

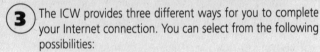

③ The ICW provides three different ways for you to complete your Internet connection. You can select from the following possibilities:

- **Automatic**   This will configure the dial-up connection and the TCP/IP protocol. This choice will also offer you a free dial-in service that allows you to select from local service providers.

- **Manual**   This lets you control the configuration process (you must provide all the dial-up information and configure the TCP/IP protocol as discussed earlier in this chapter), but ICW will make sure the proper software is copied from the Windows 95 CD-ROM. If you have received specific instructions from your service provider you may wish to do the manual installation.

- **Current**   This choice will make sure all the Windows 95 software needed to run your configuration for an Internet connection is copied to your machine. This is the best route if your MIS administrator has already configured your machine for TCP/IP on a network.

④ If you choose the **Automatic** setup, the ICW will copy the software needed from the Windows CD-ROM.

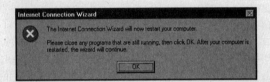

⑤ Once the appropriate dial-in and TCP/IP software is added to your computer, the ICW will restart the system. Once your computer is up and running again, the ICW will ask you for an area code and the first three digits of your phone number. This information will be used to find a local service provider (their phone number and other parameters) using the ICW's Provider locator. Once you select a local provider's number, the rest of the process is completely automated.

If you selected *Manual* or *Current* as your choices on the ICW Installation screen, the process will require that you manually configure certain aspects of completing an connection to the Internet. Since the installation will be unique for each computer, use the information in "Configure the Dial-Up Networking Program in Windows 95" on page 90 and "Install TCP/IP Software for Windows 95" on page 82.

Test Your Internet Connection

After you install and configure the TCP/IP protocol and you configure the Dial-Up Networking program (manually or using the Internet Connection Wizard), you need to test your new Internet connection to make sure it works. You'll need your login name and password for this. If you don't know them, contact your Internet service provider.

This Guided Tour contains steps for connecting to the Internet using a terminal window to log in. If your service provider doesn't require you to use a terminal window, you can connect to the Internet by performing steps 1 and 2 only. When you are ready to log off, perform step 6.

Begin Guided Tour   Log On and Off the Internet

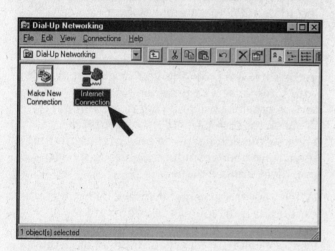

1 To connect to the Internet, double-click your new **Internet Connection** icon in the Dial-Up Networking window.

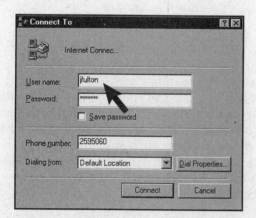

2 If you configured Dial-Up Networking to display a terminal window, do not enter your logon name and password here; you'll enter them through the terminal window itself. Click **Connect**.

If you do not have to use a terminal window, enter your logon name and password now and click **Connect.** Then skip to step 6.

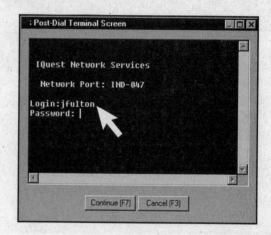

3 If a terminal window appears, enter your Login name and Password. (The password will not appear on-screen.) Then, if you are using a SLIP or CSLIP connection, continue to step 4. If not, click **Continue** and skip to step 6. (Your service provider will inform you if your log-in procedure differs from this.)

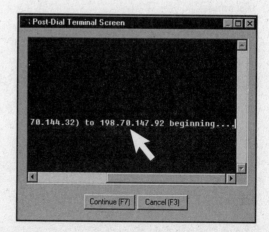

4 Use the scroll bars if necessary to see the IP address assigned to you. Write the number down and click **Continue**.

(continues)

Guided Tour Log On and Off the Internet

(continued)

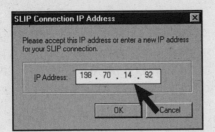

(5) Enter the IP address you wrote down and click **OK**.

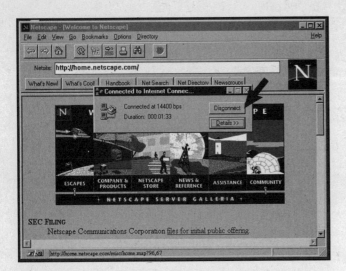

(6) You should now have a working connection, and you can use any Internet programs you have, including Netscape, Mosaic, FTP, and Gopher. You can click the **Minimize** button if you want to get this window out of your way. However, when you want to log off of the Internet later on, restore this window and then click **Disconnect**.

You can create a shortcut on your desktop for your Dial-Up Networking icon. Open **My Computer** and then open the **Dial-Up Networking** folder. Drag the Dial-Up icon for your Internet connection onto the Windows desktop. A shortcut icon will appear; it provides you with quick-click access to the Internet.

Unlike Windows 95, Windows 3.1 does not include a TCP/IP program; however, you can easily obtain one. The most common TCP/IP software is Trumpet Winsock. Trumpet Winsock is a shareware program that is usually included in the software programs you receive from your internet service provider. Normally, your service provider will also configure Trumpet Winsock for such parameters as your UP address, the domain name server (your Internet service provider's computer), and the service provider's domain name.

When you start Trumpet Winsock by double-clicking its icon, you will be prompted for a login name and then a password. Trumpet Winsock will then have your modem dial your Internet service provider's phone number. You will hear the modem connect and then you are ready to launch your e-mail package or Web browser and use the Internet.

You can set Trumpet Winsock to automatically begin the login process when you start it, and to log you out when you exit Winsock. In addition, this feature closes Trumpet Winsock any time you close all your Internet programs and don't restart any within five minutes. (If you have an Internet program open but you're not doing anything, this option will *not* close Winsock.) To set these options, open the **Dialer** menu and select **Options**. Then select **Automatic login and logout on demand** and click **OK**.

HOW TO...

Find and Install a Web Browser

The World Wide Web (known as simply WWW to its friends) is a subset of the Internet itself. You may remember from earlier discussions that the Internet is basically a set of interconnected networks. Well, the Web is a set of interconnected *documents* located on those interconnected networks.

The documents or *pages* at the various sites that make up the Web are connected through *links*. A link usually takes the form of highlighted text or a graphic. But no matter what it looks like on-screen, you simply click a link to jump from the current WWW page to some other related page on the Web. For example, you might start on a Web page that contains information about the Environmental Protection Agency, and then click some highlighted text or an icon to jump to a page that focuses on the industrial use of our national parks. What is really fascinating about the Web is that the page on the Environmental Protection Agency could reside on a computer in Washington, D.C., while the page that you jump to on national parks might be in Colorado. The Web enables you to move seamlessly from content area to content area, meaning that you are navigating through a network of computers spanning the globe.

In order to move around the Web, you'll need a Web browser. With it, you can view Web pages on-screen and navigate the links between them. In this section, you'll learn how to choose a Web browser, download it from the Internet (if necessary), and install it.

What You Will Find in This Section

Understand Web Browsers

The Web is like a vast book. You start on one page (called the home page because it's your starting point), but instead of turning from one page to another with your fingers, you click some text or a fancy picture and wham! You're on a different Web page. For example, you might be looking at a page with the latest news headlines, and then, by clicking some text that says "The Iowa Caucuses," you jump to another page with information about the '96 elections. You don't have to read the Web "book" in sequential order because links connect you to each of its various pages. In other words, you're free to browse the pages on the Web however you like.

When you log onto the Web with your Web browser, you start on what's called the *home page*. This is usually your service provider's main page on their Web site, filled with links to what they consider the best places on the Web. (However, you *can* create your own home page and fill it with your own favorite links.) Some Web browsers provide you with a free start page (such as Internet Explorer and Netscape Navigator). You can customize the start page with your own links to favorite spots and different sites.

You jump from page to page in the Web "book" by clicking on *links*, (sometimes called hypertext or hypermedia links). But how does your Web browser program find each page within the vast Internet forest? It's easy. Outwardly, a Web page appears to contain many links. Behind the scenes, however, the page contains a number of addresses called URLs that tell the Web browser where to find the information each link refers to.

Every Web page has its own address or *URL* (Uniform Resource Locator). A typical URL looks like this:

    http://home.netscape.com/home/
    internet-search.html

The first part of an URL address denotes the *protocol*, or language in which the information on that particular Web page is written. The second part denotes the address of the Web page.

Web pages are written in a language called Hypertext Markup Language—HTML. HTML is actually a bunch of codes that are used to mark the text and graphics found in the Web pages. These HTML codes can link certain text or a picture to another Web site's page. So when you are in your Web browser and click a particular link and jump to a new site, it is the HTML code that takes you to the new destination.

HTML codes used in conjunction with other program languages like Java and ActiveX allow programmers to place interactive content on a particular page. HTML is now quite easy to use and a number of products are available on the market for building Web pages without programming. These easy-to-use HTML packages operate much like a word processor and use wizards and pre-built Web content to help you construct your own home page.

Web browsers support other protocols as well, such as FTP, Gopher, Telnet, and news. This is one of the things that make Web browsers so versatile. Each protocol follows a particular format for addressing a Web page. The following table contains a list of common protocols and sample addresses.

Some Web browsers come with built-in newsreaders and mail readers; others require you to supply those programs, as well as separate Gopher, Telnet, and FTP programs. If your browser does not offer such programs, during setup you can tell your Web browser where the programs are located, and it uses them to display the corresponding data on-screen.

Web Browser-Supported Protocols

Protocol	Address Format and Sample Address
HTTP	http://*server_name/document_path/document_name* http://www.memphis.edu/egypt/main.html
FTP	ftp://*server_name/file_path/file_name* ftp://winsite.com/pub/pc/winzip.exe
Gopher	gopher://*server_name/document_type/selector* gopher://gopher.senate.gov/1
Telnet	telnet://*user_name:password@server_name* telnet://jfulton:secret@delphi.com
News	newsrc://*newsgroup:first_article-last_article* newsrc://news:/misc.writing

In addition to being able to jump from page to page on the Web by clicking links, you can jump directly to a particular page by typing its address. And if you don't know the address but you know the information you want to locate, you can use one of several Web search tools such as Lycos, Web Crawler, or Yahoo! to look for applicable pages. See "Search for Information on the Internet" on page 169 for more information. Once you find a page that's useful, you can save its address so that you can visit it later. You can also print a page or save a page image so you can open it later using your word processor.

Begin Guided Tour   Tour a Typical Web Browser

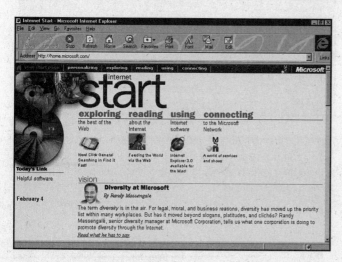

Internet Explorer and Netscape support framed windows, which divide a single Web page into several smaller windows. Frames make it easy to organize large amounts of information for a user to locate.

(continues)

1 When you start your Web browser, you automatically begin at the home page. The home page is usually the main page of your Internet provider, but you customize your own home page.

Guided Tour Tour a Typical Web Browser

(continued)

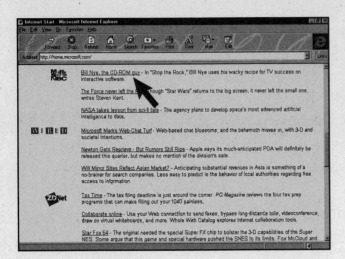

2 To jump to another Web page, click a link. Many links look like highlighted or underlined text, as shown here.

4 You can save your favorite URLs (addresses) and jump directly to a particular page.

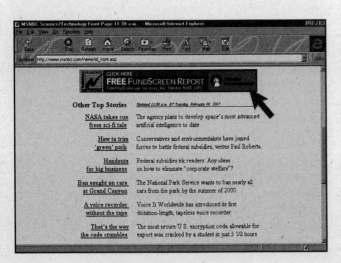

3 Some links look like a simple graphic or icon, as shown here.

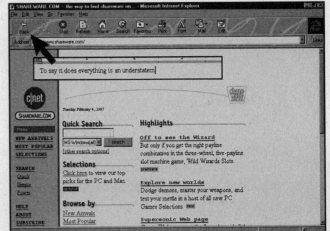

5 By clicking a button, you can jump backward to the previous page you were on, and then you can return to your starting page by jumping forward. You can also jump to the home page at any time.

Guided Tour Tour a Typical Web Browser

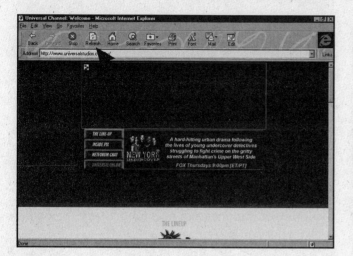

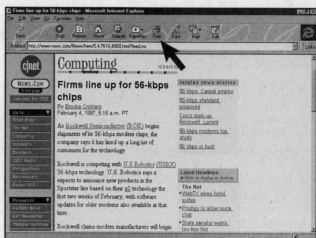

6 Sometimes your Web browser will have a problem loading the page you want to view. If that happens, you can stop the current loading process and reload the page.

8 If you find a page you like, you can click the **Print** button to print it.

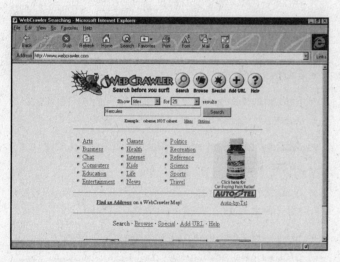

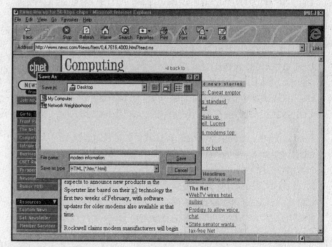

7 You'll find many search tools on the Web that can help you find a particular page. The one shown here is called WebCrawler.

9 You can also save the image of a page you like to your hard drive.

Choose a Web Browser

There are a number of Web browsers on the market, and more are being created every minute. The three most popular right now are Netscape Navigator, Microsoft Internet Explorer, and NCSA Mosaic. Check out one of these Web browsers:

- Netscape Navigator 3.0 for Windows 95, Windows 3.1, and Macintosh

- Internet Explorer 3.0 for Windows 95, Windows 3.1, and Macintosh

- NCSA Mosaic for Windows 95 and Windows 3.1

Internet suites are a popular alternative. A *Net-suite* is a package of programs that you can use on the Internet. The individual programs in the suite (such as the Web browser program) probably won't be as nice as programs marketed separately (such as Netscape Navigator), but getting a suite assures you of complete compatibility and ease of use. Popular suites include Internet Chameleon, Internet in a Box, Emissary, Cyberjack, Mariner, and Netshark.

Netscape currently has a suite product available in preview form called Netscape Communicator. It uses Netscape Navigator as its Web browser. Even if you choose a suite, you may want to use Netscape Navigator or Internet Explorer as your Web browser; they are far superior to most others.

What qualities should you look for when you're searching for the best Web browser for you? Here's a list:

- **Speed** This is possibly the most important factor because it is time-consuming for any Web browser to display a page on-screen (especially a page filled with complex graphics); you want your browser to be as efficient as possible. The best way to judge the efficiency of a Web browser is to measure how long it takes to load graphics on-screen.

- **Video and sound support**

- **Mail, news, and FTP support** The ability to send e-mail messages, browse the Usenet, and receive (download) files.

- **Java, VRML, and Plug-In support** Used to extend the capabilities of your browser.

- **Forms support**

- **Security features** Such as the ability to block access to certain Web pages.

- **Ability to open multiple windows at the same time**

- **Supports Frames** Giving you access to Web sites that divide their content.

- **Supports ActiveX technology** A new protocol from Microsoft that makes it very easy for the Web browser to play special content such as Java applications and other special content.

Begin Guided Tour   Look at What Your Web Browser Should Do

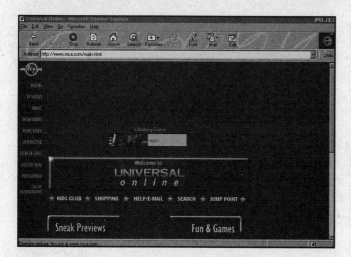

1 A good Web browser displays text on-screen as it processes graphics.

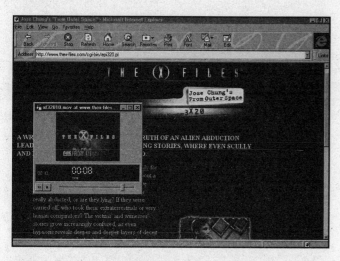

2 With a good Web browser, you can play all those video and sound clips you keep hearing about.

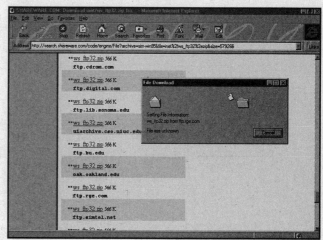

3 Your Web browser should allow you to perform common Internet functions such as downloading files with FTP.

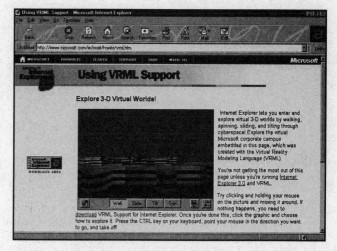

4 A new feature to look for is the capability to display 3-D animations—that is, pictures that look three-dimensional.

(continues)

Guided Tour   Look at What Your Web Browser Should Do

(continued)

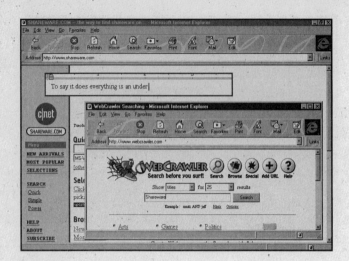

5 Being able to open several windows at the same time allows you to get your work done quickly and more easily.

Find a Web Browser on the Internet

Some Web browsers are available for purchase at software stores. This is especially true of those that come in suite packages. Browsers that come in suites are usually coordinated with a newsreader, an FTP program, and other programs.

Many of the more popular Web browsers are available for downloading from the Internet. Many of these programs are *shareware* (not freeware), which means you can "test drive" your browser before you buy it. Shareware works under the principle that you will register your program after a reasonable evaluation period. So if the Web browser you decide to use is listed as shareware, you will need to pay a small fee for its use. And even if your service provider included a Web browser with its startup files, you'll still have to pay to register the Web browser and any other shareware programs you decide to keep.

A major exception to the rule that most good software for the Internet is shareware (which means you should eventually pay for a copy) is the Internet tools that have recently been developed by Microsoft Corporation. Microsoft Internet Explorer is freeware; the only string attached is that Microsoft would like you to register the Web browser with them. Microsoft also offers other free tools for the Internet— chat clients, conferencing software, and even HTML development tools.

> Some Web browsers are free to nonprofit organizations and schools. Check the documentation for details.

A very popular Web browser, Netscape Navigator, is available at software stores and on the Internet. The fee to register the program is the same either way, so if you want to save yourself some hassle, you can simply buy Navigator instead of downloading it.

Microsoft Internet Explorer can be downloaded from the Web or with an FTP program. Internet Explorer is also available as part of Microsoft's new application suite package Microsoft Office 97, and the newest version of Windows 95.

If you decide to download your Web browser from the Internet, you must currently have another Web browser so that you can download the new one via the Web.

> You can also download the file using File Transfer Protocol, but you will need to know the address of the FTP site where the file is located and an FTP program to download (receive) it. Either a Web browser or FTP program was probably included with the files you downloaded from your service provider. See "Find and Install an FTP Program" on page 184 if you need more help.

Keep Your Browser Up-To-Date

With the rapid technological advances taking place in World Wide Web content the Web browsers are evolving too. Both Netscape Navigator and Internet Explorer have gone through updates in the last year. Currently Microsoft Internet Explorer is in release 3.01. Version 4.0 is supposed to be available some time this year.

Netscape Navigator is currently in version 3.01. However, this past month a new product from Netscape, Netscape Communicator, has been released in preview form. This Internet application suite offers an e-mail package, a Web page design tool, an Internet Newsreader, and Netscape Navigator 4.0. Navigator 4.0 has increased security features and takes excellent advantage of multimedia-rich web pages.

To download the newest version of Internet Explorer on the Web, go to **http://www.windows.microsoft.com/windows/download/msie20.exeftp1.microsoft.com/msdownload/ieinstall/msie301.exe**. For the latest version of Netscape Navigator go to the Netscape home page at **http://home.netscape.com**.

In the following Guided Tour, you will learn to download and install Netscape Communicator. You will download the file via the World Wide Web using Netscape Navigator. If you use a different Web browser, the steps may vary a bit.

Begin Guided Tour   Download and Install Netscape Communicator

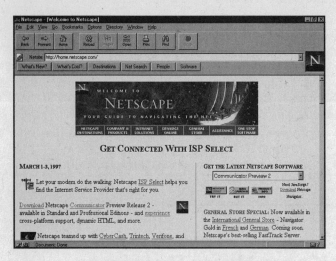

1 Connect to the Internet and start your Web browser (Netscape Navigator).

2 Connect to Netscape's home page at **http://home.netscape.com**.

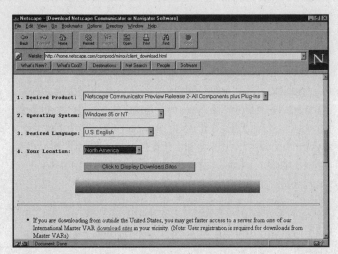

4 On the download page specify the product, your operating system, a desired language, and your location, then click the **Click to Display Download Sites** button.

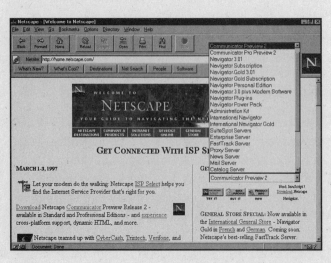

3 Select the **Communicator Preview** (or release version if available) in the **Get The Latest Netscape Software** drop-down box. Once you've selected the software, click the **Try It** icon.

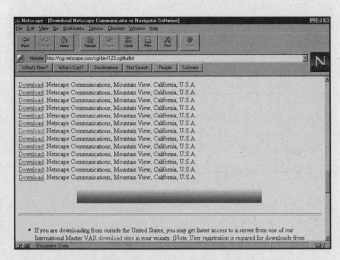

5 Select a download site from the list provided.

Guided Tour Download and Install Netscape Communicator

6 When the download begins, designate an appropriate directory for the installation file.

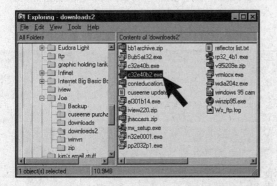

7 Once the download is complete, use Windows Explorer to locate the Communicator installation file. Double-click **c32e40b2.exe** to start the installation process.

8 You will find the process to be a typical Windows 95 software installation.

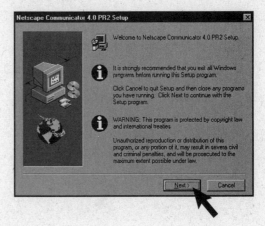

9 Advance through the installation screens by clicking the **Next** button and selecting a typical installation. This will install the most commonly-used components of Communicator on your computer.

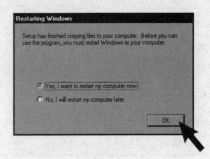

10 When the installation is complete, you will be asked to restart your machine. Click **OK** to restart.

11 Connect to your service provider. When you start Communicator for the first time (double-click the icon on the Windows desktop), the software will walk you through the process of creating a user profile. Click **Next** to continue.

(continues)

Guided Tour   Download and Install Netscape Communicator

(continued)

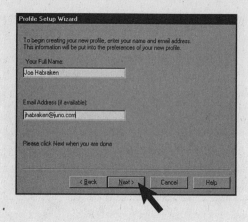

12 Fill in your name and your e-mail address and then click **Next**.

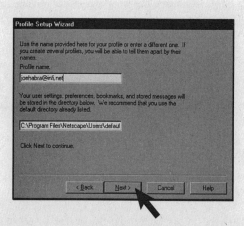

13 Supply a name and a path for your profile and you're ready to go to the next step; click **Next**.

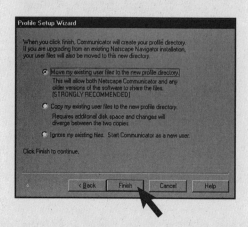

14 You can have Communicator share files with your previous version of Netscape Navigator, copy your user files to a new directory, or start Communicator as a new user. Make your selection and then click **Finish**, and the profile creation process will be complete.

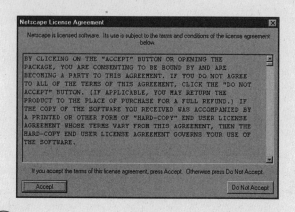

15 A license agreement will appear; read and accept it to continue.

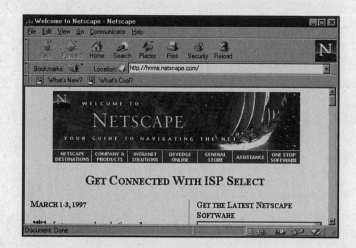

16 Navigator 4.0 will open and take you to the Netscape home page; you are ready to browse the Web.

Guided Tour Download and Install Netscape Communicator

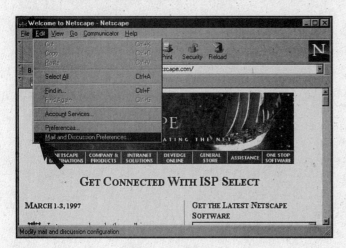

17 To set up the e-mail and newsgroup preferences for Netscape Communicator, click **Edit** and then click **Mail and Discussion Preferences**.

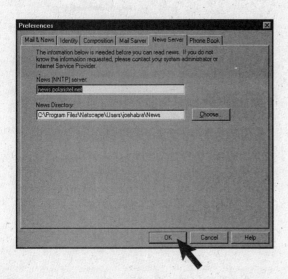

18 Select the appropriate tabs in the Preference dialog box, and fill in your e-mail address, e-mail server, news server, and other preferences. Once you've supplied the necessary information click **OK**.

After installing your Web browser, in this case Netscape 4.0 beta, you may want to find and install a series of helper applications or plug-ins for it. These applications can include: an MPEG movie viewer, a QuickTime movie viewer, a chat client, a RealAudio/Video client, or a VRML viewer. See "Play Sound and Video Clips with Helper Applications" on page 129 for more information.

19 You can activate the Communicator Messenger e-mail service or the Newsgroup feature by clicking the appropriate icon on the Communicator toolbar, which is in the lower right-hand corner of the Communicator window.

20 Communicator is now ready for Web browsing, e-mail, newsgroups, and Web page design. Enjoy.

If you plan to use a 32-bit browser such as Netscape or Internet Explorer in Windows 3.1, you'll need to install something called Win32s before you actually install the browser. It helps your Web browser run properly under Windows 3.1. The file that is used to install Win32s, pw1118.exe, can be obtained from the Microsoft FTP **FTP1.microsoft.com**. Once you download the file using your Web browser or an FTP client, place it in a separate directory and double-click it to decompress the file. A number of files will be generated by this decompression. Double-click the **wb2s120.exe** file to install the Win32s files.

Explore the World Wide Web

As you learned in previous sections, the World Wide Web is a subset of the Internet. The Internet is a group of interconnected networks, and the Web is made up of special sites along the Internet that support Web browsing.

On the Web, you navigate from one place to another by selecting a *link* that appears on a Web page. A link might be a picture or some highlighted text that appears on-screen. You just click the picture or text, and your Web browser links you to the requested spot on the Internet. With a Web browser, surfing the Net is as simple and easy as using Windows.

As you learned in "Find and Install a Web Browser" on page 97, there are a number of Web browsers from which you can choose. Right now, the most popular Web browsers are Netscape Navigator and Microsoft Internet Explorer. In this section, you'll learn how to use Netscape Navigator 4.0 to explore the World Wide Web.

What You Will Find in This Section

Connect to the World Wide Web

In order to connect to the World Wide Web part of the Internet, you'll need a special program called a Web browser. In "Find and Install a Web Browser" (page 97), you learned how to download your choice of Web browsers from the Internet and how to install it. In this section, you'll use Netscape Navigator to connect to the WWW. If you're using a different Web browser, the steps in the Guided Tour may vary slightly; however, all Web browsers work basically the same way.

> In the Guided Tour, we use Netscape Navigator version 4.0 for Windows 95. You will find that both Netscape and Microsoft update their browsers periodically, adding new features and fine-tuning the browser's performance. To download a current version of Netscape, see "Find a Web Browser on the Internet" (page 105).

Each Web site has its own address, called an URL (Uniform Resource Locator). The URL for the Netscape Navigator's home page looks like this:

http://home.netscape.com/

The *home page* is your starting point. When you start Netscape Navigator, it connects you to Netscape's home page, from which you can jump to other pages on the Web. You can jump back to the home page at any time by clicking the **Home** button, as you'll see in a moment. Later, as you become more familiar with the Web, you can select a different home page from which to start, if you want. See "Select a New Home Page" on page 120 for help. This new home page can be one of your favorite pages on the Web, or it can be a page designed by someone in your company or school, linked to Web pages that you find most useful.

If you received your Web browser from your Internet Service Provider, it will probably be configured so that your home page is the provider's Web site. Many providers offer home pages that provide you with local news and services and links to other Web sites.

Each page contains links to other pages, providing a quick way for you to browse around and view pages on similar topics. You can also jump directly to a specific Web page by entering its address (URL) into the Web browser. In upcoming Guided Tours, you'll learn how to navigate the Web, but first you must connect to it.

Begin Guided Tour   Connect to the WWW with Netscape

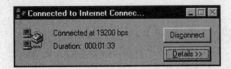

1 Connect to the Internet in the usual manner.

If you need help connecting to the Internet, see "Configure Your TCP/IP Software" on page 81 for help.

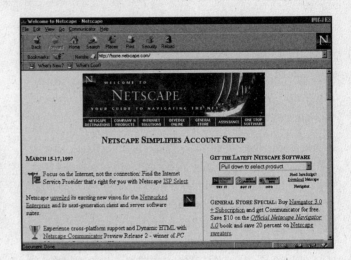

3 The Netscape home page opens, providing you with a number of links to other Netscape content areas. Notice that the links can be highlighted text, choices in a drop-down box, or graphics. The Netscape home page is pretty typical fare for the Web.

4 When you are ready to close your Web browser, open the **File** menu and select **Exit**, or click the **Close** button.

Remember that even when you close Netscape, you're still connected to the Internet. To disconnect from the Internet, return to the Connect To dialog box and select **Disconnect**.

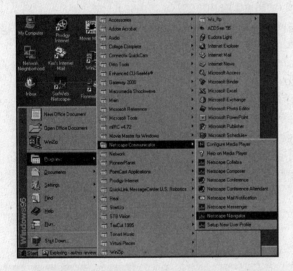

2 Click **Start**, **Programs**, and select **Netscape Communicator** to open the Netscape folder. Click **Netscape Navigator** to start the browser.

You can also start Netscape Communicator by double-clicking its shortcut icon, which you'll find conveniently located on the Windows 95 Desktop.

Use Links to Jump Around

Links are by far the easiest way to explore the World Wide Web. Links can be pictures, items in a selection box, or specially highlighted text that automatically jumps you to a different Web page when you choose them.

In Netscape Navigator 4.0 (which is now part of the Netscape Communicator Internet suite product), text links are marked in blue by default. When you visit a particular link, Navigator changes its text color to purple so you can easily tell where you've been. Of course, like many things on the Web, even this minor convention is changing. You might run into colors other than blue and purple, but you get the idea.

What to Do When a Link Fails

Normally, when you click a link or enter an URL, meteors flash across the Netscape icon (the big "N" in the upper-right corner). This is good. If the meteors stop flashing, it means that Netscape Navigator is hung up—which means you're getting nowhere. Click the **Reload** button at the top of the Navigator window. If the meteors move again but then stop, and nothing happens for a minute or two, something's hung up again. Click **Stop** to discontinue loading the Web page. Then try clicking the link again. Chances are, particularly if you've found an URL using a Web search tool, you will eventually happen upon a site that is no longer available. When this happens you will receive a message on your screen that says "Not Found." When this happens, just click the **Back** button to return to the previous page.

Begin Guided Tour   Using Links

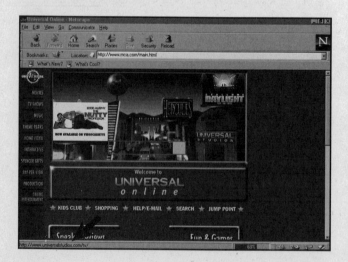

1 When you move the mouse over a link, the address of the Web page it links to appears at the bottom of the Netscape Navigator window.

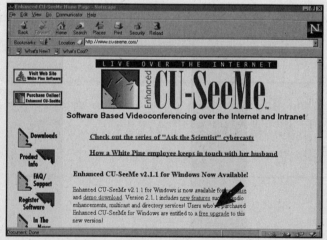

2 To connect to a linked Web page, click the link.

3 After you visit a linked site, the text link changes color from blue to purple.

Guided Tour Using Links

4 Some links are graphic images instead of text. To connect to the linked Web page, just click the graphic.

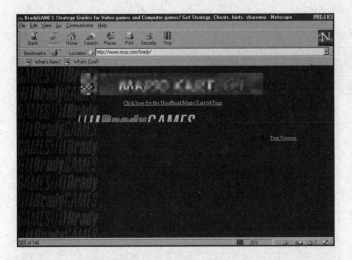

5 If a link fails, you can click **Reload** to reload the page. (You might have to do this, for example, if a page contains a lot of complex graphics; graphics often cause loading problems.) If the downloading of the page seems to take forever, you can click **Stop**. This will stop the connection to the page.

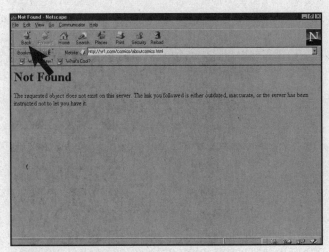

6 There will be times when you run into a site that is no longer available. This usually means that it has been removed from the site that a link carries you to. When you end up on a non-existent site, click **Back** to return to the previous page.

Many times 403 or 404 errors (not found) will appear on your screen because of heavy server traffic. The site probably still exists, but your connection quits before you are able to access the page. Try the tips above before you totally give up on a Web site. You may have to try it a couple of times or at a later time to make the connection.

Back Up and Move Forward

As you change from one page to another on the Web, you create a kind of working history of where you've been. Your Web browser saves this history for you, making it easy for you to return to any previously-viewed page. The most recent of the previously-viewed pages remain in Netscape's memory. If you ever need to see one again, you can click a button, and the page pops back up in about a second.

The history that Netscape Navigator tracks is for the current session only; it is erased when you exit the program (Microsoft Internet Explorer keeps a running history of all your sessions). However, if you find a Web page that you like, you can save its address permanently so that you can return to it at any time.

See "Return to Your Favorite Pages" on page 122 for more information.

Using the history feature in Netscape Navigator is a lot like reading a book. To return to a previously viewed page, you move backward in the "book." You can move as many pages backward as you like. After moving backward, you can return to your starting point by moving forward through your Web pages. You can also jump directly to a previously-viewed page by selecting it from the history list.

Even if you are using a Web browser other than Netscape Navigator, your browser probably has a history feature that works very much like Netscape's. The Guided Tour shows you how to use this handy feature.

Begin Guided Tour   Back Up and Move Forward

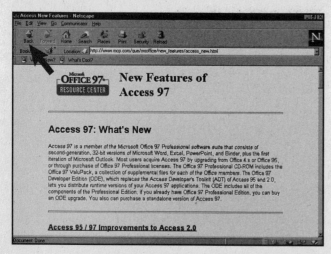

1 To return to the Web page you just viewed, click the **Back** button.

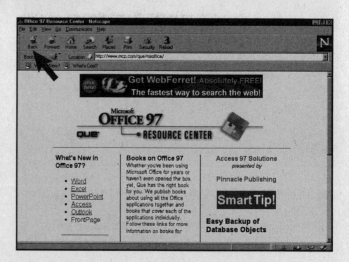

2 Move backward one more page by clicking the **Back** button again. You can repeat this action over and over to return to a previously-viewed page.

Guided Tour   Back Up and Move Forward

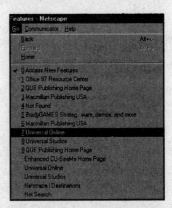

3 To return to the page you were just on, click the **Forward** button. As with the Back button, you can click the **Forward** button as many times as necessary to return to your starting position.

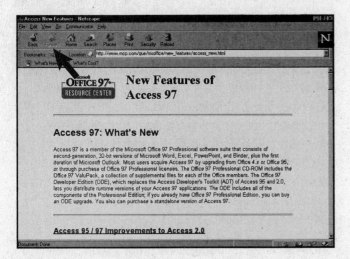

4 If the Forward (or Backward) button is gray, you have moved to the end (or the beginning) of the history. You can't select the gray button because you've moved as far forward (or backward) in history as you can.

5 To jump directly to a previously-viewed page, open the **Go** menu and a list of the sites that you visited appears.

6 Click the page address that you want to go to. Click the **Close** button to remove the History dialog box. The page you selected appears in the Navigator window.

Go to a Specific Web Page Using an URL

As I've mentioned, each Web page has its own address, or URL. A typical URL looks like this:

http://pages.nyu.edu/~liaos/indigo.html

With the right address, you can jump directly to the Web page you want. If you don't know the address or even which pages you might want to view, you can search for applicable pages using a Web search tool such as Lycos. See "Search for Information on the Internet" on page 169 for more information. You can also get addresses for hot Web sites from any of several Internet magazines such as *The Net*, *Websight*, and *Internet World*. Electronic newsletters, such as *TipWorld*, are also good resources for finding cool Web sites.

To jump directly to a Web page, enter its address in your Web browser. A Web address identifies an official Internet resource, whose "name" is known formally as its URL. (If you hear a person talk about his site's "earl," he's referring to its URL.) Every URL has two parts: a content identifier and location.

The first part, the content identifier (or content-id for short), tells you what protocol or language was used to create the current page. For most Web pages, the basic content-id is http:// because the Web pages are written in HTML (HyperText Markup Language) and can be addressed using the HyperText Transport Protocol or http (it's not unlike FTP or File Transfer Protocol—a way to move data on the Internet). Web browsers do support other protocols such as ftp://, gopher://, telnet://, and news:// (the protocol for UseNet newsgroups). But those protocols aren't used for Web pages; they connect you to other resources you can reach through the Web. An HTTP Web page can link directly to any resource that uses one of these protocols. You can easily identify such a resource by its content-id. For instance, you can link to a site's FTP directory or to a UseNet newsgroup just as easily as you can link to another Web page—just by clicking the link. If you want to see what type of resource you're linking to before you link to it, move your pointer over the link but don't click. The URL of the link appears in your browser's status line. The content-id at the beginning of the URL tells you whether the link is a Web page (http://) or some other type of resource.

The second part of every URL identifies the location of the resource. Every resource and every Web page has its own unique location name. This name looks suspiciously like a directory path—which is exactly what it is. Every Web page is a document file that exists on someone else's computer somewhere. These directory paths follow the UNIX format, using forward slashes (/) in place of the backslashes (\) you're used to seeing in DOS and Windows. The paths also contain periods (.), which are used to categorize the resource. So, looking at the address www.microsoft.com, you see that the address refers to the Web-managing portion (www) of the computer called microsoft.com. See "Understand Web Browsers" on page 98 for examples of other types of addresses.

Once you enter an address into your Web browser, you can save it so that you can revisit it again later. See "Return to Your Favorite Web Pages" on page 122 for details.

Begin Guided Tour Entering a Web Page's Address (URL)

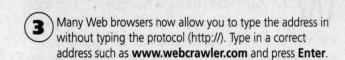

1 Type the address of the page you want to go to in the **Location** or **Go to** text box (whichever is currently visible). Make sure that you use forward slashes (/) to separate the parts of the address. Make sure you've typed the URL correctly, and then press **Enter**.

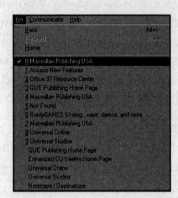

2 After you enter an address, your Web browser keeps it in a list of most recently visited addresses. To return to a previously entered address, click the **Go** menu and select an address from the list.

3 Many Web browsers now allow you to type the address in without typing the protocol (http://). Type in a correct address such as **www.webcrawler.com** and press **Enter**.

4 You will be taken to the designated address.

Select a New Home Page

When you install Netscape Navigator, it sets the home page (the page at which you start your Internet session) to the Netscape home page (if you got your copy of Navigator from your Internet Service Provider, your home page may be different). This is a good place to start, especially if you're new to the Internet. But as you gain confidence and a certain preference for particular sites, you may want more from your home page.

Netscape and other Web browsers allow you to set the home page to any Web page. For example, if you always start your Internet session by checking out CNN for the latest headlines, you might want to set the CNN Web page as your home page. Or suppose someone in your company or school may have designed a local Web page with links tailored to your interests, so you may want to set your home page to that.

Netscape Navigator and Internet Explorer also provide you with the ability to create your own home page consisting of links that you choose. Navigator creates the custom start page via a special Web site: **http://home.netscape.com/custom/index.html**. Follow the steps provided to create the custom page. Internet Explorer provides a link at the top of the Internet Explorer default start page named Your Start Page. Click this link to define a custom home page.

No matter what you choose, when you're ready to change your home page, take the following Guided Tour to learn how (in Netscape Navigator 4.0).

Begin Guided Tour   Set Your Home Page

1 Open the **Edit** menu and select **Preferences**.

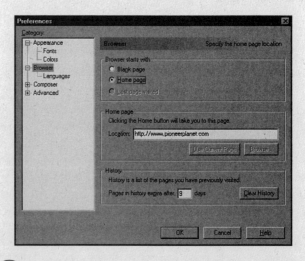

2 Make sure **Browser** is selected in the Category window.

Guided Tour Set Your Home Page

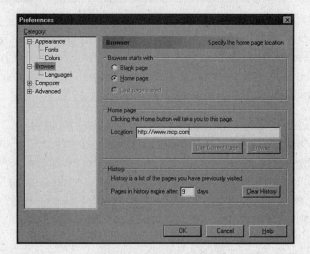

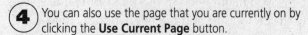

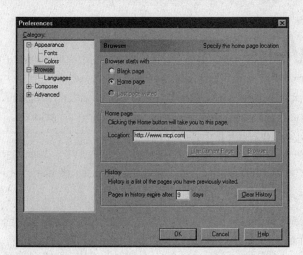

3 In the **Location** text box, enter the URL (address) of the Web page you want to use as your home page. For example, to start at Macmillan Computer Publishing's home page, type the address **http://www.mcp.com**.

4 You can also use the page that you are currently on by clicking the **Use Current Page** button.

5 Click **OK**.

Return to Your Favorite Web Pages

Web addresses (URLs) are often long and complex, which can make it difficult to enter them correctly. And there will be times when you happen upon a great Web site that you will want to return to again and again. When you finish typing an address into your Web browser, you may not want to lose it. There's no need to worry about it. Every Web browser provides a means of saving the addresses of the Web pages you visit.

Browsing the Web is like browsing through the pages of a large book. When you find a particular passage in a book that you will want to find again quickly, insert a bookmark. You can do the same thing with your Web browser. To return to a page you've marked, you select it from the Bookmark list.

> Microsoft Internet Explorer also has the ability to create bookmarks; they are called Favorites. You will find that Netscape and Explorer have many of the same features and abilities. This is why they are the two top tools for browsing the Web.

One of the most important things to know about Internet Web pages is how likely they are to change. Whereas you'll find the same Web page at a given URL address from day to day, the contents of that page may change at any time. If the address is a news-related site, such as a magazine or headline service, you can count on the contents changing. So if you like a certain Web page for what it contains more than for who's bringing it to you, keeping a

bookmark for it will not be enough. You'll want to save a copy of the page to your own computer, which is usually no more difficult than saving a word processor file.

Occasionally, the URL location of a page changes. Many companies that produce Web pages rent computer storage space from a type of computer called an Internet Service Provider (ISP). And because there's a big market in Web space rental these days, some companies tend to move from one provider to another. When that happens, their URL addresses change (just as their U.S. postal addresses would if they moved their home offices). So a bookmark that you can count on one week to take you to a favorite site may not be valid the next week. When that happens, you might need to use one of the Internet's many search tools to find the new address; then you can use the browser's bookmark editor to change the old address.

Some sites put up a message that tells you they have moved and their new address. Also, sometimes these pages will take you directly to the new address after a short wait (around 3 seconds) and you don't have to do anything but just sit there.

In the Guided Tour, you'll use Netscape Navigator 4.0 to set up and edit bookmarks. This particular version of Navigator provides a more advanced bookmark feature than most other Web browsers; it enables you to sort bookmarks, organize them in folders, and add comments.

Begin Guided Tour Set a Bookmark

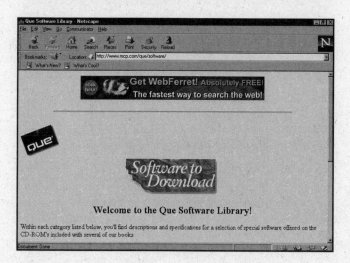

(**1**) First, jump to a page whose address you want to save.

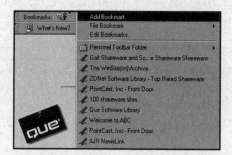

(**2**) Click **Bookmarks** icon and select **Add Bookmark**. Your browser saves the address of the current Web page.

(**3**) To return to a page whose address you've saved, open the **Bookmarks** menu and select the page from the list.

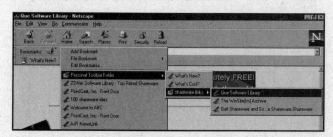

(**4**) If you store the address in a bookmark folder (a group of related bookmarks), select the folder from the Bookmarks menu.

(**5**) Select the page you want to jump to from the cascading menu that appears.

Begin Guided Tour Edit a Bookmark's Name and Description

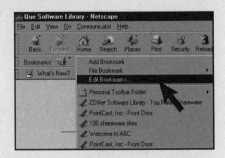

1 Click the **Bookmarks** icon and select **Edit Bookmarks**.

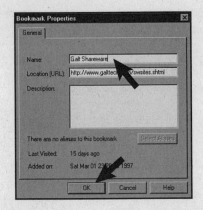

3 In the **Name** text box, change the name of the item if necessary.

4 In the **Description** area, add a description if you want. This is a great place to save user IDs and passwords for sites that require you to log on. The description shows up at the bottom of the Netscape Navigator window when you select the item from the Bookmarks list. Click **OK**.

> When you move the mouse pointer over a link, its URL (address) appears at the bottom of the Netscape Navigator screen.

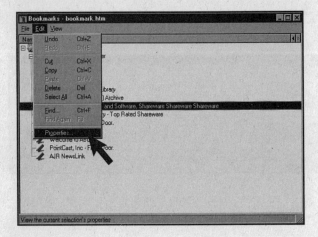

2 To change the description for a particular item, select it, open the **Edit** menu, and select **Properties**.

Begin Guided Tour Organize Items into Bookmark Folders

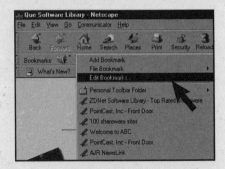

1 Click the **Bookmarks** icon and select **Edit Bookmarks**.

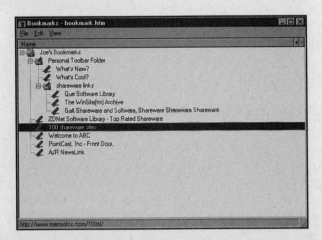

2 To keep similar items together, you can create a folder. In the Bookmarks list, click where you want the folder to appear.

Guided Tour Organize Items into Bookmark Folders

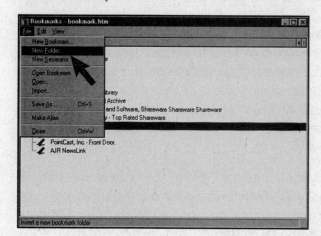

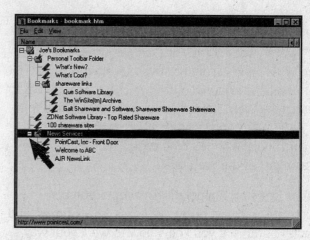

3 Then open the **File** menu and select **New Folder**.

6 You can hide the items in a folder by clicking the folder's minus sign. To redisplay the items, click the plus sign that appears next to the folder name.

7 Close the Bookmarks window by clicking its **Close** button.

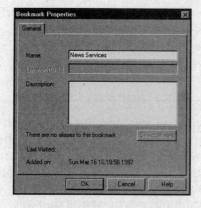

4 Type a name and a description for the folder, and then click **OK**.

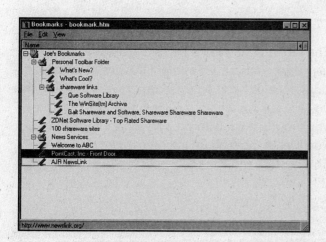

5 To add a bookmark item to the folder, click the bookmark item and drag it into the folder.

Fill Out Forms

At some Web pages you visit, you may be asked to fill out a form. For example, when you visit the Lycos page (a common Web search tool), you'll fill out the basic information for which you want Lycos to search the Web. Similarly, you might complete a form to order merchandise on the Web or to leave an opinion on someone's Web page. The uses for forms are as vast as the Web itself.

An on-screen form looks like a large dialog box, complete with text boxes, list boxes, check boxes, and option buttons. If you know how to work your way around a basic Windows dialog box, you'll do fine with Web forms. To complete a form, make your selections and type in data as needed. There's always some kind of button—such as Send Now, Accept, or Search—to tell the system when you've finished completing the form. Just click the appropriate button, and your information is saved for the owner of the Web page.

About Security

The Internet is basically an open system. This means that much of the information you send over the Internet is not completely secure. However, some systems are more secure than others. In Netscape Navigator, secure Web pages use the protocol **https** instead of the usual **http**, so you can look at the address of the page you're on to see if it's secure. Another way to tell if you're on a secure page in Navigator is to look at the key icon in the status bar. A broken key represents a nonsecure channel. You need to be aware of a page's security level when you're completing forms that ask for personal information such as your social security number or credit card numbers.

Navigator 4.0 also includes some other security innovations. A Security button is available on the Command toolbar that can be used to show the current security status of a page and check other security issues related to sites such as site certificates (certificates identify a secure site), Java applets, and e-mail.

Microsoft Internet Explorer also possesses security features. It offers encryption protocols that allow you to send information over the Web securely. Microsoft has also taken steps to start an authentication program that would allow "legitimate Web sites" to be authenticated by the Web browser. Security will continue to be an issue on the Web as more and more users use it as an avenue for credit card transactions. For more information on security issues and the Web, see "Secure Your System and Practice Proper Netiquette" on page 271.

> The Internet is subject to the same credit card fraud dangers as the regular mail and the telephone system. Be careful when completing any Internet form that asks for private information such as your social security number, credit card numbers, or phone number. The Internet is not completely secure, so there's always a chance that someone could get the information you provide.

The World Wide Web is becoming a more secure venue for transactions as more businesses and institutions open up shop on their own sites. Make sure that you are familiar with the company or group before you provide them with your personal information. You'll learn more about Internet security in "Secure Your System and Practice Proper Netiquette" on page 271.

Begin Guided Tour   Fill Out a Form

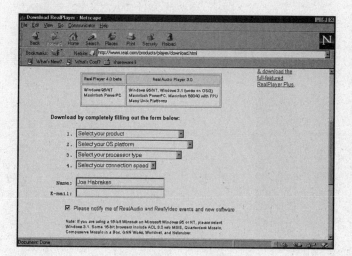

1 When you encounter a form on a Web page, treat it like you would a Windows dialog box. To enter text, click in the text box and type your information.

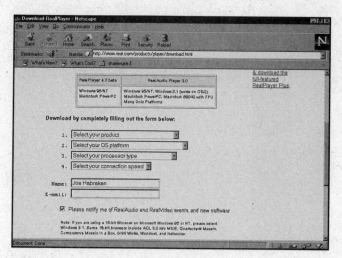

2 Many forms utilize option buttons and check boxes. Simply click the option you want to select.

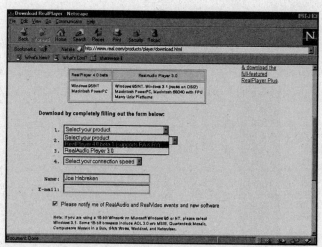

3 If the form utilizes list boxes, click the drop-down arrow to open the list. Then make your selection.

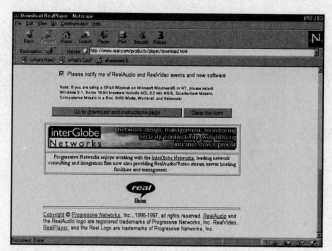

4 Click the button your system provides for letting it know you've finished making selections. In the case of the system shown here, click **Go to download and instructions page**.

HOW TO...

Play Sound and Video Clips with Helper Applications

Although your Web browser (or Gopher program) may not be able to play some types of files directly, it can automatically run a *helper application* that can play the file. Helper applications are small programs that typically run very quickly and require little memory. Whenever your Web browser (or Gopher program) encounters a file it cannot play, it copies the file to your computer and runs the helper application. The helper application automatically opens the file and plays it or displays it on the screen.

Microsoft Internet Explorer takes advantage of helper applications built into the Windows 95 operating system software (Media Player) and a helper application (ActiveMovie) that now comes with Explorer when you download it from the Microsoft Web page. These two helpers take care of many of the audio, video, and other media files that you run across on the Web.

Special file types such as sounds and video clips can also be played by other special programs called plug-ins and controls. For more information on Netscape Plug-ins and Internet Explorer ActiveX controls, see "Find and Install Browser Plug-ins and ActiveX Controls" on page 145.

In this section, you will learn how to copy helper applications from the Internet and set them up to run automatically from your Web browser or Gopher program.

What You Will Find in This Section

Copy Helper Applications from the WWW and the Internet

There are a number of special Web sites, such as **http://www.shareware.com**, that provide you with the links you need to download all the Helper Applications you will need for your Web browser. There are also various FTP (File Transfer Protocol) servers on the Internet that have the helper applications (also called *viewers*) you need. You can connect to these servers with your Web browser or with an FTP program (as explained in "Find and Copy Files from the Internet" on page 179). You can then download the helper application files. This Guided Tour shows you how to use your Web browser to get the files you need.

The procedure is fairly straightforward: In your Web browser, you enter the URL of the Web site or the address of the FTP server. Web sites containing the helper applications connect to the appropriate FTP server or Web server via a hyperlink, such as text or a graphic. When you connect to an FTP site with your Web browser, you may have to negotiate a list of folders and files that get you to the helper file that you wish to download. Whichever route you take, you'll find that it's fun and easy to acquire the helper applications that will turn your Web browser into a multimedia playback machine.

All the helper applications and other files that you will add to Microsoft Internet Explorer can be found on Microsoft's Web site. Use your Web browser to go to **http://www.microsoft.com/ie/**. For Netscape Navigator, go to this site for add-on goodies: **http://home.netscape.com/comprod/mirror navcomponents_download.html**.

Which Helper Applications Do You Need?

In general, you should have at least three helper applications: one for displaying graphics, one for playing sound (audio) files, and one for running video clips. The following table shows common file types you'll find on the Internet, along with the names of popular helper applications that can handle these file types.

Find the Right Helper Application

To Play	With These File Name Extensions	You Need This Helper Application
Graphics and Photos	JPG, JPEG, GIF, BMP	LView or PaintShop Pro
Sounds	AU, AIF	Windows 95 Media Player or Netscape Navigator Audio Player
	WAV	Windows 95 Media Player
Video Clips	AVI	Video for Windows, Avi Pro, or ActiveMovie
	MPG, MPEG	MPEGPlay, VMPEG, or ActiveMovie
	MOV	QuickTime
Compressed Files	ZIP, TAR	WinZip or PKZIP

Your Web browser might already be equipped to display graphics and play sounds. For example, Netscape Navigator and Internet Explorer have built-in capabilities to display JPG and GIF files. Navigator also has an audio player that can play audio clips. Internet Explorer, which is heavily integrated with the Windows 95 operating system, uses the Windows Media Player to take care of playing sounds. If you are satisfied with the way your Web browser plays certain file types, you don't need to set up helper applications for those particular file types.

Find Helper Applications

Fortunately, the Web has a few sites that can help you track down popular helper applications. Both Microsoft and Netscape maintain special Web pages that give you quick access to the helpers that you need. Try **http://www.microsoft.com/ie/** first if you use Internet Explorer and **http://home.netscape. com/assist/helper_apps/windows_helpers.html** if you use Netscape Navigator. Other great sites exist; using your Web browser, try loading any of the following Web pages (as instructed in the Guided Tour). Then click the links to download the helper applications you want.

> **http://www.download.com/**: Links on this page provide you with easy access to Internet utilities such as helper applications and other useful programs.

http://www.voicenet.com/~mmax/help/ win.html: This site, Windows Central, has direct links to most of the popular helper applications.

http://quicktime.apple.com/sw/ qtwin32.html: Many video clips found on the Internet are stored in the .mov file format. Quicktime, from Apple, provides you with a helper application that plays .mov files.

http://www.unl.edu/websat/tools.html: A page that provides links to many Internet tools including helper applications for your browser.

http://www.shareware.com: One stop-shopping for just about every shareware or freeware application available. An easy-to-use search engine provides you with a way to find the helper applications that you need.

One of the first applications you should download is WinZip. You will find that many files have an extension that reads .zip. This means that the file has been zipped *or compressed* so that it doesn't take as long to download (or take up as much room on the server). You will use WinZip to unzip these files.

One word of caution: The file name or folder in which the file is stored may change at any time. When looking for files to download, you may have to poke around a number of folders or search for a file name that's close (not necessarily identical) to the name listed in the following table.

Where to Find Helper Applications

Application	Location
LView	ftp://oak.oakland.edu ftp://ftp.download.com
PaintShop Pro	ftp://ftp.download.com ftp://support.lotus.com
QuickTime	ftp://ftp.support.apple.com ftp://ftptoo.support.apple.com
MpegPlay	ftp://wuarchive.wustl.edu ftp://ftp.the.net
WinZip	ftp://ftp.satlin.com ftp://ftp.digital.com

Begin Guided Tour   Download a Helper Application Using HTTP

1 Connect to the Internet, and then run your Web browser as explained in "Connect to the World Wide Web," on page 112. Once on the Web use a search engine to find a specific helper application.

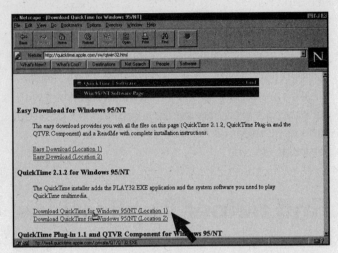

3 You can also go directly to one of the URLs referenced in the figure above to download a helper application such as Apple's Quicktime page at **http://quicktime.apple.com/qtwin32.html**. Click the link for the Windows 95 version of Quicktime to download the software.

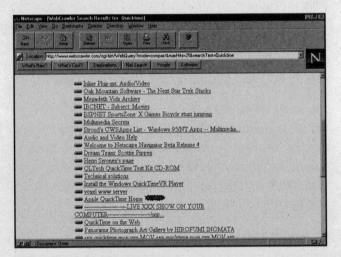

2 The results of your search for a specific helper application will provide you with links that you can follow, and then download the program.

4 A dialog box will appear that allows you to specify the directory; the file will be downloaded to your computer.

5 Once the file has been downloaded, you can use the Windows Explorer to locate and then install the helper application on your computer.

In some cases, the download will be made from a Web site via HTTP. In other cases, an FTP site will be accessed. Since your browser can handle both of these download protocols, all you have to do is sit back and relax while the file is downloaded to your computer.

Begin Guided Tour   Download a Helper Application Using FTP

1 You can also use your browser to go directly to an FTP server by typing the server name in the Location box. Just click inside the box to highlight the current text.

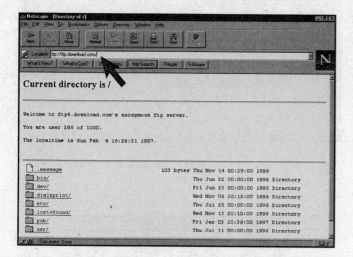

2 Type the address of an FTP server that has the helper application file you want to download, such as **ftp:// ftp.download.com**, and then press **Enter**.

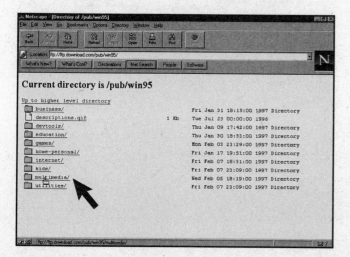

3 Your Web browser connects to the FTP server and displays a list of folders. Click a link for the folder to which you want to go. Continue to click links until you reach the folder that contains the helper application.

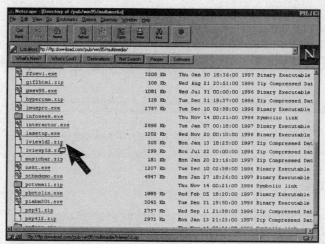

4 Eventually, you change to the folder that contains the helper application file you need. If you have Netscape Navigator, click the link to download the file.

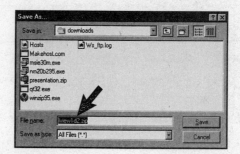

5 Click the file name to begin the download process.

6 Designate an appropriate directory for the file, and then click **OK** or **Save** to save the file.

Begin Guided Tour   Download WinZip with Your Browser

One of the most important and useful helper applications is WinZip. This application is used to uncompress the files that you downloaded from Web pages or FTP sites as discussed in the previous Guided Tours. This Guided Tour will show you how to download WinZip using your browser.

1 One of the best places on the Web to find helper and other applications for the Internet is **http://www.shareware. com**. Type the address in your browser's Netsite box and press **Enter**.

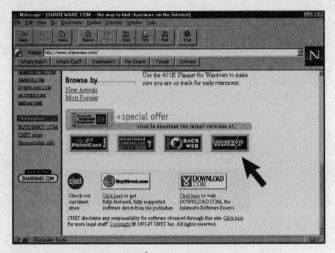

2 Scroll to the bottom of the shareware.com page. A link is provided for the most recent version of WinZip. Click the link.

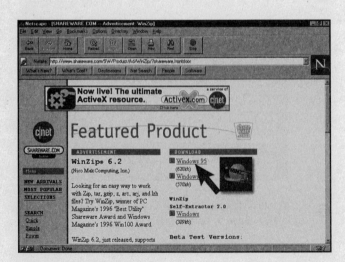

3 You will be taken to a page that provides links for several different versions of the popular WinZip software. Click the **Windows 95** link.

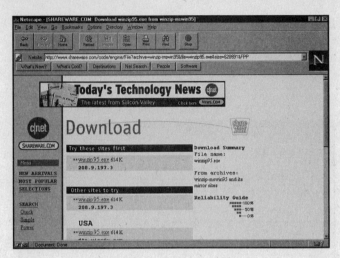

4 Select one of the download sites for WinZip and click the link.

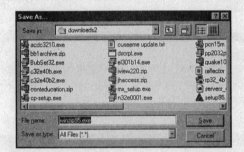

5 The Save As dialog box will appear. Select an appropriate directory on your computer for the WinZip software, and then click **Save**. The WinZip program will be downloaded to your computer.

Install a Helper Application

The helper applications you just downloaded are in zipped (compressed) files. Each zipped file (any file whose name ends in .zip) contains all the files that make up one of the helper applications. To install a helper application, you use a file decompression program such as PKZIP or WinZip, which extracts the compressed files from the zipped file.

You may have downloaded and installed WinZip in "Install Your Files" (page 79). If you haven't installed WinZip, that's okay. The Guided Tour walks you through installing WinZip so you can use it to unzip the other helper applications you downloaded.

Where to Store Your Helper Applications

You should create a separate folder for each of your helper applications. For example, you might create a folder called LVIEW, another folder called MPEG, and still another folder called QuickTime. You can then extract the zipped files for each helper application to its own, separate folder.

Although you can create these folders anywhere on your hard disk, they are usually placed under the WinApps folder. This is where most Windows applications place their *applets* (small programs that bigger programs share), and many Web browsers are set up to look under the WinApps folder for helper applications. If you place the helper applications under this folder, you might save yourself a little work.

Do you have to run a setup program? Whether or not you have to run a setup program depends on the helper application. Some are ready to run as soon as you unzip them. You simply extract the zipped files to a folder, and you're ready to roll. In some cases the files are downloaded as executable files (they have the extension .exe). This means that they are self-extracting. Place them in a directory (such as the ones you created above or your windows temp directory) and double-click the file. It will automatically unzip the files that are needed to either run or install the application. WinZip is a self-extracting zip file. When you run it (by double-clicking it in My Computer or Windows Explorer), WinZip extracts its files and automatically runs the setup program, which leads you through the process of installing WinZip.

Begin Guided Tour   **Extract Helper Applications**

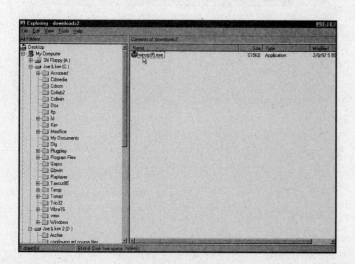

1 Double-click the WinZip95 icon to begin the installation process. The file will automatically extract its files and run a setup program.

(continues)

Guided Tour Extract Helper Applications *(continued)*

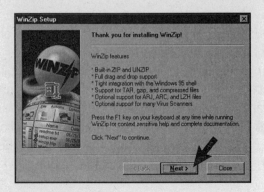

2 Follow the instructions to complete the installation.

You will find that most of the latest versions of shareware programs that you download for Windows 95 use a setup Wizard to install the software. All you have to do is answer questions concerning where you want the files installed, what Web browser you are using, or what modem speed you connect to the Internet with. Setup Wizards often look at your computer's configuration and help you make the correct installation choices.

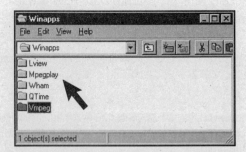

3 Create a folder for each of your helper applications under the WinApps folder in Windows 95. You will extract the zipped helper application files to these folders.

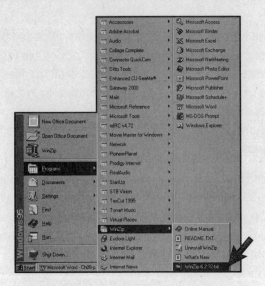

4 In Windows 95, the WinZip installation places WinZip on the Start menu. Click the **Start** button, point to **Programs**, point to **WinZip**, and then click the **WinZip** option.

5 The WinZip window appears. To open an archive (one of your ZIP files), click the **Open** button on the toolbar.

Guided Tour   Extract Helper Applications

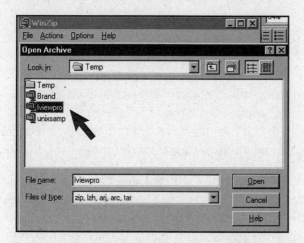

6 In the dialog box that appears, select one of your zipped helper application files. (If you followed the download instructions given earlier, they should be in the TEMP folder.) Click the **Open** or **OK** button to proceed.

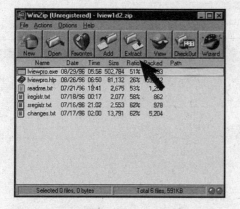

7 WinZip displays the names of all the files in the selected ZIP file. Click the **Extract** button in the toolbar.

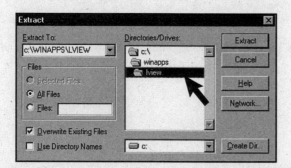

8 A dialog box like the one shown here appears. Select the drive and the folder that you created for this particular helper application. (That folder should be under the winapps folder.)

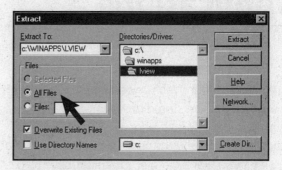

9 If necessary, select the **All Files** option to have WinZip unzip all of the files in the zipped file.

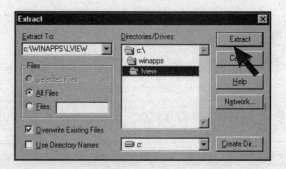

10 Click the **Extract** button. WinZip unzips the ZIP file and stores all the extracted files in the specified folder.

11 You can repeat steps 6 through 10 to unzip other zipped files. When you are done, proceed to the next section, in which you learn how to tell your Web browser where to look for helper applications.

After you unzip your helper applications, you can delete the original files you downloaded (the ones with the .zip extension). This will free up some disk space.

Set Up Your Web Browser to Use Helper Applications

Even though the helper applications are on your hard disk, your Web browser doesn't know where the applications are stored or when it should use them. To remedy the situation, you must *associate* particular file types with the helper applications that can play them. For example, you might have to tell your Web browser that whenever it encounters a GIF or JPG file, it should run LView.

The steps you take to associate file types to helper applications vary according to which Web browser or Gopher program you're using. Most programs offer an Options menu, a Preferences menu, or a Configure menu that contains the command you need. That command may be called "Preferences," "Options," "Edit Viewers," or "Helper Apps." You'll have to poke around your own menu system to find the command for setting up helper applications (or viewers).

When you enter the required command, you'll see a dialog box that is basically the same no matter which Web browser or Gopher program you're using. The dialog box allows you to pick a file type (such as JPG graphic files), and then assign a helper application to that file type. Follow the Guided Tour to associate file types to your helper applications.

Begin Guided Tour   Associate File Types with Helper Applications

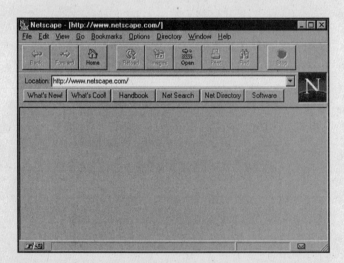

1 You don't need to be connected to the Internet to set the options for your Web browser or Gopher program. Run the Web browser or Gopher program for which you want to set up helper applications.

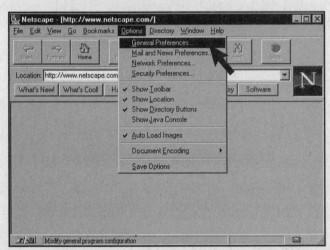

2 In your Web browser, enter the command for setting your preferences. In Netscape Navigator (shown here), you open the **Options** menu and select **General Preferences**.

Guided Tour   Associate File Types with Helper Applications

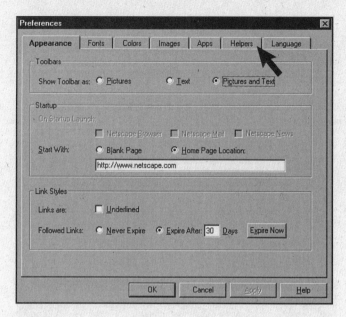

3 If the dialog box that appears has several tabs, click the **Viewers** or **Helpers** tab to bring its options to the front.

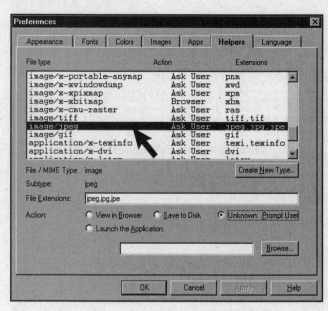

5 Click the file type (for example, **image/jpeg**) that you want to associate with one of your helper applications.

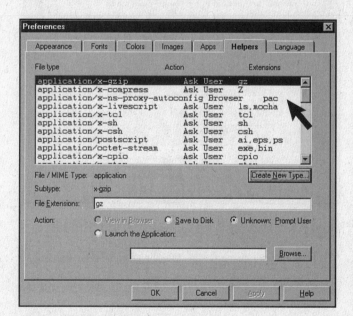

4 The File type list shows the file types that you can associate with a helper application. The right-most column shows the file name extensions for each file type. (You can ignore most of the file types listed.)

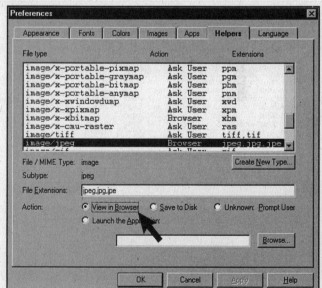

6 If your Web browser can open the file type you selected, you can choose **View in Browser** to use the Web browser to play the file. Or, you can choose to play the file type in a helper application, as explained in step 7.

(continues)

Guided Tour Associate File Types with Helper Applications *(continued)*

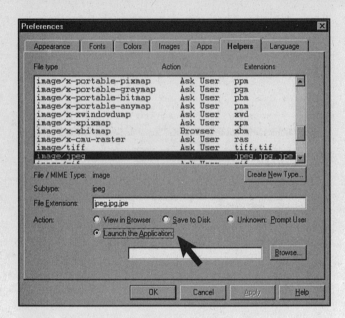

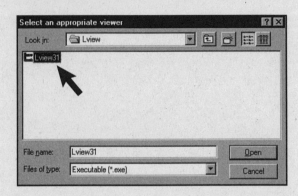

9 A dialog box appears, allowing you to select the helper application. Select the drive, folder, and name of the file that runs the helper application. Click **Open** or **OK**.

7 To use a helper application to play the file type you selected, select the **Launch the Application** option (or the comparable option in your program).

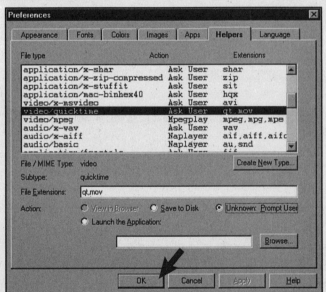

10 Repeat steps 5 through 9 to associate additional file types to your helper applications. Click **OK** when you are done to accept your changes and close the Preferences dialog box.

8 Next you must specify where the helper application is located. Click the **Browse** button.

Play Multimedia Files

After you have associated the most common file types with helper applications, playing multimedia files is easy. You just click a link for the file you want to open or play. Your Web browser or Gopher program downloads the file, runs the associated helper application, and opens the file in the helper application. You can then use the commands in the helper application to play the file, save the file to disk, or perform other actions.

As you select files to play, keep in mind that some files may be rather large. A short movie clip, for example, might be larger than one megabyte. Even if you have a fast modem, it can take well over a minute to download the file. Most Web browsers display a dialog box showing the progress of the file transfer. Don't expect the file to immediately pop up on your screen.

The Guided Tour shows how easy it is to play graphics, video, and sound clips on the Web and from a Gopher program.

Save Files to Your Disk

There may be times when you want to save a graphic, sound, or movie clip to your hard disk. After you play a file, you can usually save it using the **File**, **Save** command in your helper application. Most Web browsers also have commands that let you bypass the helper applications in case you want to save a file without playing it.

In Netscape Navigator, for example, you can right-click the link for a file, click the **Save** option on the shortcut menu that appears, and respond to the resulting dialog box. In Mosaic and some other Web browsers, you can save a file by holding down the **Shift** key while clicking the file's link. This brings up the Save dialog box, in which you select the drive and folder to which you want the file saved.

Some Web browsers, such as Netscape Navigator, let you associate a file type to the Save to Disk option (instead of to a helper application). If you select this option, anytime you select a file of the specified type, a dialog box appears, asking you if you want to save the file instead of playing it. This option is useful if you want to copy a bunch of files of a particular type to your disk.

Begin Guided Tour Play Files from the Web

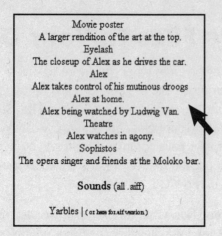

1 Connect to the Internet and run your Web browser. As you wander the Web, you will come across files that may require a helper application. Click a file's link to play or open the file.

2 The Web has a place for you to test your helper applications. Enter the following URL to go to the test page: **http://www-dsed.llnl.gov/documents/WWWtest.html**.

3 Click the test button for one of the file types you set up a helper application to play. (If you find a file type you can't play, this page also has links you can use to find and download helper applications.)

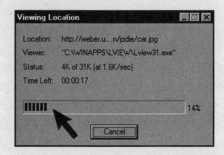

4 If you selected a file for which you've associated a helper application, your Web browser downloads the file. A dialog box like the one shown here displays the progress of the file transfer. (If the file type is not associated with a helper application, you'll see a dialog box saying so. Skip to step 8 for further instructions.)

5 When the file transfer is complete, the Web browser runs the associated helper application and opens the downloaded file in the application. Here, LView displays the contents of a GIF file—a simple test pattern.

6 If your file is a sound or video clip, you may have to click a **Play** button to start playing the downloaded file. If it's a simple graphic (such as a GIF or JPG file), the helper application displays the contents of the file immediately.

Guided Tour   Play Files from the Web

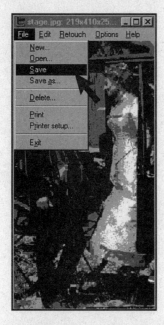

7 Many helper applications allow you to save a file to disk. Simply open the application's **File** menu and select **Save**. Fill in the information in the dialog box that appears to specify where you want the file saved.

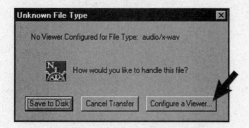

8 If you click a link to play a file, and you see a dialog box indicating that no helper application has been assigned to this file type, you can choose to save the file to disk (to play later).

9 Some browsers let you set up file associations on-the-fly. With Netscape Navigator, you can click the **Configure a Viewer** button to assign a helper application to this file type.

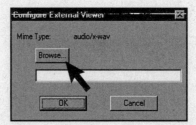

10 The Configure External Viewer dialog box displays the file type you selected. Click the **Browse** button to pick the helper application you want to use.

11 In the dialog box that appears, select the drive, folder, and name of the file that runs your helper application. Then click **Open** or **OK**.

12 After you configure a viewer for the selected file type, your browser downloads the selected file and opens it in the specified helper application.

HOW TO...

Find and Install Browser Plug-Ins and ActiveX Controls

With the incredible explosion of new sites on the World Wide Web, the Web has really become the preferred avenue to the Internet for most users. Web browsers offer a rich and constantly-evolving interface to an incredible repository of information.

You've already learned in the section "Play Sound and Video Clips with Helper Applications" beginning on page 129 that you can install helper applications that allow you to play and view Web content that is beyond the capabilities of your Web browser. The helper information is played outside of the browser window actually in the helper application. Well, hold onto your hat because there are two other types of software that can greatly expand what your Web browser can do: Browser Plug-Ins and ActiveX Controls. Whether you use Plug-Ins or ActiveX controls to soup up your Web browser will depend on which Web browser you use: Netscape Navigator uses Plug-Ins and Microsoft Internet Explorer uses ActiveX controls.

What You Will Find in This Section

Netscape Navigator and Plug-Ins

Plug-Ins are software programs that extend the capabilities of the browser. They are similar to helper applications; however, plug-ins become immediately operational after installation and many of them play their special content (multimedia files—sound, video, virtual reality content) within the confines of the Web browser. An example would be Macromedia's Shockware that allows you to play and interact with special multimedia Web content within your Netscape browser. Another great Netscape Navigator Plug-In is the Real Audio/Video player, which can play real-time (or recorded) audio and video via your Web browser. For a detailed discussion of helper applications see the section "Play Sound and Video Clips with Helper Applications" beginning on page 129.

The easiest places to find Plug-Ins for Netscape Navigator are two Netscape sites:

http://home.netscape.com/comprod/ products/\navigator/version_2.0/plugins/ index.html

http://home18.mcom.com/comprod/ products/navigator/version_2.0/plugins/ whats_new.html

Although the sites say they are for version 2 of Navigator, you will find all the 3.01 and Windows 95/ Windows NT 32 bit Plug-Ins at these sites. Another good site for Navigator Plug-Ins is **http://home. netscape.com/comprod/mirror/navcomponents download.html.**

Microsoft Internet Explorer and ActiveX Controls

Microsoft Internet Explorer can also be enhanced with special programs that extend the capabilities of the browser. The way that this is done, however, is somewhat different than the plug-in strategy used by Netscape, although the results are similar. Internet Explorer uses ActiveX controls to play and interact with special Web content.

What is ActiveX? It is a technology that allows your Web browser, specifically Internet Explorer, to access information (mainly multimedia content) that relies on an outside program to play.

> You're probably wondering how ActiveX controls work. It's really quite easy; for instance, when you go to a Web page that uses ActiveX, an ActiveX control will be part of the page. This control tells Internet Explorer what program it should use to play the special content (not unlike a Plug-In) associated with the control. Internet Explorer basically functions as a container that allows the special multimedia files associated with the ActiveX control to be played directly in the Web browser.

The ActiveX versions of software add-ons such as Macromedia Shockwave and the Real Audio/Video player are available on the Web. In fact, there are a number of sites that provide you with links to ActiveX controls for Internet Explorer. C/Net actually maintains a page called ActiveX.com. You can find it at **http://www.activex.com/library/mult.html**. It keeps an updated list of ActiveX controls. Another good place to find controls is **http://www.stroud.com/95activex.html**; this Web page is part of Stroud's Consummate Winsock site. For more information and additional links to ActiveX see **http:/www.microsoft.com/activex/gallery/**.

You can also find Navigator plug-ins and Explorer ActiveX controls at shareware sites such as **http://www.shareware.com, http://download.com**, the Sams Publishing TUCOWS mirror **http://tucows.mcp.com/at** and Strouds at **http://cws.iworld.com/**.

Netscape Navigator users can also take advantage of ActiveX content on the Web. An ActiveX Plug-In made by NC Compass Labs is available for Navigator. You can find this Plug-In at **www.nccompasslab.com/products/scriptactive.htm**.

To begin your exploration of these add-ons for your browsers, you will download a Navigator Plug-In, install it and use it to view multimedia content on the Web. You will also have an opportunity to explore ActiveX controls. The Guided Tour takes you to the sites where you can find the software and shows you the ins-and-outs of installation. You will also play multimedia content with your new Plug-Ins and controls.

Begin Guided Tour　Find and Install a Netscape Navigator Plug-In

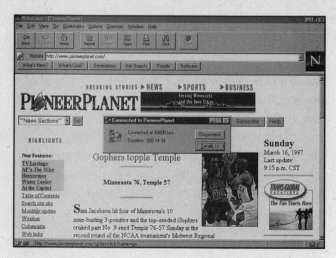

1 Establish your Internet connection, and run Netscape Navigator.

If you need help establishing a connéction with the Internet see "Prepare to Connect to the Internet" on page 27.

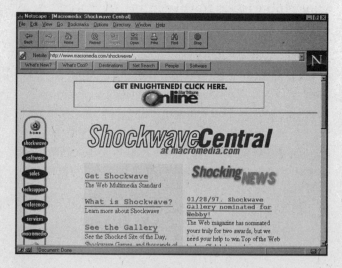

2 Enter **http://www.macromedia.com/shockwave/** in the Netsite box and then press **Enter**.

3 Click the **Get Shockwave** link.

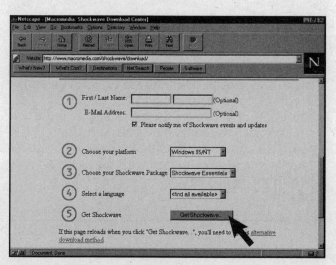

4 Fill out the form on this Web page (the name and e-mail information are optional) and then click the **Get Shockwave** button.

Guided Tour Find and Install a Netscape Navigator Plug-In

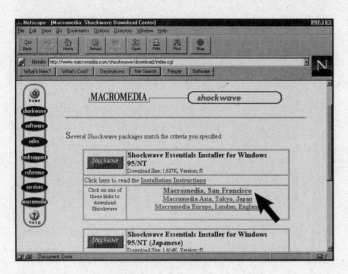

5 A list of sites for Shockwave Essentials is listed. Click the **Macromedia San Francisco** link.

6 You will be asked where you would like to store the file that is downloaded. Select the appropriate directory on your hard drive such as downloads or the Windows temp directory. Then press the **Save** button.

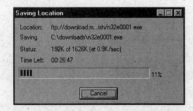

7 The file will be downloaded to your computer. When the Saving Location box disappears, the download will be complete.

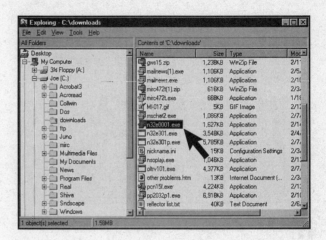

8 Open the Windows 95 Explorer and locate the Shockwave installation file that you downloaded—n32e001.exe (it will be in the directory that you specified). Double click **n32e001.exe** (this is a self-extracting program) to begin the installation procedure.

9 The installation process for Shockwave begins. Click **Yes** to continue.

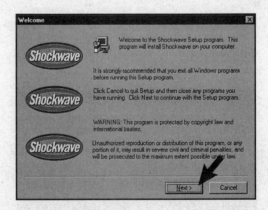

10 A series of screens walks you though the steps needed to get the software onto your computer's hard drive. Click the **Next** button to continue.

(continues)

Guided Tour Find and Install a Netscape Navigator Plug-In

(continued)

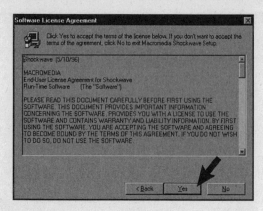

11 Read the license agreement provided for you. To accept click **Yes**.

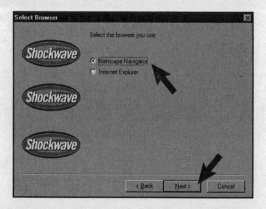

12 Shockwave can be set up for use with Netscape Navigator or Internet Explorer. Make sure the radio button for Netscape Navigator is selected and then click **Next**.

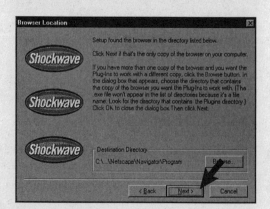

13 Check the Destination Directory listed in the dialog box to ensure that is where your browser is located. If the information is correct, click **Next** to continue.

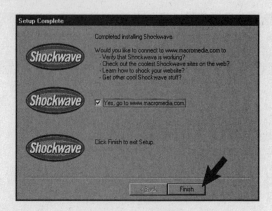

14 Check **Yes go to www.macromedia.com** if you want to test Shockwave; then click **Finish**.

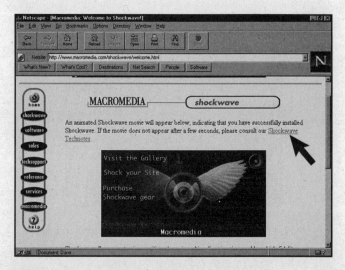

15 Click the **Shockwave Technotes** link if a Shockwave movie does not appear on the page.

Shockwave presentations are interactive multimedia content that has been created in programs called Director and Authorware by Macromedia. This content is "shocked" or altered so that it can be presented on the Web and viewed with your browser using the Shockwave Plug-In or ActiveX control.

Play Special Web Content with a Plug-In

Once you've installed a particular plug-in (or several plug-ins), you're ready to take advantage of the Web content that the plug-in offers through your Web browser. There are many plug-ins for Netscape. And while you can keep up on the advent of new plug-ins by checking out the Netscape home page, there will be times when you go to a Web site that contains special content that you do not have the plug-in for. This is a minor problem, however, and one that Netscape Navigator can remedy in many situations.

Navigator will look at the Web information that cannot be viewed and let you know that a plug-in is needed. Clicking the appropriate button in the dialog box that appears takes you to Netscape's Plug-In Finder page. This page shows you a list of plug-ins that can play the particular content. In this Guided Tour we'll show you how easy it is to play Web information with a Plug-In and what happens when you don't have a particular Plug-In.

Begin Guided Tour Play Shockwave Content on the Web

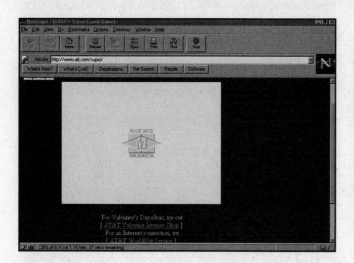

1 Go to the Web address: **www.attt.com/cupid/**. When you locate special Web content such as a Shockwave movie or interactive content, it may take a moment for the Shockwave content to load.

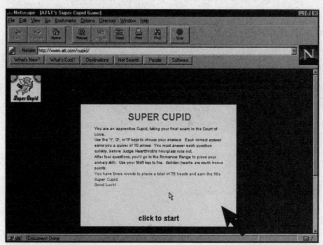

2 Once the Shockwave material is loaded, you're ready to interact within your Web browser. In this case, a mouse click begins an interactive quiz.

(continues)

Guided Tour Play Shockwave Content on the Web *(continued)*

3 The "shocked content" can contain animation, sound, and interactive abilities. In this "shocked" quiz participants must answer a question before the judge calls time.

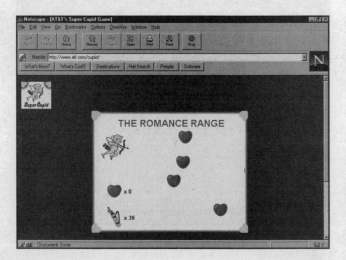

4 Once the quiz is completed the "shocked" presentation becomes an interactive shooting gallery, where you have to click the falling hearts with your mouse to score. Sound effects accompany the visuals.

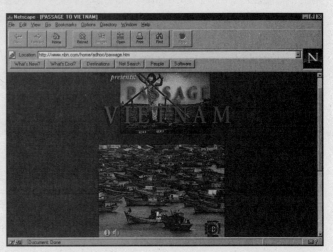

5 "Shocked" sites might contain some incredible content. The Passage to Vietnam site at **http://www.nbn.com/ home/adhoc/passage.htm** is a preview of material found on the popular *Passage to Vietnam* CD-ROM product.

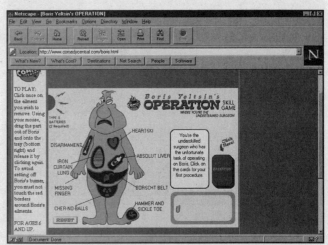

6 The Comedy Central Web site contains a "shocked" game that's a knock-off of the old standard: *Operation*. See if you can cure Boris Yeltsin at **http://www.comedycentral.com/ boris.html**.

Macromedia has a site that lists tons of sites that contain "shocked" material. There is even a Shocked site of the day. Go to **http://www. macromedia.com/shockwave/epicenter/** to check these sites out.

Guided Tour Play Shockwave Content on the Web

7 You will happen upon Web sites that contain special content that need a Plug-In that you have not installed. A dialog box will appear letting you know that an unknown file type is being downloaded. Click **More Info** to get some direct help from Navigator.

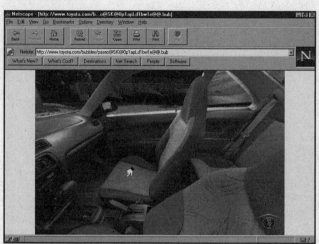

9 This particular Plug-In, BubbleViewer, allows you to view Photobubbles—3-dimensional pictures of various objects such as the interior of an automobile.

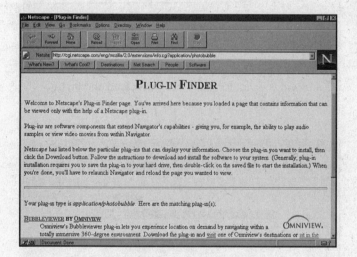

8 Navigator will take you to a special page (the Plug-In Finder) to help you locate the needed Plug-In. Once you find and install the plug-in using the steps shown earlier in "Find and Install a Netscape Navigator Plug-In" on page 148, you can return to the site that holds the special content and view it.

Begin Guided Tour Find and Install an ActiveX Control

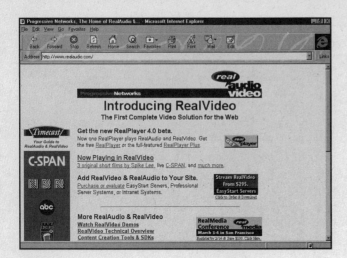

1 You can install ActiveX controls for Internet Explorer in the same way that you installed Plug-Ins for Navigator. RealPlayer is an add-on that plays both recorded and real-time video and audio through your Web browser. The link to download RealPlayer can be found at **www.realaudio.com**. Once you've located the real audio page, Click the **RealPlayer** link to download the program.

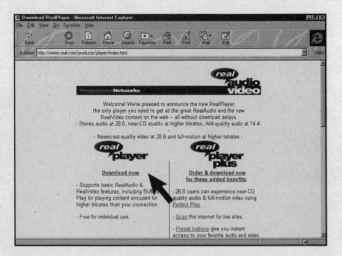

2 Click the **Download now** link to begin the download process.

3 Fill out the form. Once you've completed the form, scroll down and click the **Go to the Download and Instructions Page** button.

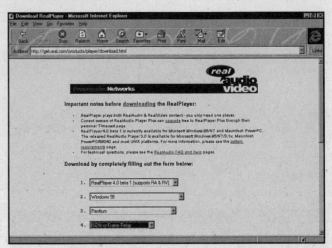

4 Once you are on the download page, click one of the sites shown.

Guided Tour Find and Install an ActiveX Control

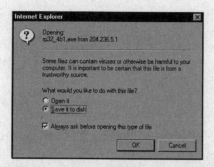

5 Select the **Save it to disk** radio button on the dialog box that appears and then click **OK**. .

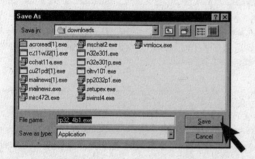

6 Select the folder that you want the RealPlayer file saved to and then click **Save**.

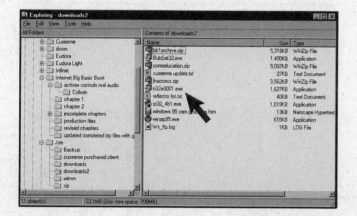

7 Locate the file using the Windows Explorer and then double-click it.

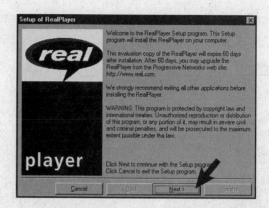

8 Answer the questions on the screen to complete the installation process.

9 Select a browser to run the RealPlayer. After you have made your selection, click **Finish**.

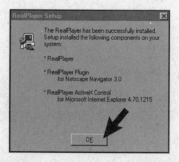

10 The setup lets you know that RealPlayer has been installed and the ActiveX control (and plug-in if you had Navigator installed) is now available for use by Internet Explorer. Click **OK** to end the installation process.

Begin Guided Tour Play Special Web Content with an ActiveX Control

1 Now you're ready to try out the RealPlayer ActiveX control and see how it works with Internet Explorer. Go to **http://www.timecast.com/spikelee/theater/lobby.html**. This site offers three short films that can be played using the RealPlayer control. Click the **John Turturro** link.

2 Click the Video Start button. The RealPlayer ActiveX control allows Internet Explorer to play the video content within the Web browser.

You will find that the number of ActiveX controls and Netscape Plug-Ins available seems to grow daily. Most add-ons now come with an installation program that can either set up the software to run as a Plug-In or an ActiveX control.

HOW TO...

Find and Play Java and Other Applets

One of the hottest Web topics is Java, a programming language that lets people create interactive multimedia applications for the World Wide Web. Using Java, programmers can create small programs called Java applets that can be placed on a Web page. A Java applet can be an animation (like a cartoon), a movie clip that plays automatically, or a form that gives you immediate feedback.

Java Applets can be found all over the World Wide Web. Many pages use them for animated effects, and you will find that the complexity of Java applets can also vary. At **www.bulletproof.com/ wallstreetweb/**—WallStreet Web— you will find a Java applet that allows you to view the latest stock prices on Wallstreet and actually do online trading. A somewhat simpler but no less impressive Java applet is the PacMan-like game, Gobbler, found at **http:// www.magnastar.com/games/gobbler/**.

In this section, you will skip around the Web to find and play some of the more interesting Java applets and other small online programs.

What You Will Find in This Section

Play Sample Java Applets

S hortly after the Java genesis, programmers used the programming language to create small, interesting applications that showed the capabilities of Java. These demos included an online painting application, a tic-tac-toe game, an animated Christmas card that played a jingle, a crossword puzzle, a loan calculator, and other nifty playthings.

Today Java programmers are developing online applications that can be accessed via the Web. As this technology is perfected, you will be able to perform all sorts of tasks online as you cruise the Web.

What Makes Java Special?

On the surface, Java might seem like just another programming language. What makes Java so special is that its applets can be run on nearly any type of computer (a PC running Windows, a Macintosh, a UNIX workstation, or any other computer that can connect to the Internet). The only essential you need for running a Java applet is a Web browser that can handle Java applets.

Currently, there are three Web browsers that can play Java applets: Netscape Navigator, Microsoft Internet Explorer, and HotJava (a Web browser created by the same company that developed Java—Sun Microsystems). By the time you read this, most Web browsers should have this capability. Because Java

applets can run on virtually any computer system, they are ideal for the Internet. And, because these applets can easily be placed on any Web page, they are very accessible.

> Unlike full-fledged applications that can run on their own, Java applets need a host program in which to run. The Web browser acts as the host program for Java applets.

Find Java Applets

You will be surprised at how many Web pages take advantage of Java applets. Some use Java for simple animations on their pages; others use Java for applications that can help you perform all sorts of tasks, or just entertain you. As the use of Java increases on the Web, you'll be bumping into Java applets at every turn. And, because Java applets are embedded in Web pages, you probably won't even realize that you're using Java applets. You'll just point, click, and type, while the applet performs its magic behind the scenes.

To begin your exploration of Java applets you will check out some sample Java applets that can be found on the Netscape Java page and the Sun Microsystems page—both major promoters of Java. The Guided Tour takes you to these sites and shows you some sample Java applets in action.

Begin Guided Tour Play Java Applets

① Establish your Internet connection, and run a Java-compatible Web browser, such as Microsoft Internet Explorer or Netscape. Internet Explorer is shown here.

② Highlight the entry in the Address text box, and type **http://java.sun.com**. Press **Enter**.

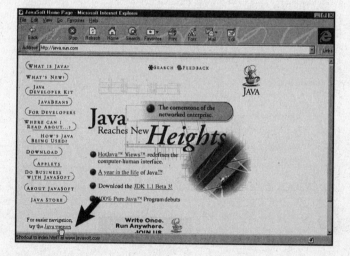

③ Click the link that says **For easier navigation, try the Java version**.

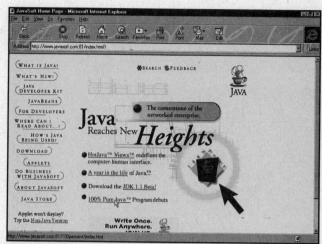

④ Point at a graphic with your cursor. The Sun Java page contains a Java applet that changes the graphics on the page when you point to them.

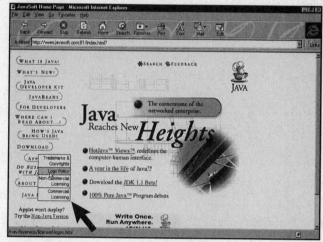

⑤ Move the cursor to the left side of the page; another applet on the page provides you with drop-down menus when you place the mouse on various links.

(continues)

Guided Tour Play Java Applets *(continued)*

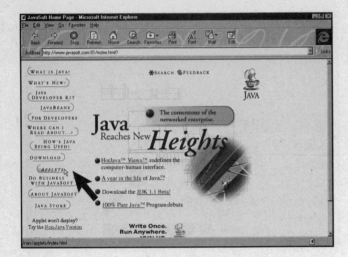

6 Click the Applets link on the left side of the page to take a look at other Java applets.

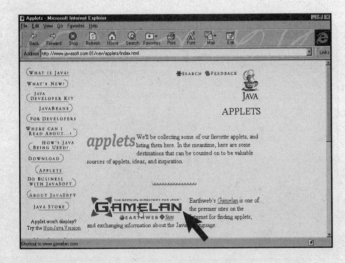

7 This page provides you with a link to Gamelan, a great place to find Java applets. Click the Gamelan link.

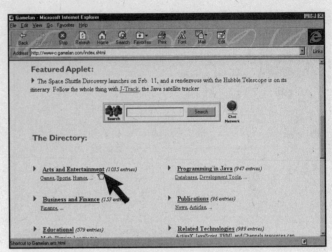

8 The Gamelan page provides you with access to tons of applets. Scroll down the Gamelan page and you will find directories of Java applets organized by categories. Gamelan also provides a search tool for finding applets. Click the **Arts and Entertainment** link.

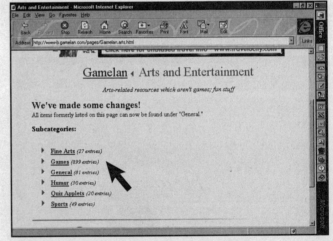

9 On the next page, the Arts and Entertainment Java applets are listed in subcategories; click the **Games** link.

Guided Tour   Play Java Applets

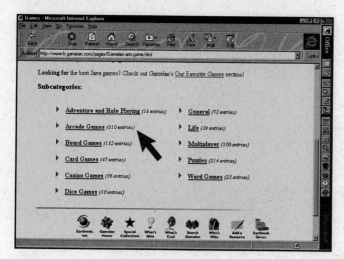

10 Still more subcategories, click **Arcade Games**.

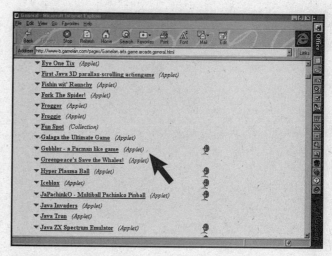

12 Click the **Gobbler** link to play a Java game.

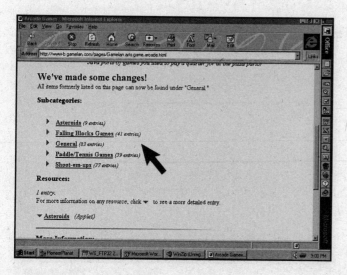

11 Now click the **General** link. Gobbler, a PacMan-like game, can be found in this list of games, so scroll down until you see it.

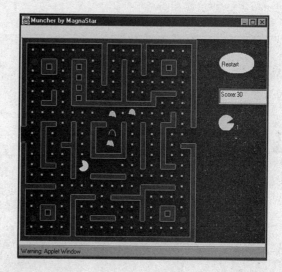

13 A fully functional Java version of the popular PacMan game appears. To play the game, check-out the directions on the page directly behind the applet.

(continues)

Guided Tour Play Java Applets (continued)

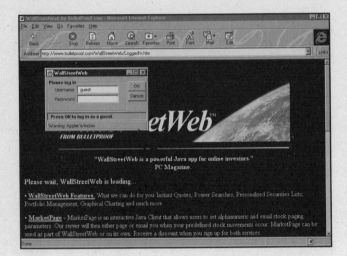

14 Another great Java applet to check out is the WallStreet Web at **www.bulletproof.com/wallstreetweb/**. When you first enter the site, a Java applet log-in will appear. Click **OK** to log onto the system as a guest.

Since Java applets are applications, they may take a while to load. Some of the larger ones may seem to take forever; be patient.

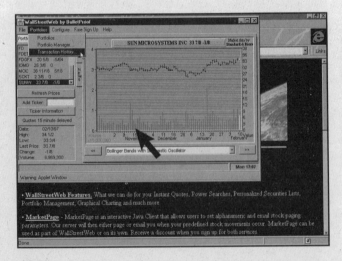

15 Once you are logged on, you can use the applet to track the performance of various companies' stock. Just choose a company in the company scrollbox to see a graph of their performance.

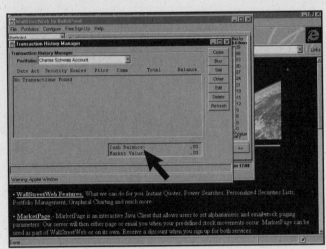

16 This system can also provide you with online trading options, if you are a subscriber. By clicking the **Portfolios** menu you can view the history of your stock trades.

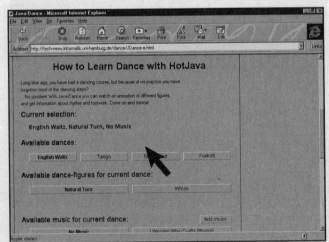

17 Another great example of a Java applet is the Learn to Dance with HotJava demo at **tech-www.informatik. uni-hamburg.de/dance/JDance-e.html**. This applet plays music and will show you the dance steps of the selected dance.

Understand JavaScript

As you encounter Java applets, you might come across a reference to JavaScript. Don't confuse JavaScript with Java. Java is a full-featured programming language, which is somewhat difficult for the average computer user to learn (as is any programming language). JavaScript is simply a coding system that allows Web page creators to embed Java applets in Web pages.

If you don't plan on creating your own Web pages, you don't have to worry about JavaScript. It works behind the scenes. However, if you decide to try your hand at creating Web pages, you might want to insert a Java applet on your page, or use JavaScript to make your Web page more interactive.

The following Guided Tour shows you some sample JavaScript codes and demonstrates how they are used. If you're serious about writing your own Java applets, grab a copy of *The Complete Idiot's Guide to JavaScript*, Second Edition, by Aaron Weiss.

Begin Guided Tour   Look at a Sample JavaScript

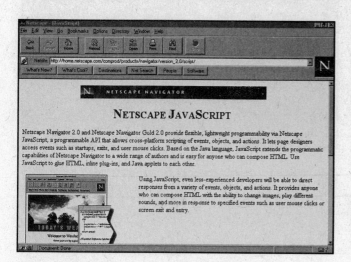

1 The best place to check out JavaScript is at Netscape's Web site. In your Web browser (Netscape Navigator is used here), enter the following URL: **http://home.netscape.com/ comprod/products/navigator/version_2.0/script/**.

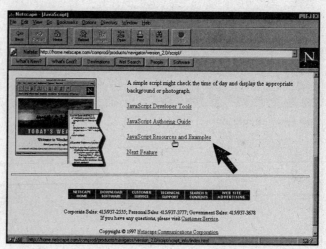

2 Scroll down the page to view some samples of how JavaScript can be used. Click the **JavaScript Resources and Examples** link to learn more about JavaScript.

(continues)

Guided Tour   Look at a Sample JavaScript

(continued)

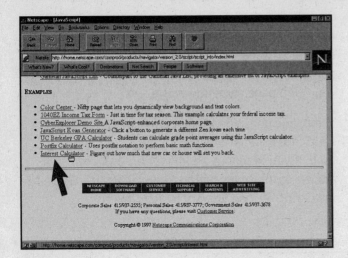

3 This page provides you with several JavaScript resources, including a tutorial. Scroll down to the examples of JavaScript and select the **Interest Calculator**.

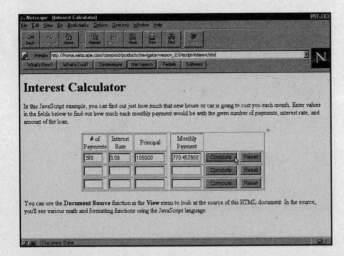

4 This calculator determines your monthly payment amount based on the amount borrowed, the interest rate, and the length of the loan. Enter the requested data, and click the **Compute** button.

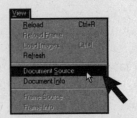

5 To see how this JavaScript applet is constructed, open Navigator's **View** menu and select **Document Source**.

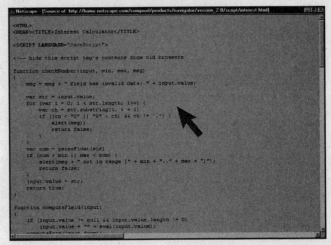

6 Navigator displays the coding behind the JavaScript applet. Note that the applet's programming code is set off from the rest of the document by the <Script> code.

Guided Tour   Look at a Sample JavaScript

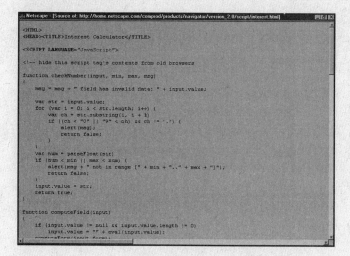

7 Following the <Script> codes are the programming commands that perform the calculations required to determine the monthly payment amount. This is a fairly complex JavaScript applet.

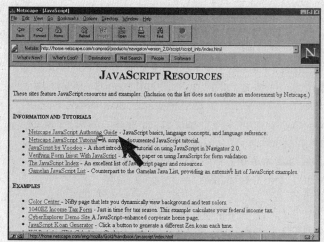

9 The Netscape Web site offers additional information about JavaScript. If you are interested in learning more, click the **Back** button to return to the previous page. Click **Netscape JavaScript Authoring Guide**.

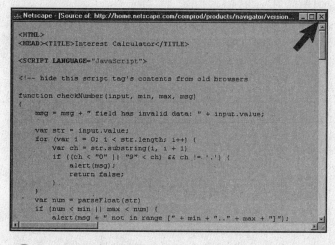

8 Click the **Close** button to close the Document Source window and return to Netscape Navigator.

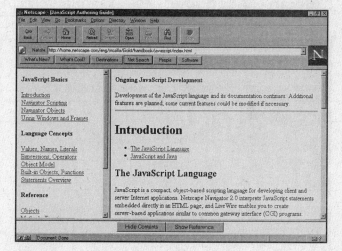

10 Netscape presents complete documentation to help you learn how to use JavaScript. Click a link in the left frame to display information about a specific JavaScript topic.

Play VRML Applets

Although Java has received the most press coverage, there are other programming languages designed for the Internet. The strongest contender is VRML (rhymes with "gerbil" and stands for *Virtual Reality Modeling Language*). Like Java, VRML is used by programmers to create small applications that can be placed on Web pages. These applications are just like Java applets, in that they can display animations, video, and interactive forms on a page.

VRML has been used a great deal to create 3-D objects, places, (yes, even worlds) that can be navigated with a VRML-ready Web-browser. To view VRML content, you need a special VRML-compatible Web browser, or a helper application, plug-in, or ActiveX control. Both Netscape and Microsoft Internet Explorer can be set up to run VRML code. See "Find and Install Browser Plug-ins and ActiveX Controls" on page for more information on setting up your browser to play special Web content such as VRML. To quickly prepare Internet Explorer for VRML, download the VRML add-in at: **http://www. microsoft. com/ie/download/**. Once you download the file, run it (by double-clicking the file) and follow the on-screen instructions to install the program; Internet Explorer will then be ready to view VRML content. Now you can take the Guided Tour to play some sample VRML files.

Begin Guided Tour   Play Sample VRML Applets

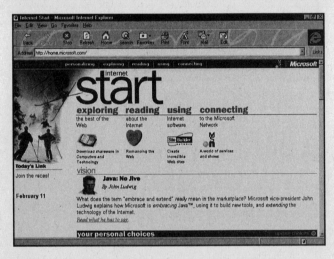

1 Establish your Internet connection, and run your Web browser. The picture here shows Internet Explorer.

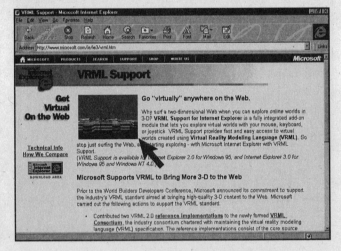

2 A good place to get your feet wet with VRML is a page sponsored by Microsoft: **http://www.microsoft.com/ie/ie3/vrml.htm**. This site contains information on VRML and a VRML object that you can immediately click and explore.

Guided Tour   Play Sample VRML Applets

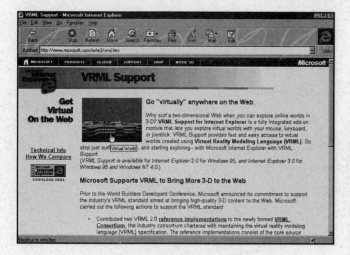

3 Click the VRML Virtual World on the page to activate it.

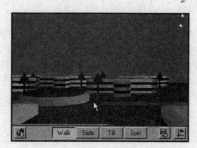

4 The VRML code loads and the virtual world appears in a box that contains a set of controls. You can walk through this three-dimensional scene, slide through the scene (faster than walking), or you can rotate the entire world on its axis. You move through the virtual world by placing your mouse where you want to go and then pressing the mouse button. Release the mouse button when you wish to stop.

5 You can return to the starting point of the virtual world by clicking the reset button.

6 Another good place to check out VRML objects is **http://www.ocnus.com/models/models.html**. The items are divided into categories.

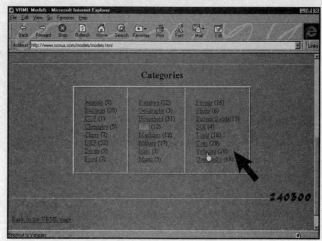

7 Now for some cool stuff. Click the **Vehicles** link.

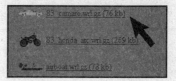

8 Scroll down through the list and select the 83 Camaro.

(continues)

Guided Tour   Play Sample VRML Applets   *(continued)*

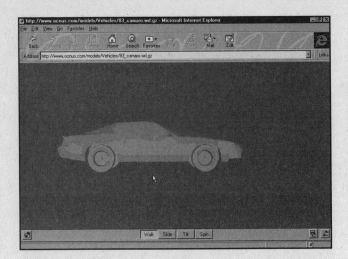

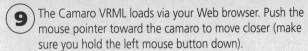

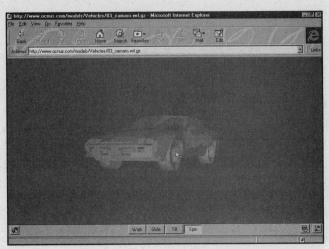

9 The Camaro VRML loads via your Web browser. Push the mouse pointer toward the camaro to move closer (make sure you hold the left mouse button down).

10 Click the **Spin** button and then use the mouse to rotate the vehicle.

> If you become interested in making a career out of running VRML applets on the Web, make sure you have a fast modem connection, lots of memory, and a quick microprocessor. VRML can be huge and require a tremendous amount of processing power.

HOW TO...

Search for Information on the Internet

U p to this point, you've been wandering the Web like some disori-
ented nomad, relying on links and recommended URLs to carry you
where they may. That's fine if you're using the Internet to pass the
time or for the sheer enjoyment of stumbling upon interesting
sites. But if you have to use the Internet to research a topic or do
some serious work, wandering is not the most efficient method.

Fortunately, the Internet offers several search tools that you can
use to find specific information. On the Web, you can use Yahoo!'s
home page to search various categories for information, or you
can type a search term (a key term that zeros in on what you're
looking for). Three other popular Web search tools, Lycos, Alta
Vista, and WebCrawler, work in much the same way.

What You Will Find in This Section

Search for Information on the Web

The best Internet search tools are on the World Wide Web. To search for general information about movies, for example, you can go to any of several Web pages that contain lists of categories. You simply click a category, such as Movies or Food, and the page displays a long list of links. You can then poke around for the general information you need.

If you need specific information in a hurry, the Web offers *forms-based* search tools. A forms-based search tool is simply a fill-in-the-blanks Web page that asks you what you're looking for. You type a specific search term, such as **Casablanca** or **Harrison Ford**, and then click a button (usually labeled **Submit** or **Search**). Within seconds, the search tool displays links that can carry you to Web pages that have the information you need.

Take the Guided Tour to try out some of these Web search tools. You'll find that the Web search tools often turn up additional information that you'll find on non-Web servers (such as newsgroups, FTP servers, and Gophers).

Understand How Search Tools Work

When you perform a search, you might get the impression that the search tool is rummaging through the Internet to find the information you asked for. Actually, the search itself has already been done. Each search tool uses a *search engine* that regularly explores the Internet for new information. When it finds new information, it catalogs or indexes that information, referencing each topic with an URL (an address that tells where the information is stored).

When you enter a specific search term, the search tool simply dips into the index, finds all the items that match your search term, and displays a list of links that point to the URLs where the information is stored. By handling searches in this way, a search tool can perform a search in a matter of seconds.

> Search tools that regularly wander the Web, indexing its many pages, go by many names including knowbot, robot, webcrawler, spider, and infobot. These names all focus on the nature of the search tools: They are automated and persistent. The Yahoo! search tool, however, is not a robot; its directory is compiled and maintained by humans.

Narrow Your Search

If you choose to use a forms-based search tool, you should select your search terms carefully. Searching for a general term such as "food" or "books" will give you a list of links too long to be of any use. Try to pick a term that is more specific, such as "desserts" or "Crime Novels." You can further narrow the search by looking for "pies" or "Devil in a Blue Dress."

In addition, many search forms allow you to set additional options for narrowing your search. These search tools, for example, are set to find all topics that match any of the search terms you enter. So if you enter "Coral Snake," the search tool will find a bunch of references to "coral" and to "snake." You need to specify that you want only those items that have *both* "coral" and "snake" in the title. The Guided Tour shows you how to enter search options for the most popular search tools.

Stop Words and Hits

As you type search terms, keep in mind that the search tool may not look up all the terms you type. Search tools are set up to ignore certain common words, called *stop words*. These include "a," "the," and "what," and such commonly used nouns as "computer" and "internet." So, for example, if you type "What is a web robot?" the search tool is likely to search only for "robot." When you type search terms, type one or two unique words.

Other Search Tools

The Guided Tour covers the three most popular search tools on the Web. However, the Web offers other search tools. Here's a list of other search tools to try, along with their URLs:

InfoSeek: http://www2.infoseek.com/

WebCrawler: http://www.webcrawler.com

Alta Vista: http://altavista.digital.com/

Excite: http://www.excite.com/

Magellan: http://searcher.mckinley.com

Lycos: http://www.lycos.com

HotBot: http://www.hotbot.com/

Begin Guided Tour   Search from the Yahoo! Home Page

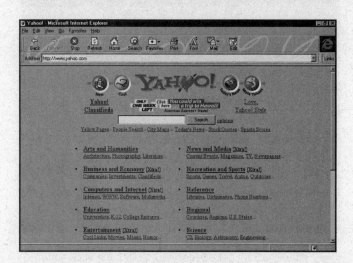

1 The Yahoo! home page is one of the most popular places to start wandering the Web. To go to Yahoo!, type **http://www.yahoo.com** in the **Location** or **Go to** text box of your Web browser and press **Enter**.

(continues)

Guided Tour Search from the Yahoo! Home Page *(continued)*

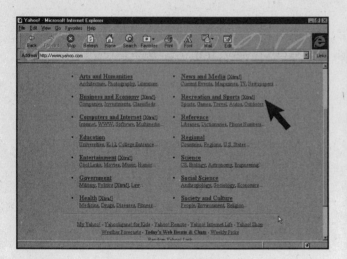

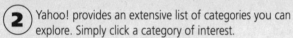

2 Yahoo! provides an extensive list of categories you can explore. Simply click a category of interest.

3 When you click a major category, such as **Recreation and Sports**, Yahoo! presents you with a list of subcategories. Continue clicking links until you find the information you want or reach a dead end.

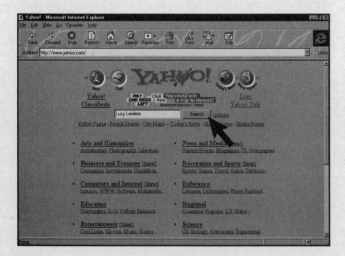

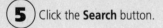

4 To perform a more structured search, return to Yahoo!'s home page and type one or two search terms in the text box at the top of the page.

5 Click the **Search** button.

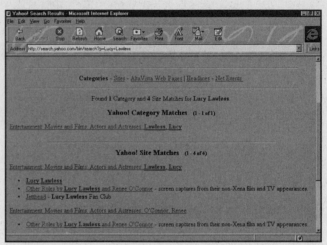

6 Yahoo! searches for the requested topic and displays a list of links that match your entry. Click a link to display the Web page or other Internet resource.

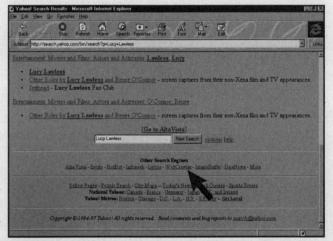

7 After checking out a page, you can click the **Back** button to go back to the list of items that Yahoo! found and click on another link. Also look at the end of the list of found items for links to other search tools. You can click one of these links to search for the same information using another tool.

Guided Tour   Search from the Yahoo! Home Page

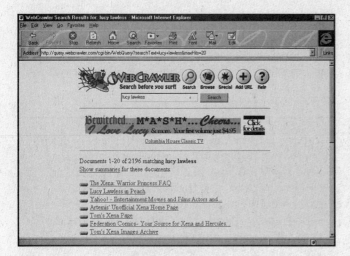

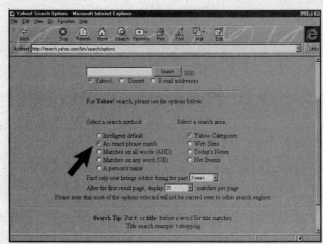

8 If you click a link for another search tool, the tool automatically performs the search and displays a list of items it found in its index.

10 Yahoo! normally treats your search terms as substrings, so if you type "book," Yahoo! will find "book," "books," "bookstore," "bookkeeper," and so on. You can select the **An exact phrase match** option to narrow the search.

(continues)

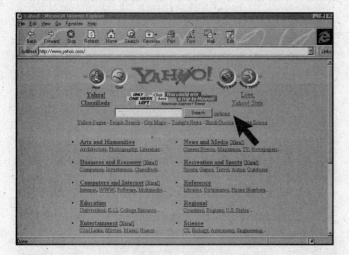

9 Although a basic Yahoo! search usually finds the information you need, you can set Yahoo! search options. Return to Yahoo!'s home page and click the **Options** link.

Guided Tour   Search from the Yahoo! Home Page   *(continued)*

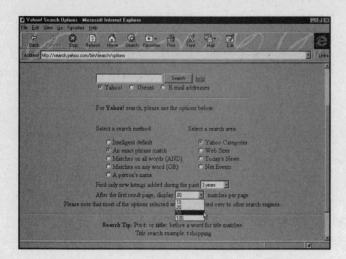

11 Yahoo! typically displays up to 25 found items per page, but provides a link at the bottom of the page that allows you to change that number. If you want more items displayed per page, open the **After the first result page, display __ matches per page** drop-down list and select the desired number.

Yahoo! is unlike most of the other Web search tools in that its index of sites is actually generated by Web users, like yourself, who submit URLs to Yahoo!. It is these sites that are included in its database when you search for Web pages related to certain topics. Lycos is a true Web search engine in that it crawls the Web searching for documents and catalogs them. When you search Lycos, you are looking through the results of the latest crawl by this powerful Web finder tool.

Begin Guided Tour   Search with Lycos

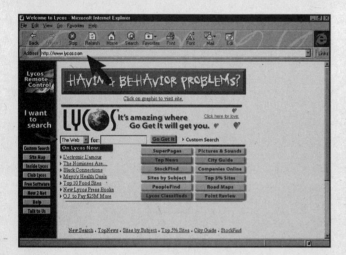

1 Lycos provides one of the most thorough Internet indexes you can find. To display the Lycos search page, type **http://www.lycos.com** in the **Location** or **Address** text box and press **Enter**.

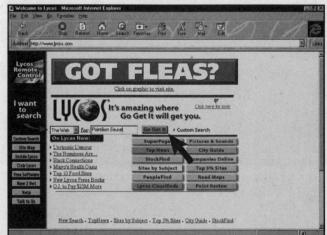

2 To perform a simple search for one or two terms, type the terms in the text box (as shown here) and click the **Go Get It** button. Lycos will find any items that have any of the search terms you enter.

Guided Tour Search with Lycos

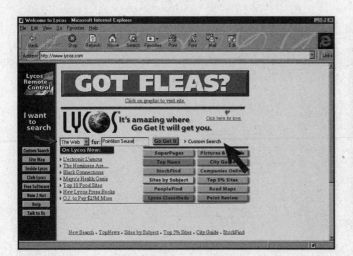

3 You can take more control of the search by setting the search options. To do so, click the **Custom Search** link.

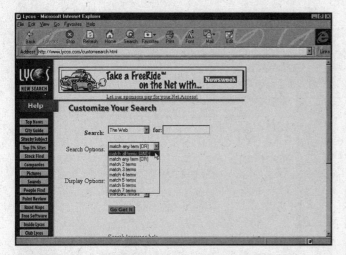

4 To narrow the search, open the **Search Options** drop-down list on the left, and click **match all terms (AND)**.

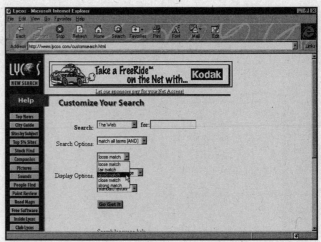

5 You can further narrow the search by specifying how exact you want the match to be. Open the second **Search Options** drop-down list and select an option that specifies how close you want the match to be.

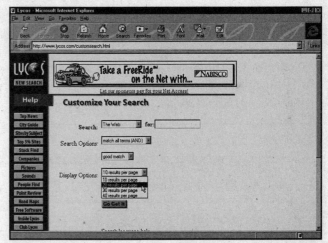

6 By default, Lycos displays 10 of the items it finds per page and displays a link at the bottom of the page that allows you to see additional items. To display more items per page, open the **Display Options** drop-down list and select a number.

(continues)

Guided Tour Search with Lycos

(continued)

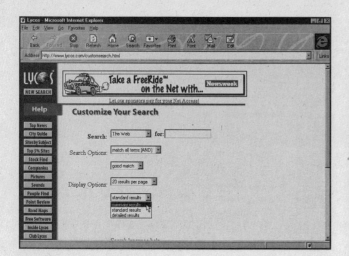

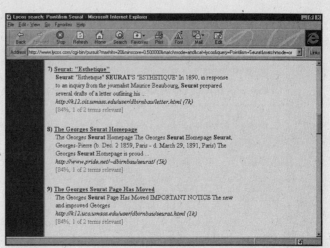

7 Lycos displays a brief description of each item it finds. To specify the length of each description, open the **Display Options** drop-down list and click the desired detail option: **summary results** (short), **standard results** (longer), or **detailed results** (longest).

9 Lycos searches its index and displays a list of items that match your search instructions. You click a link for an item to access that item.

If you are doing a custom search, you need to type in what you want to search for (at the top of this form). The search engine doesn't automatically pick up the search term from the standard search page.

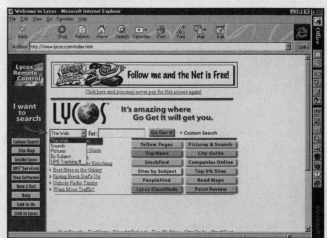

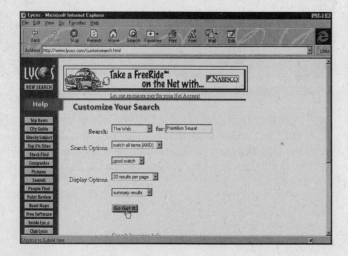

10 While many of your searches using Lycos will be for items on the Web, you can also use Lycos to search sounds, pictures, sites by subject, and even search for a particular UPS tracking number. For these special searches, click the drop-down box on the Lycos main search page.

8 Click the **Go Get It** button to start the search.

Begin Guided Tour   Find Information with WebCrawler

1 For a quick, no-frills Web search, connect to WebCrawler. Type **http://www.webcrawler.com/** in the **Location** or **Address** text box and press **Enter**.

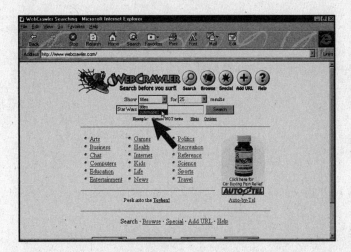

2 WebCrawler displays a form that prompts you to type your search terms. Type your search terms in the text box.

3 WebCrawler does offer search options. You can decide to view the titles of the matches or to view summary information for each of the matches to your search parameters. You can also choose the number of matches that you would like to appear based on your search parameters.

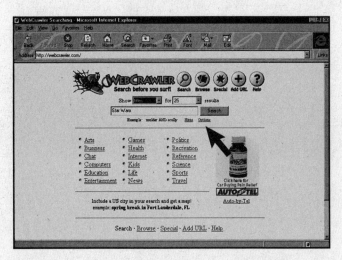

4 Click the **Options** link and you can customize WebCrawler even more.

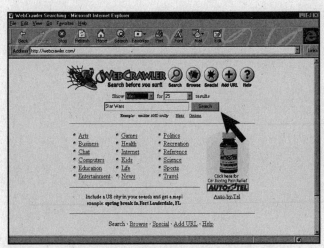

5 Set options and press the **Apply Preferences** button to return to the search page; click the **Search** button.

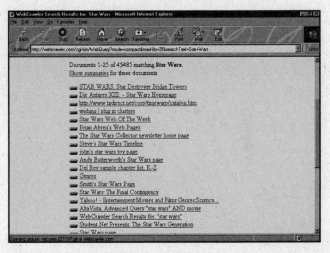

6 WebCrawler finds the items that match your search terms and displays a list of links. Click a link to go to the desired site.

Find and Copy Files from the Internet

You've already seen that there are a lot of software files available on the Internet. And while a lot of them are programs and information related to the Internet itself, there are also tons of software packages (both shareware and freeware) that you can download for your own use.

One of the most complete resources of files (applications, Internet add-ons, games, and all sorts of other stuff) is **www.Shareware.com** maintained by C/Net. Other sites such as Stroud's Consummate Winsock site at **http://cws.iworld.com/** maintain archives of specific types of software such as Internet tools.

While your Web browser is probably the most straightforward method of downloading new files, you can also use a dedicated FTP program such as WS-FTP. Some users prefer to download via an FTP client while they surf the Web with their browser. This is just one strategy for getting double duty out of your Internet connection time. This section explains how to find and download files quickly and how to efficiently use your Web browser. It will also show you how to use a dedicated FTP client.

What You Will Find in This Section

Copy Files with Your Web Browser

Sure you can upload (send) or download (receive) files from the Internet using your FTP program, but why bother when you can use your Web browser instead?

> One reason that there may be occasions to use a dedicated FTP client is sites that do not accept an anonymous login. This would be a situation where you have to give a specific user-name and password to log on to the file server.

As you've probably learned by now, your Web browser is what makes the Internet fun—mainly because it's so easy to use and understand. Just click a link, and you jump to that page. Want to go back? No problem. Want to jump directly to a particular Web page? No sweat. Want to search for stuff? Easy.

Well, your Web browser also makes downloading files as simple as point-and-click: You point to a link that is connected to a file on a Web site or FTP site, and then click to begin the downloading process. Then all you have to do is select an existing folder or create a new folder in which you want the downloaded file placed. Internet Explorer and Netscape Navigator also have the ability to download a file or files while you continue to surf the Web. That way you don't have to sit on your hands staring at one Web page while you wait for the file to download.

> You may want to create a single folder called Downloads for all the files you get off the Internet. That way, you can keep everything in one place until you've had a chance to use your antivirus program to verify that the files you've received are virus-free. I don't want to scare you, but downloading contaminated files from the Internet (or anywhere, for that matter) is the most common way a system becomes contaminated. So protect yourself (and your data) by double-checking the files you receive.

To download any file from the Internet, you have to find the file first. See "Search for Information on the Web" on page 169 for help finding the information you want. You can also try any of the following Web sites when you are looking for a file:

Shareware.com at **http://www. shareware.com/**

Stroud's Consummate Winsock Site at **http://cws.iworld.com/**

Windows95.com at **http://www. windows95.com/**

Galt Shareware Zone at **http://www. galttech.com/**

www.32bit.com at **http://www.32bit. com/software/index.phtml**

Sams Publishing TUCOWS mirror at **http://tucows.mcp.com/**

Begin Guided Tour   Search for Files on Shareware.com

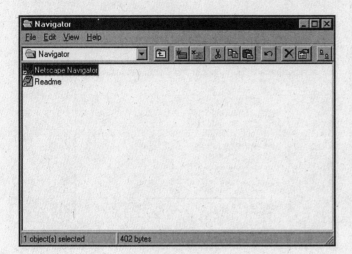

1 Connect to the Internet and start your Web browser. For example, to start Netscape Navigator in Windows 95, open the **Start** menu, point to **Programs**, and select **Netscape**. Then double-click the **Netscape Navigator** icon.

2 A good source of files is shareware.com. To jump there, type **http://www.shareware.com** in the **Go to** text box, and then press **Enter**.

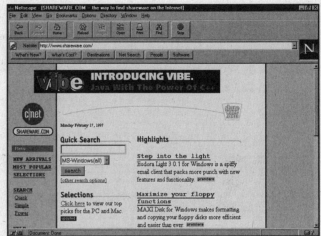

3 The shareware.com site offers an easy-to-use search engine.

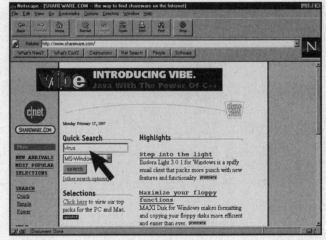

4 Type **virus** in the search text box.

If you know the file name of the program you want to search for, you can enter it in the search text box.

(continues)

Guided Tour Search for Files on Shareware.com

(continued)

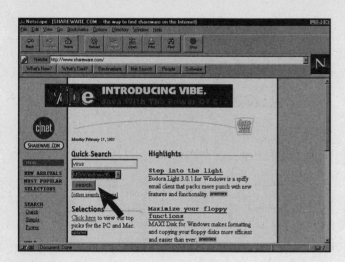

5 Select your operating system in the drop-down box and then click **search** or press the **Enter** key.

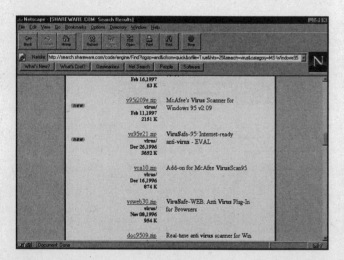

6 Scroll down to see the results of your search.

If you didn't get the results you wanted, click the **Back** button and change the information on the form, making it as specific as possible. For example, I originally searched for "anti-virus" and got nothing. When I searched for "virus," I got results.

7 Select a file to download by clicking its name.

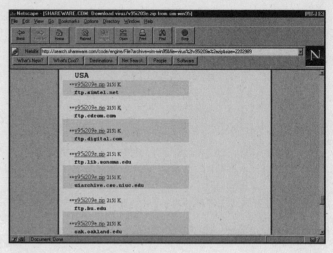

8 The page that appears has links to various FTP sites that contain your file.

9 When you're ready to download the file, click a site. You do not have to use a site close to you, but that might be faster. Often, however, the sites closest to you are busy. Your best bet is to pick a site that's in a time zone where it is the middle of the night; such sites are often less busy.

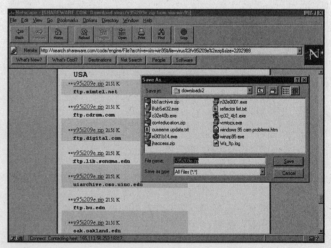

10 Select a directory in which to save the file and click **Save**.

Guided Tour Search for Files on Shareware.com

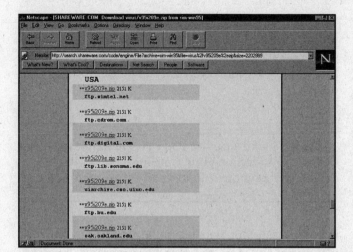

11 When you have saved the file, you're returned to your Web browser.

The route to saving a downloaded file will vary among Web browsers. Depending on how your preferences are set, Navigator might bring up the unknown file type box. Internet Explorer brings up a dialog box that will ask you if you want to open the file or to save it.

Begin Guided Tour Copy a File Directly from an FTP Site

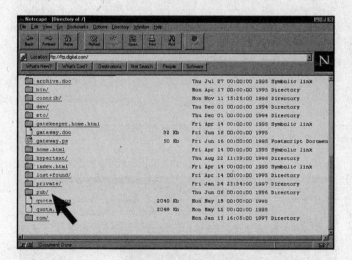

1 If you know the FTP site that a particular file is on, you can go directly to that site. For example, type **ftp://ftp.digital.com** in the **Location** or **Go to** text box and press **Enter**.

2 Scroll down until you see the Pub directory and then click it. This is where all the files are stored for public download.

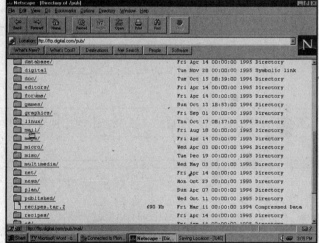

3 Scroll down again and click the **mail/** folder. Each time you click another folder you are deeper into the FTP directories.

4 From here, you can dig deeper for a file such as an e-mail package like Eudora.

5 To download a file, just click its name.

Find and Install an FTP Program

While your Web browser will probably be your most-used tool as you cruise the Web and download files, you can also use a dedicated FTP to download files from the Internet. The FTP program is usually a no-frills freeware or shareware program that is designed to download files from FTP sites. One good thing about having an FTP program is that you can set it up to download files while you continue to browse the Web with Navigator or Explorer. You can use your Web browser to download an FTP program.

After you download your FTP program, you must install it. But before you can install most programs you get from the Internet, you need to decompress them. Most files that you find will be *zipped*, which means they've been compressed with a utility called PKZIP. Compressing a file makes it smaller so that it takes less time to download. The files that make up your FTP program have been zipped into one small file. To make the files usable, you have to decompress (unzip) them. The easiest way to deal with this

unzipping nonsense is to use WinZip, which you can download from many FTP sites. For example, you'll find it at the **ftp.winsite.com** site in the **pub/pc/win95** directory.

> Always make sure the you have WinZip available (installed on your machine) in case the files that you download need to be unzipped.

In the Guided Tour, you'll learn how to download WS-FTP, one of the more common FTP programs. If you're looking for something easier to use, you might want to try downloading Cute FTP instead. Another good FTP program is FTP Explorer. If you are sometimes disconnected from your service provider in the middle of the download, this program may be for you. FTP Explorer caches what you have saved and when you reconnect, it starts downloading where you left off.

Begin Guided Tour Download a Different FTP Program

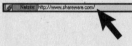

1 Connect to the Internet as usual and start your Web browser.

2 Connect to the shareware.com site by typing **http://www.shareware.com** in the **Location** or **Go to** text box and pressing **Enter**.

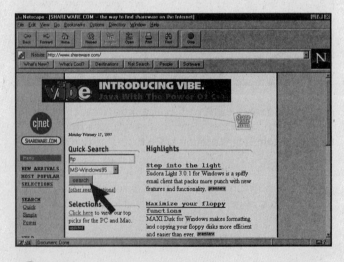

3 Type **ftp** in the Quick Search box, select your operating system, and then click **search**.

Guided Tour   Download a Different FTP Program

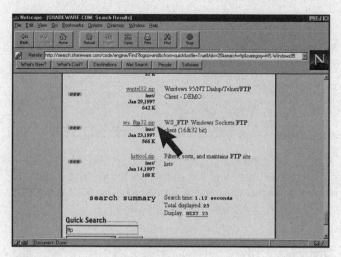

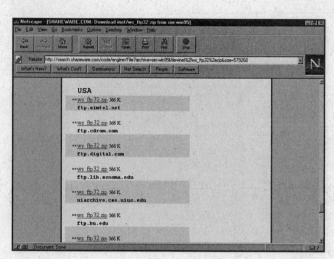

4 Scroll down and select **ws_ftp32.zip**.

7 When you finish downloading the program, click the **Close** button to close Netscape and then disconnect from the Internet so you can set up your FTP program.

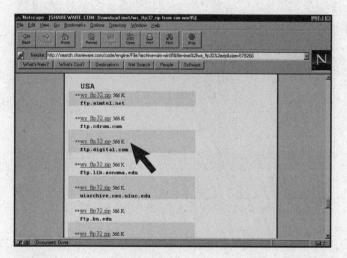

5 Click one of the sites to download ws_ftp32.zip.

6 Make sure you designate a directory for the file and then proceed with the download as you did above.

Don't download the file into your existing FTP folder (if you have one). You won't be able to install WS-FTP in the same folder into which you download it.

Begin Guided Tour   Install Your FTP Program

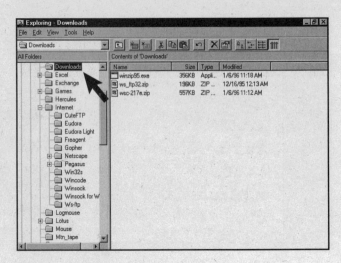

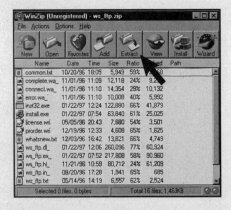

1 Start Explorer and change to the folder to which you downloaded your file.

2 Double-click the **ws_ftp32.zip** file to start WinZip.

3 Click the **I Agree** button and the contents of the zipped files appear. Click the **Extract** button; the Extract dialog box appears.

Before you unzip the file, you can use WinZip to check it for viruses, provided you have an antivirus program on your system. Just click the **Actions** menu and then click **Virus Scan**.

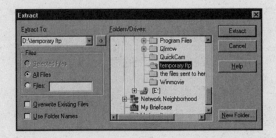

4 Select the folder in which you want the files placed and click **Extract**. WinZip decompresses the files and places them in the folder you selected. Now all you have to do is run the WS-FTP installation program. Close WinZip.

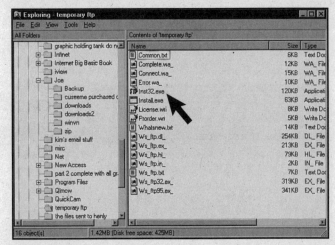

5 Use Windows Explorer to open the directory to which you unzipped the WS-FTP files. Double-click **Inst32.exe**.

Guided Tour   Install Your FTP Program

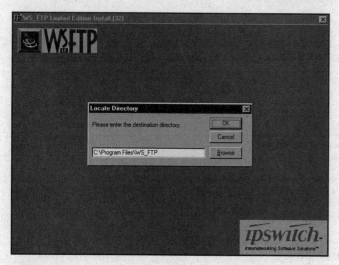
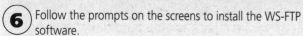

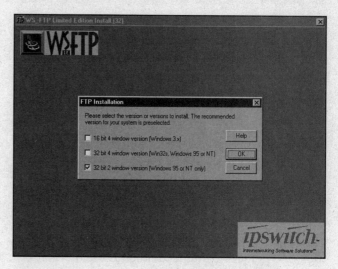

6 Follow the prompts on the screens to install the WS-FTP software.

7 Make sure you choose the appropriate version of the WS-FTP software during the installation. Click **OK**.

8 Once you complete the installation you can start the WS-FTP software via the **Start** button.

Use an FTP Program to Copy Files

Although you can copy (download) files from the Internet with your Web browser, the process is a bit slower than if you used a separate FTP program. Of course, there is a trade-off. You'll probably find that locating files you want to download is easier with your Web program.

In any case, the bottom line is this: In order to connect to any computer out there and grab a copy of one of its files, you're going to need the computer's address. You might get the address in any number of ways. You might, for example, find the address in a book or a magazine that recommends the FTP site, or you might get the address through a program called Archie that helps you locate files on the Internet. The table lists some sites where you can start.

A computer that allows you access to its files is called a host computer. You are its guest. To gain entrance, you need the password. In most cases, the password is a simple one: "anonymous." In other cases, it is something like "guest." Without a doubt, you *will* need a password in order to gain access to an FTP site. If "anonymous" or "guest" doesn't work, the server probably requires that you have a special type of account with it, in which case you're given a special password. This doesn't necessarily have

anything to do with money, but it might. Some restricted-access FTP servers do charge fees. Generally, those servers (brokerage houses or research labs, for example) are in the business of selling information. Nonpublic information, after all, needs to be protected somehow.

Once you log onto an FTP site, you'll see its public folders (those files and folders to which you've been given some level of access). You can move about these folders in much the same way that you move from folder to folder within File Manager or Explorer. When you find the right folder, select the file you want. If you have "read" rights to that file, the FTP program copies it back to your hard disk. (Read rights designate a file you can see, but you can't touch.) Of course, you can also select to which folder on your system your FTP program copies the file.

In the Guided Tour, you'll learn how to copy files using WS-FTP. If you use another FTP program, the steps will vary slightly. Another popular FTP program is Cute FTP (it comes in both Windows 3.1 and Windows 95 versions); you'll discover tips on where it differs from WS-FTP in the next section.

Recommended FTP Sites

Site	URL
CICA Windows Archive	ftp.winsite.com
Netscape	ftp1.netscape.com
Oakland Archives	oak.oakland.edu
Microsoft	ftp1.microsoft.com
America Online	ftp.aol.com
Mirrors to Popular Sites	mirrors.aol.com
SimTel Archives	ftp.coast.net

Tips on Using Cute FTP

If you choose Cute FTP, here's how it differs from what you'll find in the Guided Tour:

To connect to an FTP site, select it from the Sites Manager and then click **Connect**. If your site is not in the list, click the folder to which you want to add the site, and then click **Add Site**. Add the required information and click **OK**. To edit an existing site (for example, to edit the CICA site information as mentioned in the Guided Tour, then select the CICA site and click **Edit Site**. Make the necessary changes and click **OK**.

With Cute FTP, your local system is not displayed initially. To get to it, right-click in the left window panel and select **Change dir** from the shortcut menu. Enter a directory such as **C:** and click **OK**. You can change from folder to folder on your local system the same way that you do on the remote system—by double-clicking the folder to which you want to change.

Another way in which Cute FTP differs from WS-FTP is the way it handles file descriptions. The moment it assimilates a remote directory, Cute FTP looks for a file called index.txt and automatically downloads it—without permission from you. As a matter of courtesy, most systems have an index.txt file for each directory, which contains a list of all the files in that directory, along with descriptions of what those files are. You'd probably download this file yourself anyway. Cute FTP then reconciles the information in the index.txt file with the directory listing it actually sees, and automatically writes each file's description next to its listing in the download folder. This is all automatic.

Begin Guided Tour   Copy Files with WS-FTP

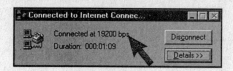

1 Connect to the Internet as usual.

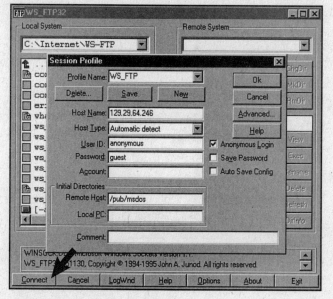

2 Start an FTP program, such as WS-FTP.

3 Click **Connect**, and the Session Profile dialog box appears. (If this is your first time using WS-FTP, you can skip this step.)

(continues)

Guided Tour   Copy Files with WS-FTP   *(continued)*

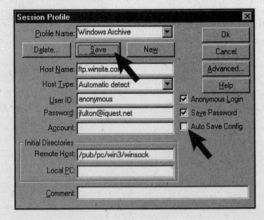

4 In the **Profile Name** drop-down list, select the FTP site you want to visit. For example, select **CICA WinSock Files**.

If the site you want to visit isn't in the list, you can add it within WS-FTP. Click the **New** button, type a description in the **Profile Name** text box, and type the FTP address (such as **ftp5.netscape.com**) in the **Host Name** text box. Select the **Anonymous Login** check box, and then click **OK**.

5 You'll need to change the password to your e-mail address. For example, I changed mine to jfulton@iquest.net. Type your e-mail address and click the **Save Password** box.

6 Click **Save** to save your changes, and then click **OK** to dial into the FTP site.

If you skip step 4 and try to log on to the Windows Archive, you'll get an error message telling you that you need to change the password to your e-mail address. To see errors that occur during logon, you have to scroll back through the log-in list in the lower part of the main WS-FTP window.

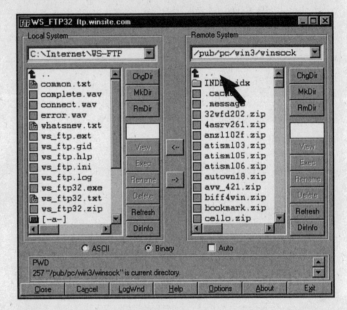

7 After you connect to the FTP site, change to the directory that contains the files you want. For example, change to the pub/pc/win95 directory by clicking the dot-dot (..) to move up one level. Then double-click the **win3** folder and the **util** folder.

Guided Tour   Copy Files with WS-FTP

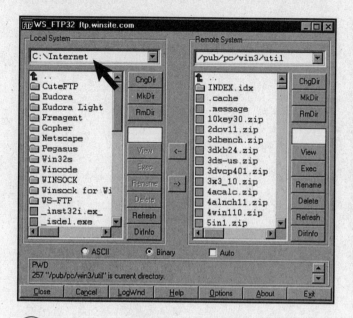

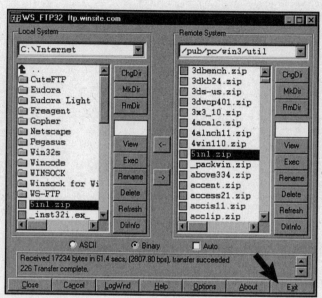

8 On your Local System, change to the temporary folder into which you want to download the file.

11 Click **Connect** if you want to connect to another FTP site. When you finish, click **Exit** to exit WS-FTP.

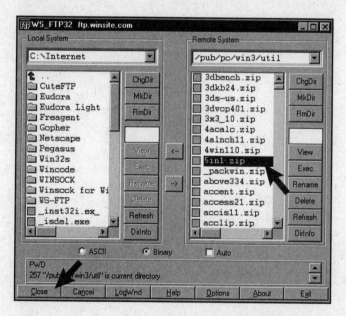

9 Double-click a file to download it into the folder you selected. For example, double-click the **5in1.zip** file.

10 After the file has been copied to your system, click **Close** to disconnect from the FTP site.

HOW TO...

Send and Receive Electronic Mail

Electronic mail (e-mail for short) is a system that enables users to send messages via modem, or over a network, from one computer to another. E-mail messages sent over the Internet were restricted to text only (as in a letter, memo, or report) until quite recently; under normal circumstances, they usually cannot include graphics or special text enhancements such as bold, italics, or underline.

Depending on what program you use, it is also possible to attach graphic images, even a spreadsheet or a highly formatted document, to an e-mail message. The complexity of the actual process of attaching a file to an e-mail message will vary with the e-mail package you use. You'll learn more about that in "Send Files as Messages over the Internet" on page 209.

When you receive an e-mail message, open it and read the message just as you would if it were a real letter. If other files have been attached to the e-mail message, you can detach them for use in some other program.

What You Will Find in This Section

Find and Download an E-Mail Program

In order to send and receive e-mail through the Internet, you need an e-mail program. A lot of Web browsers such as Netscape Navigator include a built-in e-mail program. Internet Explorer uses an add-on called *Internet Mail*. There are also stand-alone packages that are quite popular, such as Eudora and Pegasus Mail.

> If you already use Lotus Notes or cc:Mail, these programs can handle your Internet e-mail if you like. Likewise, if you use Windows 95, you can use Microsoft Exchange as your e-mail program. However, many Internet users (especially those with SLIP or PPP accounts) still prefer a separate Internet e-mail program such as Pegasus Mail or Eudora, so that's what I will concentrate on here.

You can purchase a variety of e-mail programs at any software store. However, you'll find a larger variety of software available on the Internet. Like Web browsers, the e-mail programs you'll find on the Internet are mostly shareware (not freeware), so you will need to register your program and pay a small fee after a reasonable testing period. Even if your service provider included an e-mail program with its startup files (either on disk or files that you downloaded from the provider), you'll still have to pay to register the e-mail program if you decide to keep it.

The easiest way to locate and download an e-mail program from the Internet is with your Web browser. If you haven't installed yours yet, see "Find and Install a Web Browser" on page 97 for help. Once you download your e-mail program, you'll need to install and configure it for your use.

Follow the Guided Tour to download an e-mail program called Eudora Light using Netscape Navigator. If you use a Web browser other than Netscape, the steps may vary slightly. To download the e-mail program, you'll jump to a Web site called Stroud's, which provides access to a lot of good Internet programs.

If you prefer a more direct method for downloading a particular e-mail program, you can connect to that program's FTP or Web site directly using one of the addresses listed here:

Eudora **http://www.qualcomm.com/quest**

Pegasus **http://www.pegasus.usa.com/**

But the fastest way to shop around for the best e-mail program is to go to a Web site such as Stroud's, which provides links to each program along with comprehensive reviews. Another such Web site is called *The Ultimate Collection of Winsock Software*, or *TUCOWS*. Here are their Web locations:

Stroud's main site **http://cws. iworld.com**

Stroud's second main site **http://www. stroud.com**

TUCOWS main site **http://sunsite. auc.dk/tucows/**

You can always look for software files at **www. shareware.com**—one of the biggest collections on the Web.

Other e-mail alternatives exist. Two possibilities from Microsoft are Microsoft Exchange and Microsoft Internet Mail. Exchange ships with the Windows 95 software and can be configured for Internet e-mail. This e-mail package allows you to maintain a phonebook of contacts with their e-mail addresses. Exchange can also be configured to send and receive faxes. Internet Mail is now part of the latest version of Internet Explorer and can be installed as an option. It's a simple e-mail package but it boasts special features such as a spell checker.

Microsoft Office 97, the latest version of Microsoft's application suite package, also contains a new e-mail client—*Microsoft Outlook*. Outlook is more than just an e-mail package. You can also use it to track appointments and maintain an electronic phone book.

Netscape has recently launched a new product called Netscape Communicator. Communicator is really a suite of products that (among other things) will provide you with browser and e-mail capabilities. The e-mail client for Communicator is much more robust than the current Navigator e-mail. You can download Communicator from **www.netscape.com**.

Stroud's is an excellent one-stop shopping place for all your Internet software needs. You'll probably visit it often, so you might want to create a bookmark in your Web browser to save the Stroud's Web address permanently. If you use Netscape Navigator, you create a bookmark by jumping to Stroud's, opening the **Bookmarks** menu, and selecting **Add Bookmark**.

Begin Guided Tour   Download Eudora

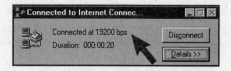

1 Connect to your Internet service provider in the usual manner.

2 Start your Web browser and in the **Location** or **Netsite box**, type **http://cws.iworld.com**. Then press **Enter**.

If you have trouble connecting to the main Stroud's site, then try its other main site: **http://www.stroud.com**.

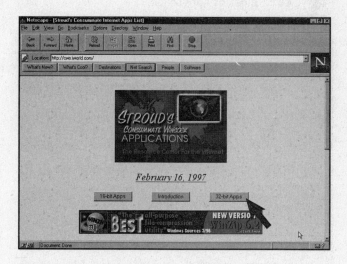

3 After connecting to Stroud's, click the **32-bit Apps** button logo.

If you need help connecting via modem, see "Configure Your TCP/IP Software" on page 81. If you need help connecting to the Internet through your office network, see your system administrator.

(continues)

Guided Tour   Download Eudora   *(continued)*

4 Click the **Index of Apps** botton.

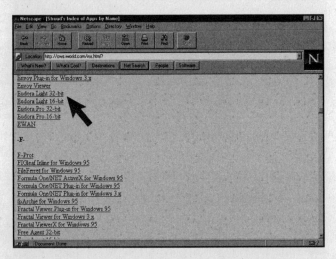

5 Scroll down the list until you reach the list of applications beginning with E; click the **Eudora Light 32-bit** link.

Eudora comes in two flavors: Eudora Light and Eudora Pro. Eudora Light is a stripped-down shareware version of the Eudora e-mail client. Eudora Pro (now available in a 30-day trial version) is the full-featured version of this popular e-mail client.

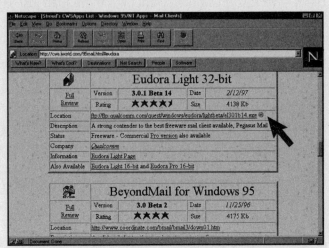

6 You'll be taken to another screen where you can click the file's location.

Also, if you want to read about any e-mail program before you download it, click the **Full Review** box next to the program name.

7 Select the folder into which you want to download your e-mail program. You might want to create a new folder called Eudora Light.

8 Click **Save**.

9 Once the program is downloaded, disconnect from the Internet by clicking the **Close** button so you won't waste online time while setting up Eudora.

Install Your E-Mail Program

To install Eudora (or any e-mail program), you'll need some information from your Internet service provider. For example, you'll need to know:

- The address of your Internet provider's POP (Post Office Protocol) server.
- The address of your Internet provider's SMTP (Simple Mail Transfer Protocol) server.

- Your specific e-mail address.
- Your password for getting mail (which is probably the same as your Internet logon password).

In the Guided Tour, you'll learn how to set up and install Eudora. If you downloaded a different e-mail program, the steps for installing it may vary. Look for a README.TXT file for help installing it.

Begin Guided Tour   Install Eudora Light

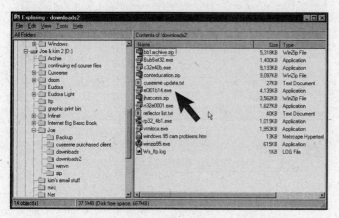

> Your file name may differ slightly from the one shown here if you downloaded a more recent version of Eudora Light.

1 Start Explorer and change to the directory where you downloaded Eudora Light.

2 Double-click the **el301b14.exe** file.

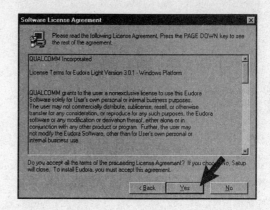

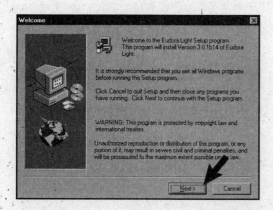

3 The installation process begins; click **Next** to continue.

4 Read the software agreement and then click **Yes** to continue.

(continues)

Guided Tour Install Eudora Light *(continued)*

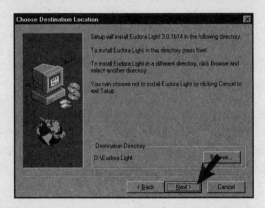

5 Verify the directory into which Eudora will be installed. If you want, click **Browse** and select a different directory.

6 Click **Next**.

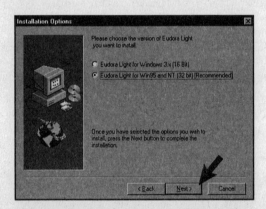

7 Select **Eudora Light for Win 95 and NT** if it's not already selected, and then click **Next**.

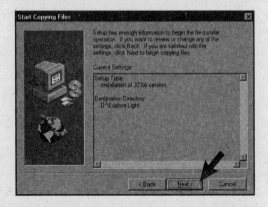

8 Verify your settings and click **Next**.

9 The setup is complete. Click **Yes**.

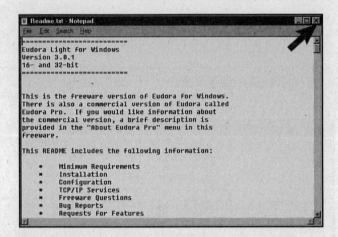

10 After you read about Eudora, click the **Close** button, or open the **File** menu and select **Exit** to close the window.

Begin Guided Tour   Configure Eudora Light

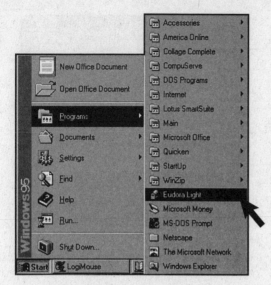

1 Start Eudora by clicking the **Start** button, selecting **Programs**, and selecting **Eudora Light**.

2 In the **POP account** text box, enter your e-mail address, such as **jhabraken@juno.com**.

3 Enter your name in the **Real Name** text box.

4 Select **Winsock** if you plan to dial into the Internet directly or through a network. Select **Shell Account Access** if you're going through an online service such as CompuServe or America Online. Do not click **Offline** unless you will be sending your mail through a network to the Internet.

5 Click the **Personal Information** icon on the left side of the window.

6 Enter your **Return Address**.

7 Enter a **Dialup Username** if you use an online service or a network where you need to log in with a different username from the one in the POP account.

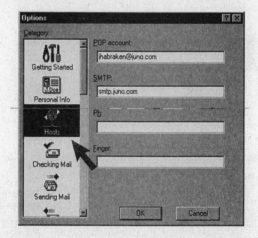

8 If your Internet provider uses a separate SMTP, Ph, or Finger handler, click the **Hosts** icon and enter the appropriate address.

The SMTP server's address may be the same as the POP server's. In that case, you can just skip to step 9.

(continues)

Guided Tour Configure Eudora Light *(continued)*

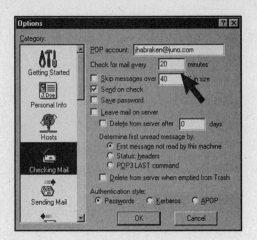

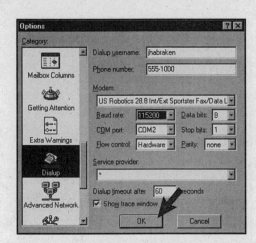

9 If you want Eudora to check for mail periodically while you're online, click the **Checking Mail** icon.

10 Enter a time interval in the **Check for Mail Every __ Minutes** box.

13 If you connect to the Internet via modem, click the **Dialup** icon and enter the information required for connecting to your service provider.

14 You can make additional changes to the setup if you want. Simply click a button or icon on the left side of the screen and change the settings on the right. (For example, you can change the font used in e-mail messages.) Once you've made all your selections in Eudora, click **OK**.

11 You should tell Eudora where to put files that you receive as attachments to e-mail messages. Click the **Attachments** icon, and then click the **Attachment Directory** button.

12 Select the directory in which you want Eudora to store attached files. Then click **Use Directory**.

Send an E-Mail Message

When you finish installing your e-mail program, you're ready to send a message. Remember that an e-mail message can only contain text. If you want to send a file as an e-mail message, see "Send Files as Messages over the Internet" on page 209.

You can send e-mail—either directly or indirectly (such as through CompuServe or America Online)—to anyone who is connected to the Internet. All you need to know is his or her e-mail address. An Internet address looks something like this:

jnoname@que.mcp.com

The first part of the address is the person's user name (the name by which she is known to her home system). Most user names consist of the person's first initial and last name run together. An at symbol (@) always comes after the user name. The part that follows the @ sign is a location, in this case, the address of Que (the company that published this book). The smaller parts of that address tell you that Que is part of Macmillan Computer Publishing—hence que.mcp—and that it is a commercial (.com) venture. The last part of an address will always be .com (commercial), .edu (educational), .net (an Internet server),.gov (government), or .mil (military).

When you're on the Internet, you must be careful to use upper- and lowercase letters exactly as they are given to you. If someone tells you that his address is **SAMBeldon@ imagineTHAT.com**, you must type the address exactly that way. He will not receive his mail if you send it to **sambeldon@imaginethat.com** because that is a completely different address.

If you're sending e-mail to a person who connects to the Internet through an online service such as CompuServe, you'll find that entering the address may be a little different than you are use to. And CompuServe is definitely the trickiest to handle. When a CompuServe user gives you her e-mail address it will be a series of numbers such as 71354 separated by a comma from a second set of numbers and the CompuServe domain name—**1234@compuserve.com**. You should convert the comma separator to a period before you attempt to send mail to the address.

The following list shows you the format of an e-mail address for each of the most popular online services.

Online Service	Sample Address
CompuServe	71354.1234@compuserve.com
America Online	joeblow@aol.com
Prodigy	joeblow@prodigy.com
The Microsoft Network	joeblow@msn.com

If you have several e-mail messages to send, you can create each one while you're offline (that is, not connected to the Internet) and save it in your Outbox. Then when you're ready to send the messages, you can connect to the Internet and send all the messages in the Outbox at once. This Guided Tour walks you through the process of sending e-mail from the program Eudora Light. The process will be similar in any other e-mail program.

Begin Guided Tour   Send an E-Mail Message with Eudora Light

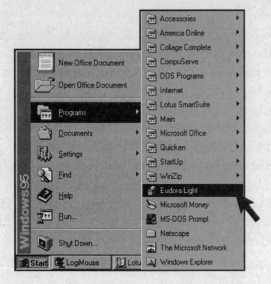

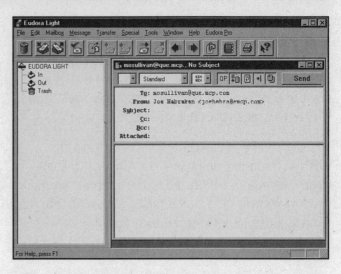

1 Click **Start**, select **Programs**, and then select **Eudora Light**.

3 In the **To:** line, type the Internet address of the person to whom you want to send your e-mail message. To enter a second address, separate it from the first address with a comma.

You do not have to connect to the Internet in order to use your e-mail program. In fact, it's less expensive to create your e-mail messages offline and then connect to the Internet and send all your messages at the same time. If you have unlimited access for a flat fee, the connection time is unimportant.

Eudora lets you save the addresses of people who send you e-mail (see "Retrieve and Read E-Mail Messages" on page 204). To create a new e-mail message for a person whose address you have saved, skip steps 2 and 3. Instead open the **Message** menu and select **New Message To**. A list of saved addresses appears. From this list, select the name of the person to whom you want to send a message.

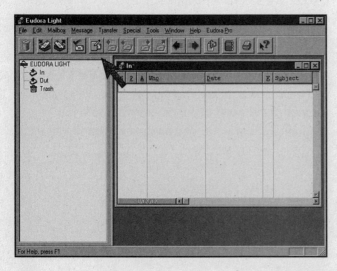

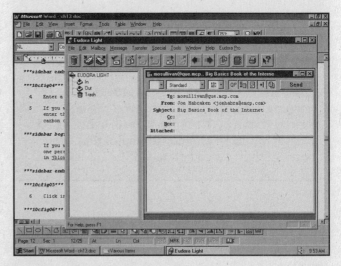

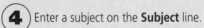

2 Click the **New Message** icon.

4 Enter a subject on the **Subject** line.

Guided Tour   Send an E-Mail Message with Eudora Light

5 If you want to send a copy of this e-mail to other people, enter their addresses on the **Cc** (carbon copy) and or **Bcc** (blind carbon copy) lines.

If you want to send copies of this message to more than one person, use a comma in front of each new address as in **jblow@fake.com, tsilly @duh.net.**

You don't have to connect to the Internet before you click the Send button to send your messages. If you click the Send button while you are offline, the message or messages will be queued in the Out box and you can close the mail program. The next time you connect, use the **Send Queued Message File** menu option to send the messages.

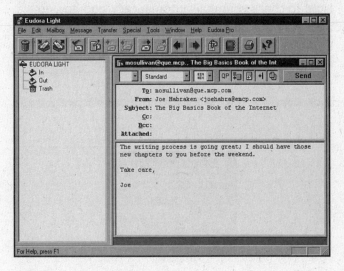

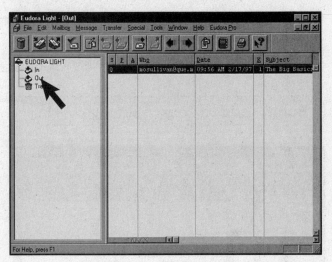

6 Click in the message area and type your message.

8 Click the **Out** folder to view the messages that it contains. Your message is in the Out box. Your message will be sent the next time you connect to your service.

9 To send additional messages, repeat the steps above.

Messages that have been sent are marked with an **S** in the Outbox.

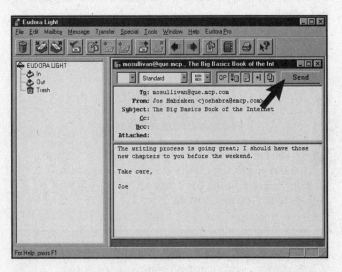

7 When you finish entering your message, connect to the Internet via your provider and then click the **Send** button. If you want to send additional messages, however, click the Close button for the message Window.

Retrieve and Read E-Mail Messages

Besides sending messages, the other basic function of a good e-mail program is retrieving messages. Retrieving an e-mail message is like going to your mailbox and checking for mail. If there's mail in your mailbox, you take it out, open it, and read it. Your e-mail program does the same thing: It goes to your electronic mailbox, located on your Internet provider's computer, checks for mail, and brings back anything it finds.

You can configure your e-mail program to automatically check for mail every so often, or you can initiate the checking process whenever you want. Once you retrieve your mail, you "open" it to read it. You can print an open message if you want, save the contents of the message in a file to use in another program, or reply to the message by sending a message back to the originator (see "Respond to a Message" on page 207).

In this Guided Tour, you'll learn how to retrieve your mail using Eudora Light, how to configure Eudora Light to check your mail automatically, and how to print your mail. If you use another e-mail program, the steps may vary.

Begin Guided Tour   Retrieve Mail

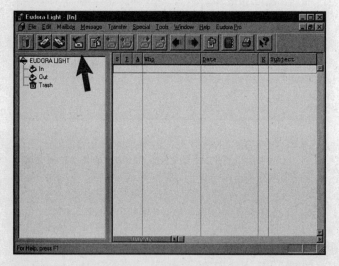

1 Connect to the Internet in your usual manner and start your e-mail program, such as Eudora Light.

2 Click on the **Check Mail** button.

3 Type your password and click **OK**. Eudora connects to your Internet service provider's computer and searches your mailbox.for new mail. If you have new messages, it copies them to your system.

4 If you have new mail, the New Mail dialog box appears, telling you so. Click **OK**, and Eudora places your new e-mail in the In box. If you don't have any e-mail, you'll get a message telling you so. Click **OK**.

Once you get your e-mail, disconnect from the Internet so you don't have to pay connect charges while you view each message.

Guided Tour   Retrieve Mail

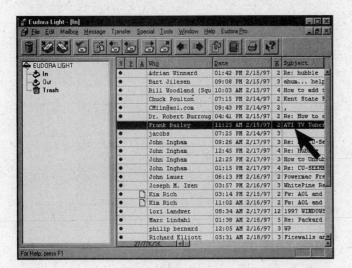

(7) To save the contents of the message in a file, open the **File** menu and select **Save As**. The Save As dialog box appears.

(5) To view the contents of a particular message, double-click the message in the In box.

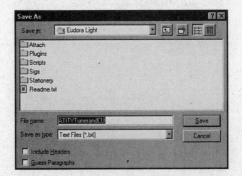

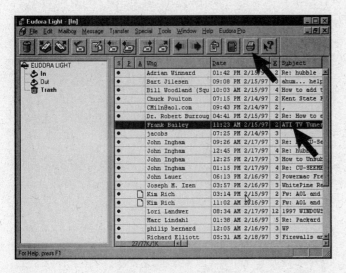

(8) Change to a different folder if necessary. Then type a name for the new file and click **Save**.

(6) If you want to print your e-mail message, click the **Print** toolbar button or open the **File** menu and select **Print**.

Begin Guided Tour   Check Your Mail Automatically

1 Open the **Tools** menu and select **Options**.

2 Click the **Checking Mail** icon.

3 Enter a time interval in the **Check for Mail Every __ Minutes** box.

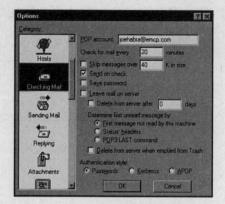

4 Click **OK**.

Respond to a Message

You can reply to, forward, or redirect any message you receive. When you reply to a message, your e-mail program automatically fills in the address of the originator in your new message. All you have to do is type your reply and then send the message.

When you forward a message, your e-mail program sends a copy of the original message to the person you indicate. Redirecting a message is similar to forwarding a message, except that when you redirect, the program adds your address to the From text box.

When you forward, redirect, or reply to a message, most e-mail programs include the text of the original message for reference. You can customize your e-mail program so that the original text is not included if you want, or you can simply delete the text if you don't want to include it in a particular reply.

The Guided Tour shows you how to reply to a message using Eudora Light. If you use a different e-mail program, the steps may vary.

Begin Guided Tour   Reply to a Message with Eudora Light

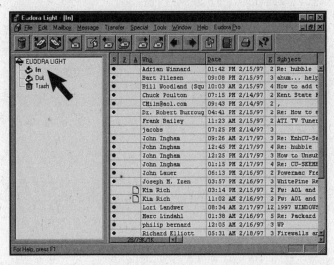

1 Double-click the **In** icon if necessary.

If you want to reply to a message that's already open, don't worry about following steps 1 or 2. Just skip to step 3.

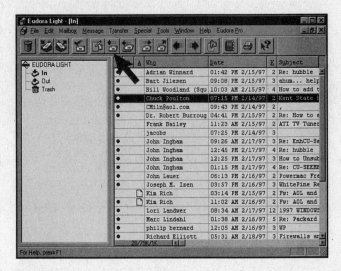

2 Select the message to which you want to reply.

3 Then click the **Reply** button.

(continues)

Guided Tour   Reply to a Message with Eudora Light   *(continued)*

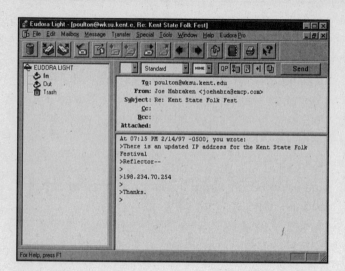

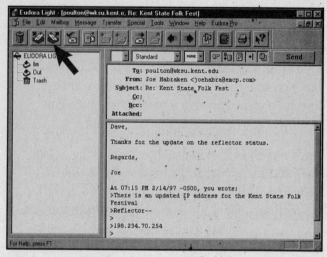

4 Your e-mail program updates the header information, filling in the To:, From:, and Subject: lines. In the message area, the text from the original message appears. Each line of the original message is marked with an arrow (>).

5 Type your message under (or above) the copy of the original message.

6 Save and send your message as usual.

If you want to delete any of these original lines, just select them and press **Delete**. In addition, you can type your reply in between lines of the original message; simply place the cursor at the end of an original line and press **Enter** to create a blank line on which you can type.

Send Files as Messages over the Internet

You can send files over the Internet attached to e-mail messages. And if you and the recipient have your e-mail packages set up correctly, you can exchange graphics, sounds, even files created in various application packages like Microsoft Word and Excel.

An attached file can contain just about anything. For example, you might send someone a spreadsheet file, a graphic, or even a report complete with graphic images in a word processing file. Your recipient needs some way of reading the contents of the file. For example, if you send a Word document attached to an e-mail message, your recipient must have a copy of Word (or some other program that can read Word files such as the Word Viewer which is freely distributed by Microsoft) in order to read the information in the file.

Normally, messages sent over the Internet contain text only, with none of the coding necessary to display fancy fonts, text enhancements (such as bold), or graphics. Therefore, before you can send a file over the Internet, it has to be converted into these basic text codes (7-bit characters). There are several ways to convert files for transmittal over the Internet, each of which has its pros and cons.

One process that's included in most e-mail programs is called MIME (Multipurpose Internet Mail Extension). MIME places a header in the e-mail message just before the file's data to show that what follows is not text. The MIME header also indicates the file type (such as a bitmap graphic or a word processing document). The recipient's e-mail recognizes the MIME header and sends the data after the header to the indicated program for translation. Unfortunately, if the recipient of your file uses an online service to access the Internet, his e-mail program may not make sense of MIME coding.

The most dependable process for sending files over the Internet is called *UUEncoding*. Some e-mail programs (such as Microsoft Exchange and Netscape Mail) automatically uuencode a file when you attach it to an Internet message. Others, such as Eudora, require you to uuencode the file manually using a program called a uuencoder. Once the file is encoded, you can attach it to an e-mail message within Eudora and send it.

A good uuencoder is WinCode, which you can download from the Stroud's site (**http://www.stroud.com**). Follow the Guided Tour in the section "Find and Download an E-Mail Program" (page 194) to locate and download a UUEncoder.

Another common encoding scheme is BinHex, which began as an encoding format for Macintosh computers and later spread to PCs. The theory behind BinHex and uuencoding is much the same, but the methods and results are somewhat different. Because UUEncoding is the method of choice among UNIX users, and UNIX forms the backbone of much of the Internet, BinHex is a less common encoding scheme. If you're sending your file to someone who uses a PC, BinHex is a not a good choice.

In the Guided Tour, you'll learn how to use Eudora to send files. Because Eudora does not automatically UUEncode files, you'll learn how to use WinCode to UUEncode your file first. You can then attach the UUEncoded file to an e-mail message. You'll also learn how to attach a file to an e-mail message using an e-mail program such as Pegasus that automatically uuencodes the file for you. (To learn how to use Netscape Mail to send a file, see "Send and Receive E-Mail with Your Web Browser" on page 214.)

Begin Guided Tour   Send a File with Eudora

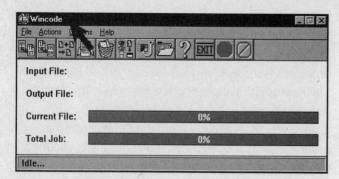

1 Start WinCode (or whatever UUEncoder you downloaded and installed).

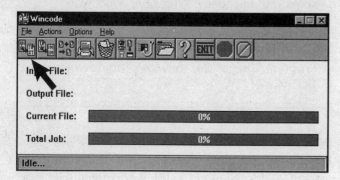

2 Click the **File Encode** button.

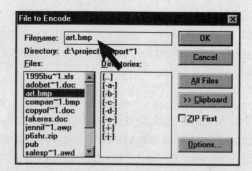

3 Select the file you want to encode and click **OK**. The program uuencodes your file and places it in the WinCode directory.

4 Click **OK**.

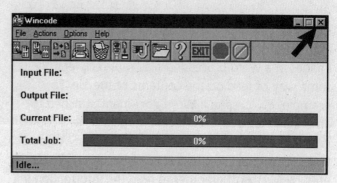

5 Click the **Close** button to close your UUEncoder program.

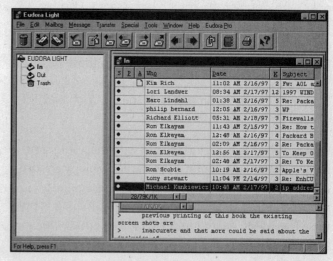

6 Start Eudora Light. Then click the **New Message** button.

Guided Tour Send a File with Eudora

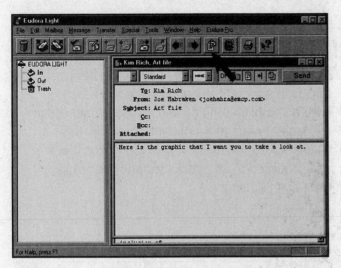

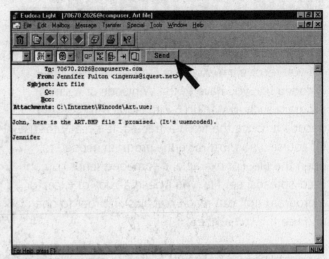

7 Enter the appropriate information in the **To:**, **Subject:**, **Cc:**, and **Bcc:** lines.

8 Click in the message area and type a message that indicates the contents of the file. Also make sure that your message tells the recipient the format of the file that you are attaching.

9 Click the **Attach File** button.

10 In the Attach File dialog box, select the file you want to attach to the message and click **Attach**. Your attached file will have the same file name, but it will have a .UUE extension.

11 Click the **Send** button to send the message.

When you send attached files with your e-mail messages, it is a good idea to zip the files first with WinZip. This makes the transfer of the file over the Net faster. Eudora users should zip the file first and then UUEncode the zipped file. Other e-mail package users (Microsoft Internet Mail, Netscape Mail) can zip the file and attach it directly to the e-mail message. Compressing your files with a zip program will not only make the transfer faster but will also keep your Internet Service Provider happy. As a general rule, try to keep attachments under 50K.

Retrieve a File Sent as a Message over the Internet

If you receive a message in Eudora with a UUEn-coded file, you have to use WinCode or a similar program such as WinZip 6.2 to extract the file and decode it. Once the file is extracted, it is ready for use. Of course, you must have the program needed to open the file. For example, if someone sends you an Excel spreadsheet file, you'll need a copy of Excel (or a program that can read Excel files) in order to open and use the spreadsheet.

Most e-mail packages such as Netscape Mail, Microsoft Internet Mail, and Microsoft Exchange have no problem sending and receiving uuencoded messages. In fact they do it automatically. This Guided Tour shows you how easy it is to retrieve a file attached to an e-mail message opened in Microsoft Exchange.

Begin Guided Tour   Open an Attached File in Microsoft Exchange

1 Open Microsoft Exchange by double-clicking its Desktop icon—the Inbox.

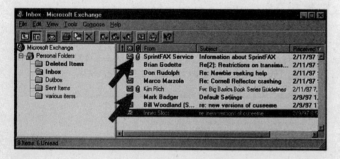

2 Messages that have attached files are denoted by a paper clip symbol.

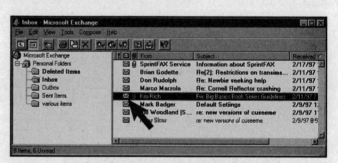

3 Double-click a message that has an attached file.

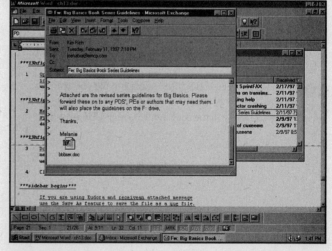

4 The attached file appears as an icon in the e-mail message. In this case, a Word document is attached to the e-mail.

Guided Tour Open an Attached File in Microsoft Exchange

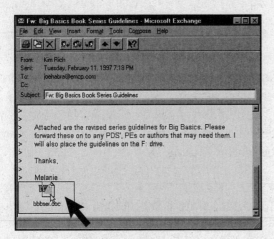

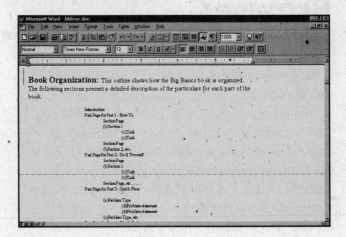

5 Double-click the attached file.

6 If you have the necessary software to open the attached file (in this case Microsoft Word) the file will open in the application. You can then use the Save As feature to save the file anywhere on your hard drive.

If you are using Eudora and receive an attached message use the Save As feature to save the file as a .uue file. Then use Wincode to decode the message. Once you've decoded the message you can open the file in the application that it was created in.

Send and Receive E-Mail with Your Web Browser

With some Web browsers, such as Netscape Navigator, you don't need a separate e-mail program because they come with one built-in. Internet Explorer also has its own e-mail package called Internet Mail. As browsers have become more full-featured, their e-mail packages have become as sophisticated as the stand-alone packages. Netscape Communicator (now in preview from Netscape) contains a very robust e-mail client.

If you use Netscape Navigator or Internet Explorer and their built-in e-mail packages, you will have to

configure the e-mail package as you did for Eudora earlier in this section. The Guided Tour shows you how to set up the e-mail program in Netscape Navigator. Setting up any other Web browser's program will be much the same.

> Flip back to "Install Your E-Mail Program" on page 197 if you need a refresher on the basic information you have to fill in when configuring an e-mail program.

Begin Guided Tour   Configure Netscape Navigator for E-Mail

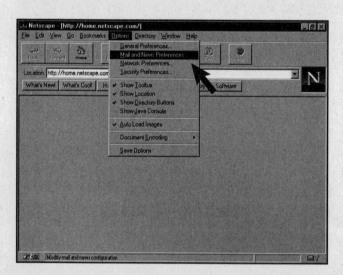

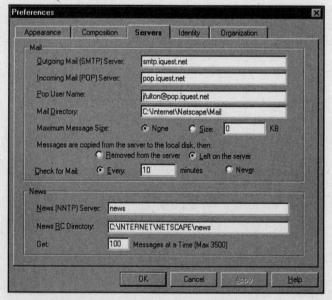

1 Start Netscape Navigator. (You do not need to be connected to the Internet.)

2 Open the **Options** menu and select **Mail and News Preferences**.

3 Click the **Servers** tab.

4 Enter the address of your incoming and outgoing mail servers.

5 In the **Pop User Name** text box, enter your address on the POP server.

Guided Tour   Configure Netscape Navigator for E-Mail

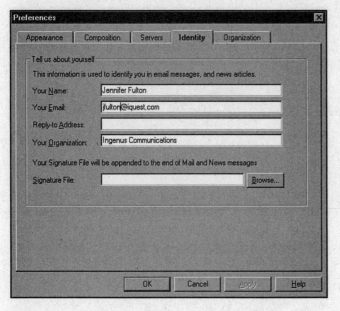

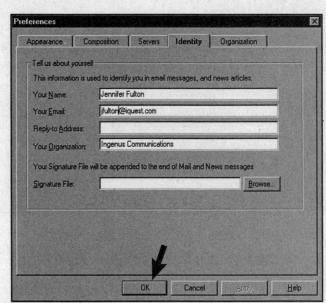

6 Click the **Identity** tab.

7 Enter your name, e-mail address, reply-to address, and organization in the appropriate text boxes.

8 If you use a signature file, click **Browse**, select the signature file, and click **OK**.

9 Click **OK** to save your settings.

A signature file is a text file that usually includes your name and some kind of logo/ picture, created using only spaces and other keyboard characters such as x, l, and -. By putting such characters together in a particular pattern, you can form a crude picture like the one shown here:

```
J Byrd            x
                =~xxx
                 | |
                 ^ ^
```

To create your own signature file, open WordPad, type your name, and then create a simple picture. Save the file as SIGN.TXT. Then if you tell Netscape to use the file, it attaches your "signature" to the end of each message you send.

Begin Guided Tour   Send E-Mail

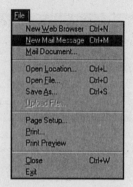

1 In Netscape Navigator, open the **File** menu and select **New Mail Message**.

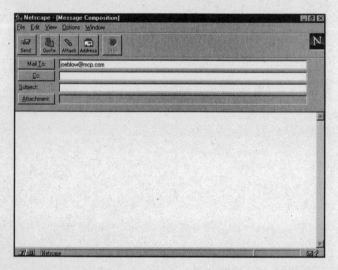

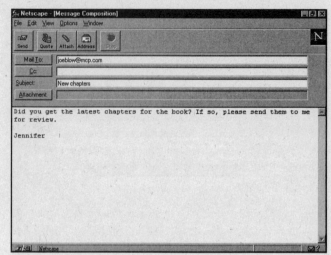

3 Enter a subject in the **Subject:** text box, and then type your message.

4 Click the **Send** button to send your message.

You can attach a file to send with your message, and Netscape Mail will UUEncode it automatically. To attach a file, click the **Attachment** button, click **Attach File**, select your file, and click **Open**. Select **As Is** and click **OK**.

2 Enter the recipients' addresses in the **Mail To:** and **Cc:** text boxes.

Netscape Navigator enables you to save addresses of the people from whom you receive mail so you can reuse them if you want. To send a message to someone whose address you've saved, click the **Address** button and select the address to which to send your message.

Begin Guided Tour   Receive E-Mail

1 In Netscape Navigator, open the **Window** menu and select **Netscape Mail**.

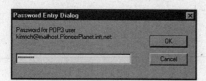

2 Enter your password and click **OK**.

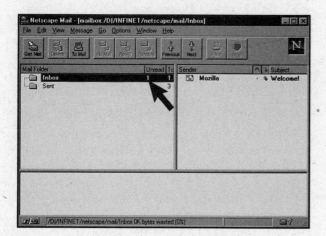

3 To check for new mail, click the **Get Mail** button.

4 In the Mail Folder list (on the left), click the **Inbox** folder. Your messages appear in the list on the right.

5 Click the message you want to open.

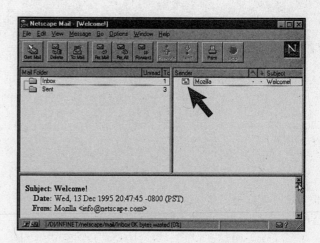

6 The e-mail message appears at the bottom of the window. If necessary, scroll down to read the complete message.

You can reply to or forward a Netscape Mail message just as you would any other e-mail. Click the **Reply, Reply All**, or **Forward** button, and then type your message.

Read and Post Messages in Newsgroups

When you walk into a library or grocery store, you invariably see a bulletin board plastered with brochures, announcements, and want ads. When you wander around the Internet, you find *newsgroups*, electronic bulletin boards where users with a particular hobby or interest post questions, answers, and information that can help others.

The Internet offers thousands of newsgroups, each of which focuses on a specific interest. You can find a newsgroup for any topic imaginable—from using a PC to tattooing your body. With a special program called a *newsreader*, you can open any of these newsgroups and read messages that other people have posted, or you can post your own messages. For example, if you have a tax question, you can post your question in a tax newsgroup and then check every day to see if anyone has answered it (chances are, somebody will try to help).

In this section, you'll learn how to find and download a newsreader from the Internet and use it to read and post messages in newsgroups.

What You Will Find in This Section

Find and Install a Newsreader

To access newsgroups, you need a *newsreader*, a program that connects to a news server and enables you to read and post messages. You can get a freeware (no charge) or shareware (use now, pay later) version of the program you need off the Internet from an FTP server or Web site. A standard newsreader that has been available for some time is WinVN. Microsoft also has its own newsreader, Internet News, which works with Internet Explorer. Netscape has a Web browser built-in.

For details on how to download (*copy*) files from the Internet, see "Find and Copy Files from the Internet" on page 179. The following list provides a list of sites where you can find the WinVN newsreader featured in this section. Remember that file names and directories can change at any time; when you get to the FTP or HTTP site, look for a file name that is similar to one of the names in the list.

Follow the Guided Tour to download the newsreader and install it on your computer. Remember, if you ftp from your Web browser, be sure to add **ftp://** before the FTP server's URL.

Where to find WinVN (WV32 for Windows 95):

> **ftp.satlink.com**
>
> **ftp.cdrom.com**

ftp.digital.com

ftp.lib.sonoma.edu

uiarchive.cso.uiuc.edu

oak.oakland.edu

You can also use Microsoft Internet News as your reader whether you use Internet Explorer or not. To download Internet News go to **http://www. microsoft.com/ie/imn/**.

Another popular news reader is FreeAgent. It supplies several nifty features which save you time, including the ability to read messages offline.

You can also search for a newsreader using any of the search tools described in "Search for Information on the Internet" (page 169). For example, go to Yahoo!'s home page and search for **newsreader**. This gives you a list of links you can follow to download the news-reader of your choice. And remember that one of the best places to look for shareware and freeware on the Web is **www.shareware.com**.

Begin Guided Tour   Download the WinVN Newsreader

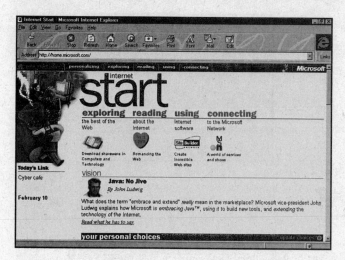

1 Connect to the Internet and start your Web browser (as explained in "Connect to the World Wide Web" on page 112).

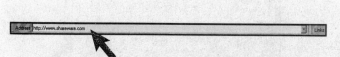

2 The best place to start your software search is **www. shareware.com**. Type the URL of a FTP server that has the newsreader file you want to download. (You can use an URL from the previous list.) Press **Enter**. You can also choose a site from your Favorites list, if you've previously bookmarked the location of a Web site.

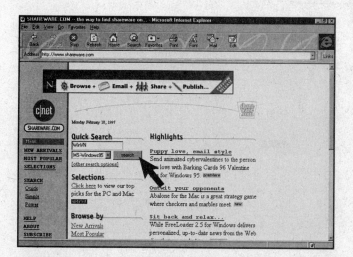

3 Your Web browser takes you to the shareware site, which uses a search engine to help you find your software. Type the software name, such as **WinVN** or a keyword into the search box. Specify your operating system and then click **Search**.

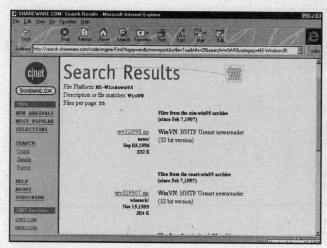

4 A list of software archives that hold the software package or packages related to your search parameters will appear. Click the archive you want to explore.

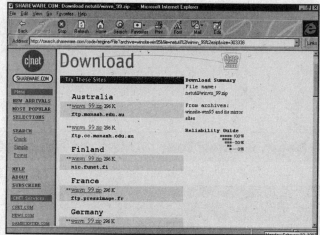

5 You will be given a list of FTP sites around the world that hold the file that you want to download. It makes sense to choose a location that is in the same country where you reside.

(continues)

Guided Tour Download the WinVN Newsreader *(continued)*

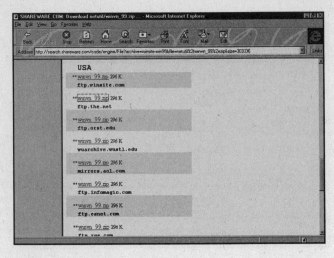

6 Click the location from which you want to download the file.

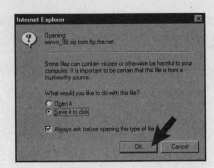

7 Your browser (Internet Explorer is shown here) will let you know that a file is about to be downloaded. Click **OK**.

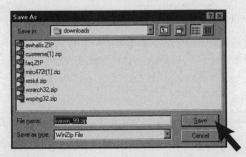

8 A dialog box appears; designate where you would like the file to be saved on your computer. Once you decide this, click **Save**. The file will downloaded to your computer.

Begin Guided Tour Unzip the Newsreader File

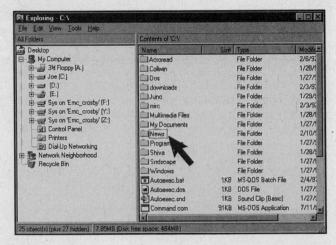

1 Use My Computer, or the Windows Explorer, to create a folder called **News**. This is the folder in which you will store your newsreader program files.

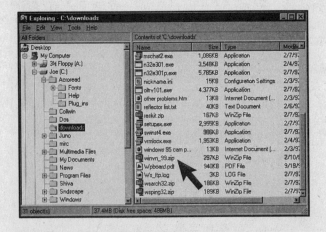

2 Once you have the directory created, use My Computer or the Windows Explorer to locate the file you want to install, in this case **winvn_99.zip**. Double-click the file.

Guided Tour Unzip the Newsreader File

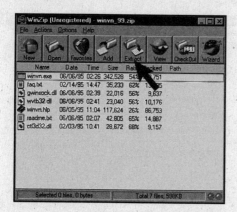

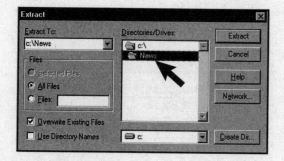

3 The WinZip window appears, showing the files that are contained in the WinVN zipped archive. Click the **Extract** button on the toolbar.

4 The Extract dialog box appears. Select the **News** folder to extract the files to it.

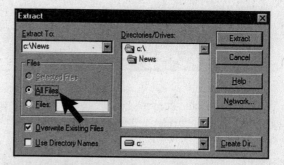

5 Select the **All Files** option, if necessary, so WinZip will extract all the files in the zipped file.

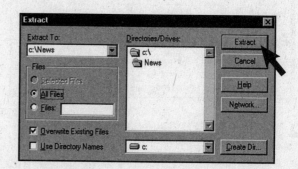

6 Click the **Extract** button. WinZip unzips the file and stores all the extracted files in the specified folder.

Begin Guided Tour   Set Up Your Newsreader

1 Establish your Internet connection, as explained in "Configure Your TCP/IP Software" which begins on page 81).

2 Use My Computer, or the Windows Explorer, to change to the **News** folder, and then double-click the **winvn** or **winvn.exe** file.

In Windows 95, you can use the right mouse button to drag the WinVN icon from My Computer to the Windows desktop. Release the mouse button over the desktop and click **Create Shortcut(s) Here**. This places an icon on the Windows Desktop that you can double-click to run WinVN.

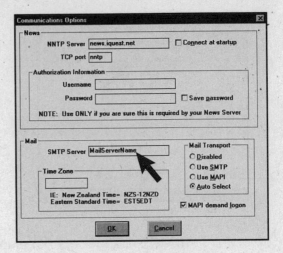

3 The first time you run WinVN, it displays the Communications Options dialog box, asking you to specify the URL of the news server you will connect to. Type the URL specified by your service provider in the **NNTP (News) Server** text box.

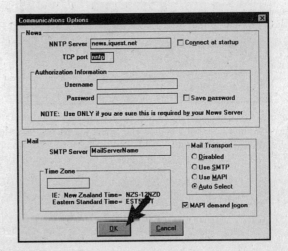

4 The TCP port entry is **nntp** for most news servers. For some servers, you might have to enter a port number—usually 149. Unless your service provider specified otherwise, leave this entry alone.

Guided Tour Set Up Your Newsreader

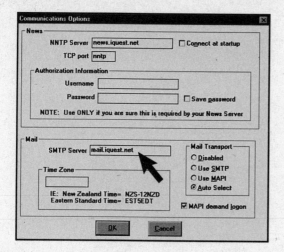

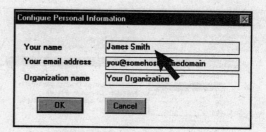

7 WinVN displays another dialog box that asks for information about you. Type your name in the **Your Name** text box.

5 WinVN doubles as an e-mail program. It allows you to send e-mail directly to people who have posted messages in the newsgroup. If you want to use WinVN as an e-mail program, type your e-mail server's URL in the **SMTP Server** text box. To learn more about e-mail, see "Send and Receive Electronic Mail" on page 193.

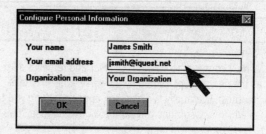

8 Type your e-mail address in the **Your Email Address** text box.

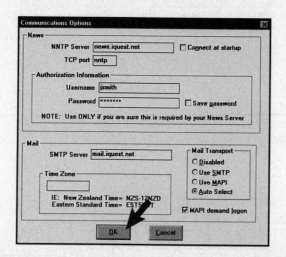

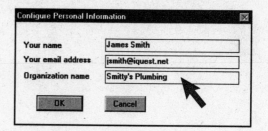

9 (Optional) If you want to supply a company name, type it in the **Organization Name** text box.

10 Click **OK**.

6 Most news servers do not require you to enter a username or password to access the server. If your news server requires this login information, type it in the appropriate text boxes and click **OK**.

(continues)

Guided Tour   Set Up Your Newsreader   *(continued)*

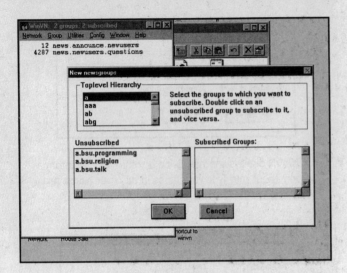

11 WinVN connects to your news server and retrieves a list of all the newsgroups carried by the server (this may take several minutes). Eventually, a dialog box appears, asking you to specify to which newsgroups you want to subscribe. See "Subscribe to Newsgroups" on page 230.

Set Up Your Web Browser To Read Newsgroups

Some Web browsers double as newsreaders. For example, Netscape Navigator has a built-in newsreader called Netscape News that enables you to both read and post messages. If you click a link for a newsgroup or enter its URL in the Location text box, Navigator runs the newsreader and displays a list of messages. You can then click a message's description to read it.

Although several Web browsers function as newsreaders, many don't offer all the newsreader features that Netscape Navigator does. With some Web browsers, for example, you can read the messages in

a newsgroup, but you can't respond to them or post your own messages.

Before you can use your Web browser as a newsreader, you must tell the Web browser which news server to use. In most Web browsers, you do this by selecting the Options or Preferences command and then typing the URL for the newsreader. The Guided Tour shows you how to enter a newsgroup URL in Netscape Navigator and how to use Netscape News to read newsgroup messages. The steps may differ slightly if you use a different browser.

Begin Guided Tour   Use Your Web Browser as a Newsreader

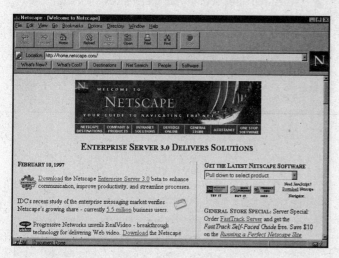

1 Establish your Internet connection and start your Web browser. This figure shows Netscape Navigator in action.

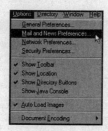

2 Enter the command that allows you to specify a news server. In Navigator, you open the **Options** menu and select **Mail and News Preferences**.

(continues)

Guided Tour Use Your Web Browser as a Newsreader *(continued)*

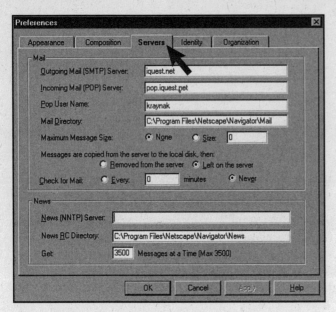

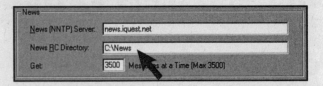

5 Some browsers let you set additional news preferences. In Navigator, for example, you can specify the folder in which you want to save news messages.

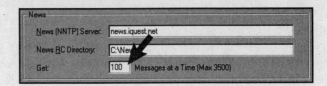

6 You can also specify the maximum number of news messages you want the program to retrieve from any one newsgroup. Drag over the entry in the **Get _ Messages at a Time** text box and type the desired number.

7 When you finish setting your preferences, click **OK**.

3 Enter your preferences in the dialog box that appears. If the dialog box has tabs, click the tab for the news server option. In Navigator, click the **Servers** tab.

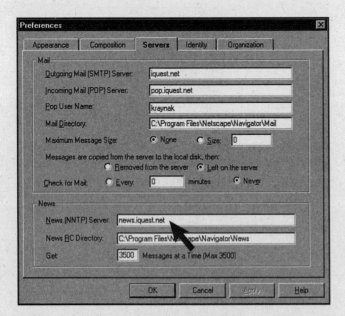

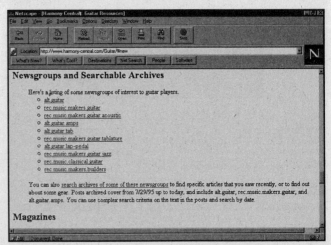

8 There are a number of ways to access a newsgroup with your Web browser. If you encounter a link for a newsgroup, click the link.

4 Drag over the entry in the **News (NNTP) Server** text box, and then type the URL of the news server you want to use. (NNTP stands for Network News Transfer Protocol.)

Guided Tour Use Your Web Browser as a Newsreader

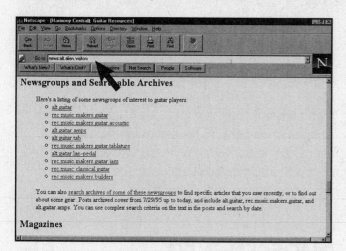

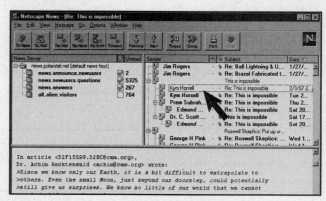

9 You can also view a list of messages in a specific newsgroup by entering the newsgroup's URL in the Location, Go to, or URL text box. As you can see here, a newsgroup URL starts with **news:**. Note that it does not contain the forward slashes (/) you find in most URLs.

11 From here, you can read newsgroup messages, reply to them, or post your own messages, all of which are explained later in this section.

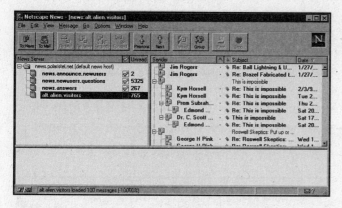

10 If you use Netscape Navigator to go to a newsgroup, Navigator runs its newsreader, Netscape News, and displays a list of messages in the selected newsgroup.

Retrieve a List of Newsgroups

Before you can become involved in a newsgroup, you need to use your newsreader to retrieve a list of available newsgroups from your news server. The first time you run your newsreader, it should display a dialog box that asks if you want to retrieve newsgroups. You simply click the OK or Yes button, and the newsreader does the rest. Because there are thousands of newsgroups, it may take your newsreader several minutes to retrieve their names.

Once you have a list of newsgroups, you can open a newsgroup and start reading and posting messages. However, as time passes, your newsgroup list will become dated. New newsgroups are created daily, and old newsgroups in which interest has faded are destroyed just as quickly. To keep your newsgroup list current, you must refresh your list as shown in the Guided Tour.

Understand Newsgroup Names

In order to know which newsgroups might interest you, you must know how to read a newsgroup name (or URL). Unlike most URLs, you read newsgroup URLs from left to right. For example, **alt.comedy.british** stands for "alternative comedy of the British persuasion."

The first part of the address indicates the newsgroup's overall subject area: **comp** stands for computer, **news** is for general information about newsgroups, **rec** is for recreation (hobbies, sports), **sci** stands for science, **soc** is for social topics, **talk** is for controversial debates, **misc** is for general topics such as jobs and selling, and **alt** is for topics that are somewhat offbeat.

The second part of the address indicates, more specifically, what the newsgroup offers. For example, **comp.ai** is about computers (comp), but specifically covers artificial intelligence (ai). If the address has a third part, it focuses even further. For example, comp.ai.philosophy discusses how artificial intelligence can be applied to philosophical questions. And, of course, **rec.arts.bodyart** discusses the art of tattoos and other body decorations.

Subscribe to Newsgroups

In most newsreaders, you can subscribe to newsgroups that interest you—and ignore the 15,000 that cover topics that are of no interest to you. To subscribe to newsgroups, you simply select the newsgroups you want from a list of all available newsgroups. The names of the newsgroups you've subscribed to then appear at the top of the newsgroup list or in a completely separate area, making them easy to access. However, you can still read and post messages in newsgroups to which you haven't subscribed.

WinVN treats all newsgroups the same, whether or not you've subscribed to them. But it places subscribed newsgroups at the top of the newsgroup list. More advanced newsreaders enable you to create a separate folder for each subscribed newsgroup, and still others display only the names of those to which you've subscribed.

Begin Guided Tour   Make a List of Newsgroups

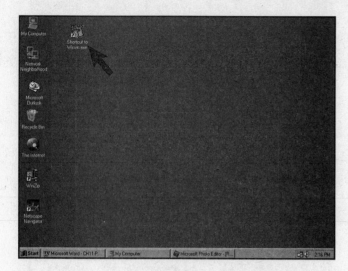

1 Establish your Internet connection and start your newsreader. If you installed WinVN earlier in this section, you can run it by double-clicking the **WinVn.exe** icon.

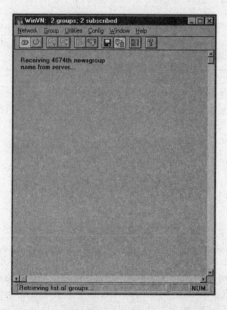

2 When you connect to your news server for the first time, WinVN retrieves the names of all the available newsgroups. A message appears, showing its progress.

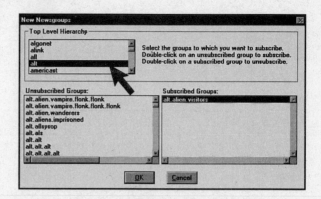

3 After retrieving the names of all the newsgroups, WinVN displays a dialog box in which you subscribe to specific newsgroups. In the Top Level Hierarchy list, click a general newsgroup category.

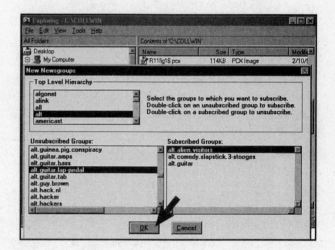

4 A list of the specific newsgroups in the selected category appears in the Unsubscribed list. Double-click the name of the newsgroup to which you want to subscribe. Click **OK**.

(continues)

Guided Tour Make a List of Newsgroups

(continued)

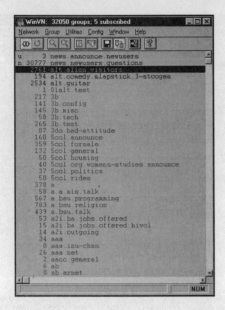

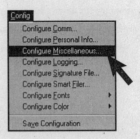

8 Newgroups are created and deleted daily. To have WinVN refresh your newsgroup list, open the **Config** menu and click **Configure Miscellaneous**.

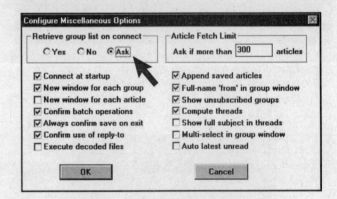

5 The name of the selected newsgroup moves to the Subscribed Groups list. You can remove a newsgroup name from the Subscribed Groups list by double-clicking it.

6 Repeat steps 3 through 5 to subscribe to additional newsgroups. When you finish, click **OK**.

9 Under **Retrieve Group List on Connect**, select **Ask** to have WinVN prompt you each time you connect. (If you select Yes, the list will be updated each time you connect, but that takes a long time.) Click **OK**.

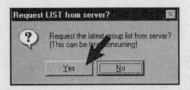

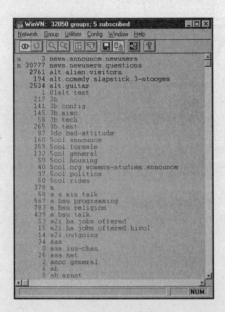

10 From now on, whenever you run WinVN, it displays a dialog box asking if you want to retrieve the newsgroup list. Click **Yes** to retrieve the latest list.

7 WinVN returns you to the opening window and displays a list of all the newsgroups. At the top of the list are the newsgroups to which you subscribed.

Because the list of newsgroups is long, you might have trouble finding the newsgroup you want. To help, WinVN offers a search feature. Open the **Group** menu and select **Find**. In the dialog box that appears, type a few characters of the newsgroup's name, and click **OK**. WinVN displays an arrow next to the first newsgroup it finds that matches what you typed. Press **F3** to find the next newsgroup.

Read and Respond to Newsgroup Messages

Once you have subscribed to a list of newsgroups, you can start opening the newsgroups that interest you. When you open a newsgroup, your newsreader displays a list of recently posted messages. You can then select the messages you want to read (and possibly respond to).

Before you post your own messages in a newsgroup, familiarize yourself with the newsgroup. Hang out and read existing messages so you have a clear idea of the focus and tone of the newsgroup. Reading messages without posting your own messages is known as *lurking*. Newsgroups encourage lurking because it provides you with the knowledge you need to respond intelligently and to avoid repeating what has already been said.

Most messages you encounter in newsgroups are text messages. A newsgroup participant may post an opinion, a question, an answer, or simply an informative tidbit of general interest. However, you may encounter messages that have files attached. For example, in a photography newsgroup, people may trade their favorite photos. These files are usually encoded so they can be transmitted across the Internet. You will have to decode the files to view them. For information on how to decode files, see "Encode and Decode Messages" on page 237.

The Guided Tour shows you how to read and respond to text messages in newsgroups using WinVN. The steps may differ slightly if you are using a different newsreader.

Begin Guided Tour   Read and Reply to Newsgroup Messages

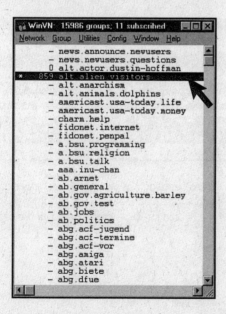

1 Establish your Internet connection and run your newsreader. The figure here shows the opening WinVN window, which displays the list of available newsgroups. Double-click the name of a newsgroup.

2 The newsreader retrieves a list of recently posted messages in the newsgroup you selected (this may take several seconds). Note that each message is dated and has a description. To read a message, double-click its description.

(continued)

Guided Tour Read and Reply to Newsgroup Messages

(continued)

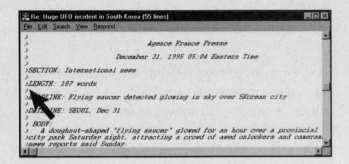

3 The newsreader displays the contents of the message. The angle brackets (>) indicate quoted material that has been lifted from a previous message. This particular message is a response to the previous message.

4 To respond to a message, enter the Reply or Respond command. In WinVN (shown here), you open the **Respond** menu and click **Followup Article**.

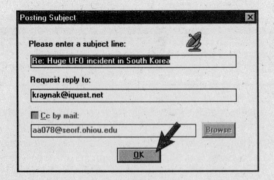

5 The Posting Subject dialog box appears, asking for a message description. Because you are responding to a message, WinVN uses the same description as the message to which you are replying. Click **OK**.

In most newsreaders, you can respond to a message privately by sending your reply using e-mail. You simply address your reply directly to the person who posted the message. This ensures that the person receives the message even if he or she does not check the newsgroup postings again.

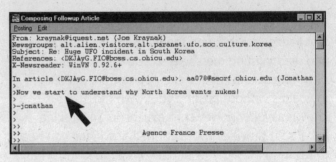

6 WinVN displays a window in which you can enter your message. Note that WinVN automatically inserts the contents of the original message as a quotation, marking each line with a right-angle bracket (>).

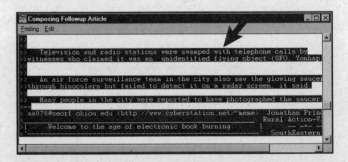

7 You should quote only as much of the original message as is necessary to remind the sender of its contents. To delete a portion of the quoted message, drag over it and press the **Delete**.

Guided Tour   Read and Reply to Newsgroup Messages

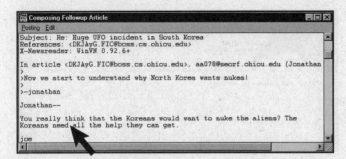

8 Click after the quoted material, and then type your response to the message.

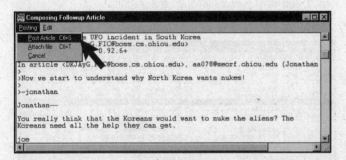

9 Enter the command to send or post your response. In WinVN, you open the **Posting** menu and select **Post Article**.

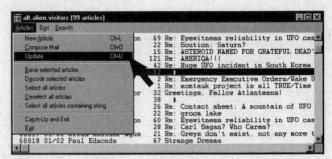

10 Your newsreader sends your message to the current newsgroup. Don't expect your message to appear immediately; it can take several minutes for your reply to be posted. To see if your message has been posted, refresh the list of messages. In WinVN, open the **Articles** menu and select **Update**.

Many newsreaders enable you to sort messages by date, author, or description. They may also display *threaded* messages, which means they keep the original message and all of its responses together. This makes it easier for you to follow a newsgroup conversation. Look for a Sort menu in your newsreader to see your sorting options.

Begin Guided Tour   Post a Message in a Newsgroup

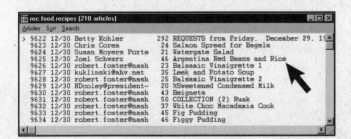

1 In addition to responding to other people's postings, you can start your own conversations. To post a message in WinVN, first open the newsgroup in which you want your message to be posted.

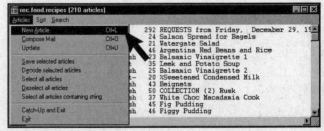

2 In your newsreader, enter the command for posting a message. In WinVN, open the **Articles** menu and select **New Article**.

(continues)

Guided Tour   Post a Message in a Newsgroup   *(continued)*

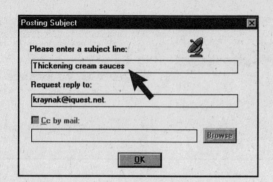

3 A dialog box appears, asking you to type a subject for your message. Type a description and click **OK**.

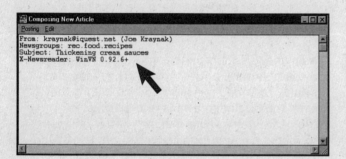

4 Your newsreader displays a window in which you can compose your message. At the top of the window, it adds a header that will be sent with the message. This header includes your e-mail address and the message description you entered.

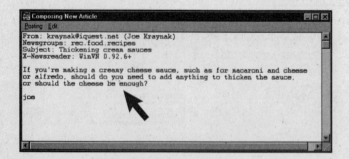

5 Click below the header area and type your message.

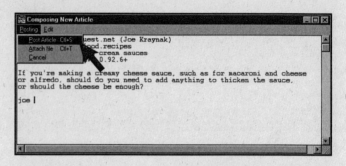

6 When you finish composing your message, you're ready to send it. In WinVN, open the **Posting** menu and click **Post Article**. In a matter of minutes, your article appears in the newsgroup, and other people can open and read it.

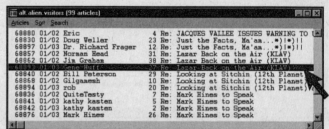

7 Check the newsgroup daily (or more frequently, if necessary) for responses to your message. When you see a response, double-click its description to read the message.

Encode and Decode Messages

Most newsgroups are essentially discussion groups where people send messages back and forth, share trade secrets, and attempt to carry on intelligent dialogue. However, in some newsgroups, people swap more than just text. For instance, in a movie newsgroup, people might post photos of their favorite movie stars, or short video clips of films.

Because these types of files are binary (not just text), newsgroups have a special way of transferring them over the Internet. A special coding system called *UUEncode* is commonly used to convert binary files into text. If you encounter a binary file in a newsgroup, you must get the encoded file (in its text form) and decode it to return it to its binary form.

Likewise, if you want to include a binary file with your own text message, you must encode the file before sending it. The Guided Tour shows you how to encode and decode files using WinVN. A more advanced newsreader may be able to encode and decode files automatically.

Some advanced newsreaders allow you to view the photo directly in the newsreader. Navigator News and Internet News from Microsoft are good examples. These readers also make it very easy for you to attach a photo or other file to a News post.

> You have probably heard about newsgroups that focus on pornography. In these newsgroups, users commonly swap pornographic material, including nude images. If you have children who use your system, or if you find this material offensive, steer clear of any newsgroup that has "sex" or "erotica" in the title. For more information, see "Prevent Your Children from Accessing Specific Sites and Content" on page 280.

Begin Guided Tour   Decode Uuencoded Files

1 If you see a message that indicates a binary file is attached, or if you see something like (0/2), (1/2), or (2/2) next to a message, you must decode the file to use it. Long files are posted in sections; notations such as (0/2) and (1/2), indicate the order of the sections.

2 In WinVN, you must first select all the sections of the file you want to decode. Click each message description that contains a section number for the file.

(continues)

Guided Tour Decode Uuencoded Files

(continued)

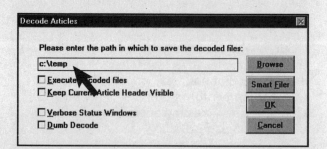

3 Having selected all the sections of an encoded file, you can decode the file. In WinVN, you open the **Articles** menu and select **Decode selected articles**.

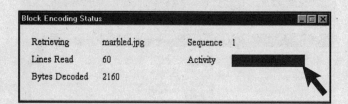

4 A dialog box appears, asking where you want the decoded file stored. Type a path to the drive and folder in which you want the file stored. In this example, the file will be stored in the temp folder on drive C. Click **OK**.

5 Your newsreader begins to decode the file, keeping you updated on its progress. Wait until the operation is complete.

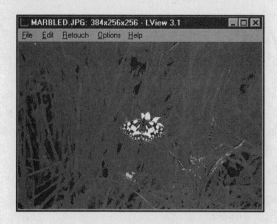

6 Most newsreaders cannot "play" or open the binary file you just downloaded. You need to run another application (usually a helper application), and then open the file in that application. This picture shows a helper application called LView 3.1 displaying a downloaded JPG file. See "Play Sound and Video Clips with Helper Applications" on page 129 for details.

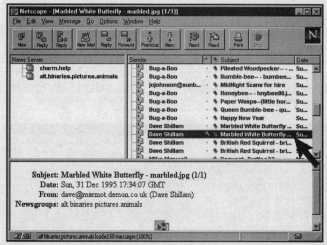

7 Netscape News is a sophisticated newsreader that comes with Netscape Navigator. In Netscape News, you simply double-click the first section of the file you want to decode.

Guided Tour   Decode Uuencoded Files

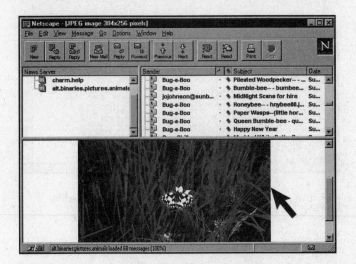

8 Netscape News automatically finds all the sections of the encoded file, decodes the file, and (if the file is one that News can handle) displays the file on-screen.

Begin Guided Tour   Encode and Post a File

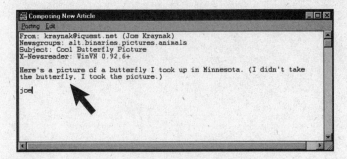

1 If you want to post a binary file—say, a picture of yourself—in a newsgroup, first you compose a message (as explained in "Read and Post Messages in Newsgroups" on page 219).

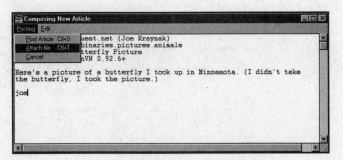

2 After composing your message, you can attach a file to it. Open the **Posting** menu and select **Attach File**.

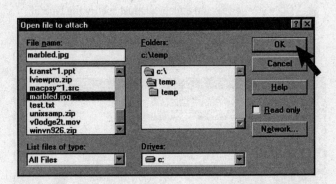

3 A dialog box appears, prompting you to enter the name of the file you want to send. Select the drive, folder, and name of the file you want to send. Click **OK**.

(continues)

Guided Tour   Encode and Post a File

(continued)

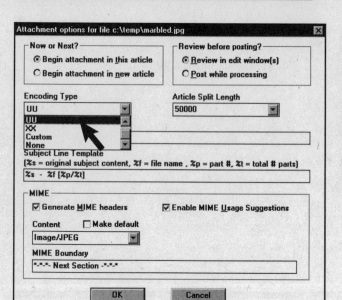

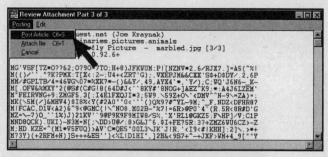

6 You can now send your message with the encoded file. Open the **Posting** menu and select **Post Article**.

4 Once you've selected a file, you must specify the type of encoding you want to use. Open the **Encoding Type** drop-down list and select **UU** (for UUEncode). Click **OK**.

5 WinVN encodes the file and inserts the encoded (text) version at the bottom of your message. This figure shows the text version of a graphic file.

HOW TO...

Chat with People on the Internet

One of the most popular pastimes on the Internet is *real-time chat*. Real-time chat is a conversation with other users who are logged on at the same time you are. It's called *real-time* because the words you type instantly appear on the screens of everyone else who is participating in this activity. There's no waiting for a posted message or e-mail; the conversation happens live.

Traditionally, the live chat system on the Internet has been *IRC*, which stands for Internet Relay Chat. IRC is actually a program designed to let multiple users communicate, and it is made up of many channels. Chat channels work like electronic "rooms" where people gather to talk about a common subject or just anything at all.

To use IRC, you need an IRC program, and you need to locate an Internet server that uses the IRC network. There are various ways to enter IRC, depending on your type of Internet access. If you're using an account that doesn't have a graphical interface program, you'll probably have to type IRC commands to navigate the chat channels. If you're using a SLIP or PPP account (also called a dial-in direct account), you may be using a graphical browser program such as Netscape to access the Internet, and you will be able to enter IRC commands using icons and toolbar buttons.

What You Will Find in This Section

Find and Install an IRC Chat Program

Online services such as America Online have always provided their users with the ability to chat. For example, the America Online software includes a chat function that allows you to communicate with other AOL users. You click the **People Connection** button, connect to an AOL server, and then you're ready to chat. You can even create private chat rooms for your online conversations.

If you've decided to make your connection to the Internet via a local service provider, they probably won't supply you with a chat client in the software that you are given. More than likely you will have to find a chat client yourself. You know from previous chapters that you can find all the Internet-related software you need either on the World Wide Web or an FTP site.

There are many popular programs for chatting—most take advantage of the IRC servers around the globe. Other chat software such as Virtual Places and Microsoft Virtual Chat use other avenues to connect users who wish to chat. All of these chat clients are available for download from the Internet. Most of them also have shareware (or in some cases freeware) versions. IRC programs vary in terms of how much disk space they take up on your computer and how they look and perform. As usual, some are easier to use than others. Here are a few you might look for:

- **mIRC**   This software has gone through several overhauls by the programmer and is one of the most-used IRC packages; mIRC has an easy-to-use menu system. It also lets you enter commands indirectly with a menu option or directly with a conversation window preceded with a slash (UNIX-style).

- **WS-IRC**   This is another very popular IRC program for Windows users with PPP or SLIP accounts. It's available in both shareware and freeware versions, and it's updated often. WS-IRC offers toolbars and icons, and it's very intuitive.

- **Winsock IRC**   A smaller program for Windows users, Winsock IRC is a new freeware Internet Relay Chat program for novice users. Setting up the program and configuring its various options is simple.

- **Netscape Chat**   Although it's a separate program, Netscape Chat is used with Netscape Navigator to access the Internet. It's easy to use, and it comes complete with toolbar and icons. (You can learn how to install it on your computer in the Guided Tour.)

- **Microsoft Comic Chat**   This interesting and unusual offering from Microsoft allows you to chat on typical IRC channels in a visual way. Each participant is represented by a comic character and the chat plays out as a comic strip. Once you master more typical IRC chat, try this software.

> Another type of software that you can use for communication via the Internet is a *MUD* or Multi-User-Domain client. While they are not chat programs in the strictest sense, these software interfaces allow users to interact via text. MUDs are usually tied to some type of virtual world in which the users role play.

Many of the newer IRC programs not only enable you to chat but also support file exchange, enable you to play sound files and trade Web pages. By far, the most popular IRC programs you'll come across are those that offer graphical interfaces and these extra features.

Locate an IRC Program

The best place on the Web to start your search for an appropriate IRC program is Stroud's Consummate Winsock Applications: **http://www.stroud.com**. Microsoft Comic Chat can be found at **http://www.microsoft.com/msdownload/#chat**. Two other sites to check out for the latest and greatest in IRC software and other shareware is The TUCOWS mirror at Sams Publishing, **http://tucows.mcp.com/** and Que's Software Library at **http://www.mcp.com/que/software/**.

You can also find the IRC programs mentioned, by finding an FTP site that stores them. Because the more popular FTP sites are often busy, you may not be able to sign on to them. However, most offer mirror sites (alternate FTP sites) that contain copies of the same files. Once you ftp to a site, look for directories with names such as irc, clients, or windows to help you find the IRC program you're looking for.

Try the following sites for the latest IRC programs:

> **ftp.netscape.com**
>
> **ftp2.netscape.com** (mirror site)
>
> **ftp.winsite.com**
>
> **ftp.eskimo.com**
>
> **cs-ftp.bu.edu**
>
> **ftp.undernet.org**
>
> **ftp1.microsoft.com**

European sites:

> **ftp.demon.co.uk**
>
> **ftp.funet.fi**
>
> **src.doc.ic.ac.uk**

For more information about downloading files, turn to "Find and Copy Files from the Internet" (page 179).

Another good place to start your search for IRC software is **www.shareware.com** on the Web. For general information about IRC check out **http://http1.brunel.ac.uk:8080/~cs93jtl/IRC.html**.

Once you find an IRC program and copy it to your computer, you can install the program and set it up to access an IRC server. (For more information about locating a chat server, read "Connect to a Chat Server" on page 249). The Guided Tour will show you how to find and install Netscape Chat and connect to an IRC server.

Find and Copy the Netscape Chat Program

If you're using Netscape to access the Internet, you may want to install Netscape Chat as your IRC program (although, you can use any of the IRC software mentioned previously). You can find the program at Stroud's Consummate Winsock Applications Web site or any of the Netscape ftp sites referenced previously. Use your Web browser or an FTP package to download the file. For more information, turn to "Find and Copy Files from the Internet" on page 179. In the meantime, follow the Guided Tour to copy and install Netscape Chat.

Using your Internet Browser's FTP feature, click the **Location** or **Go to** text box, type **ftp://ftp.netscape.com** or **ftp://ftp2.netscape.com**. Once you're connected, use the directory list to change to the **pub/powerpack** directory. Select the **pp2032p1** file. Netscape Chat has been made part of the Netscape Navigator Power Pack. You must download the entire Power Pack if you wish to use Netscape Chat. Download the file to an appropriate directory on your computer.

Begin Guided Tour   Install Netscape Chat

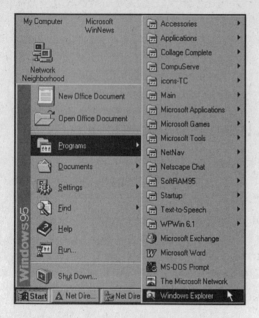

1 Click the **Start** button, select **Programs**, and click **Windows Explorer**.

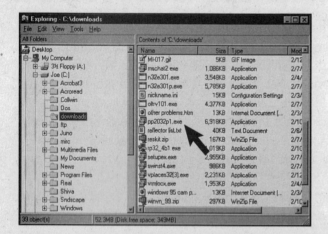

2 Open the folder into which you downloaded the Netscape Chat file, and double-click the file named **pp2032p1.exe**.

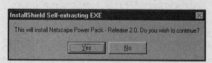

3 A dialog box starts the installation process; click **Yes**.

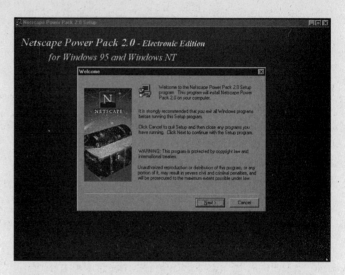

4 The installation screen opens for the Netscape Power Pack (which includes Netscape Chat). Click **Next** to continue.

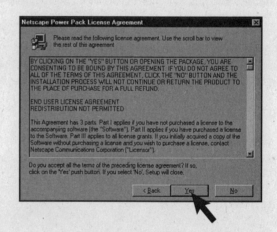

5 Read the License Agreement and then click **Yes** to continue.

Guided Tour Install Netscape Chat

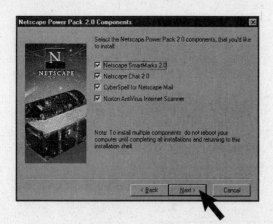

6 Select the Power Pack components that you want to install. Make sure you choose at least Netscape Chat 2.0, then click **Next**.

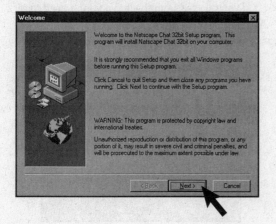

7 The setup program for Netscape Chat will begin; click **Next**.

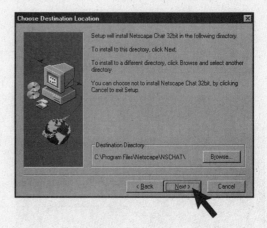

8 Choose the directory that you want to place the Netscape Chat software in (or use the default selected by the installer). Click **Next** to continue.

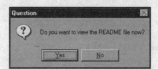

9 At the completion of the installation you will be asked if you want to view a readme file. If you click **Yes** the file will appear. When you are finished reading the file click it's **Close** button.

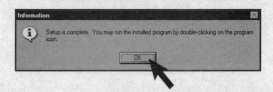

10 The installation is complete. Click **OK** to finish.

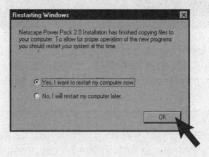

11 You will have to restart your computer for the changes that were made during the installation process to take effect. Click **OK**. When Windows 95 restarts, you will be ready to run the Netscape Chat program.

Begin Guided Tour Set Up Netscape Chat

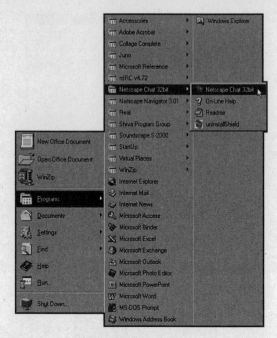

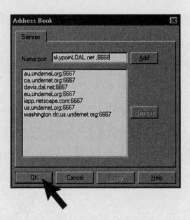

3 Select a server from the Address Book list or type in a server name as shown. (If you type in a new server name, you must also include the port number—usually 6667 or 6668.)

4 Click the **Add** button if you've added a new server to the list (if you selected from the list you don't need to click the Add button). Click **OK**.

1 To set up Netscape Chat for use and make your first IRC connection, start with your Internet connection up and running. Click the **Start** button, select **Programs**, and click **Netscape Chat**.

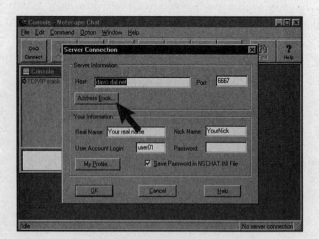

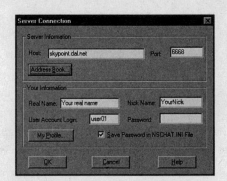

5 Under Your Information, type your full name in the **Real Name** text box. In the **Nick Name** text box, type in the name you want to use when you chat. For example, you might type Joe Habraken in the Real Name box and then J-Guy (a nick name) in the Nick Name box.

2 The Server Connection dialog box appears. The first thing you need to do is either type a chat server name or select a server from the Address Book. Click the **Address Book** button.

For a list of IRC servers, turn to "IRC Chat Servers" on page 444 in the reference section of this book.

Guided Tour Set Up Netscape Chat

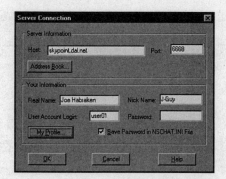

6 Click in the **Nick Name** text box and enter the nickname or "handle" that you want to use in the chat channels. You can use up to nine characters, but spaces aren't allowed.

A few chat channels require you to enter a password in order to use them. If you already know the password, you can type it in the **Password** text box in the Server Connection dialog box. Then click the **Save Password in NSCHAT.INI File** option to select it.

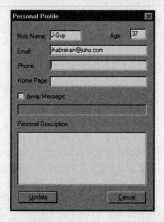

7 Click the **My Profile** button. Type your e-mail address in the **Email** text box. (If you don't want anyone you meet in IRC to e-mail you, leave this text box blank.) You can also place other personal information in the Profile box such as your age, phone number, and home page (if you have your own). Once you've completed your entries, click the **Update** button.

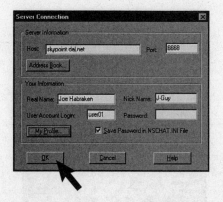

8 Once you've completed the Profile and the other setup options, click **OK**. If you entered the name of a specific chat server, Netscape Chat attempts to connect you. If the connection doesn't work (it might be busy), you may have to select another chat server. If you get a list of conversation channels, select one and click **Join**.

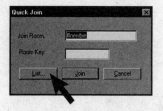

9 If the connection is successful, information about the server will scroll by, telling you the location of the server, how many users are logged on, and any other rules or messages. A dialog box with a suggested channel (#Newbie) appears. This channel is set up for new users who would like to ask for help from veteran channel sysops (system operators—the people who serve as moderators for the channel). To join the channel, click **Join**.

10 To look at a list of all the channels available on the server, click **List**.

(continues)

Guided Tour Set Up Netscape Chat *(continued)*

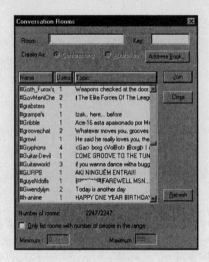

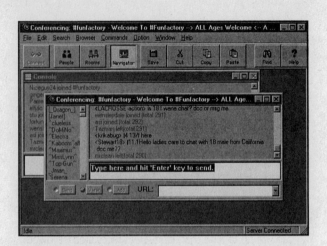

11 To connect to a particular channel and begin chatting, double-click on a channel.

12 The Chat window for the particular channel will open and you will be ready to chat.

Connect to a Chat Server

As you have seen with Netscape Chat, when you log onto your chat program, you have an opportunity to choose a particular chat server to use. There are several IRC networks you can tap into to find chat servers. The various networks differ in philosophy, in terms of how the network is run, and in number of users. These are some of the more popular IRC networks:

EFNet is the largest IRC network, with over 100 connected servers. It has the most users (averaging 7,000–11,000) and the most channels, but that means it's very busy.

Undernet, formed in 1992, is one of the more famous renegade nets, offering more "attitude" and freedom than the other nets. With 200–500 users and up to 27 servers, it's considerably less congested than the EFNet.

DALnet, formed in 1994, is also less busy than the EFNet, making it a good source for IRC activity. It uses 16 servers and averages 130 users at any given moment.

UpperNet, a very new network for IRC, has 10 servers available.

ChatNet, one of the newest IRC networks, was created as a family-oriented network. It has 20 worldwide servers (including Superlink) boasting over 100 registered channels making it the fourth-largest IRC network.

Despite the fact that all of these networks support IRC, you can't chat with users on other networks. For example, if you're using EFNet, you won't stumble across any Undernet users in your EFNet chat channels.

Because each IRC network has servers, you have a choice of which one to use to start chatting. Unfortunately, not all servers will allow you to log on and use them. With some servers, you can log on only if you're near their site, and some allow only certain Internet domains to use them. Other servers have various other restrictions on who uses their site. You may have to look around for a chat server you can use. Check with your service provider or try subscribing to the **alt.irc** newsgroup (see "Read and Post Messages in Newsgroups" on page 219 for information on using Internet newsgroups).

To get you started, here are just a few of the many IRC servers you can try:

irc.colorado.edu (EFNet)

irc.indiana.edu (EFNet)

irc.netcom.com (EFNet)

davis.ca.us.undernet.org (UnderNet)

milwaukee.wi.us.undernet.org (UnderNet)

chicago.il.us.undernet.org (Undernet)

irc.ucdavis.edu (DALnet)

glass.dal.net (DALnet)

skypoint.dal.net (DALnet)

Portland.OR.US.Chatnet.Org (ChatNet)

SF.CA.US.Chatnet.Org (ChatNet)

WalnutCreek.CA.US.ChatNet.Org (ChatNet)

Begin Guided Tour Change Chat Servers on mIRC

One of the more popular IRC chat clients is a shareware product called mIRC. It works pretty much the same as Netscape Chat and provides you with some advanced yet easy-to-use features that can make your chat experience a lot more fun. You can download mIRC **http://pebbles.axi.net/mirc/** or find the latest version of the software at **Shareware.com**.

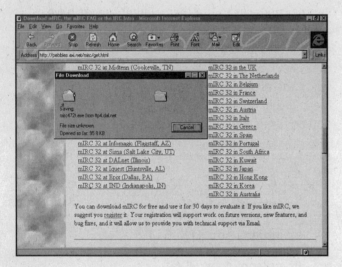

1 Download mIRC from one of the sites listed above using your Web browser.

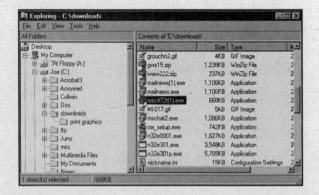

2 Open the Windows Explorer, locate the folder that you downloaded mIRC to, and double-click **mirc472.exe** to install the software (it's a typical Windows 95 installation and will create the appropriate directory and Start menu icons).

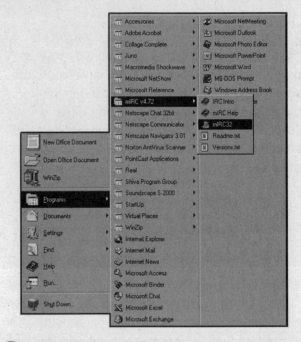

3 Click the **Start** button, point at Programs, and then click the **mIRC** icon to start the program.

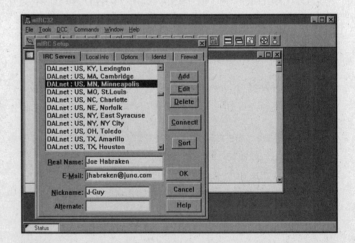

4 The first time that you start the mIRC software you will be asked to provide personal information such as your e-mail address and the nickname that you will use on the various chat channels. Enter the information.

5 You can also pick a Chat server from a list that is provided. The default choice assigns you randomly to an available server. If you know of a server in your area, or have a particular server preference, choose it from the list.

Guided Tour Change Chat Servers on mIRC

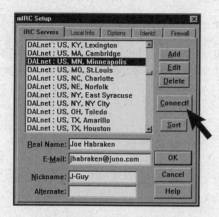

6 Once you've completed the personal information and chosen a server, click **Connect**.

If the connection doesn't work (the first one you select might be busy, for example), you may have to try selecting another chat server.

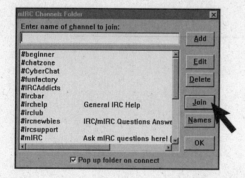

7 After you are connected, a window will open giving you a list of commonly-used channels and channels for new users. You can select a channel from the list and then click **Join**.

8 If you want to view all the channels available on a particular chat server, click **OK** without selecting a channel.

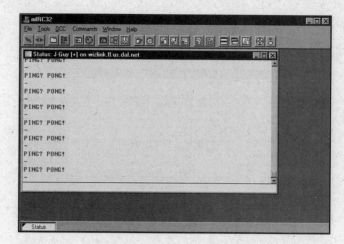

9 To list all the channels on a chat sever, click the **List Channels** button.

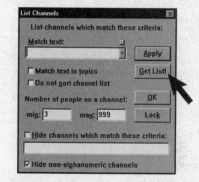

10 A dialog box will appear that allows you to list channels that meet certain criteria, or to list all the channels. To list all the channels on a server, click the **Get List!** button.

(continues)

Guided Tour   Change Chat Servers on mIRC

(continued)

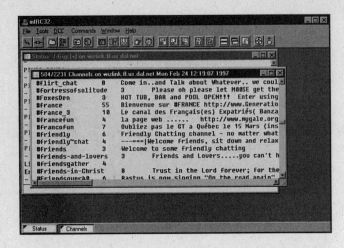

11 A list of channels on the server will appear (the list will be tailored to the criteria that you set in the channel dialog box). The number of users on a particular channel is listed along with information concerning the subject of the channel discussion. To log on to a channel double-click the channel name.

Converse in Channels

Having installed a chat program and connected to a chat server, you're ready to be a part of IRC. At this point, you might display a list of the various channels so you know what's available, you might create a nickname for yourself, or you might jump right into your favorite channel. If you use Netscape Chat, or mIRC, you can join and exit channels using icons and buttons. There are still a very small number of IRC clients that require you to know some IRC commands before you get started. The following table shows some common IRC commands you can use to navigate the live chat areas. Remember to press **Enter** after any IRC command. (You won't need to know these commands if you use Netscape Chat or mIRC. However you can still use these commands in their chat windows if you want.)

You'll learn more about channels and nicknames in the following sections.

What Goes On in a Chat Channel?

IRC's chat channels are smaller areas in which people usually talk about a particular subject. When you're tuned in to an Internet chat channel, you can sit back and watch conversations scroll across your screen. When a person talks, her name appears to the left of the screen, and her text appears to the right of her name. For an observer, it's sort of like reading a script for a play or movie.

Depending on how busy the channel is, following the scrolling conversation may be easy—or it may be extremely difficult. If everyone is talking about the same thing, the text will probably appear in a logical order. Everyone takes turns "talking," and you can easily follow the conversation. However, if some participants are carrying on separate conversations, the lines of text can appear on-screen without any logical flow. You have to learn to read the words and associate them with the person who "spoke" them. This association can be a little tricky sometimes.

Common IRC Commands

Use This Command	To Do This
/join #*channelname* or /channel #*channelname*	Log onto the specified channel
/part #*channelname* or /leave #*channelname*	Exit the channel
/whois *nickname*	Find information about another person, such as his real name and Internet domain
/nick *nickname*	Change your nickname
/quit *message*	Exit the channel and display a personal message (such as "See you later," for example)
/hop #*channelname*	Exit the current channel and enter the new channel that you designate
/help	List IRC commands and information

When you connect to IRC, you might want to see a list of available channels, or you might just go directly to a channel you already know about. The Guided Tour shows you how to get to a channel both ways. If you go to a channel and you don't see any "talk," either no one is talking or they're all engaged in private messaging. To find out if anyone's "home," try typing **hello** and press **Enter**. Wait a few minutes, and if no one answers you, switch to another channel.

Some channels sponsor special conferences with guest speakers. During such events, the channel operator sets the mode to moderated channel. In a moderated channel, only the designated guest speaker is allowed to converse freely; other users are given limited abilities to ask questions.

The channels are started and run by channel operators, called *ops* or *channelops* for short. Channelops ultimately have total control over the channel, including the topic name, who's allowed in, and who gets kicked out. Channelops can easily be identified in the IRC channels; they have @ symbols in front of their names.

Using Nicknames

Anybody with a modem and an Internet connection can participate in live chat. You'll find a variety of people from all walks of life and from all over the globe. In addition, you'll encounter all kinds of personality types. One of the best ways to express your personality is with a nickname. Before entering IRC, you need to select your own nickname (also called a handle or screen name) that will identify you to others; it can be your login name or a fun creation.

Even if you know a user's nickname, you may never really *know* exactly who you're talking to in IRC. There's no audible voice to help you determine the person's gender or age. Just because someone's screen name is Bob doesn't necessarily mean it's a guy you're talking to. It could be a woman, a child, or even a famous celebrity. That's part of the fascination of online chat: No one really knows who you are, so you can be whoever you want to be. For example, for a normally quiet, shy person, IRC offers a chance to play a vibrant role. However, that can work to your advantage or disadvantage. Some people in the chat channels are very bold, often saying things they normally wouldn't say in a face-to-face conversation. Because of this, you need to approach Internet chat with a little bit of skepticism. Remember that not all the participants are genuine and sincere. Keep in mind that some users may have sinister motives and be cautious.

The Internet isn't the only place where people chat electronically. Online chat is also very popular among commercial online services, such as CompuServe and America Online, as well as the smaller BBSs (Bulletin Board Services).

Chat Rules and Guidelines

You might be ready to jump into a channel and chat as soon as you connect to IRC. However, before you do that you need to consider some guidelines.

IRC doesn't follow the strict rules that some areas of the Internet do. But that's not necessarily a good thing. That means it's not always easy to figure out the prevailing attitudes of the various channels and their members. So it's always best to look before leaping into the fray.

Generally, you should conduct yourself in the chat channels the same as you would in real life. Be polite and civil as necessary. Don't use crude language, sexual innuendo, or harassment unless that's what the channel is all about. Remember, you never know who might be reading what you say.

Common sense is the best way to approach live chat on the Internet. Here are a few guidelines:

- Always observe the conversation first before you jump in.

- Apply the Golden Rule: Treat others as you would have them treat you.

- If you're in the middle of a conversation and must leave the room for a moment, it's a good idea to send a *brb* (be right back) message to let others know what happened to you.

- If someone says hello to you, it's polite to at least answer them, even if you're planning to *lurk* (observe) for awhile.

- If you join a channel that requests that you speak a foreign language, don't start speaking in English. For example, if you join the #spanish channel and everyone seems to be speaking spanish, don't assume that you can just start speaking English.

If you're concerned about your children being able to access the more risqué IRC channels, you might consider using a program such as Cyberpatrol to block out certain IRC channels. You can find the program on the Web at **http:/ /www.cyberpatrol.com**. For more information, see "Secure Your System and Practice Proper Netiquette," on page 271.

If you violate chat guidelines or channel rules, you can be kicked off the channel. If you continuously violate those rules, you might be reported to your Internet Service Provider, in which case you could find yourself expelled from the service. Chat participants often stick together, so if someone continually annoys the rest of

the group, that person may be verbally attacked by the crowd and driven from the channel. For more information about chat etiquette, see "Secure Your System and Practice Proper Netiquette," starting on page 271.

Online Emoticons and Abbreviations

It's not always easy to convey your emotion or tone while engaging in IRC conversations. For example, if someone types in "You're a looney," you can't tell from the words alone if he actually thinks you're crazy, or if he's just kidding around. To compensate for the lack of facial expressions and voice inflections, online users have created symbols, called *smileys* or *emoticons*, to express emotions.

A smiley is a face created out of keyboard symbols, such as **:)** or **: -)** (the dash for the nose is optional). To read a smiley properly, you must tilt your head to the left and look at the symbols. With a smiley, the message "You're a looney :)" takes on a light, friendly meaning. For a complete list of emoticons, turn to the Handy Reference section on page 445.

Another way to express emotions or actions on-screen is with the use of brackets of some kind, such as **<grin>**, **[sigh]**, ***thump***, or **::slap::**. Some of the graphical-based IRC programs have action icons you can select to show physical movements. There's also an IRC command you can use, such as **/me hits head on desk**, which others on the channel read as "*Chatldiot* hits head on desk" (or whatever your nickname is).

Not only will you come across strange keyboard symbols in the chat rooms, you'll also encounter a hip abbreviated form of online shorthand. Common words or phrases are abbreviated or reduced to acronyms to speed up typing. If you're not sure what a person's acronym means, don't hesitate to ask. For a list of acronyms, see the Handy Reference section in Part 4.

Chat on the Web with Virtual Places

While IRC has remained one of the most popular avenues of chat on the Internet, software now exists that allows you to chat directly on the World Wide Web. Every page on the Web becomes a potential chat site replacing the chat servers and channels used by IRC. Virtual Places (one of a number of Web chat software products) is chat software that works with your web browser. When you are located on a page that is occupied by other users of the Virtual Places software you will be able to chat with them. Each user is represented by a picture called an *avatar*. When you chat (type information into a chat window) your responses appear as a word balloon next to your avatar.

Web-chat software like Virtual Places allows you to navigate the Web with your web browser with the added facility of being able to chat with the other users that you come across. Virtual Places even has a Tour feature that allows you to load a group of users (their avatars actually) into a tour bus and then move the group from Web site to site. This Guided Tour will show you how to get Virtual Places up and running and how to use it with your Web browser.

Begin Guided Tour   Install and Configure Virtual Places

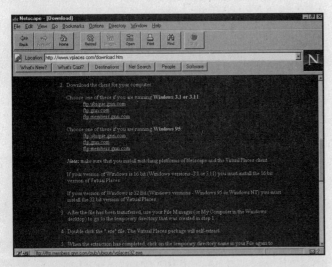

1 Download the Virtual Places software using your Web browser. The link for the software download can be found on the Web at **http://www.vplaces.com/download.htm**.

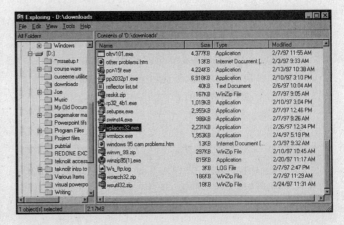

2 When the file download is complete, use the Windows Explorer to locate the Virtual Places installation file, and double-click it.

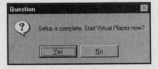

3 The Virtual Places installation is a typical install for Windows 95. Follow the screen prompts to advance through the process.

Guided Tour   Install and Configure Virtual Places

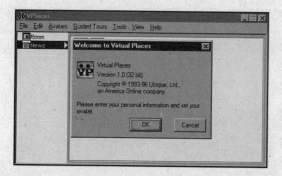

4 Once the installation is complete the Virtual Places software will start and ask you to enter your personal information. Click **OK** to begin the process.

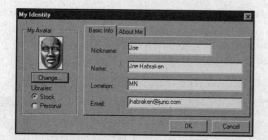

5 Enter your information in the Basic Info text boxes.

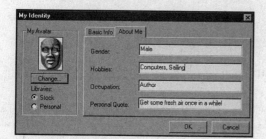

6 Click the **About Me** tab and enter the appropriate information in the text boxes.

7 The last step in the setup process is to pick an avatar that will represent you on the Web as you chat. Click the **Change** button and a gallery of avatars will appear. Choose an avatar and then click the **OK** button.

You can also use a custom avatar in Virtual Places such as a scanned photo of yourself or a picture of your favorite movie star. A number of Web sites dedicated to Virtual Places house avatar galleries where you can download a variety of pictures for your use.

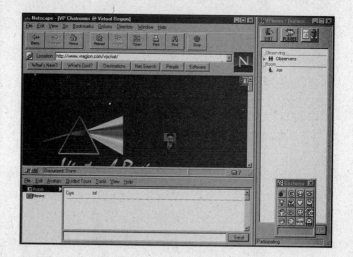

8 After selecting your avatar, you are ready to chat on the Web; Virtual Places will start your default Web browser (in this case Netscape Navigator) and set up the Virtual Places Chat window and the various Virtual Places tools such as the Gestures palette. You will be taken to a default Web page dictated by the Virtual Places software. Your avatar will appear in the Web browser window.

(continues)

Begin Guided Tour   Chat on the Web with Virtual Places   *(continued)*

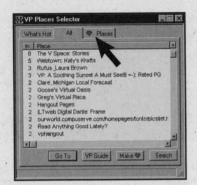

1 To find other users who you can chat with click the **Places** button on the right side of the Virtual Places screen.

2 The Places window shows you where other users are chatting and the number of other users on a particular page.

3 To go to one of the pages and join a chat session click a particular place and then click the **Go To** button.

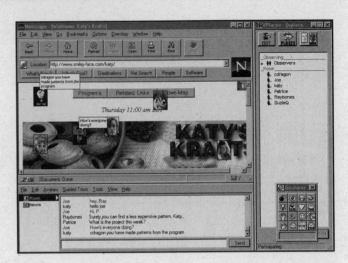

4 Once you are on a site with other users you can chat; type in the chat window and then press **Enter** to send you conversational tidbits. Your chat text will appear in the chat window and as a word balloon over your avatar.

5 You will find that special Web pages have been created for Virtual Places chatting such as the Glade shown here at **www.vplaces.com/vpnet/glade.html**.

Guided Tour   Chat on the Web with Virtual Places

6 Virtual Places also gives you the ability to add gestures to your conversation. Select a gesture from the Gestures palate and it will be sent with your chat text when you press **Enter** or click **Send**.

7 Once you've completed a chat session and said your good-byes, you can close the Virtual Places window by clicking its **Close** button. Your Web browser will remain on the desktop until you close it.

HOW TO...

Use Internet Video Conferencing

While Internet Relay Chat and other real-time chat clients provide a way for users on the Internet to hold conversations via their keyboards, recent innovations in computer hardware and software have made it possible for you to take advantage of video and voice communication over the Internet using a typical service provider dial-in account and your modem.

Real-time video and voice conferencing on the Net takes you way beyond the capabilities and possibilities offered by IRC and other chat clients. The fact that you can potentially see and hear other users as you communicate with them is quite remarkable, making conferencing ideal for business and personal use. This communication avenue also offers you the capability of "meeting" with a number of people or one person at a time.

To take advantage of real-time conferencing on the Net you need a conferencing program and a couple of additional hardware components on your computer; specifically video input from some kind of video camera and sound input from a microphone plugged into a sound card. You will find that the conferencing software is available on the Internet in both freeware and shareware packages. The hardware that you need can actually be quite inexpensive and take advantage of the existing sound card in your computer or the family video camera.

What You Will Find in This Section

Hardware Considerations for Internet Conferencing

To take advantage of video and voice conferencing on the Internet you need two hardware enhancements for your computer—a microphone and a video camera. Most sound cards (which are practically standard on any new PC) have an input port where you can plug in a variety of microphone types. Most computer and electronic stores offer a selection of microphones at very reasonable prices.

Readying your computer for video input may require a little more thought and effort. Two routes are provided to you to add the video input you will need for Internet video conferencing: You can add a video capture card to your computer and hook a typical home video camera to it, or you can buy a small digital video camera that hooks directly into your parallel port. Both of these options will supply you with suitable video input. Video capture boards can range from 200 to 400 dollars (some come with a digital camera). Digital cameras that hook directly to your computer's parallel port can run under 100 for a black and white version and less than 250 dollars for a color camera.

The final hardware consideration for Internet conferencing is your modem speed. Video and sound requires greater bandwidth than the still images and the text that you normally view on your Web browser or send via e-mail. So, a slower modem that provides satisfactory connection speeds for Web browsing may make Internet conferencing a very time-consuming and frustrating endeavor. It is best to have a modem that can connect at a baud rate of 28.8, although any speed between 14.4 and 28.8 will give you a satisfactory connection for Internet video conferencing. However, the connection speed is directly related to the number of frames per second that you will see in the video window; a faster connection gives you more frames per second, supplying a smoother (less jumpy) video feed.

Find and Install a Video Conferencing Program

Video and voice conferencing do have certain similarities to Internet Relay Chat; you need a PPP account to connect to a server that provides you with a place to meet and communicate with other users. These servers will often provide a number of different conferences that you can log onto. And while many public servers are available, servers also exist that require membership for access.

Several conferencing software packages exist (both shareware and freeware) and are available on the Internet for downloading. Microsoft provides a freeware product called NetMeeting. This software provides you with voice and video conferencing potential and also provides tools for conducting a group meeting, such as a shared whiteboard. You can download NetMeeting from Microsoft at **http://www.microsoft.com/msdownload/default.asp#chat**. Intel also has a voice/video communication package called Intel Internet Video Phone. You can download Internet Video Phone (currently a beta version) from **http://connectedpc.com/sites/connectedpc/**.

One of the most widely-used video conferencing software programs on the Internet—CU-SeeMe—has also been around the longest. CU-SeeMe was originally created by student programmers at Cornell University, which still maintains a much-used server for video conferencing. A freeware Windows version of CU-SeeMe is available from Cornell at **http://cu-seeme.cornell.edu/PC.CU-SeeMeCurrent.html**.

An enhanced version of the Cornell CU-SeeMe software has also been developed by White Pine Software. The White Pine version of the CU-SeeMe software for Windows offers additional features, including an interactive Whiteboard for conference meetings. White Pine offers a shareware trial version of Enhanced Cu-SeeMe, which you can download from the White Pine Web site at **http://goliath.wpine.com/cudownload.htm**.

> The White Pine version of Cu-SeeMe also supports color digital cameras such as those made by Connectix. If you use a color camera with the Cornell version, you will still have to use a black and white protocol to run the camera.

When you use CU-SeeMe for video conferencing you log onto a server, which is called a *reflector*. Each reflector can support one or a number of conferences at a time. Once you log onto a reflector server and choose a conference, you're ready to chat in a live video/audio environment.

Begin Guided Tour   Find & Install Enhanced CU-SeeMe Video Conferencing Program

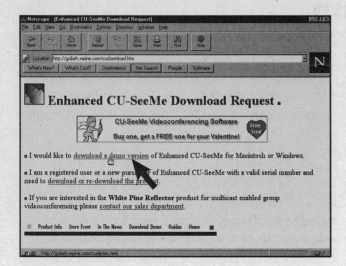

1 Connect to the Internet and start your Web browser. Enter **http://goliath.wpine.com/cudownload.htm** in the Location box of your Web browser and press Enter. Once on the White Pine download page, click the **download a demo version** link.

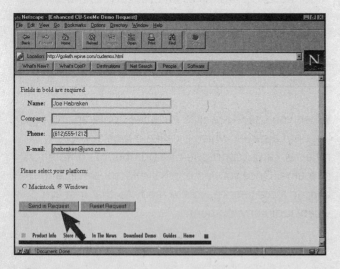

2 On the download request page, fill in the Demo request form and then click the **Send in Request** button.

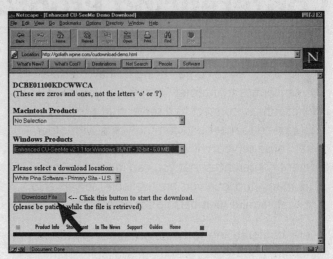

3 Select the appropriate version of the software in the Windows product drop-down box and the click the **Download File** button.

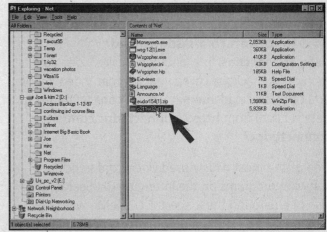

4 Once the download of the file is complete, use the Windows Explorer to locate the CU-SeeMe installation file c211w32.exe. Double-click **c211w32.exe**.

The CU-SeeMe installation program does a very good job at identifying your sound card type and your video input device. If you find that these parameters have not been set correctly check your hardware before attempting to re-install the software program.

Guided Tour   Find & Install Enhanced CU-SeeMe Video Conferencing Program

5 Follow the steps provided by the Enhanced CU-SeeMe installation program to install the software.

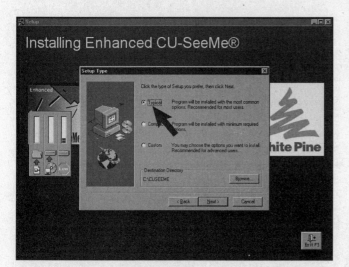

6 You can perform a typical or custom installation of the software. Choose **Typical**. You might also choose the directory location for the CU-SeeMe software.

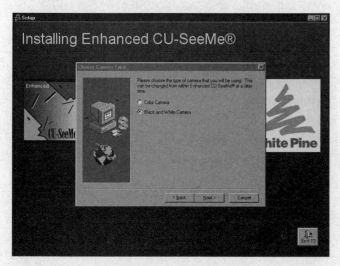

7 You will be asked to choose the type of camera that you will be using with the software (color or black and white).

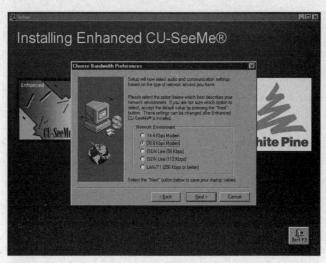

8 You will also need to supply information on the speed of your modem or your network connection to the Internet so that the software can be installed with the correct video and sound settings.

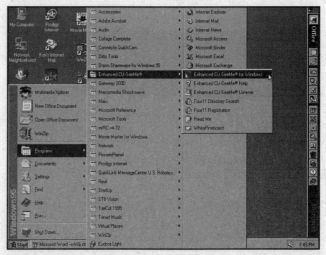

9 Once you've completed the installation process, make sure that you have your camera and microphone attached correctly to your computer. Click the **Start** menu, point at **Programs**, point at **Enhanced CU-SeeMe**, and then click **Enhanced CU-SeeMe for Windows** to start the video conferencing software.

Begin Guided Tour Connect to a Conferencing Reflector Site

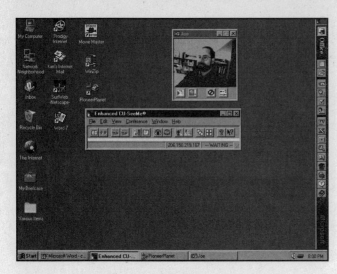

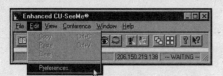

1 After you load the CU-SeeMe software via the Start menu, you will find two things on your Windows desktop: A local video window, which should show you (or whatever appears in your camera viewfinder) and the CU-SeeMe main application window, which gives you access to all the features and preferences of the CU-SeeMe software.

2 Before you attempt to connect to a reflector and join a conference, you may wish to check the preferences that were set for the software during the installation process. Click the **Edit** menu, then click **Preferences**.

3 The Preferences dialog box will appear. You can use this box to set the various parameters associated with the operation of the CU-SeeMe software. General preferences include whether or not the toolbar is visible in the software window. Click the **Conferencing** tab, which controls the name of your local video window and the maximum number of participant windows that can be open when you join a conference.

The Communications tab is where you can set the transmission and reception speeds you use to communicate. These parameters are set during the installation of the software based on your connection speed. In most cases, you will use the default settings for transmission and reception. When you click the **Audio** tab you will notice that your sound card has been identified for sound recording and playback and that an audio compression scheme has been selected for you based on your connection speed and installed sound card. Again, the software does a very good job configuring these items and you can more than likely go with the selections set during the installation.

Guided Tour Connect to a Conferencing Reflector Site

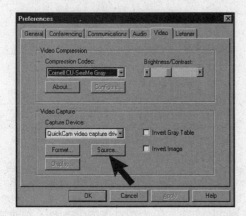

4 Click the Video tab if you need to adjust the picture in your local video window. The video capture drop down box will display the currently installed video device. To adjust it, click the **Source** button.

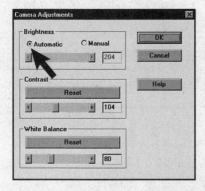

5 The Camera adjustment window allows you to fine-tune the image that appears in your local video window. You can adjust the brightness, contrast, and white balance for the camera. You can also set the camera to automatic adjustment; click the **Automatic** radio button. This allows the camera to automatically adjust the picture in relation to the light in the room.

6 To close the Preferences dialog box, click the Close button.

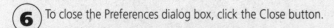

You can experience video conferencing without a video camera using the CU-SeeMe software. When you connect to a reflector site, you will be categorized as a "Lurker," meaning that you can see and communicate with those participants who appear in video windows.

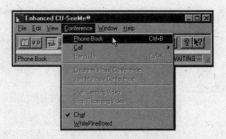

7 Once you have checked your preferences you are ready to connect to a conference reflector. Click **Conference** menu and then click **Phone Book**.

8 The CU-SeeMe Phone book appears. It contains a list of a number of public reflectors that you can use for video conferencing. Select a reflector and then click the **Call** button.

9 When you connect to the reflector, the Reflector Active Conference window will open showing you the conferences currently underway. Choose a conference and then click the **OK** button to join.

Begin Guided Tour Take Part in a Video Conference

1 As soon as you join the conference, the video windows for the other participants will begin to appear.

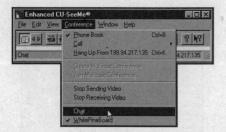

2 Although audio communication is an option, many users prefer to use a chat window (very much like an IRC chat window) to communicate. Click the **Communication** menu, then click **Chat** to open the chat window.

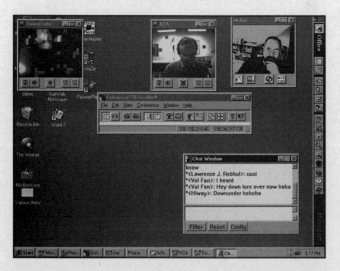

3 Type text into the Chat window and then press **Enter** to broadcast it.

4 Participants will come and go doing the conference. You can also close video windows that are not providing a good picture. To keep track of all the video windows and participants, click the **Window** menu and select **Participants**. A Participant List will appear showing who is in the conference and whether they have audio and video capabilities.

5 Audio communication is also an important part of CU-SeeMe. If you have a microphone and speakers, you will want to take advantage of their potential. Click the **Windows** menu and then click **Audio**. An Audio control window will appear that allows you to control the volume of incoming and outgoing audio.

Believe it or not, audio quality is more of a problem than video when you video conference on the Internet. Good audio requires a lot of bandwidth, which means that you will need to connect at 28.8 or faster to get real sound quality.

Guided Tour   Take Part in a Video Conference

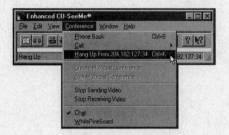

6 When you send audio, a level meter will register the strength of your audio transmission.

9 When you have said your good-byes and are ready to leave a conference, click the **Conference** menu, then click **Hang Up From** (the current reflector). This will close the connection to the conference.

10 To exit the CU-SeeMe software click the Close button for the CU-SeeMe window.

7 When another participant broadcasts video, their user name will be highlighted in the Participant List window.

The courtesy and netiquette rules of CU-SeeMe video conferencing are basically the same as those followed for participation in Internet Relay Chat. Most of the public reflectors are G-Rated, so it's important to act accordingly.

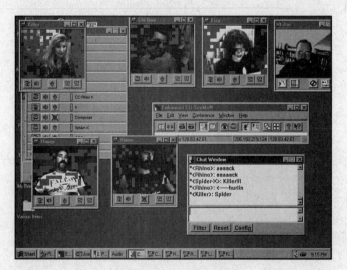

8 The quality of the video that you receive will depend on your connection speed and the connection speed of the other users that you are conferencing with. The number of users on a reflector can also affect audio and video quality.

HOW TO...

Secure Your System and Practice Proper Netiquette

As a citizen of the Internet, you have special concerns and responsibilities. You need to protect your computer and yourself from intrusions, and you must follow the rules of the Internet to avoid insulting another user or tying up a connection during the Internet "rush hour."

In this section, you will get the information you need to become a good Internet citizen. You'll learn how to protect your system against viruses that might infect your computer (and spread to other systems on the Internet). You'll find out how to send sensitive material (such as credit card numbers) safely through Internet connections. You'll learn how to act in newsgroups to prevent sparking unproductive arguments. And, if you have children, you'll learn how to screen out material that may (or at least should) offend them.

What You Will Find in This Section

Understand Internet Security

The Internet is like a big, electronic city, which offers everything from massive electronic libraries and art museums to electronic pornography and online criminals. And, because the Internet is a computer playground, it has the added threat of computer viruses—bugs that can bring your computer to a grinding halt, and wipe out all the programs and data you spent months to accumulate.

In order to protect yourself, your family, and your computer from harm, you should give some thought to securing your system. To ensure that your system is secure, you must take the following three steps:

- Use a secure Web browser (such as Netscape Navigator or Microsoft Internet Explorer), and make sure that if you enter any information (using an online form), that you do it at a secure site. See "Send Information Securely" on page 274 for details.

- If you have children, obtain and use a program that filters out inappropriate information and prevents your kids from accessing specific sites. You can use a free program such as Cyber Patrol. For details, see "Prevent Your Children from Accessing Specific Sites and Content," on page 280.

- Back up your system regularly, and use an antivirus program to check for viruses. Because you will be downloading and running programs from the Internet, you risk infecting your system with a virus. Although viruses are uncommon, they can do a lot of damage if not detected early. See "Avoid Viruses," on page 288, for details.

The following Guided Tour provides a basic overview of what you must do to secure your system. Other Guided Tours in this section provide details on various programs that ensure that your system is secure.

Begin Guided Tour   Secure Your System on the Internet

1 If all you do is wander the Internet with a Web browser, looking at Web pages, you don't have to worry too much about securing your system.

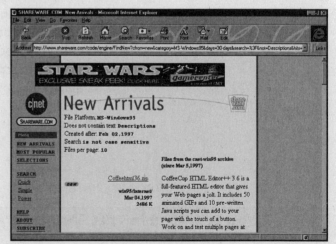

2 If you download and run programs (even small helper applications) from Web and FTP sites, you run the risk of infecting your computer with a virus.

Guided Tour   Secure Your System on the Internet

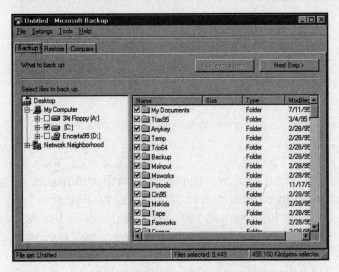

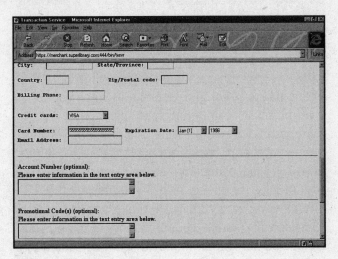

3 To prevent viruses from damaging your system, the best defense is a recent backup of your programs and data. Be sure to back up your system regularly.

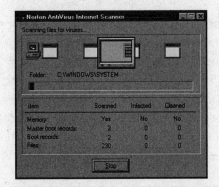

4 Although most antivirus programs cannot prevent a virus from infecting your system, they can detect a virus early and help you get rid of it, so it does as little damage as possible. Run your antivirus program regularly.

5 Whenever you fill out a form on the Internet, you risk having the information you enter fall into the wrong hands. To be extra safe, give sensitive information (credit card numbers, phone numbers, and so on) only to reputable companies.

6 Some forms have special security features that prevent other users from intercepting the data you enter. When entering sensitive data, make sure you are at a secure site. For instance, Internet Explorer displays a lock in the lower-left corner of the Web browser window if the site is secure for transactions.

When you send your kids out on the Internet, you're sending

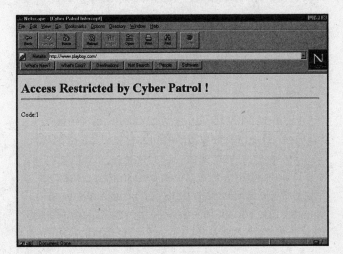

7 them into a big city. Protect them from the criminal element by installing a special filter that screens out pornography and prevents your kids from accessing inappropriate material.

Send Information Securely

Whenever you use a credit card, or give someone your telephone number or address, you run some risk of having that information fall into the wrong hands. You run the same risks when you transmit sensitive information on the Internet. For that reason, you should never give someone your phone number or credit card number on the Internet unless you feel confident that the company taking your order is legitimate. Also, if you transmit the information over a connection that is not protected by some security system, you run the risk of having your credit card number or phone number intercepted by a nefarious computer hacker.

Digital IDs and Certificates

A recent technical innovation is making the Internet a safer place for transactions and the transfer of important information: the Digital ID or certificate. Digital IDs are encrypted files that identify a user or a site. For instance, your personal Digital ID would identify you by name, e-mail address, and a digital signature key that would be read by a site when you send them information, such as a Web form that includes your credit card number.

More importantly to you as a possible consumer on the Web, Digital IDs and certificates can be used to identify secure Web sites. For instance, when you go to a Web page that has been designated as secure, a series of messages pass between your browser and the site. The server, in essence, proves its identity to your Web browser, which checks the validity of the ID

certificate of the site. If the certificate is valid (the Browser checks the site address, the certificate, and the certification authority that issued the certificate) your Browser will let you know that it's a secure site.

Digital IDs are granted by special Certificate Authorities, which is kind of a digital Department of Motor Vehicles providing licenses to users and sites. You can sign up for your own Digital ID at **http://digitalid. verisign.com/** (when you first install Navigator or Internet Explorer, you are given the choice of signing up for a certificate). The Guided Tour shows how to use Netscape Navigator to ensure that you are entering information at a secure Web site.

Server Firewalls

Corporations and Institutions are using other strategies to make the Internet safer for transactions. Many sites are now protected by software programs called firewalls. Firewalls can control access into and out of a site. And while firewalls can potentially increase Internet security, their main purpose is to protect the information on a corporate server from hacker intrusion and vandalism.

> Most credit card fraud associated with the Internet has involved some scofflaw Hacker intercepting, uncovering, or generating a list of valid credit card numbers issued by a particular bank or institution. On secure sites your personal transactions are actually quite safe and fairly unimportant to these computer criminals.

Begin Guided Tour Use Netscape Navigator's Security Options

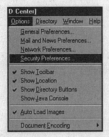

1 Before you enter any sensitive information on the Web, make sure Navigator's security features are turned on. Open the **Options** menu and select **Security Preferences**.

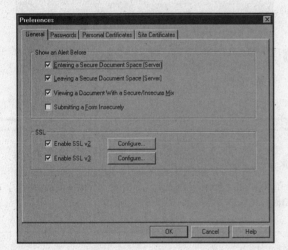

2 Navigator's security options tell you when you are entering and leaving a secure site, and when you are about to enter information (any information) at an insecure site. Make sure all the options have a check mark next to them. Navigator (3.0 and above) also provides special encryption schemes that help secure information that you send over the Web (Internet Explorer also provides advanced encryption methods); make sure that both the SSL encryption radio dials are checked.

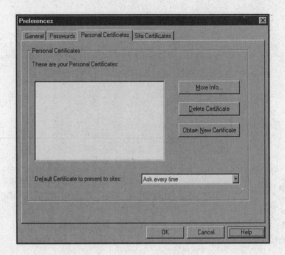

3 If you wish to identify yourself on the Web with a Digital ID, click the **Personal Certificates** tab. Click the **Obtain New Certificate** button.

4 You are taken to a Netscape page that provides a list of Certificate Authority Services that can provide you with your own Digital ID. Click a link and you will be taken to an Authority page.

(continues)

Guided Tour Use Netscape Navigator's Security Options

(continued)

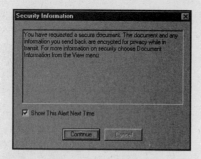

5 Whenever you connect to a Web server that is protected by Netscape's security features, a dialog box appears, telling you that the site is safe. Companies have to register with a certification authority to prove they are "safe" sites. Click **Continue**.

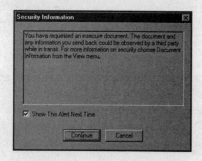

6 If you enter information at a site that is not secure, Navigator displays a dialog box, warning you that the information you've entered might get intercepted. If the information is not of a sensitive nature, don't worry about entering it. Click **Continue**.

7 If you never enter any sensitive information on the Web, you can turn off the security warnings. Open the **Options** menu and select **Security Preferences**.

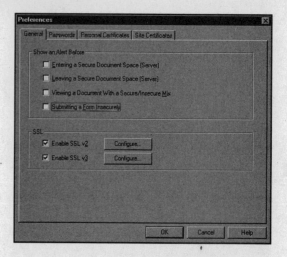

8 The security warnings can become annoying. To turn them off, click each warning option to remove its check mark. Click **OK**.

9 Even with the warnings off, you can tell when you are at a secure site. First, look in the Location or Go To text box. If the URL begins with **https** instead of **http**, the site is secure.

You will receive Navigator's warning messages even if you submit a form to search for a particular topic. You can ignore these warnings, because you are not entering data that anyone else might want.

10 The key icon in the lower left corner of the Navigator window also indicates whether a site is secure. If the key is broken, the site is not secure.

Practice Proper Internet Netiquette

Although the Internet is a massive network of computers, it is also a network of people, and whenever people assemble, you have to start worrying about etiquette—the proper way to behave in social situations. Proper behavior on the Internet is called *netiquette*. In addition to making you look bad, improper behavior (bad netiquette) may result in you losing privileges to some sites, being kicked out of chat channels, or being inundated with angry e-mail messages. This is known as being *flamed* via e-mail and it can be less than fun.

The rules of the Internet are simple. First, be considerate when downloading big files. You may want to set up your computer to download big shareware or freeware items just before you go to bed. That way you're not adding to the slow-down that the Net can face during business hours. Second, don't make people angry. Antagonizing people on the Net can be a real mistake.

Downloading files during the off hours is best for everyone. It benefits the Web or FTP site by reducing traffic during the busiest times. It benefits you, because you're more likely to be able to connect during off-hours, and the file transfer will proceed much more quickly.

If you type in ALL UPPERCASE characters, for example, users think you're shouting at them, and they become suitably annoyed. If you ask questions that have already been answered earlier in a newsgroup, or if you voice an opinion in a newsgroup about which you know little or nothing, people are likely to become upset. Likewise, spouting off in chat rooms is considered bad form.

The following Guided Tour shows you how to behave on the Internet. With this Guided Tour, and a little common sense and empathy, you will be well on your way to becoming the Miss Manners of the Internet. (If you want to be the Attila the Hun of the Internet, you can skip this tour.)

Begin Guided Tour   Behave Yourself on the Internet

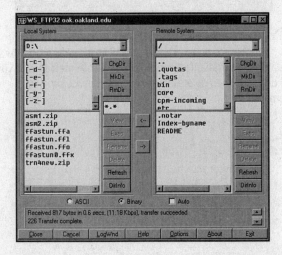

1 When you connect to an FTP site, there is usually a text file (often called README) that contains the rules of the site. Click the link to read this file.

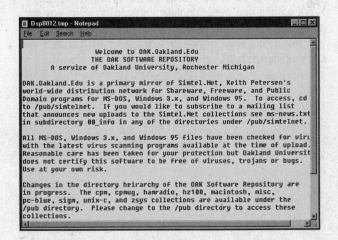

2 The README file usually contains an explanation of where files are stored and instructions on how to access files. README might also tell you the best times to download files.

(continues)

Guided Tour   Behave Yourself on the Internet

(continued)

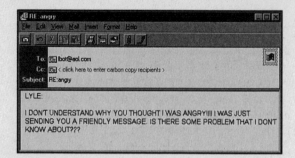

3 When composing e-mail or talking in a chat room, don't shout. Using ALL UPPERCASE characters and overusing exclamation points is the equivalent of shouting, and it is very annoying.

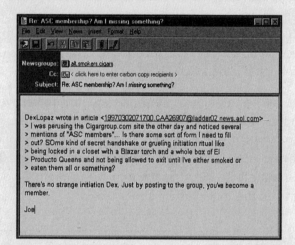

4 When composing e-mail or a response to a newsgroup posting, you should quote any message to which you are responding. If the e-mail program doesn't quote the message for you, type a right angle bracket (>) to the left of each quoted line, and keep quotes brief.

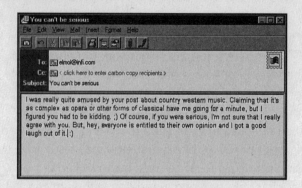

5 Word your e-mail messages tactfully. Humor and sarcasm can easily be misinterpreted in typewritten messages. You can often use *emoticons* to add a smile to a phrase that might be taken wrong, to show you are joking. See page 445 for a list of emoticons.

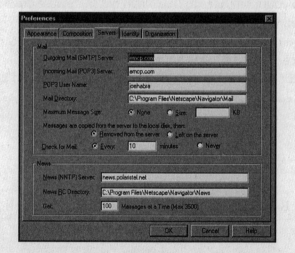

6 Delete any e-mail messages you've received and read from your service provider's computer. Most e-mail programs have an option that automatically copies e-mail messages to your hard disk, and then deletes them from the service provider's system.

Guided Tour　Behave Yourself on the Internet

7 Spend some time in a newsgroup reading messages before you post your own messages or respond. Many newsgroups have a FAQ (frequently asked questions) file that you should read to learn more about the group. The more you know about a newsgroup, the more intelligently you can respond to messages.

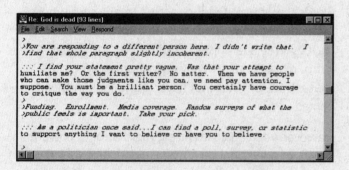

8 Avoid insulting a particular newsgroup member's opinion. This can start a *flame war* (a typically unproductive war of words).

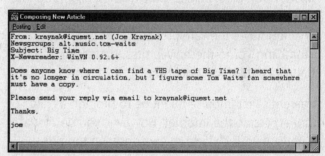

9 Don't use newsgroups as a way to advertise, unless the newsgroup is specifically for listing services or products for sale.

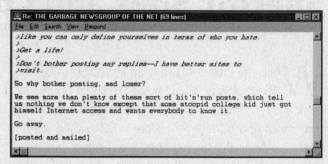

10 If you encounter a newsgroup that annoys you, avoid it. Don't enter a newsgroup simply to insult its members.

11 If you ask a specific question in a newsgroup, request that answers be sent to you via e-mail. That way, the newsgroup won't become cluttered with 20 of the same answers to the same question. You can post the best answer later, for those who might be curious.

In addition to these proper manners, keep in mind that you must follow state and federal laws as well. You cannot use the Internet to harass people, sell or trade child pornography, steal, or destroy a person's work or reputation.

Prevent Your Children from Accessing Specific Sites and Content

While the Internet is truly an incredible information highway, it also has its share of seedy back alleys—meaning that there is content on the Net that is not appropriate for children. Many Web sites, chat channels, and newsgroups are G-rated, but others exist that are strictly for adults. And while we all want to protect First Amendment rights and free speech, you are probably concerned about your children stumbling across some of these inappropriate content areas. And since kids are incredibly clever, and very inquisitive, they are probably a lot better at "stumbling" onto these Web sites, newsgroups, and chat areas, than we would like.

A parent's first impulse might be to prohibit a child from accessing the Internet. However, you don't want to prevent your child from encountering the fun, educational Internet sites. Instead, a parent must find an Internet escort: a program that can prevent a child from accessing the adult areas of the Internet.

One such program is Cyber Patrol. This shareware program is made available by the creators of Cyber Sentry, a program designed to prevent workers from accessing certain Internet sites during work hours. The following Guided Tour shows how to download, install, and use Cyber Patrol to limit a child's Internet access.

Parents can try the complete software package for a seven-day trial period. If you like Cyber Patrol, they ask that you register and pay $29.95 for the product.

Take Control of Cyber Patrol

Cyber Patrol comes with a built-in set of safeguards. It has a list of Web sites that are off limits and a list of words that it uses to block access to any sites whose name or URL suggests indecency. For example, the Playboy Web site is listed as off limits, and Cyber Patrol blocks access to any newsgroups, Web sites, chat rooms, or URLs that have "bondage" in their names.

However, you can customize Cyber Patrol to prevent access to additional sites. The Guided Tour shows you how to modify the list of words that Cyber Patrol uses to block access, and update the list of Web sites that are blocked.

Begin Guided Tour   Download and Install Cyber Patrol

1 The easiest way to download files is to use your Web browser. Enter the following URL to go to the Cyber Patrol Web page:

http://www.cyberpatrol.com

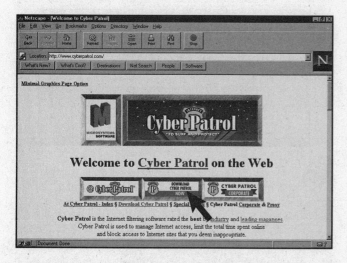

2 Cyber Patrol is a shareware program; you can try it and then buy it if you like it. To download it, click the **Download Cyber Patrol Now** icon.

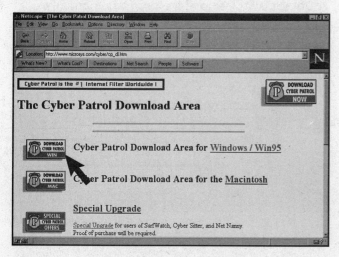

3 Cyber Patrol is available for Windows and Macintosh. Click the **Download Cyber Patrol Win** icon to go to the Windows download page.

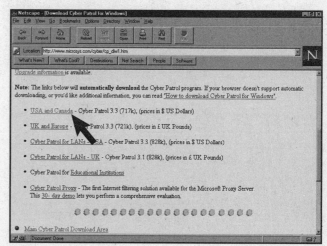

4 The next page provides you with information on how to purchase Cyber Patrol. It also provides links so that you can download the software and try it for free. Click the **USA and Canada** link to download the software.

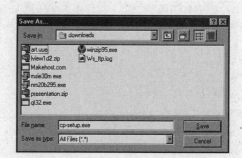

5 Pick an appropriate folder on your hard drive for the downloading of the Cyber Patrol installation file and then click **Save**.

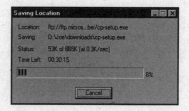

6 The Saving Location dialog box will keep you apprised of the progress of the download.

(continues)

Guided Tour Download and Install Cyber Patrol *(continued)*

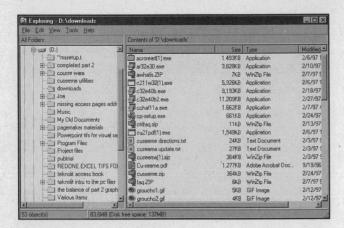

7 The file you downloaded is self-extracting and automatically runs the installation program. Close your Web browser and disconnect from your provider. Next, run My Computer or the Windows Explorer; change to the folder where you saved the file; and then double-click the **cp-setup**.**exe** file to run it.

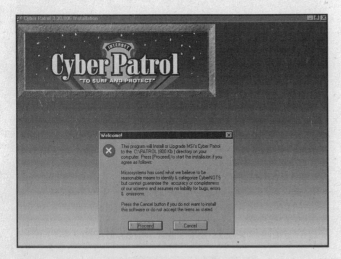

8 The Cyber Patrol installation program leads you through the setup process. Follow the on-screen instructions to install Cyber Patrol. Click the **Proceed** button to continue.

9 When Cyber Patrol is finished installing itself, you're ready to configure the software. The software is already running and will open whenever you start Windows 95. Click the **Cyber Patrol** button on the Windows Taskbar.

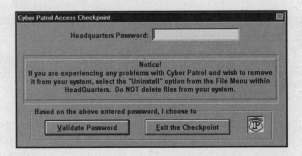

10 The Cyber Patrol Access Checkpoint will open. This is where you choose your Cyber Patrol password and configure the access constraints on certain types of Internet content.

> If you decide to remove Cyber Patrol from your system, switch to Cyber Patrol (by clicking it in the taskbar or by using **Alt+Tab**). Then, open the **File** menu and select **Uninstall Cyber Patrol**. Do not try to remove the program manually.

Begin Guided Tour   Control Internet Access with Cyber Patrol

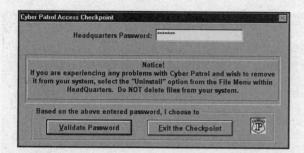

1 Type a password into the Headquarters Password box and then click **Validate Password**. Make sure that you choose a password that you will remember and one that your kids won't guess.

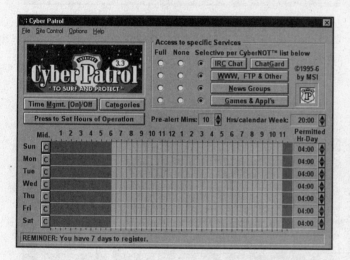

2 Cyber Patrol Checkpoint lets you change the Internet access limitations. To prevent someone from using the Internet during certain hours, click the **Press to Set Hours of Operation** button.

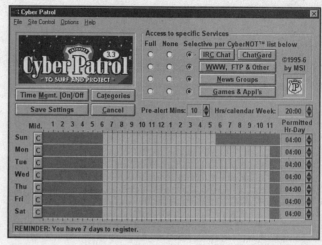

3 Red blocks mark hours during which Internet access will be blocked. Green blocks show hours where Internet access is permitted. Click a red block to turn it green, or click a green block to turn it red. You can drag over blocks to select them.

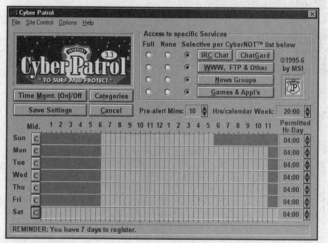

4 To allow Internet access for all hours, click the **C** button for a given day. (C stands for Clear.)

(continues)

Guided Tour Control Internet Access with Cyber Patrol (continued)

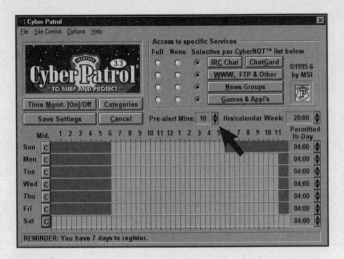

5 Click the arrows next to **Pre-alert Mins** to specify the length of time a user will be warned that he is nearing a prohibited time period.

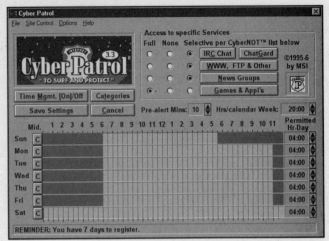

7 The **Access to Specific Services** area lets you prevent access to specific Internet features. The **Full** option gives complete access to a feature. **None** completely locks out the feature. **Selective** blocks access to areas that are known to offer inappropriate material.

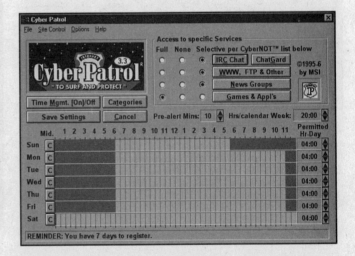

6 You can specify the number of hours per day or per week that users can access the Internet. Use the scroll boxes next to **Hrs/calendar Week** and **Permitted Hr-Day** to set the allowable times.

8 Cyber Patrol has a list of prohibited Internet services. To prevent access to additional services, or to allow access to features on Cyber Patrol's list, click a button in the **Access to Specific Services** area.

Guided Tour   Control Internet Access with Cyber Patrol

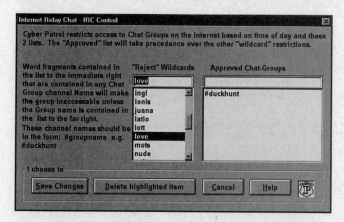

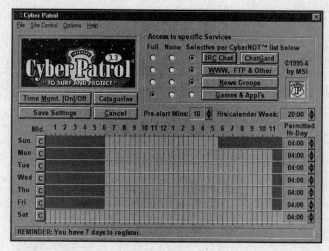

9 If you click the **IRC Chat** button, a list of keywords appears. Cyber Patrol will prevent access to newsgroups that have these words anywhere in their names. To add a word, type it in the **"Reject" Wildcards** text box, and press **Enter**.

10 To remove a word from the "Reject" Wildcards list, click the word, and then click **Delete Highlighted Item**.

12 The **WWW, FTP & Other** button allows you to limit access to certain sites based on their URLs. Cyber Patrol already prevents access to a list of known adult sites, but if you want to lock out additional sites, click this button.

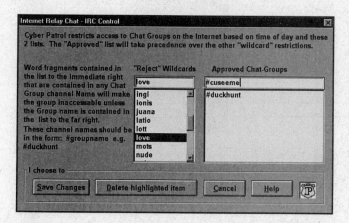

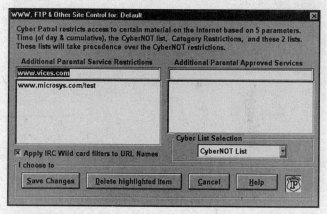

11 To approve a specific chat room that Cyber Patrol may not allow access to, type its name in **Approved Chat-Groups** list, and press **Enter**. When you are done, click **Save Changes**.

13 To prevent access to a specific site, type its URL in the **Additional Parental Service Restrictions** text box, and press **Enter**.

If the entire URL won't fit inside the text box, you can chop the end off the URL.

(continues)

Guided Tour   Control Internet Access with Cyber Patrol   *(continued)*

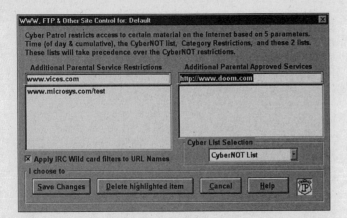

14 To override Cyber Patrol's no-no list and allow access to a site that's on the list, type the site's URL in the **Additional Parental Approved Services** text box, and press **Enter**.

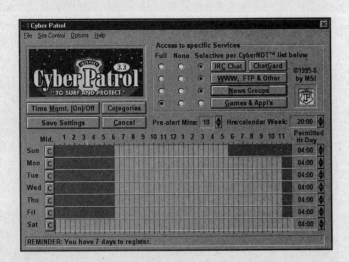

15 Now that you have the hang of this, try using the other two buttons to control access to newsgroups and to applications on your computer.

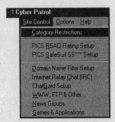

16 To prevent or allow access to certain off-beat topics, open the **Site Control** menu, and select **Category Restrictions**.

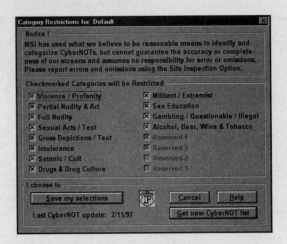

17 The dialog box that appears allows you to block areas that you feel are inappropriate. Initially, all the topics are blocked (checked). To remove the X and allow access to a topic, click its name. Click **Save My Selections** when you're done.

18 The makers of Cyber Patrol are constantly updating their no-no list as more sites appear on the Internet. To update the list, open the **File** menu and select **Update CyberNOT List**.

19 To bypass Cyber Patrol and open access to all Internet services, open the **File** menu and select **Deputy ByPass**.

Guided Tour   Control Internet Access with Cyber Patrol

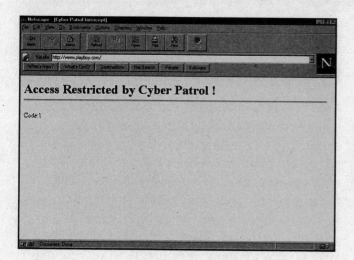

20 When Cyber Patrol is active it will stop access to the sites and content that you specified in the program's configuration.

The shareware version of Cyber Patrol gives you seven days to check out the features of this great piece of software. If you decide to use it as your Internet watchdog, make sure that you pay for and register the software.

Avoid Viruses

The only way to completely protect yourself against viruses on the Internet is to disconnect your modem and stop using the Internet. As long as you are connected to other people's computers, and are downloading and using software from FTP sites, there is some risk that a virus in one of those programs will infect your computer.

However, you can minimize the risk by downloading files only from reputable sites. Most companies are careful to regularly check for viruses on their sites, and in the programs they offer for downloading. If users catch a virus from one of the company's programs, the company can lose business and develop a bad reputation. As long as you download files from well-known companies or from online services, you are relatively safe.

Try to avoid programs from individuals on the Internet. If someone offers to send you a file, ask the person where they received the file, and then download the original file from that FTP site. If you don't know the individual, he might be intentionally trying to infect your system. Even if you *do* know the individual, the person's computer might be infected with a virus, and the program might carry the virus to your computer. Work with only original files.

In addition, avoid getting and running programs from newsgroups. Although some newsgroups are monitored, others allow anyone to post files, and these files might contain viruses.

The following Guided Tour shows you how to download a virus-checking program, called Norton Anti-Virus Scanner, and use it to check your system for known viruses.

> Most viruses are transmitted through program files. Before running a program on your computer, you should check it for viruses, as explained in the Guided Tour.

How Antivirus Programs Work

AntiVirus programs protect your system by waging a three-pronged attack against viruses. First, the antivirus program scans all the files on your computer for *signatures* of known viruses. A signature is a piece of computer code that is unique to a virus. Second, the antivirus program scans for the effects of viruses, such as modified system files, unauthorized file deletions, and so on. Finally, antivirus programs help identify viruses in programs you haven't yet run, thus preventing your system from becoming infected.

To prevent your system from becoming infected, and to reduce the amount of damage in the event that your computer becomes infected, you should perform the following tasks:

- Scan all the files on your computer every week or so for known viruses. By detecting and eliminating a virus early, you prevent it from causing more damage.

- Before running any programs you download from the Internet, scan the program files for known viruses. This prevents your computer from becoming infected in the first place.

- Update your virus list regularly. Every antivirus program has a list of known viruses. If a new virus is developed, it won't be on the list. By updating your list, you enable the antivirus program to check for the latest viruses.

- Before you place any files on the Internet or send them to an individual, check the files for viruses. This prevents spreading the virus to other computers.

Back Up Your System

Viruses typically infect program files and destroy both program and data files. They don't destroy the hardware that makes up your computer. The best way to protect your program and data files is to back them up regularly. I further recommend that you back up your data files (the files you create) separately from your program files.

This book does not cover the steps required for backing up your files. You can use Microsoft Backup (which comes with Windows 95 and DOS versions 5.0 or later) to perform the backups. Or you can purchase and use a specialized backup program. Refer to your Windows documentation for details.

Following are a few tips for using backups to protect your system against viruses:

- Write-protect your program disks before installing a program, so your original program disks will not become infected. If the program becomes infected on your hard disk, you can then delete it and reinstall it from the floppy disks. (Don't worry about CDs.)

- Back up program files and data files (the files you create) separately. Because data files rarely become infected, if your system does catch a virus, you can delete all the programs, reinstall them, and then restore the data files from your backups.

- Some backup programs can check for viruses during the backup operation. If your backup program has this option, turn it on.

- If your system becomes infected, reinstall clean copies of your programs from the original disks, not from the backups. The backed up files might be infected. Restoring the files could reinfect your system.

> Create a separate folder (or directory) for the files you create and save called DATA. You can create subfolders under the DATA folder. You can back up all the files in this folder separately from your program files.

Begin Guided Tour   Download and Install Norton AntiVirus Scanner

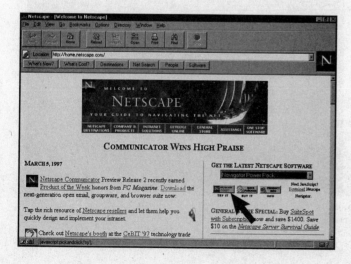

1 The Netscape Navigator Power Pack, which can be downloaded from the Netscape home page, includes a great Windows 95-based antivirus program called Norton AntiVirus Scanner. Use the **Get the Latest Netscape Software** drop-down menu to select Navigator Power Pack and then click the **Try It** icon.

(continues)

Guided Tour Download and Install Norton AntiVirus Scanner

(continued)

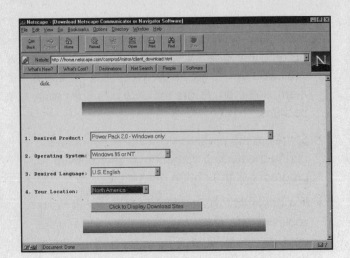

2 You will be taken to the download page where you specify product, operating system, and language. After filling in the form, click the **Click to Display Download Sites** button.

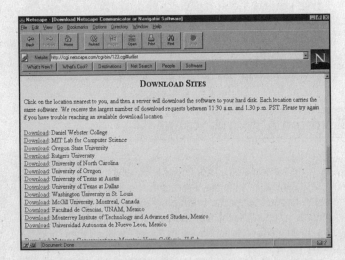

3 Choose a download site and then click the link. Download the software to an appropriate directory.

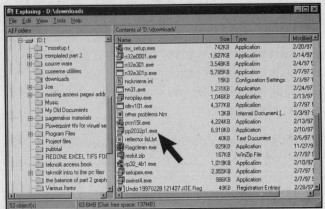

4 Use the Windows Explorer to open the appropriate folder on your computer and double click the **pp2032p1.exe** installation file.

5 The installation process will begin; click **Yes** to continue.

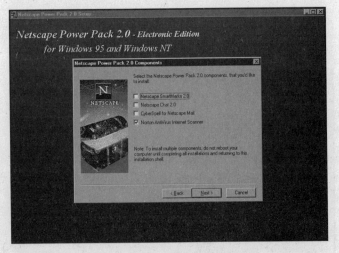

6 Follow the screen prompts to complete the installation of Norton AntiVirus Scanner. Make sure that you select Norton AntiVirus at the component installation screen.

Guided Tour Download and Install Norton AntiVirus Scanner

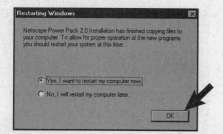

7 You must restart your computer at the completion of the installation. Click **OK**.

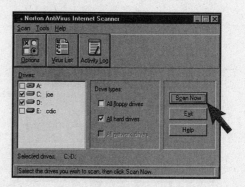

9 The AntiVirus Scanner allows you to specify the drives that you want to scan. Select the drives and then click **Scan Now**.

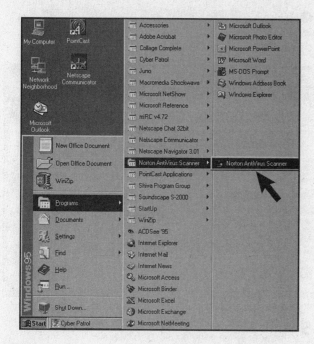

8 To scan your computer for viruses start **Norton AntiVirus Scanner** via the Windows **Start** button.

Begin Guided Tour Scan Your Computer for Viruses

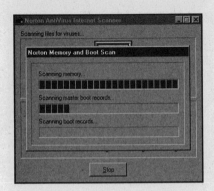

1 First the program checks the computer's memory and the boot sectors of the disks for any hiding viruses.

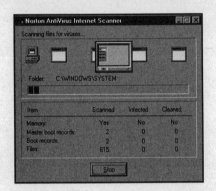

2 The software then checks each file on the specified drive or drives for virus infection.

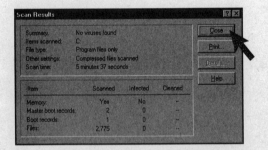

3 Once the virus scan is complete, you are given a summary of the files checked. If the program file finds an infected file it will ask you if you would like the file cleaned. Click **Close** to close the scan summary box.

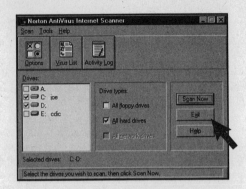

4 You can exit the AntiVirus Scanner software or scan another drive or a disk. Click **Exit** to close the program.

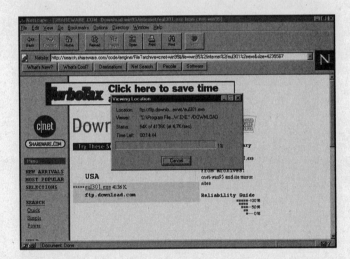

5 Norton AntiVirus Scanner also works with your Web browser when you download software.

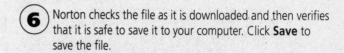

Guided Tour   Scan Your Computer for Viruses

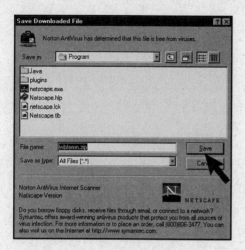

6 Norton checks the file as it is downloaded and then verifies that it is safe to save it to your computer. Click **Save** to save the file.

If a virus is detected, follow the on-screen directions to remove it from your system.

PART 2

Do it Yourself

n Part 1 of this book, you learned how to establish an Internet connection and use a Web browser, an FTP program, and Gopher. In addition, you learned how to send and receive e-mail, read newsgroup messages, chat and video conference. By now, you should be feeling fairly comfortable with those various Internet programs.

But just knowing how to use these programs won't make you feel at home on the Internet. As a matter of fact, you're probably thinking, "OK, so I can get on the Internet. But what do I do once I'm there?" In this part, you'll explore the possibilities of what you can do by working through some simple step-by-step projects. Of course, these projects don't represent all that you can do on the Internet, but they will show you how to accomplish some of the more common tasks. And they might just inspire you to explore some of the other things you can do on the Internet.

What You Will Find in This Part

Take an Internet Scavenger Hunt

Now that you know your way around the Internet, you've probably developed some techniques for sniffing out the information you want. Maybe you have a favorite search tool (such as Yahoo!), or maybe you've developed a knack for just guessing a site's URL. However you decide to cruise the Internet, you'll continue to find topics that pose new research challenges.

This project is designed to intentionally challenge your ability to cruise the Internet and find specific items. This project includes a list of topics, Web pages, files, and other Internet goodies for you to find. Use your favorite Internet search tool or technique to find the item, and then chalk up a point for each item you find. Don't stop until you've found all 20 items! Use the following form to keep score.

In searching for these items, try to go beyond the World Wide Web. You can look for answers in newsgroups or chat rooms (where you can ask other people for the answers), you can use Archie to find files, and you can even send a Gopher to root out a server.

Score	Item Found	Score	Item Found
	Fisherman's Wharf "live" cam		The Jerry Garcia Memorial page
	Interactive model railroad		The Hercules home page
	Seinfeld Page		NetSurfer Digest
	Chocolate chip cookie recipe		Newbie chat room
	Painting of Mona Lisa		Hate Barney newsgroup
	Today's *Dilbert* cartoon		Michael's Baby
	The Shakespeare Web		Monty Python Page
	Encyclopedia Britannica's *Britannica Online*		Cool Site of the Day
	The Caffeine archive		Online Scavenger Hunt
	China's home page		

Begin Do It Yourself   Find Lost Treasures

1 Some Web sites use Web cams to broadcast "live" pictures of such scenes as the Space Needle in Seattle and San Francisco Bay. Find the picture of Fisherman's Wharf.

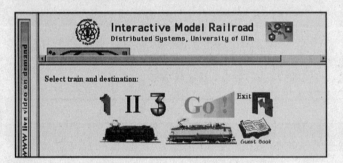

2 In addition to "live" video, some sites have *telerobots*, devices that you can control from your computer. Find the model railroad at the University of Ulm.

3 See if you can find the ShockWave multimedia fairy tales—The Nightingale, Jack and the Beanstalk, and The Three Little Pigs—on the Web.

4 See what Jerry and the rest of the cast of Seinfeld are up to.

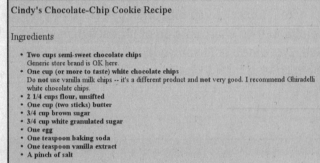

5 Find a recipe for chocolate chip cookies.

6 Where's Mona Lisa? She's on the Internet somewhere. Track her down, and chalk up another point (hint: she is also known as the *La Gioconda* and was painted by a guy named Da Vinci).

Do It Yourself   Find Lost Treasures

7 If you've never seen *Dilbert*, you're in for a treat. This cartoon character has been keeping Internet surfers in stitches for years. Take a break from your wanderings to have a laugh.

8 Shakespeare is making a comeback, this time in Hollywood. Find the Shakespeare Web and learn more about this famous playwright.

9 If you don't want to clutter your house with a set of encyclopedias, consider using an encyclopedia on the Internet. Find *Britannica Online* from the editors of *Encyclopedia Britannica*.

10 If this scavenger hunt is making you sleepy, maybe you need a lift. Visit the Caffeine archive…if you can find it.

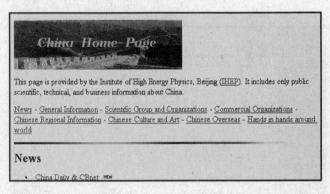

11 Anyone can find the White House, but can you find China's home page?

12 Are you a Dead Head? Pay tribute to Jerry Garcia at the Jerry Garcia Memorial page.

(continues)

Do It Yourself   Find Lost Treasures

(continued)

13 One of the hottest syndicated shows on television is *Hercules: The Legendary Journeys*. Can you find this show's official home page?

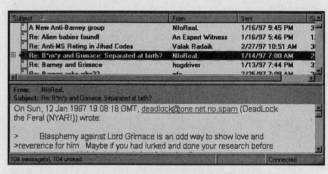

16 Use your newsgroup reader to find out why so many people dislike Barney the purple dinosaur (there is more than one newsgroup devoted to the topic, believe it or not).

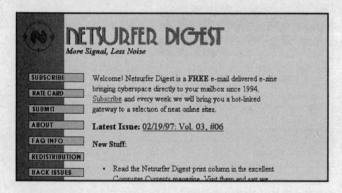

14 Keep up-to-date with the latest developments on the Internet with *NetSurfer Digest*. Find the site and subscribe to this e-mail delivered e-zine.

17 Find the right site and then use ShockWave to help Michael Jackson build a baby.

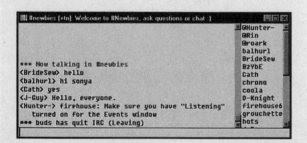

15 If you have questions about the Internet, people on the Internet are usually happy to help. Using your IRC client, visit a chat room for new users (called *newbies*).

18 Now for a surprise—find the Cool Site of the Day.

Do It Yourself   Find Lost Treasures

19 For those of you who want to see something completely different, find the Monty Python home page.

And Now...The Moment
You've All Been Waiting For...

The Typehouse Group is proud to announce
the WINNERS to the Scavenger Hunt.

GRAND PRIZE

(Trip to Disney)
Fred Link of Northborough, MA

20 If you enjoy the challenge of a good scavenger hunt, find an online version of a scavenger hunt. There are always several going on at any one time on the World Wide Web. If you're good at this, you can even win money and prizes.

Find Free Stuff on the Net

You've probably already snatched a few free programs off the Internet—maybe a couple of helper applications, a Web browser, a chat client, and some other choice tidbits. The Internet is packed with software, files, games, and other loot that's free for the taking. The only catch is that you have to know where to look.

This project takes you on a tour of the Internet in search of freebies. You'll learn where to go to get everything from computer games to shampoo samples, from online coupons to financial calculators. You'll even learn how to use some of the Internet's search tools to help you find more free stuff!

> When looking for deals and freebies, be careful. If a deal seems too good, it probably is. Avoid giving out your credit card number or any other information that someone could use to rip you off.

This project shows you a few places where you can get freebies, but don't stop there. Use other Internet search tools to search for specific items (such as vacations, cars, or shareware) that you might be able to use for free or to find out about drawings and contests you can enter and win (if you're into that sort of thing). Try searching with Lycos, Yahoo!, Web Crawler, and the other tools described in "Search for Information on the Internet" (page 169).

Begin Do It Yourself   Find Free Stuff

1 For free educational software, check out the EduMall at **http://edumall.com/center.html**.

2 Thanks to Julie Pederson for her *Next to Nothing!* online magazine of freebies (or nearly freebies). Visit this site at **http://www.winternet.com/~julie/ntn.html**.

Do It Yourself   Find Free Stuff

3 For another great clearing house for freebies and links to other freebie sites try **http://www.ft-wayne.com/ freestuff.html**.

4 If you're into sewing or crafts, visit Prime Publishing for a list of companies that give away crafty stuff. Here's the URL you'll need:

http://www.craftnet.org/prime/freestuff.html

5 Quarterdeck Software offers several demo programs of its software products, including WebCompass (a great program for searching the Web), GlobalChat (a chat client), and Hijaak Morph (a program that allows you to morph one graphic file into another). Download the demos from **http:// www.qdeck.com/qdeck/demosoft/**.

6 For a list of virtual free stuff (software, games and things on CD-ROM) grouped by category, visit Virtual Free Stuff at **http://www.dreamscape.com/frankvad/ free.software.cd.html**.

(continues)

Do It Yourself   Find Free Stuff   *(continued)*

7 For some free (and useful) financial programs, such as a mortgage calculator, visit the Debt Counselors home page at **http://www.dca.org/home.htm**.

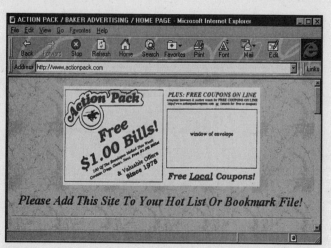

9 If you're a coupon hound, you can find coupons online at **http://www.actionpack.com/**. You can even place your name on a mailing list to receive coupons in the mail.

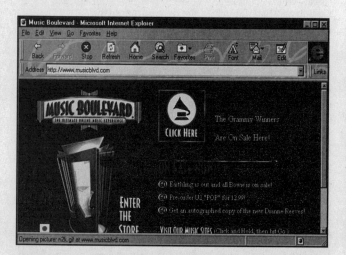

8 Are you into music? Visit Music Boulevard, where you can download audio clips of your favorite groups. To go there, use the URL **http://www.musicblvd.com**.

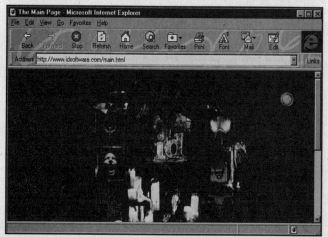

10 Do you want to try out some of the hottest computer games? Connect to ID Software's home page at **http://www.idsoftware.com/main.html**. They have demos for all their popular games.

Do It Yourself Find Free Stuff

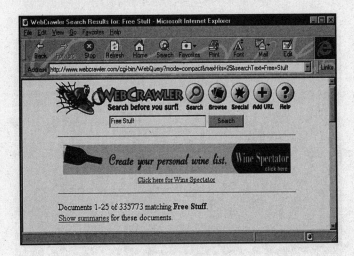

11 To look for more freebies, use a Web search tool such as Yahoo!, WebCrawler, or Lycos. Search for terms such as "free stuff," "freebies," "free offers," "contests," "demos," and "shareware."

Play Games on the Internet

Although many people like to pretend that they use the Internet mainly for business and educational purposes, if you were to sneak up on them, you very well might find them downloading GIFs, chatting, or playing one of the thousands of interactive games the Internet offers.

The biggest reasons many people *don't* play games is that they don't know where to find them or that they don't feel comfortable with the rules. In this project, you'll visit several Web sites and a couple of chat rooms where you can try your hand at some games. Play a little, until you don't feel so awkward.

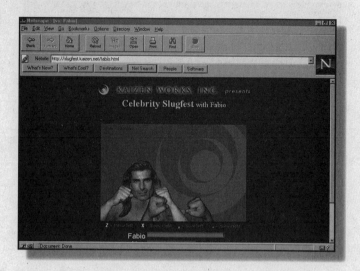

Java Games

In the section titled "Find and Play Java Applets" you learned about Java applets: small applications that you can play on the Internet. In the section titled "Find and Install Browser Plug-Ins and ActiveX Controls" you took a look at the interactive potential of ShockWave content on the Web. Many interactive games such as Tetris, Mine Sweeper, and even a Boris Yeltsen version of Operation are on the Web and have been created either as Java applets or ShockWave interactive multimedia.

This project shows you where to find the more popular Java and ShockWave games. To find more Java or ShockWave games, use a search tool such as Yahoo (**http://www.yahoo.com**) or WebCrawler (**http://www.webcrawler.com**) and search for "ShockWave game" or "Java game."

Trivia Games and Tests

Trivia games and quizzes have always been a staple of the gaming world. Whether answering questions to win prizes or just to have fun, people get hooked on testing their knowledge and their ability to remember important or unimportant information.

You can find several quiz and test sites on the Internet. You can play name-that-flag, fill out a purity questionnaire, answer questions about bats, or even determine whether you qualify as a bona fide nerd! This project shows you a few of the more unique quiz sites.

Interactive Role-Playing Games

One of the oldest and most popular types of game on the Internet is MUD. A MUD (short for Multi User Dimension) is an interactive role-playing game that involves many users from all over the world (MUD participants cringe when you call MUD a game). Originally based on *Dungeons and Dragons*, MUDs have branched out into hundreds of other role-playing games on the Internet.

You play MUDs in different ways. Some exist as a specific channel on an IRC server and are called *talkers*. Other MUDs can be accessed via the Web using your browser or by special MUD software. Some MUDs require you to *telnet* to a MUD site. That means you connect to another computer where the MUD is played, and then—by typing commands on your keyboard—you enter the commands to play the game. The easiest way to telnet is to set up your Web browser to run your Telnet program whenever you click a Telnet link.

Windows 95 has a Telnet program, cleverly called TELNET.EXE, which is stored in the Windows folder. If you're using Netscape Navigator, you can set it up to run TELNET.EXE. To do so, open the **Options** menu, select **General Preferences**, and click the **Apps** tab. Click the **Browse** button next to the Telnet Application text box and, in the dialog box that appears, select **TELNET.EXE** from the Windows folder.

Once TELNET.EXE is set up to run from Navigator, all you have to do is click a link for a MUD, and you can log in and start playing. This project shows you how to find a list of MUDs and what to expect when you enter the world of MUDs.

> A MOO (Mult-user dimension Object Oriented) is another type of Interactive Internet role-playing game that is based on MUDs. The "object oriented" part refers to the fact that MOOs use more advanced programming tools. You'll also encounter other types of games called MUSes, MUSHes, and LPMUDs.

Chat Room Games

Although most people in chat rooms are usually playing some sort of social game, special chat rooms allow you to play games. Sometimes you play these games in a normal chat room that is specifically designed for games or contests (such as punning or trivia). Other chat games use unique chat rooms in which an automated host greets you, judges your answers, keeps score, and even insults you and the other contestants. These automated hosts are known as *bots* and are programmed to recognize certain words, answers, and questions. (For example, the *Jeopardy* bot acts sort of like Alex Trebeck, greeting the contestants and listening to the contestants' responses.) This project shows you where to find some of the more interesting chat room games.

As Internet technology has advanced, the number of online games has increased. The Web is currently the home of a very wide variety of online games, quizzes, and contests. Online entertainment networks have also become commonplace on the Web. These sites offer all sorts of interactive gaming and entertainment opportunities.

Begin Do It Yourself   Play Internet Games

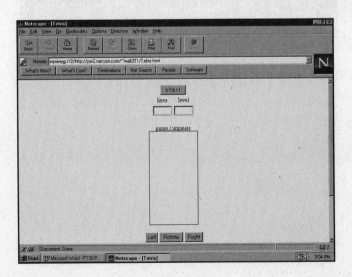

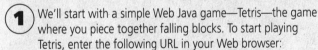

1 We'll start with a simple Web Java game—Tetris—the game where you piece together falling blocks. To start playing Tetris, enter the following URL in your Web browser:

wysiwyg://2/http://pw2.netcom.com/~walt311/Tetris.html

> Some Java applets can be run in any Java-compatible browser, such as Netscape Navigator or Internet Explorer. Other Java applets require a specific browser: They may run fine in Internet Explorer but not run at all in Netscape. Or you may need to use the special Java browser, HotJava, to load a particular applet. If you connect to a page that contains a Java applet you cannot run, you simply won't see the applet.

(continues)

Do It Yourself   Play Internet Games

(continued)

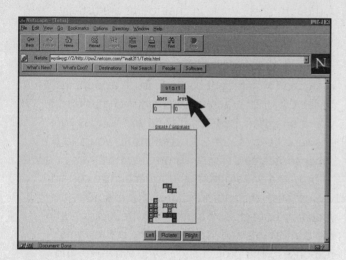

2 To play Tetris, you rotate the blocks and move them so that they interlock and form solid rows. Instructions at the bottom of the Tetris page explain the keyboard controls. Press the **start** button to begin.

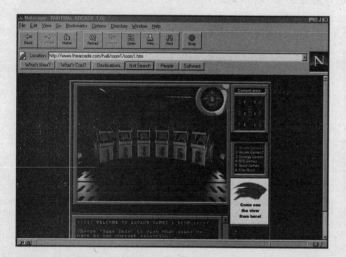

3 If you prefer arcade-style games, try the Virtual Arcade at **http://www.thearcade.com/hall/room1/room1.htm /**. Different types of games are available in the various rooms of the virtual arcade. To choose a particular game, click one of the numbered machines, such as number 2.

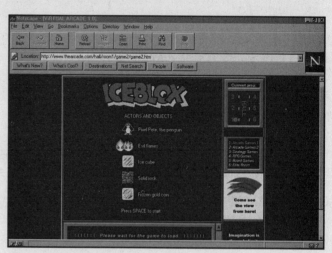

4 In this game, IceBlox, you are a penguin negotiating a hostile world.

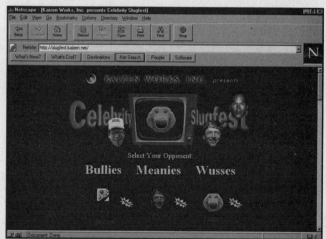

5 Great ShockWave games also exist on the Web. In Celebrity Slugfest at **http://slugfest.kaizen.net/** you get to take your aggression out on your favorite (or not-so-favorite) celebrity. Click an opponent and you're ready to slug it out.

Do It Yourself Play Internet Games

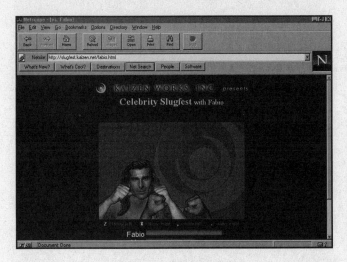

6 It may take a moment for this ShockWave game to load. Click the **Start Match** button and then use the Z and X keys to throw left and right punches.

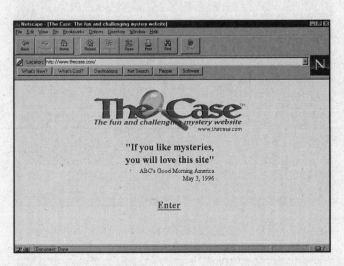

7 If you like to solve mysteries check out The Case at **http://www.thecase.com/**.

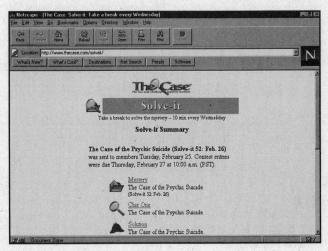

8 Once you enter The Case site you are greeeted by several icons that offer different mystery versions.

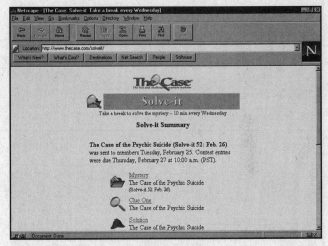

9 The Case site greets you each week with several different activities. You can read a new mini-mystery each Monday, or you can try to solve a new mystery each Wednesday.

(continues)

Do It Yourself   Play Internet Games

(continued)

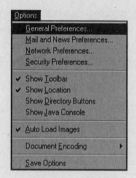

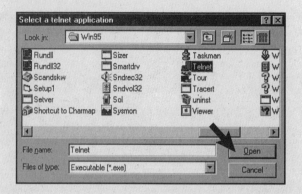

10 To play an interactive game such as a MUD or a MOO, set up your Web browser to use a Telnet program. If you are using Netscape Navigator, open the **Options** menu and select **General Preferences**.

12 In the dialog box that appears, select the **TELNET.EXE** file from the folder where you installed Windows 95. Click the **Open** button, and then click **OK** in the General Preferences dialog box.

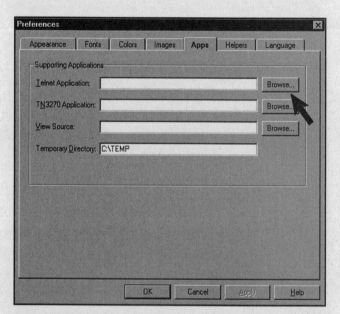

11 In the Preferences dialog box, click the **Apps** tab. Then click the **Browse** button next to the Telnet Application text box.

13 One of the best places to start learning about and playing MUDs is the Mud Connector at **http://www.mudconnect.com/**. Here you'll find a list of more than 300 MUDs, complete with a description of each.

Do It Yourself   Play Internet Games

14 At the Mud Connector, click **The Mud Connector Big List** link to view an extensive list of MUDs.

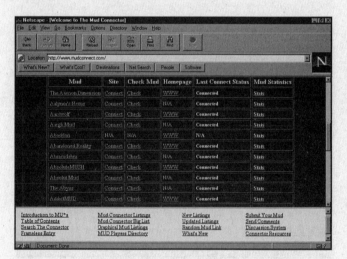

15 Mud Connector displays a table that shows each MUD's name, its Telnet site, and its Web page (if it has one). If the MUD has a Web page, click the link for the Web page.

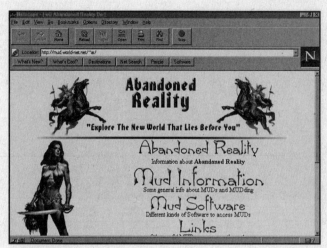

16 MUD players usually take the game very seriously. Because each MUD is different, you should learn as much as possible about the game before playing it. If the MUD has a Web page, that's a good place to learn.

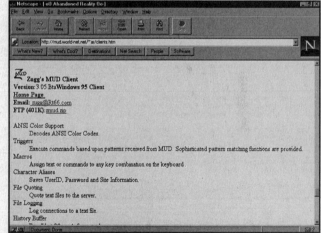

17 There is special MUD client software that you can use instead of Telnet to connect to a MUD world. An excellent download page exists at **http://mud.world-net.net/~ar/ clients.htm**.

(continues)

Do It Yourself   Play Internet Games

(continued)

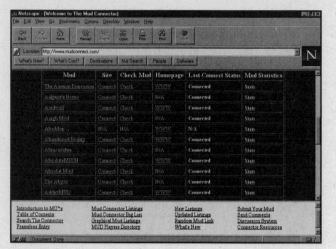

18 When you are ready to play the MUD, return to the MUD Connector and click the link for the MUD's Telnet site.

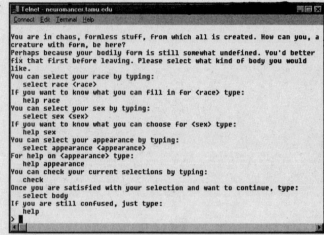

20 Each MUD has its own list of commands. To learn how to enter the required commands, you can usually type **help** and press **Enter**.

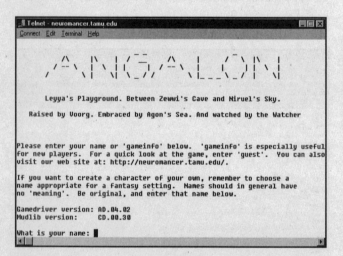

19 The Telnet program connects you to the MUD's Telnet site, which requests that you enter your name and password. If this is your first time to play the game, you can usually log in by entering **guest** as your username and **guest** as your password.

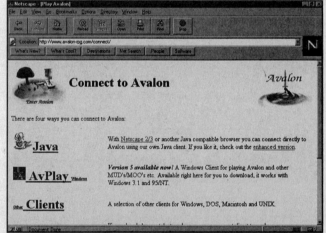

21 Some MUDs allow you to connect to them via the Web Page. The Avalon MUD has a Java interface.

Do It Yourself Play Internet Games

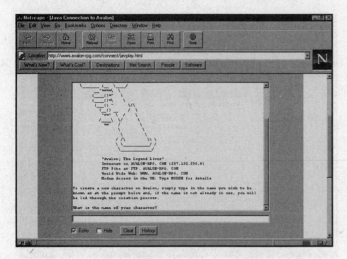

22 Select the Java interface on the Web page and you are connected to the MUD.

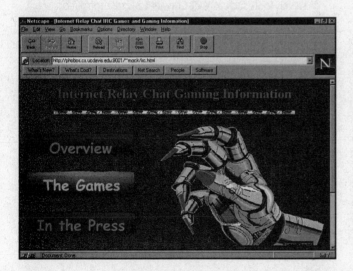

23 Chat games can also be a lot of fun. Check out the **http://phobos.cs.ucdavis.edu:8001/~mock/irc.html** page for information on all kinds of IRC games.

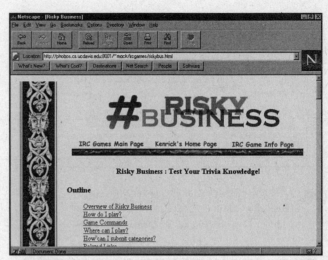

24 Information on specific IRC games is provided on the Web site. A long-running and interesting Chat game is *Risky Business*.

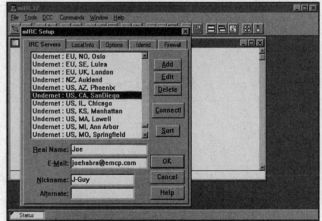

25 To enter an IRC game, run your IRC program (mIRC, for example) and connect to the specified IRC server. To play *Risky Business* (which is sort of like *Jeopardy*), try one of the following IRC servers: **irc.ucdavis.edu**, **irc.gate.net**, or **us.undernet.org**.

(continues)

Do It Yourself   Play Internet Games

(continued)

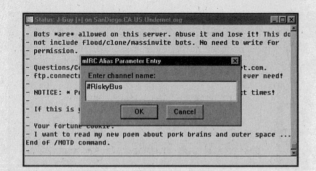

 26 After you connect to an IRC server, you must enter the **#RiskyBus** channel. (See "Converse in Channels" on page 253 for information on how to join a channel.)

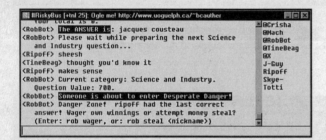

27 Here, RobBot or Mach asks the questions. When responding, type **rob** or **Mach** before your response.

28 There are many other games on the Internet. To discover additional games on your own, use any of the Internet search tools such as WebCrawler to find information.

Find a Job on the Internet

In this age of downsizing and layoffs, it's important that you are aware of the changing job market and know where to look to find a job in your field. And here in the '90s, the Sunday want ads just won't land you the best job. More and more companies are turning to the Internet to find qualified individuals—workers who know how to use a computer and make the latest technologies work for them.

The Internet is the best tool you have for finding a job in today's market. With your Web browser and some creative thinking, you can read the want ads before they reach your local paper. You can e-mail a prospective employer almost immediately and make a direct connection instead of sending your résumé, which is likely to be added to a mountain of other résumés in the human resources department. In addition, you can show off your technological savvy by posting your résumé on the Internet, where head hunters and businesses shop for people who know their way around computers.

This project shows you some of the places on the Internet where you can start job hunting and where you can find tips that may give you an edge over other applicants. In addition, the project shows you where to post your résumé so you can save some running around.

Post Your Résumé in the Proper Format

Many of the sites you will encounter in your job search, as well as many companies, will request that you submit a résumé. In most cases, you will have to submit the résumé in a specific format.

In some places, you might have to create a Web page, which you can do with Microsoft Word, Microsoft FrontPage, the HTML editor in Netscape

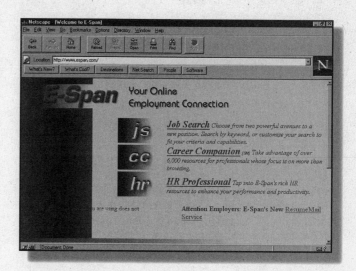

Communicator, or Windows WordPad as explained in the following section, "A Sample Web Résumé." Other sites might require you to submit your résumé as a text file. Again, you can use WordPad or your favorite word processor and save the résumé as a text file.

Because the requirements vary from site to site, you should be sure to read the specifications on format or length before you submit your résumé. If you don't, the company or résumé site may reject your résumé immediately.

A Sample Web Résumé

The listing below contains the text for a sample Web résumé that you can use as a basis for your own résumé.

For example, the code <A HREF = "#A2">Writing/ Editing Experience</A> creates a link to <A NAME="A2">, which is directly above the section of the résumé entitled "Writing Experience." These links enable a prospective employer to jump around your document quickly and easily. The sample résumé includes similar codes that enable the reader to quickly go from the bottom of the page to the top of the page or vice versa. At the top of the résumé is the `<A Name = "#Top">` code, and at the bottom is `<A HREF = "#Top">Top of page</A>`.

To keep this example as brief as possible, I've left out the salary history and references sections. However, you may want to include those items in your résumé. Check out "Submit Your Resume" on page [P2tbd] to see how this résumé looks in a Web browser.

```
<title>Keaton Résumé</title>
<A Name = "#Top">
<center><h1>Jessie Keaton</h1>
<b>5525 West Market Street</b><br>
<b>Chicago, Illinois  60629</b><br>
<b>Home/Work Phone: (312) 875-0821</b><br>
<A
HREF="mailto:jkeaton@iquest.com">jkeaton@iquest.com</
A></center><p>
<hr>

I know you're busy, so I designed this page to
make it easy to grab the information you need and
then hit the road. Just click the link for the
desired information:

<ul>
<li><A HREF = "#A1">Introduction</A>
<li><A HREF = "#A2">Writing/Editing Experience</A>
<li><A HREF = "#A3">Teaching Experience</A>
<li><A HREF = "#A4">Education</A>
</ul>

<hr>

<A NAME="A1">
<h3>Introduction</h3>

I am currently seeking a position as a writer and/
or editor of technical documentation. As my résumé
shows, I have been writing, editing, and illus-
trating computer books for the last six years.
Before that, I wrote technical training manuals
for the state of Illinois.<p>

I am trained in both task analysis and information
mapping. Both of these writing tools help break
down technical information to make it easy to
understand and to aid the reader in finding
information and skipping information. I also have
plenty of experience transforming complex ideas
into simple graphics.<p>

I am willing to relocate to anywhere with moun-
tains or oceans, but I am also willing to stay
where I am and telecommute (which I am currently
doing).<p>
```

```
Please feel free to scan this page for my qualifi-
cations. If you wish to set up an interview,
please use the information at the top of this page
to contact me.<p>

Sincerely,<p>

Jessie Keaton<p>

<hr>

<A NAME="A2">
<h3>Writing/Editing Experience</h3>

<b>1989-Present Staff Writer: Macmillan Computer
Publishing</b><p>

Authored and co-authored several general computer
books and software application books,
including:<p>

<ul>
<li>Windows 3.1 Cheat Sheet
<li>Windows 95 Cheat Sheet
<li>Complete Idiot's Guide to Mosaic
<li>WordPerfect 5.1 Bible
<li>The First Book of Personal Computing
<li>Complete Idiot's Guide to PCs
<li>First Book of MS-DOS 6
</ul>

<b>1989-1991 Production Editor: Macmillan Computer
Publishing</b><p>

<ul>
<li>Edited IBM and Macintosh software books and
Nintendo game books.
<li>Coordinated production of books from
manuscript stage until books were sent to
printer, ensuring art and text merged properly.
<li>Checked galleys and page proofs to ensure
print and graphics were of high quality and
conformed to series design specifications.
<li>In addition to my regular duties, I helped the
rest of the staff with their computer problems,
and helped develop procedures to ensure manu-
scripts proceeded smoothly through production.
</ul>

<b>1986-1989 Technical Writer: Training Special-
ists, Inc.</b><p>

Interviewed expert machine operators on the job,
and developed task analysis training manuals for
Indiana's Training for Profit (TfP) program.

Wrote more than 20 manuals explaining how to
operate various machines, including the
following:<p>
```

```
<ul>
<li>CNC Milling Machine
<li>Autoclave
<li>Vacuum Chamber
<li>Blow-Molding Press
<li>Pin-Lift Molding Machine
</ul>

Worked closely with plant personnel to ensure
accuracy of information and to target manuals to
clients' existing training program and needs.<p>

<hr>

<A NAME="A3">
<h3>Teaching Experience</h3>

1985-1986<br>
Associate Faculty: IUPUI<br>
Taught Freshman English.<br>
Developed lesson plans, lectured, directed small-
group activities, and evaluated student essays.<p>

1982-1984<br>
Teaching Assistant: Purdue University<br>
Taught English 101 and 102 half-time, while
working toward Master's degree.
Designed syllabus, developed lesson plans, ana-
lyzed professional essays in lecture, led discus-
sions, and evaluated student essays.<p>

<hr>

<A NAME="A4">
<h3>Education</h3>

1984<br>
Master of Arts in English: Purdue University.<br>
GPA: 5.8/6.0. Received highest grade possible on
Master's comprehensive exam.<p>

1982<br>
Bachelor of Arts in Philosophy: Purdue
University.<br>
GPA: 5.23/6.0.<p>

Click here to go back to the top of this page <A
HREF = "#Top">Top of Page</A>.
```

Once you've created your résumé, you can post it in any of the many Web résumé banks, as explained in the following steps. You might also be able to post it on your service provider's computer. Contact your service provider for details on how to post the Web pages you create.

Try this: Post your résumé on your service provider's computer. Then any time you're asked to send a résumé, ask your prospective employer if he has a Web browser. If the person has a browser, just send the URL of your online résumé. Talk about impressive!

E-Mail Your Résumé

Posting your résumé in an online résumé bank is a somewhat passive way to search for jobs; you basically have to wait till someone stumbles across your résumé. You'll have better luck e-mailing your résumé and cover letter directly to the people who might hire you. (Some employers do not accept e-mail applications, and you might have to resort to standard mail delivery or faxes in such cases.)

When transforming your cover letter and résumé into an e-mail message, include the cover letter and résumé in the same text file and be sure to mention (in your cover letter) where you heard about the position. Also, do not type more than 70 characters per line, and press **Enter** at the end of each line. (Some e-mail readers cannot display more than 70 characters across the screen.) Because a text editing program does not have all the fancy formatting tools you'll find in a full-featured word processing program, you'll have to rely on spaces and the Enter key to make your résumé easy to read and attractive.

You can also attach your résumé to an e-mail message as a file. A résumé and cover letter created in any word processor can be attached and sent with all the formatting and other information in the file. Make sure, however, that whoever you send the résumé to in this manner can receive attachments via their e-mail software and that they have the same word processor that you created the résumé in.

When posting your résumé, keep a log of when and where you posted it. If you move or change phone numbers, or if you gain additional job experience or training, be sure to update your résumé.

Begin Do It Yourself Read Job Postings and Other Helpful Information

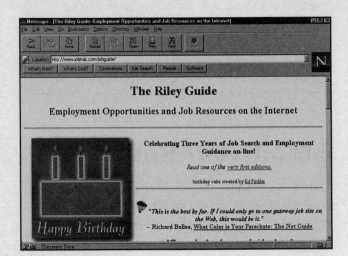

1 Listed in Point Communication's top 5% Web sites, Margaret F. Riley's Internet Job Search site is a great place to learn how to use the Internet to find a job. You can visit Ms. Riley's page at **http://www.jobtrak.com/jobguide/**.

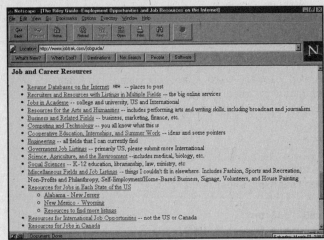

3 Scroll further down the page for files that can help you locate a potential employer. Job listings are categorized to help you locate employers in your field.

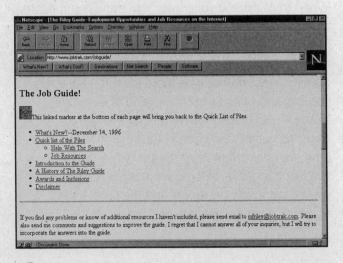

2 Scroll down the page for a list of links for files that provide general information for how to search for employment on the Internet.

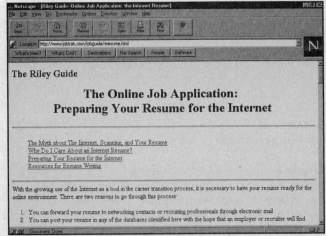

4 Before you even think about sending a résumé, read as much at this site as you can. These files contain many helpful instructions and hints on how to prepare and submit your résumé.

When you visit a Web page that has useful job search information, create a bookmark for the page so you can return to it quickly. You'll be skipping around on the Web more than usual during your job search.

Do It Yourself Read Job Postings and Other Helpful Information

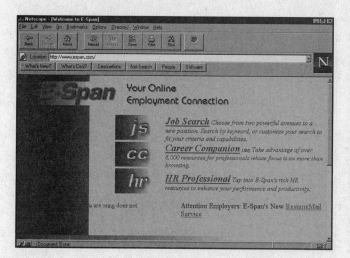

5 Another great place to start your job search is at E-Span. Enter the following URL to visit its site: **http://www.espan.com/**.

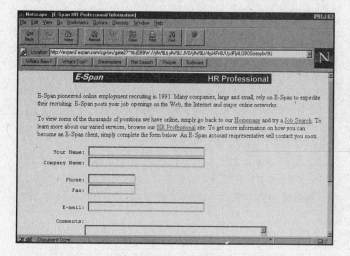

6 You can become a member of E-Span for free. Use E-Span's online HR Professional form to enter information and qualifications. E-Span enters you into its pool and can automatically e-mail you job openings in your field.

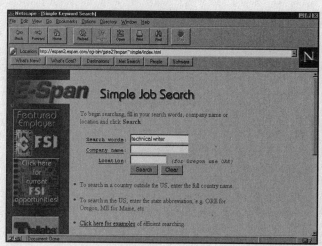

7 The online job database lets you search for job openings by keywords, company name, and location. E-Span even offers a search engine that can search for job listings in various News Groups.

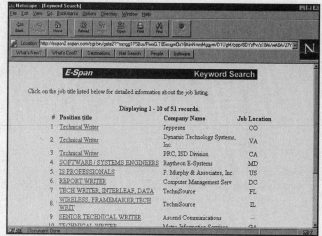

8 E-Span finds a list of employment opportunities that match your search instructions. You can click a link to view additional information about the opening.

(continues)

Do It Yourself Read Job Postings and Other Helpful Information

(continued)

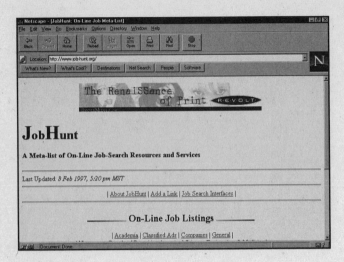

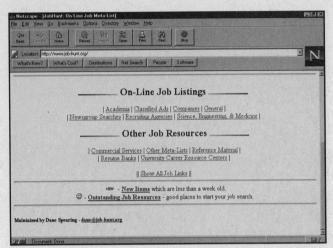

9 The Job Hunt page is another great place to start your job search. You can visit this page at **http://www.job-hunt.org/**.

10 Scroll down the Job Hunt page for links to employers, general job search information, places where you can post your résumé, and much, much more. This site contains hundreds of links.

> The job sites mentioned here are free. Many services charge the prospective employer for placing ads and finding candidates. Therefore, before you post your résumé or sign up for any of these services, you should check for hidden costs to you. And *don't* enter your credit card number.

Begin Do It Yourself Submit Your Résumé

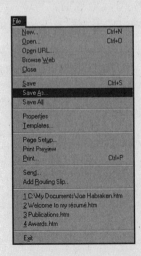

1 Before you start posting your résumé or sending it off to prospective employers, you may have to create your résumé as a text file. You might be able to save your current résumé as a text file using your word processor's **File**, **Save As** command.

Do It Yourself   Submit Your Résumé

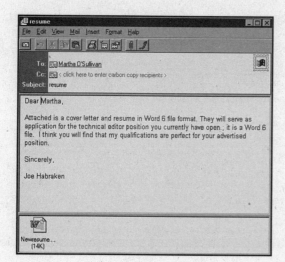

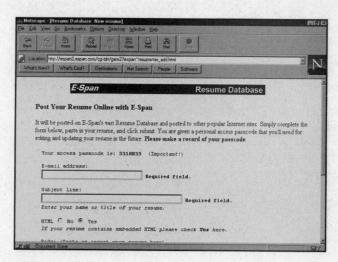

2 While a text file can certainly list your qualifications, a well-formatted word-processed résumé may even place your professional experiences in an even brighter light. Check to see if you can send your résumé to a prospective employer by attaching it as a file to an e-mail message. This may allow you to attach your résumé as a word processing file that contains great fonts and an attractive page layout.

5 If you plan to post your résumé at a Web site, the site may require that you post it as a Web document.

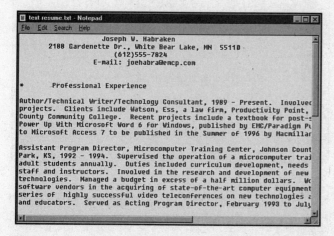

3 As a last resort, you can always put your résumé together in either of the Windows 95 text editors—Notepad or WordPad. Text editors don't offer all the fancy formatting tools you find in a word processor. However, you can use spaces, asterisks, and other basic tools to make your résumé look professional.

4 Whichever method you use to put your résumé together, make sure that you carefully proofread it.

6 Use an HTML editor such as Microsoft Word to create your HTML résumé like the one shown next.

(continues)

Do It Yourself   Submit Your Résumé   *(continued)*

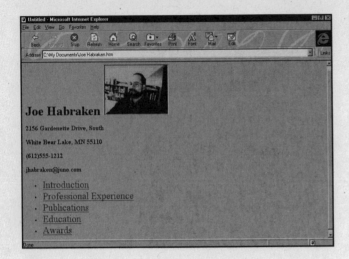

7 If you convert your résumé to a Web page, keep the opening screen brief. Include links to more lengthy material such as your résumé, references, salary history, and work samples (if applicable).

8 Before posting your Web résumé, check it for spelling, grammar, and other errors, and test it to make sure it works. If your résumé looks bad or if the links do not work, it's a bad reflection on you.

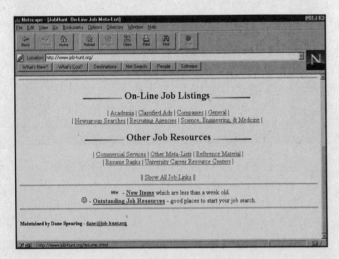

9 The Job Hunt site has links for many Internet résumé banks. To view this list, enter the following URL:

http://www.job-hunt.org

Then scroll down the page and click **Resume Banks**.

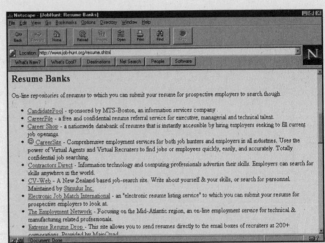

10 A list of places where you can post your résumé appears. Click a link to go to one of the many résumé banks.

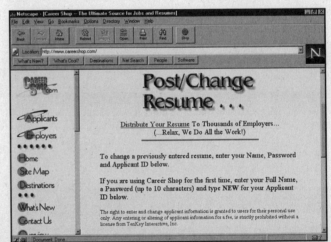

11 Each résumé bank explains its requirements for résumés. Some allow you to post only text files; others let you post HTML (Web) documents. Read and follow the requirements closely.

Do It Yourself   Submit Your Résumé

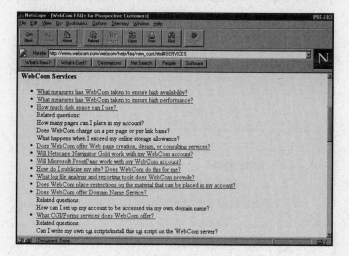

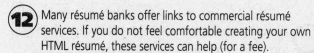

12 Many résumé banks offer links to commercial résumé services. If you do not feel comfortable creating your own HTML résumé, these services can help (for a fee).

Stay Up-To-Date on the Internet

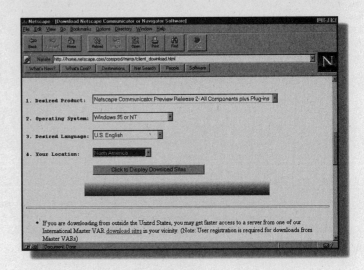

One thing about the Internet: It's always changing. You can cruise the Web every single day and still find new and interesting Web sites. They seem to pop up overnight. And along with those new sites come new ideas for putting information on the Web. Sometimes in order for you to view (and hear) the information that puts those ideas into use, you might need to get a new program or an updated version of one you already use. The best place to find the most current versions of Internet apps is on the Internet.

When looking for software, you can either dial into a known FTP site directly, or you can search for what you need on the Web. Your Web browser, as you may recall, can act like an FTP program, which makes it fully capable of downloading files for you. On the Web, you'll find many Web pages that connect you directly to files located on FTP sites. Some general Web sites allow you to search for just about any kind of software, and others cater specifically to people looking for Internet apps. The best of the latter type of Web site is Stroud's, from which you've downloaded a number of apps throughout the course of this book. Of course, you may run into times when Stroud's is busy and you have to try alternate sites such as shareware.com.

Netscape and Microsoft Internet Tools

The main tool for cruising the World Wide Web is obviously your Web browser. Netscape Navigator and Microsoft Internet Explorer have both gone through a rapid evolution and have become the pre-eminent browsers for the Web. Microsoft has recently released an updated Internet Explorer 3.0 that provides greater security for online transactions. Microsoft has promised a new version of their Web browser—Explorer 4—for the second or third quarter of 1997.

Netscape recently unveiled their newest set of Internet tools named Netscape Communicator. Netscape Communicator, which is now available as a preview (a Beta version of the software) contains Netscape Navigator 4.0, Netscape Mail, Netscape News (a newsgroup reader) and an HTML editor that provides support for dynamic HTML (multimedia-rich HTML code for interactive Web pages). Communicator also supplies GroupWare tools for use on corporate intranets (a company network that uses Internet protocols to communicate) such as a scheduling calendar. The full version of Communicator promises to be a handy bag of tricks for the Internet. And what's great is that you can try it now!

Begin Do It Yourself Download and Install Netscape Communicator

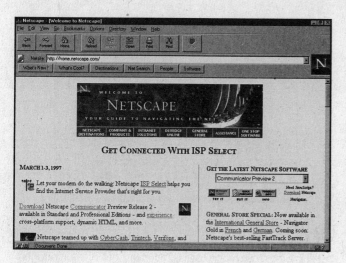

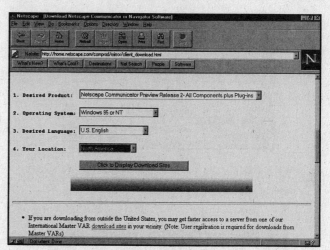

1 Connect to the Internet and start your Web browser.

2 Connect to Netscape's Home page at **http://home.netscape.com/**.

4 On the download page, specify the product, your operating system, and the desired language and your location, then click the **Click to Display Download Sites** button.

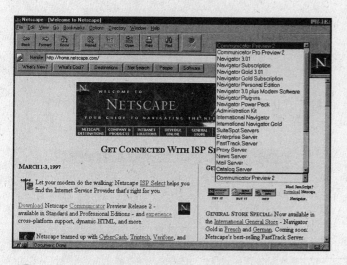

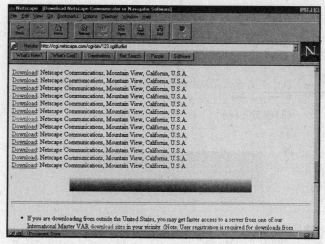

3 Select the Communicator Preview (or release version if available) in the Get The Latest Netscape Software drop down box. Once you've selected the software click the **Try It** icon.

5 Select a download site from the list provided.

(continues)

Do It Yourself Download and Install Netscape Communicator

(continued)

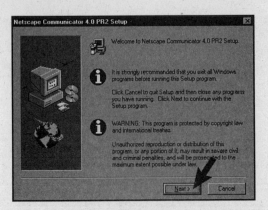

6 When the download begins, designate an appropriate directory for the installation file.

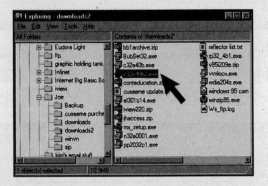

9 Advance through the installation screens by clicking the **Next** button and selecting a typical installation. This will install the most commonly used components of Communicator on your computer.

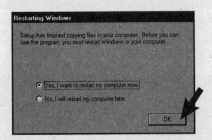

7 Once the download is complete use the Windows Explorer to locate the Communicator installation file. Double-click **c32e40b2.exe** to start the installation process.

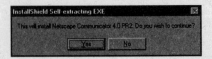

10 When the installation is complete you will be asked to restart your machine. Click **OK** to restart.

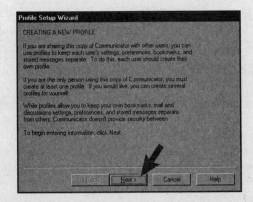

8 You will find the process to be a typical Windows 95 software installation.

11 Connect to your service provider. When you start Communicator for the first time (double-click the icon on the Windows desktop), the software will walk you through the process of creating a user profile. Click **Next** to continue.

Do It Yourself Download and Install Netscape Communicator

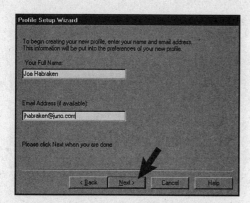

12 Fill in your name and your e-mail address and then click **Next**.

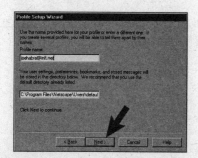

13 Supply a name and a path for your profile and you're ready to go to the next step; click **Next**.

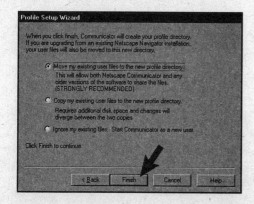

14 You can have Communicator share files with your previous version of Netscape Navigator, copy your user files to a new directory, or start Communicator as a new user. Make your selection and then click **Finish** and the profile creation process will be complete.

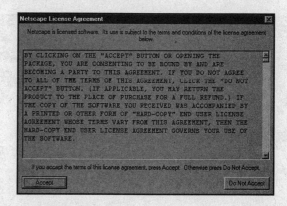

15 A license agreement will appear; read and accept it to continue.

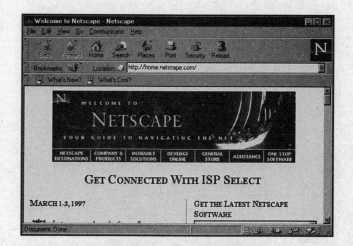

16 Navigator 4.0 will open and take you to the Netscape home page; you are ready to browse the Web.

(continues)

Do It Yourself Download and Install Netscape Communicator

(continued)

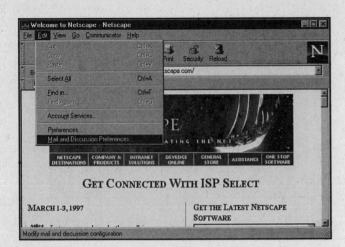

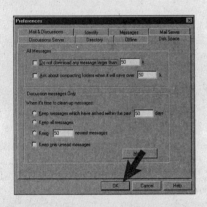

17 To set up the e-mail and newsgroup preferences for Netscape Communicator, click **Edit** and then click **Mail and Discussion Preferences**.

18 Select the appropriate tabs on the Preference dialog box and fill in your e-mail address, e-mail server, news server, and other preferences. Once you've supplied the necessary information click **OK**.

19 You can activate the Communicator Messenger e-mail service or the Newsgroup feature by clicking the appropriate icon on the Communicator toolbar, which is in the lower-right corner of the Communicator window.

20 Communicator is now ready for Web browsing, e-mail, newsgroups, and Web page design. Enjoy.

Download an Internet Application from Shareware.com

Now that you have the most up-to-date Web browser you can check out some of the other latest and greatest shareware and freeware that is available on the Web. One of the best sites for finding shareware and freeware of all kinds is **Shareware.com**, another is Stroud's Consummate Winsock Applications at **http://cws.iworld.com/**.

Another very cool site for downloading shareware and freeware is the Que Shareware Library hosted by Que publishing. All the shareware and freeware packaged with their popular computer books can be found at this site. Visit the site at **http://www.mcp.com/que/software**.

Shareware sites have rapidly proliferated on the World Wide Web as this avenue to the Internet has taken precedence over the other Net routes such as FTP and Gopher. A great place to find links to shareware sites is **http://www.mamsofco.com/100sl/**. This is the 100 Shareware Links page.

Tour Other Sites from Which You Can Download Internet Apps

Often, the best Web sites are also the busiest. You'll have the best success with the various shareware sites if you try to download your files during off-hours, which are typically between 12:00 a.m. and 5:00 a.m., local time.

Fortunately, a number of different shareware sites offer similar inventories. If one site is busy you can always try an alternative. Some of the best shareware sites and their addresses follow:

Shareware.com at **http://www.shareware.com/**

Stroud's Consummate Winsock Site at **http://cws. iworld.com/**

Windows95.com at **http://www.windows95.com/**

Galt Shareware Zone at **http://www.galttech.com/**

www.32bit.com at **http://www.32bit.com/software/index.phtml**

Begin Do It Yourself Download an Internet Application from Shareware.com.

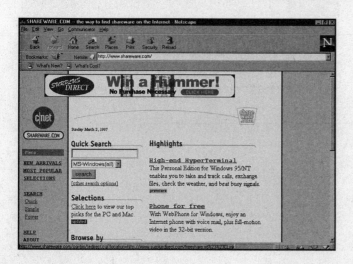

1 Connect to the Internet and start your Web browser.

2 To connect to **Shareware.com**, type the URL: **http://www.shareware.com/** and press **Enter**.

(continues)

Do It Yourself Download an Internet Application from Shareware.com. *(continued)*

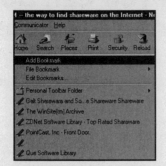

3 Once you connect to **Shareware.com**, you'll want to save its location by adding a bookmark. In Netscape Navigator 4.0, click the **Bookmarks** icon and select **Add Bookmark**.

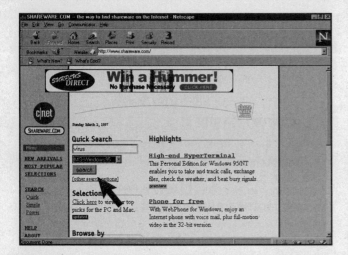

4 Shareware.com offers a search engine to help you find the applications you need. Type **virus** in the search box, select your operating system from the drop-down box, and then click **Search**.

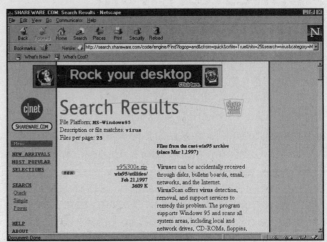

5 You will be provided with a list of applications that meet your search criteria. Select the file that you wish to download.

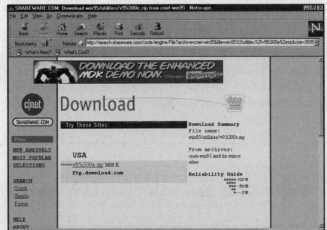

6 Once you select the file to download, you will be taken to a page that lists the FTP sites that store the particular application. Choose the site closest to you and click the link.

Do It Yourself Download an Internet Application from Shareware.com.

7 Select a folder for your new application and click **Save**.

After you download your program, you need to install it. Many of the shareware and freeware programs that you download will consist of an auto-executable file that uncompresses the files needed and installs them. However, you will also find shareware that has been compressed into a file that is not auto-executable; you will have to extract the program files (using WinZip) from the file that you downloaded. Program files that end in .EXE are self-extracting; just double-click the .EXE file, and it extracts its own files.

When you finish decompressing the files, click the **INSTALL.EXE** or **SETUP.EXE** file to install the program. If you can't find one, there may not be any real installation procedure. In that case, double-click the program's .EXE file to start the program.

Begin Do It Yourself Tour Other Sites to Download Internet Apps

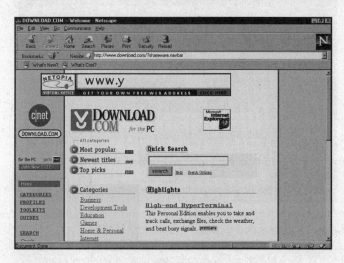

1 Another good site for downloading PC shareware is Download.com. Give it a try at **http://www.download.com/?shareware.navbar**.

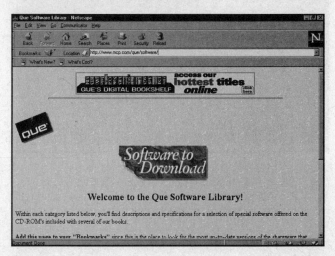

2 Don't forget to take a look at the software collection at Que Publishing. It's located at **http://www.mcp.com/que/software/**.

(continues)

Do It Yourself Tour Other Sites to Download Internet Apps *(continued)*

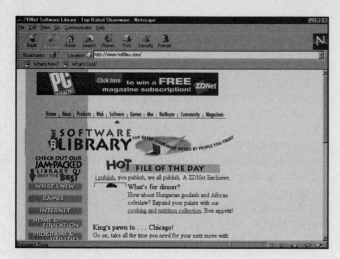

3 The ZDNet Software Library is also another good place to pick up shareware. It's located at **http://www.hotfiles.com/**.

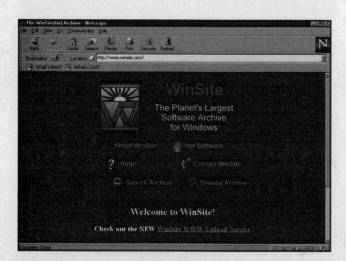

4 One of the longest-running shareware FTP sites is called Papa Winsock. You can connect to Papa via the Web using the URL **http://www.winsite.com**.

You can ftp to the Papa Winsock site if you prefer, using the address **ftp://ftp.winsite.com**. Make sure that you are familiar with your FTP client software before embarking on this journey.

5 Another great site for software is TUCOWS (The Ultimate Collection of Winsock Software) located at: **http://tucows.phx.cox.com:80/index.html**. TUCOWS is mirrored by a number of sites across the country. To choose the site closest to you go to **http://tucows.phx.cox.com:80/mirror.html** and click your location on the map to connect..

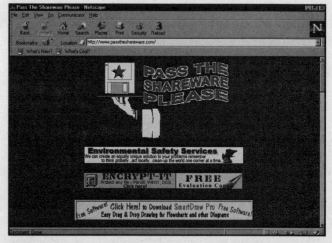

6 Another good software library is Pass the Shareware Please, located at **http://www.passtheshareware.com/**, a great place to find software other than just Internet software.

Do It Yourself Tour Other Sites to Download Internet Apps

7 If you use Windows 95, you must visit **Windows95.com**, a great source of software and help.

Get the Latest News Headlines

The worst thing about the news on the Internet is that there's almost too much of it. All the major news networks and many local news stations are online. Likewise, major newspapers (such as the *New York Times* and the *Wall Street Journal*), as well as local and international newspapers, are also online.

In addition, many specific types of news services are on the Net, including headline news, sports news, industry and business news, financial news, and weather. And if that's not enough, there's entertainment news with direct links to pages featuring many of your favorite TV shows.

To make matters even more confusing, there are now News agents that will directly download news headlines and other information, such as stock prices, directly to your PC. Some of these news agents, such as PointCast, can even be configured to operate as your screen saver. When your computer is idle, it downloads the latest news to your desktop.

As you'll see here, there definitely is not a lack of news on the Net. And the problem is not one of how to find the news, but one of how to find the news that interests you.

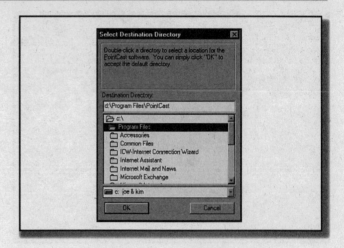

Connect to a News Source

When you're ready to get the latest news off the Net, first ask yourself, "What kind of news am I looking for, and where do I usually get it?" If the answer is that you like to get your news from the *New York Times*, start by searching for its Web page. Chances are, your favorite news source is on the Internet.

The following table lists some of the more popular national and world news sources on the Internet, along with their addresses.

Popular Internet News Sources

News Source	Address
ABC Internet Hourly News*	http://www.realaudio.com/contentp/abc.html
AP Wire Service	http://www.trib.com/NEWS/APwire.html
CBS News	http://uttm.com
ClariNet	http://www.clarinet.com
CNN Interactive	http://cnn.com
National Public Radio*	http://www.prognet.com/contentp/npr.html

* requires RealAudio

Popular Internet News Sources   Continued

News Source	Address
NBC News	http://www.nbc.com/news/index.html
The Nando Times	http://www2.nando.net/nt/nando.cgi
PR Newswire	http://www.prnewswire.com
Reuters NewMedia	http://www.yahoo.com/headlines/current/news/summary.html
TimesFax	http://www.nytimesfax.com
USA Today	http://www.usatoday.com
US Online World and News	http://www.usnews.com
Virtual Daily News	http://www.infi.net/~opfer/daily.htm
World News Today	http://www.fwi.com/wnt/wnt.html
USA Watch News	http://usawatch.com

In order to take advantage of some news sources, you must have installed a RealAudio player for your Web browser. See "Play a Radio and Video Broadcast with the RealPlayer" on page 344 for help.

For those of you who prefer local news stations and newspapers, many of them are also on the Internet. Be sure to look for your favorites. This table lists some popular online newspapers on the local level.

Popular Local-Level Online Sources

Newspaper	Geographical Location	Online Address
Boston Globe	Boston	http://www.globe.com
Detroit News	Detroit	http://detnews.com
Electronic Telegraph	United Kingdom	http://www.telegraph.co.uk
The Gate	San Francisco	http://www.sfgate.com
Houston Chronicle Interactive	Houston	http://www.chron.com
Mercury Center	San Jose	http://www.sjmercury.com
New York Times	New York City	http://www.nytimes.com
Philadelphia Inquirer	Philadelphia	http://www.phillynews.com
TribNet	Tacoma	http://www.tribnet.com/mainnews.htp
Pioneer Press	St. Paul	http://pioneerplanet.com
St. Petersburg Press	Russia	http://www.spb.su/sppress
Seattle Times	Seattle	http://www.seatimes.com

If you want to find a particular story, or if you want to look at the same story in more than one newspaper, try one of these Web pages, which provide links to multiple news sources:

Daily News	**http://www.cs.vu.nl/~gerben/news.html**
Extra!Extra!	**http://www.fyionline.com/infoMCI/update/NEWS-MCI.html**
Infoseek's News Update	**http://guide.infoseek.com/NS/ticker?DCticker.html**
Pathfinder	**http://pathfinder.com**
NewsLink	**http://www.newslink.org**
NewsPage	**http://www.newspage.com**

If time is of the essence, you can subscribe to many popular news services, and they will "deliver" the news you want to know about to your computer every morning. For example, ESPN, CBS, NewsPage, *TimesFax*, *The Wall Street Journal*, and *Investor's Daily* all offer this kind of service (just to name a few). As you visit various news sites, watch for subscription offers. Each site offers complete details on pricing and how to subscribe.

If you're looking for news that's more specific, check out the sites in the following table, which include popular financial, industrial, and political news sources.

Serious Topic News Sources

Source	Address
Business Update	http://www.fyionline.com/infoMCI/update/BUSINESS-MCI.html
BYTE	http://www.byte.com
CNBC	http://www.cnbc.com
ClNet Central	http://www.cnet.com
C-SPAN	http://www.c-span.org
Executive Lounge	http://www.rwsa.com/executive/lounge.html
Global Internet News Agency	http://www.gina.com
HotWired	http://www.wired.com
Internet Business and Industry News	http://www.lib.lsu.edu/bus/biznews.html
Mecklermedia's iWorld	http://www.iworld.com
Wall Street Journal	http://update.wsj.com
ZDNet	http://www.zdnet.com

For a lighter look at the news, try the entertainment-, weather-, and sports-related news pages listed here.

In the "Browse for a Good News Source" steps, you'll learn how to use Netscape Navigator to find many of the news sources I've mentioned. You'll connect to a Web page called NewsLink, which provides links to many news sources. I think you'll find it a good jumping off place for your tour of Web news.

Lighter Topic News Sources

Source	Address
ABC	http://www/abctelevision.com
CBS	http://www.cbs.com
Discovery Channel	http://www.discovery.com
ER	http://www.nbc.com/entertainment/shows/er/index.html
ESPNet SportsZone	http://ESPNET.SportsZone.com
Fox Online	http://www.foxnetwork.com/home.html
Friends	http://www.nbc.com/entertainment/shows/friends/index.html
Comedy Central	http://www.comedycentral.com/
INTELLICAST	http://www.intellicast.com
NBC	http://www.nbc.com
PBS	http://www.pbs.org
People Magazine	http://pathfinder.com/@@NFza14K7ZglAQKid/people
SciFi Channel	http://www.scifi.com/dominion.html
Showtime Online	http://showtimeonline.com
Sports Network	http://www.sportsnetwork.com
Sportsline USA	http://www.sportsline.com
Travel Channel	http://www.travelchannel.com
Weather Channel	http://www.weather.com
WeatherNet	http://cirrus.sprl.umich.edu/wxnet
WebWeather	http://www.princeton.edu/Webweather/ww.html
U.S. Weather Map	http://www.mit.edu:8001/usa.html

Save or Print News

From the many news sources the Internet offers, you'll soon find your favorites. And when you locate news that you're really interested in, you may want to keep a copy of it. For example, if you're doing research for an article or a report, you might want to print out a copy of several news articles so you can refer to them later.

Even if you're not writing a report, you might want to save a copy of the news you're interested in. Why go to all that trouble? Well, connecting to the Internet costs money, and it adds up fast if you spend a lot of time reading endless news reports. You can save yourself some bucks by simply printing or saving the news articles in which you're interested.

Begin Do It Yourself Browse for a Good News Source

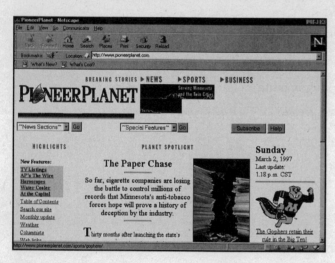

1 Connect to the Internet as usual and start Netscape or your Web browser.

2 Click **Net Search**.

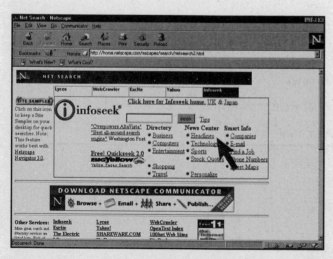

3 For a quick look at the current news (according to Infoseek), click **Headlines**.

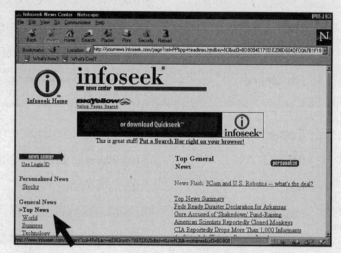

4 For a quick news update, click **Top News**.

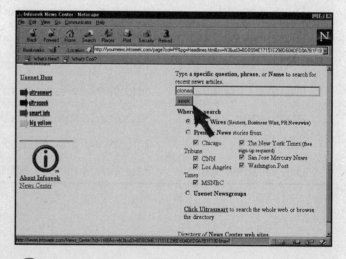

5 If, perhaps, you want more detail than the Infoseek news headlines provide, return to the main Infoseek page, scroll down and type a search phrase into the search box. Then click **seek**.

Do It Yourself Browse for a Good News Source

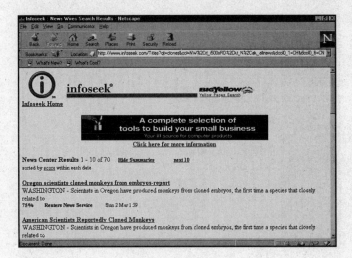

6 All the recent stories containing your search parameters will be listed.

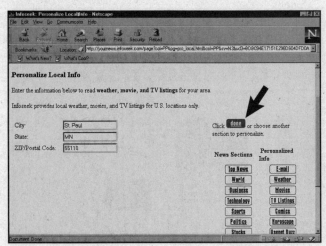

8 Enter your City, State, and Zip/Postal Code. Click **done** when you are finished.

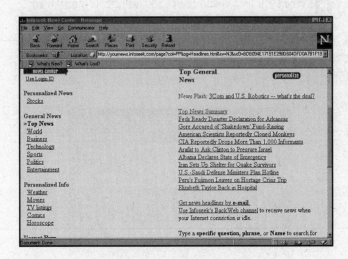

7 You can personalize the Infoseek News service. For instance, click the **Weather** link under Personalized info.

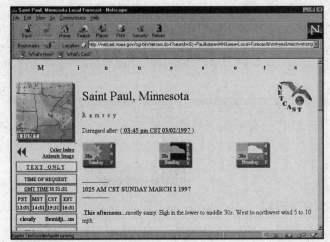

9 When you return to the main InfoSeek page and click Weather, you are provided with a weather map and forecast for your area. You can personalize many of the news features supplied by InfoSeek.

(continues)

Do It Yourself   Browse for a Good News Source

(continued)

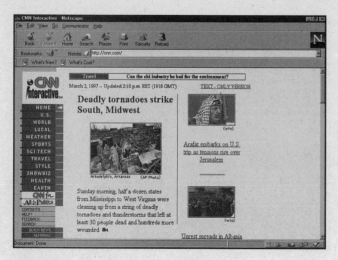

10 Another great news service is CNN Interactive at **http://www.cnn.com/.** CNN is a good source for breaking news, business news updates, and so on.

11 To check out sports go the source: ESPN. The site address for the SportsZone is **http://espnet.sportszone.com**.

12 When you find a news source you like, create a bookmark or mark it as a favorite site.

Begin Do It Yourself   Save or Print the News

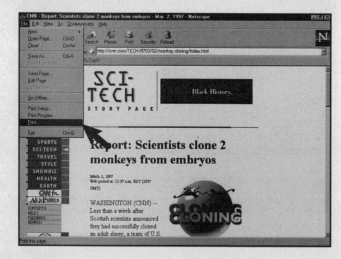

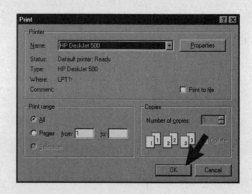

1 If you find a story that you want to keep, you can print it by clicking the **Print** button or by opening the **File** menu and clicking **Print**.

2 Click **OK**.

Do It Yourself   Save or Print the News

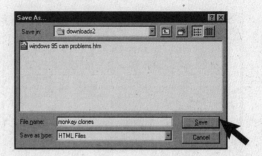

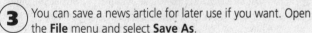

4 Type a file name for the article and click **Save**.

5 To view the article at a later date, start your Web browser, open the **File** menu, and select **Open File**.

3 You can save a news article for later use if you want. Open the **File** menu and select **Save As**.

Begin Do It Yourself   Find and Install a Webcaster News Agent

You can also have your news delivered directly to your desktop by news agent software that connects to the Internet periodically and downloads the latest headlines and other news information. Several news agents exist: PointCast, After Dark Online, Infoseek's BackWeb, and the Yahoo! Stock Ticker. The amount and type of news that they download varies. For instance, PointCast will download headlines, top stories, even graphics directly to your desktop; it delivers a full-fledged news network to your computer. On the other end of the spectrum is the Yahoo! Stock Ticker, which downloads stock prices to your desktop in the form of a stock ticker.

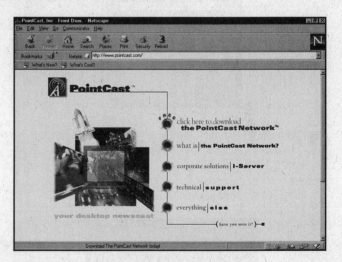

1 Go to the PointCast page at **http://www.pointcast.com** and download the PointCast Network software.

Agents are software that periodically connect to the Web and download information to your desktop. News Agents, such as PointCast, are often called Webcasters, in that they supply you with a number of different news delivery options.

(continues)

Do It Yourself Find and Install a Webcaster News Agent

(continued)

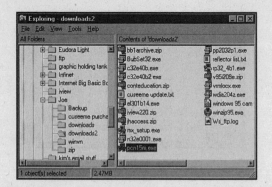

2 Once the PointCast software has been downloaded, open the Windows Explorer and then double-click the **pcn15m.exe** file to start the installation process.

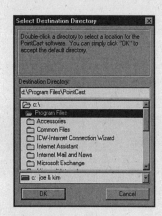

3 You will go through a typical Windows 95 software installation. Choose the location where you wish the files to be installed and follow the prompts on the screen to complete the process.

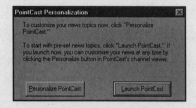

4 At the completion of the installation you can choose to personalize PointCast or start the software (if you choose to start the software, you can personalize the news that it provides later).

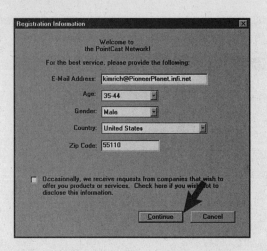

5 You will be asked to provide registration information, such as your e-mail address and zip code. Once you have completed the form, click the **Continue** button.

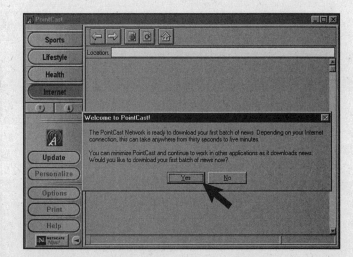

6 PointCast will download its first batch of news items. Click **Yes** to continue.

The time PointCast or any other News agent takes to download news stories will depend on the speed of your Internet connection. You may want to minimize PointCast and work on other things, while the news is being downloaded.

Do It Yourself Find and Install a Webcaster News Agent

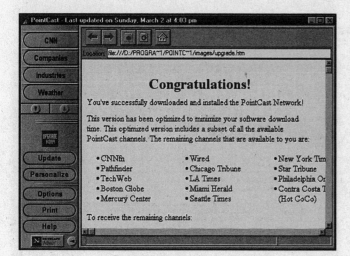

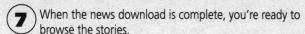

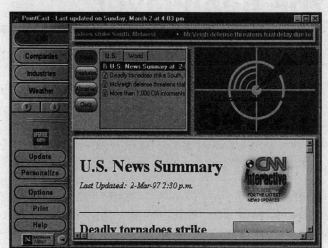

7 When the news download is complete, you're ready to browse the stories.

8 Clicking the **CNN** button gives you the latest stories from this popular news service. When you have completed reading the news stories and information provided by PointCast, you can close the software window by clicking the **Close** button.

Play a Radio and Video Broadcast with the RealPlayer

RealAudio is a standard by which near-to-live audio transmissions are sent over the Internet. It's called near-to-live transmission because there's a small delay between the time the sound signal is sent and the time you actually hear it. There are other standards, but RealAudio is by far the most popular.

Normally, when you download a sound file—such as an .AU or .wav file—from the Internet, your Web browser has to receive the entire sound file and save it to disk. Then the browser launches a sound player application, which reads the sound file in its entirety and then plays it.

RealAudio cuts a lot of time out of the audio transmission process. When you download a RealAudio sound, your RealAudio player application begins decompressing it as soon as it receives the first few thousand bytes. Then it starts playing the decompressed portion while the rest of the sound is still being transmitted. You can save a RealAudio transmission as a file if you want, but you don't have to if you only want to hear it once.

The people who created RealAudio, Progressive Networks, have taken the idea of live media on the Internet one step farther with their newest offering, RealVideo. To hear a broadcast, you'll need the RealPlayer. In this project, you'll learn how to configure the RealPlayer for audio and video, as well as how to use it.

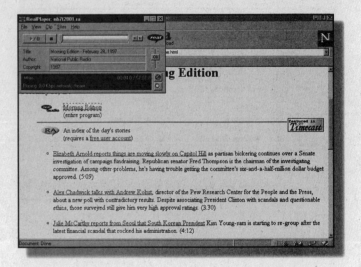

computer information. The RealAudio developers use that information to fine-tune each product to its actual user—you. During the installation process, RealAudio automatically ties itself in with your Web browser. This enables your Web browser to activate the RealAudio player whenever it encounters a RealAudio page on the Web.

The steps to download RealPlayer can be found in Part I in the section titled "Find and Install Browser Plug-Ins and ActiveX Controls" on page 145). After you download and install RealPlayer you will be ready to play audio and video on the Web.

To use RealAudio, your PC must have at least a 486 CPU (if you use Windows 95). A Pentium is recommended for RealPlayer, which plays audio and video.

When you download the RealAudio player, you must complete a form with your name, address, and

Visit the Progressive Networks Web Site

The place to get the latest version of the RealPlayer for audio and video is the Progressive Networks Web site at **http://www.realaudio.com /**.

In this project, you'll visit the National Public Radio Web site, which uses RealAudio. Another site that uses it that you might want to visit is the ABC Internet Hourly News site. The ABC News site is located at **www.realaudio.com/contentp/abc.html**. You'll find links to other RealAudio sites on the RealAudio home page.

You will also have an opportunity to test the RealPlayer's video abilities at **http://www.timecast.com/videoguide.html**, with an offering from the Children's Television Workshop.

Begin Do It Yourself Download RealAudio

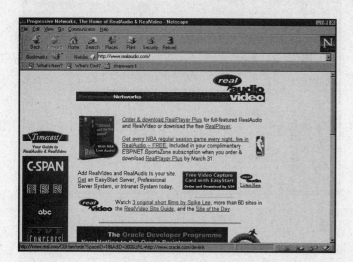

1 Connect to the Internet and start your Web browser.

2 In the **Location** or **Netsite** text box, type **http://www.realaudio.com/**and press **Enter**.

3 Follow the download and installation process for the RealPlayer found in the section title "Find and Install Browser Plug-Ins and ActiveX Controls" on page 145.

Begin Do It Yourself Visit an Audio Web Site with the RealPlayer

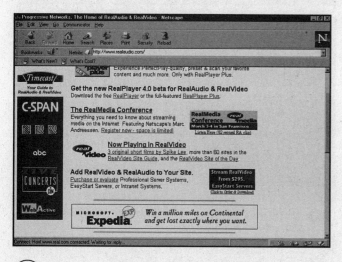

1 Connect to the Internet and start your Web browser. In the **Netsite** box, enter **http://www.realaudio.com/** and press **Enter**.

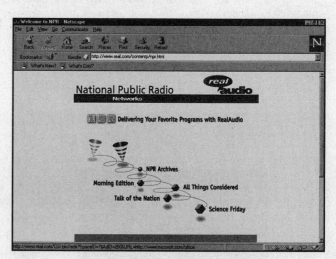

2 Scroll down to Sites and Sounds and click the **NPR** logo.

(continues)

Do It Yourself Visit an Audio Web Site with the RealPlayer *(continued)*

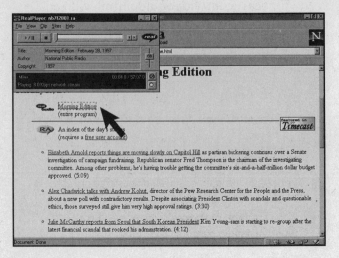

8 You can use your Web browser to visit other non-RealAudio sites, and the RealAudio transmission continues as you work. When the transmission ends, the RealAudio player closes automatically.

3 Click **Morning Edition**.

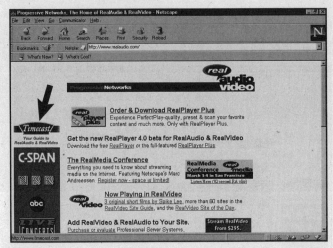

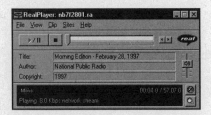

9 If you want to visit other Real Audio and Video sites, return to the RealAudio home page and click the **TimeCast logo**.

4 Click **Morning Edition** (or any of the other program links) again and the last edition of the program will begin to play in the RealPlayer audio window. (The length of the audio transmission is displayed in parentheses. This RealAudio segment is 45 minutes long.)

5 The RealPlayer starts automatically. The elapsed time appears in the lower-right corner of the RealAudio window.

6 To stop the transmission at any time, click the **Stop** button.

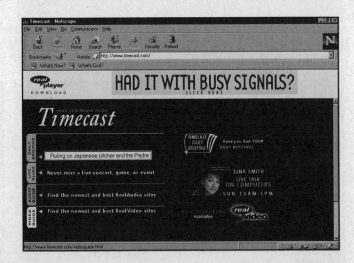

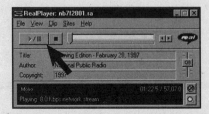

10 TimeCast provides you with links to audio and video that you can play using the RealPlayer. Click the Video Guide button to find a site that supplies video for the RealPlayer.

7 To resume the transmission, click the **Play** button.

Do It Yourself Visit an Audio Web Site with the RealPlayer

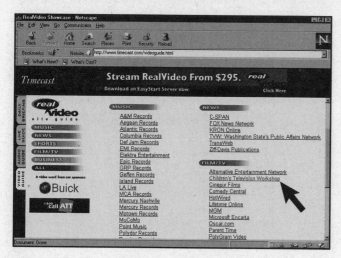

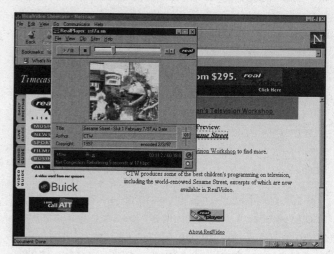

11 Click the link for the Children's Television Workshop under the Film/TV heading.

12 Click the Preview for Sesame Street. The Real Player will start and play a video/sound clip from a Sesame Street episode. When you are finished viewing the video, close the RealPlayer window.

Make an Internet Address Book

Internet e-mail addresses are about as easy to remember as international phone numbers. They can be a combination of long usernames, disjointed numbers, and domain names that snake across the screen—all separated with dots. Nobody expects you to remember these addresses, but if you don't enter them precisely, your mail will never reach its destination.

The solution to this problem is to create an e-mail address book. If you're using a browser program such as Netscape Communicator to access the Internet, you can easily create an address book using the tools provided by the e-mail package it contains. Microsoft Internet Explorer's e-mail package, Internet Mail, is capable of creating an address book, as you'll learn in this project. If you're using another Internet e-mail program (such as Eudora) you will find that it has the ability to create some kind of e-mail address book.

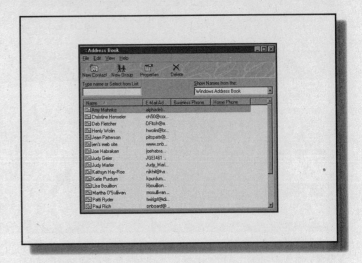

For more information on Internet e-mail addresses, turn back to "Send and Receive Electronic Mail" on page 193.

Begin Do It Yourself Create an Address Book with Microsoft Internet Mail

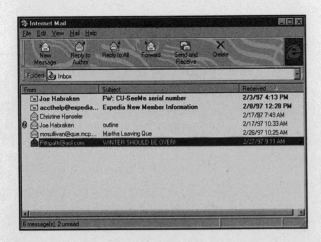

1 Open the **Internet Mail**.

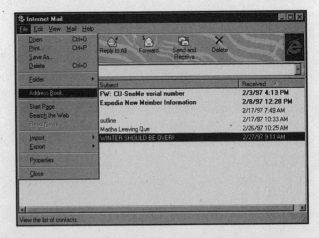

2 To add an e-mail address to your book, open the **File** menu and click **Address Book**. The Address Book dialog box appears.

Do It Yourself Create an Address Book with Microsoft Internet Mail

You may find that you need to change an address in your address book (if a person moves or picks a new e-mail address, for example). Open the Address Book window, right-click the person's name, and click **Properties**. This opens the same dialog box you used to add the person to your address book. Simply change any of the information that is no longer correct and click **OK**.

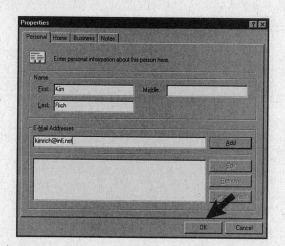

5 Click the **Add** button and then click **OK** to add the person to your address book.

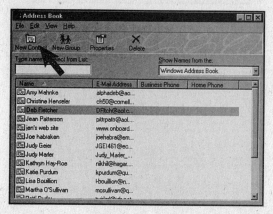

3 To add a new contact, click the **New Contact** button.

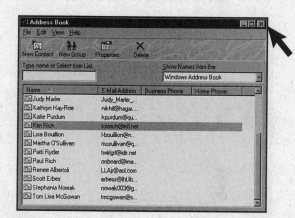

6 The person's name and e-mail address will appear in your address book. Click the **Close** button to close the address book.

7 Repeat these steps as necessary to add names to your address book.

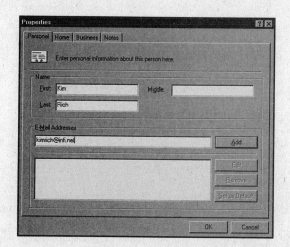

4 Click the appropriate box and fill in the person's first name, last name, and e-mail address. This is the name that will appear in your address book.

To delete a person from your address book, click the person's name and press the **Delete** key.

(continues)

Do It Yourself Create an Address Book with Microsoft Internet Mail (continued)

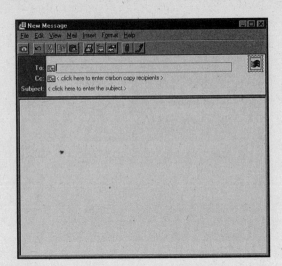

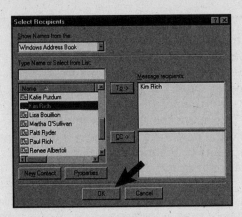

10 Select the person you want to send the e-mail message to from the list and double-click the name. The name will be copied to the Message recipients box. Once you have selected all the recipients, click **OK** and complete and send your e-mail message.

8 To use the address book and send e-mail from Internet Mail, click **New Message,** the first button on the left side of the main Internet Mail screen.

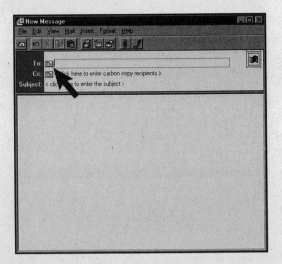

9 Make sure the insertion point is in the **To** box and then click the **Pick Recipient** button.

Take a Live Video Tour

Not only can you view text information and graphics when surfing the Internet, you can also view video clips and live video feeds. Video on the Internet has been around for a long time, but it's not always convenient to use because the video files often take a long time to download. And after you spend the time it takes to download the video file, you have to play it back from your hard drive. You've already experienced live video using the RealPlayer, which downloads streaming video information at a rapid pace. This technology is catching on quickly; however, there is still a lot of video on the Internet that is stored as files that require a helper or plug-in to play. You also have to download the entire file before you can view it.

Despite the downloading time constraints, Internet videos are still a popular element of Web surfing. Many of the hottest Web sites you can visit offer video clips you can download and view on your own computer, such as movie scenes or trailers, television scenes, music videos, and promotional videos. However, in order to view the clips, you have to have a program installed on your computer or included in your Internet browser program that allows you to see the video.

If you're using Windows 95, download ActiveMovie from Microsoft at **www.microsoft.com**. This ActiveX control can play a variety of video formats. There is also a plug-in available for Netscape that allows it to take advantage of this video player. You'll also find other viewer programs on the Net, such as QuickTime or Mpegplay, that you can download and use to view Internet videos.

A newer aspect of Internet videos is real-time or live video (also called live video feed). Live video feed is part of the cutting edge video technology that allows Internet users to view live video shots from around the world. With live video, someone sets up a TV or video camera (sometimes called a Web-Cam) to view a particular scene (a beach or a street corner, for example) and then feeds the digital images onto the Internet. When an Internet user opens a Web page containing live video feed, he sees a video picture that's only moments old. Most live videos are updated every couple of minutes, so it's not *exactly* live…it's more like a video snapshot.

For more information about using video viewer programs (or helper applications), turn to "Play Sound and Video Clips with Helper Applications" on page 129.

Because the sites you are about to visit are live video feeds, the images you see will differ from the figures shown in the project, depending on the time of day you visit a Web-Cam view. It may be night or day (don't forget to account for changing time zones). Remember, too, that the cameras update the image at different time increments. So what you see on a particular site, such as people walking by or different weather conditions, may not be what you expect.

What makes live video feed different from downloadable video clips is that the image is made into a normal data type that you can see right away on the WWW page without having to download the image onto your computer's hard drive. Most of the images appear as JPEG or GIF images, popular graphics formats.

In this project, you'll take a live video tour on the Web using Netscape Navigator 4.0, and you can take a look at "live" video snapshots from around the world.

Begin Do It Yourself   Take a Live Video Tour

Location: http://www.cybercomm.net/~szymon/cam/cameras.html

1 Connect to the Internet and start your Web browser (such as Netscape). In the **Location** or **Go to** text box, enter **http://www.cybercomm.net/~szymon/cam/cameras.html** and press **Enter**.

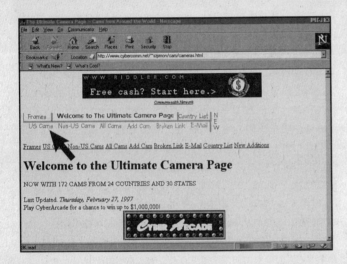

2 The Ultimate Camera Page provides a huge link to tons of Web-cams from around the world. Click the **US Cams** link.

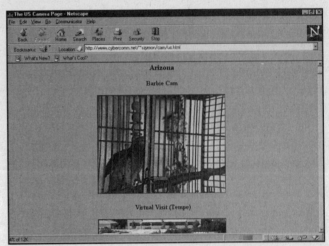

3 The download of the live video feeds may take some time, but you can scroll down through the cams to view their current images.

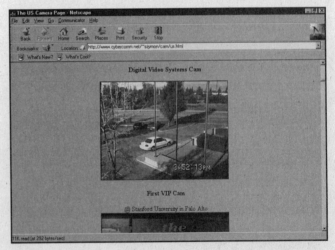

4 Scroll down to view other Web-cams.

Do It Yourself Take a Live Video Tour

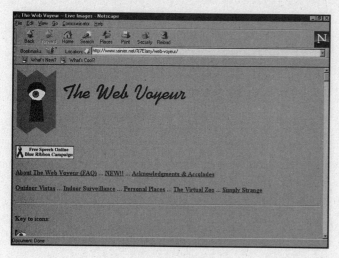

5 Another very good place to find Web-cams is the Web Voyeur page at **http://www.rainier.net/%7Elarry/web-voyeur/**. Scroll down the page until you see a list of links.

7 San Diego Bay in all its glory. Of course what you see on the Web-cam will depend on the time of day at the site you visit.

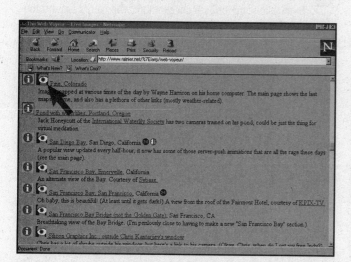

6 To check out San Diego Bay, click the eye icon next to the link.

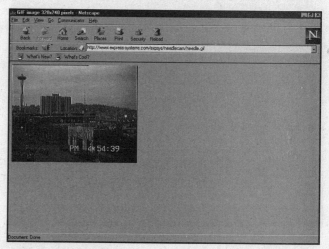

8 Another nice West Coast view is the Space Needle in Seattle.

Not all servers you contact among the Web Voyeur links may be operable at the time you attempt to connect. If you select one that's not working, try another link.

Depending on the size of the image, it may take a few seconds or a few minutes to download to the Web page. Be patient.

(continues)

Do It Yourself Take a Live Video Tour

(continued)

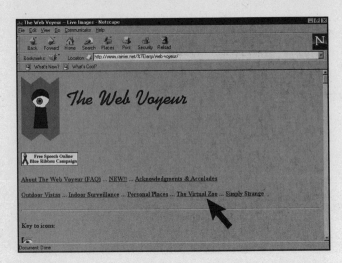

9 Back at the Web Voyeur home page, select the **Virtual Zoo** link.

11 You are transported to the offices of Netscape and have a front row seat view of their fish tank.

12 To return to the Web Voyeur site, click the **Back** button. Then take some time to check in on other spots around the world.

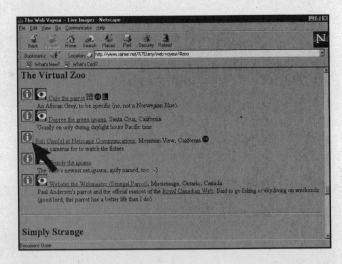

10 Click the **Fish Cams[s] at Netscapte Communicator** link.

Turn a Graphics File into Windows Wallpaper

O ne of the first things new computer users often do is experiment with the various backgrounds and wallpaper patterns available, changing the appearance of the Windows desktop. This project shows you how to take a picture you find on the Internet (such as a famous work of art) and turn it into Windows wallpaper for your desktop.

To redo your desktop at any time, open the **Control Panel** and double-click the **Display** icon. (Or for an even faster way, right-click anywhere on the desktop and select **Properties** from the menu that appears.) In the Display Properties dialog box, select the **Background** tab to see the options available for your desktop's appearance.

Microsoft Internet Explorer and Netscape Navigator make it easy for you to take any graphic from the Web and turn it into your desktop's wallpaper. It's just a matter of finding the right graphic and then right-clicking it; that's all there is to it.

The steps in this project show you how to turn an image into wallpaper using Netscape Navigator running under Windows 95.

If you are using an early version of Netscape Navigator (earlier than 3.0) or a Web browser that does not allow you to set graphics as wallpaper, you will have to download L-view or some other graphics package. Make sure that you configure your browser so that it recognizes the graphic viewer package as a helper application. When you come upon a graphic you wish to use for wallpaper, click it. The graphic file will open in the helper application and you can use the Save As function to save the graphic as a .BMP file. Make sure that you place the file in your Windows directory and you can then select it as your wallpaper.

Begin Do It Yourself Download a Graphics File and Turn It into Windows Wallpaper

Go to: http://www.artic.edu/aic/firstpage.html

1 Start Netscape Navigator and find a graphics file you want to work with. You can take a graphic from any Web page and make it your wallpaper. To give this exercise an artistic bent, we'll look for images at the Art Institute of Chicago. It has some great art that will make great Windows wallpaper. In the **Location** or **Go to** text box, type **http://www.artic.edu/aic/firstpage.html** and press **Enter**.

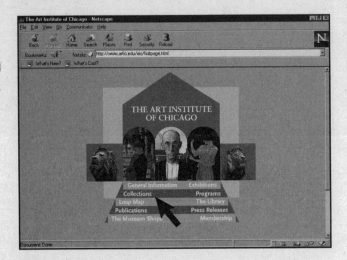

2 When the page appears, you're ready to start tracking down a graphic. Click the **Collections** link.

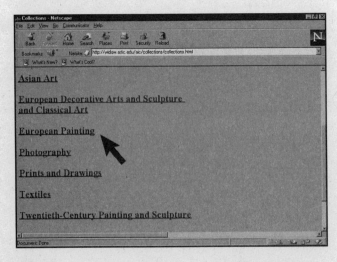

3 Scroll down the page and click the **European Painting** link.

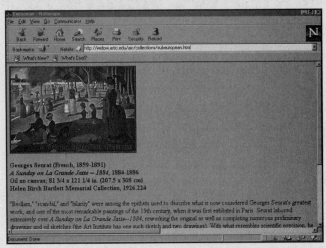

4 An example of the European paintings at the institute is shown (*A Sunday on La Grande Jatte* by Seurat).

5 Right-click the mouse on the message and select **Set as Wallpaper** from the menu that appears.

Do It Yourself Download a Graphics File and Turn It into Windows Wallpaper

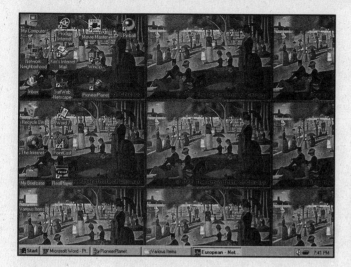

The relative size of the image that you right click to make wallpaper is important. If the image fills the maximized Web browser window, you will create wallpaper that will cover the entire desktop. Smaller images may need to be tiled to cover the desktop.

6 Minimize your Web browser and the other applications that are running on your desk. The Seurat painting now appears as your wallpaper. The picture is tiled on the desktop.

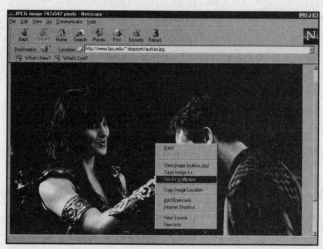

7 If you don't like the tiled look you can right-click on the Desktop and select **Properties**.

9 You can create wallpaper from all sorts of images. Find your favorites and then right-click to set them as wallpaper.

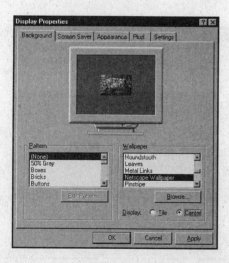

8 Make sure the **Background** Tab in the Display Properties dialog box is selected. Click the **Center** button under the Wallpaper box. This will center the wallpaper on the desktop.

10 Be creative. Wallpaper can be fun.

Find Free Legal Advice

As you've learned throughout this book, the Internet is full of information. In some cases, you can find information online that you might have to pay for elsewhere.

This is especially true of legal advice. You'll be thankful to know that you can hunt down valuable legal advice online, without paying an enormous sum of money for it. There are dozens of WWW sites you can contact and databases you can tap into to learn about legal matters and laws. There are some exceptional Web pages out there that provide you with links to other legal sources, allow you to talk to lawyers (either by live chat or e-mail questions), search through law libraries, and locate professional law services.

In this project, you'll tour the various Web pages that offer free legal advice and access to other law-related areas. The project shows you how to access this information using Netscape, but you can use any browser program to find these sites.

Don't forget that you can use Web search tools such as Yahoo! Search (**http://yahoo.com/search.html**) to look up information about law and legal data on the Internet. Turn to "Search for Information on the Internet" on page [p1s11tbd] for more information.

Begin Do It Yourself Look for Legal Advice

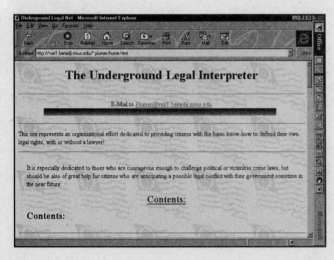

1 A good place to start your search for free legal advice is the Underground Legal Interpreter at **http://vax1.bemidji.msus.edu/~plumer/home.html** .

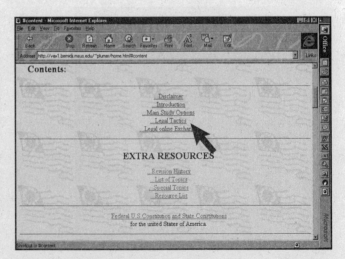

2 Click the **Contents** link to see what the Interpreter has to offer. There are links to a legal tactics section and a legal online Exchange. There are even links to the U.S. Constitution and various State Constitutions. Click the **Legal Tactics** link.

Do It Yourself   Look for Legal Advice

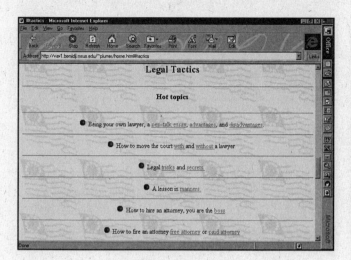

3 This page gives you legal tactics advice such as acting as your own attorney or what to do when you have to go to court.

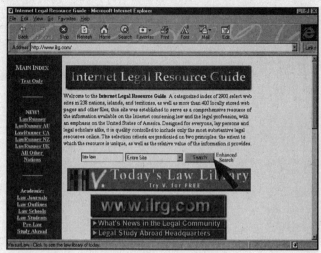

5 The Internet Legal Resources page provides a search engine to help you find what you need; type a topic in the search box and then click **Search**.

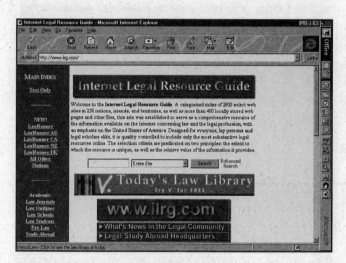

4 Another great site for legal information is the Internet Legal Resources page at **http://www.ilrg.com/**.

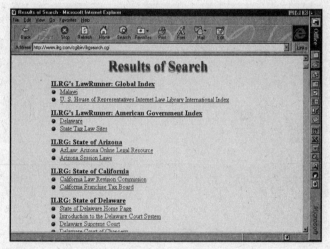

6 Your search will result in a page that provides links to information that is related to your search keywords.

(continues)

Do It Yourself   Look for Legal Advice

(continued)

7 A very comprehensive list of legal resources is provided by the legal dot Net page at **http://www.legal.net/** Click the **Dear Esquire** link.

9 Back on the Legal dot Net home page there is also a link to other legal resources, click **Legal Links**.

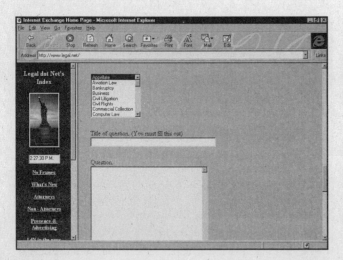

8 Scroll down the Dear Esquire page. This page allows you to ask a legal question, which will then be answered by a lawyer. Type all the necessary information into the various boxes and then click **Submit Question**.

10 You are given the choice of seeing the legal links listed by area or by name; click **By Name**.

Do It Yourself   Look for Legal Advice

11 A list of legal links is provided by name.

Another good place to search for legal sites is **http://www.pointcom.com**, the Point Review page. Click on the sites by subject link and then search **legal**. The screen that appears lists various Web sites, including the sites listed in this project.

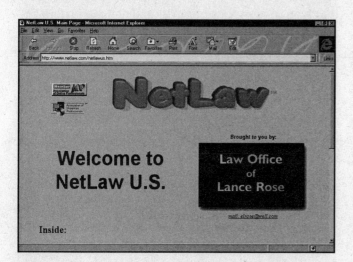

12 For those of you considering building a Web site some day, you can get advice on the legal aspects of the Net at the NetLaw page at **http://www.netlaw.com/netlawus.htm**.

13 Scroll down the page and click the **Build a Safer Web Site** link. This will take you to a page that gives you the legal ramifications of building of your own Web site.

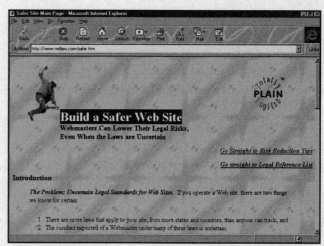

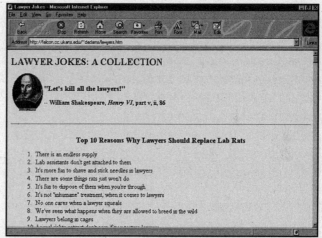

14 No search of legal advice on the Internet would be complete without a stop at a site that provides some jokes about lawyers. Go to **http://falcon.cc.ukans.edu/~dadams/lawyers.htm** and have a few laughs at the legal profession's expense.

Find Live Help Online

Most people have been in a situation at least once where they were working with a computer and something suddenly went wrong. And some people find themselves in that predicament time and time again. Where do you turn and what do you do when that happens? Unless you're working side-by-side with a computer guru, you don't have a lot of options.

Granted, most of today's software programs come with online help systems to assist with specific tasks, but often the help information in those stored databases cannot solve your problem. While you can also consult a computer manual in hopes of identifying and solving your problem, manuals are typically difficult to wade through and cannot always address your problem.

Now that you have an Internet connection, there's another alternative you can try—you can ask other Internet users. Simply log onto an IRC server and find a chat channel related to computers. Once you've found a channel, pop in and ask for help. Whether or not a channel focuses on computers, it probably has people willing to answer computer questions. All you have to do is ask. And if no one on that channel can help you, try another chat channel.

> **For more information about using Internet Relay Chat, turn to "Chat with People on the Internet" on page 241.**

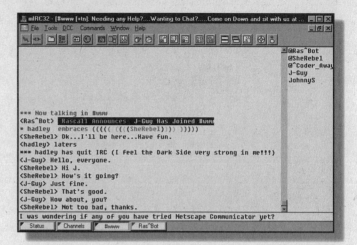

Internet Relay Chat (IRC) is a perfect place to look for live help when you're experiencing difficulties with your computer (assuming the difficulties don't keep you from using your computer to contact your Internet Service Provider or find your way online). Talking to a real person about your problem is much easier than consulting a database or manual. With a person, you can fully explain your problem, and he can respond to you—and sympathize. You won't get that type of a response from an online help system or a technical manual.

In this project, you'll learn how to find your way onto a computer-related chat channel and ask questions of other Internet users. To do this, you must have an IRC program installed, such as mIRC, and you have to log onto an IRC server (an Internet server dedicated to online chat). For a list of IRC servers, turn to the "Handy References" section on page 441. For help installing an IRC program, refer to "Find and Install an IRC Chat Program" on page 241.

Begin Do It Yourself   Find Live Help Using mIRC Chat

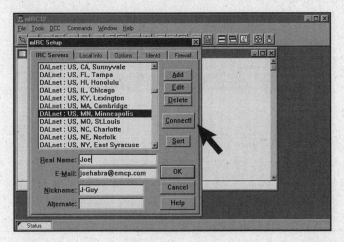

1 Start with your Internet account and mIRC running. Select the chat server you want to connect to in the Server Connection dialog box that appears when you the mIRC Chat client. Click **Connect** to make the connection.

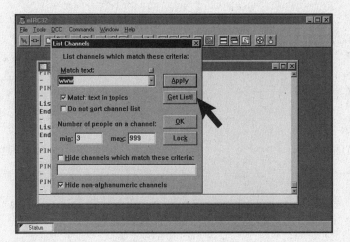

2 Click the **List Channels** button to open the List Channels dialog box. To search for a channel where you can get help on using the World Wide Web, type **WWW** in the Match Text box. Click on **Get List** to continue.

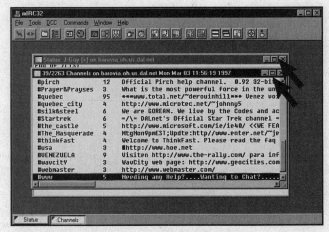

3 Double-click the channel you want to join from the list.

> To expand your chat channel window, click the window's **Maximize** button or drag the window's borders to a new size.

4 Once you're logged onto the chat channel, you can start talking. Type your question in the text box beneath the conversation window and press **Enter** to send it to the channel.

(continues)

Do It Yourself Find Live Help Using mIRC Chat

(continued)

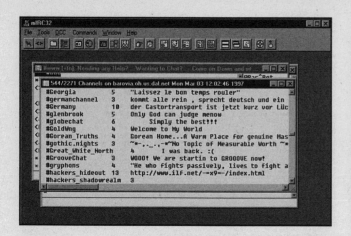

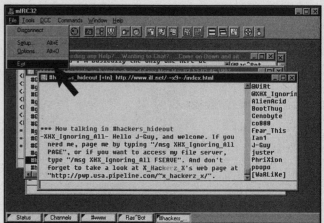

5 You may get a response to your question in no time at all—if the other people on the channel prove to be helpful. If you don't find any answers here, try another channel. To choose another channel, go back to the channel list.

6 When you're ready to leave the channel, close the channel window. To exit mIRC completely, select **File, Exit** or click the window's **Close** button.

Find the Latest Financial Report

Dozens of Web sites focus on financial information and news. But you don't have to be a Wall Street wizard to enjoy money matters on the Web. You can track the latest stock reports, find out late-breaking business news—before it's in print or on network TV—and dabble in all things financial.

The cable news network CNN has its own Web site, called CNNfn (CNN financial network), that's dedicated to financial news. You'll also find the *Wall Street Journal* online. And you can even tap into the Interactive NYSE Quote Server and view stock quotes within 15 minutes of the real thing.

Obviously, business users and those who are interested in financial reports will find plenty of sites to visit on the Internet. However, when you start visiting these Web sites, note that many of them require you to register before using their features. This simply means that you sign in and use a password each time you access the site. In most cases, these sites are free with registration, but others may want to charge you for use. Just be aware of this as you explore the many finance-focused avenues on the WWW.

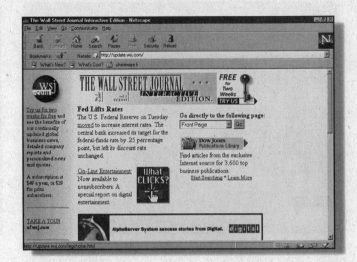

One of the best places to look up more Web sites that focus on financial matters is the Point Communications site (**http://www.pointcom.com**). Enter **financial reports** as the search text, and you'll see a long list of Web sites related to finances and investing.

This project takes you to some of the more popular Web sites that focus on financial matters. At any time, feel free to explore features or links that may be of specific interest to you.

Begin Do It Yourself   Tour Financial Web Sites Using Netscape

 Connect to the Internet and start Internet Explorer (or any other Web browser). In the **Address** text box, **http://www.cnnfn.com/** and press **Enter**.

(continues)

Do It Yourself Tour Financial Web Sites Using Netscape *(continued)*

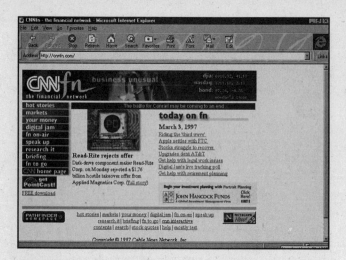

2 This is CNN's financial network site, where you'll find the latest financial news and information. The links on the left side of the page lead you to various types of financial information. To view the latest financial news, click the **hot stories** link.

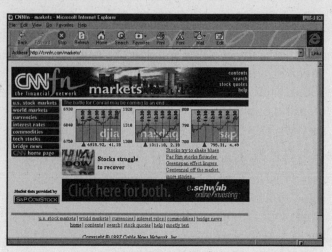

4 To explore the latest market reports, click the **Back** button and then click the **Markets** icon on the left side of the Web page. This opens the Markets Main Page, from which you can explore specific financial markets.

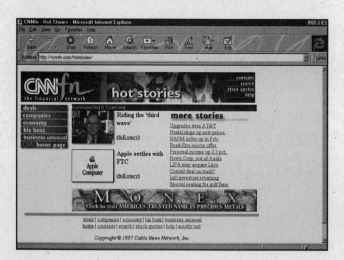

3 Explore late-breaking news reports by clicking the headlines of any stories that interest you.

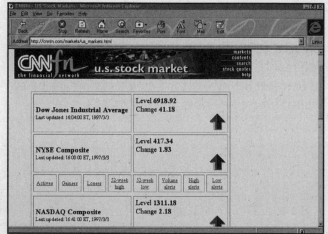

5 To take a look at U.S. stock markets, click the **U.S. Stock Markets** link.

6 On the U.S. Stock Markets page (shown here), scroll down and look at the latest figures.

Do It Yourself   Tour Financial Web Sites Using Netscape

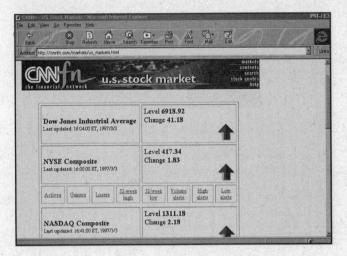

7 To get information on a specific stock, click the **stock quotes** link at the top of the page.

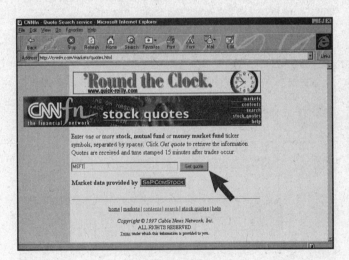

8 Enter the ticker symbol of a specific stock in the text box and click the **Get quote** button.

If you're unsure about ticker symbols (what they are or which ones to use), click the **Help** link.

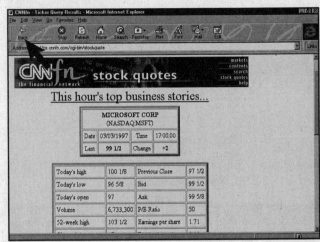

9 The information you asked for appears on-screen. You can return to the previous page by clicking **Back**.

10 One of the coolest financial stops on the Web is the InvestorsEdge site. As you might expect, it provides the latest investment information; but if you stick around the home page for a moment or two, you'll see that the stock ticker scrolls horizontally across your screen with the latest figures. To access InvestorsEdge, type **http://www.irnet.com/** and press **Enter**.

Another place you can tap into the NYSE stock ticker display is on the Interactive NYSE Quote Server (**http://www.secapl.com/cgi-bin/qs**).

(continues)

Do It Yourself Tour Financial Web Sites Using Netscape

(continued)

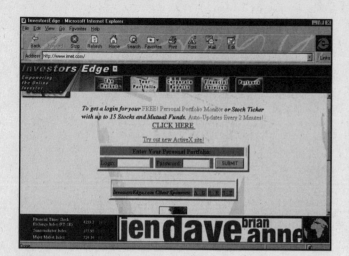

11 InvestorsEdge has a neat interactive feature that lets you build a pretend portfolio of six different stocks and then track them to see how they do. Click the **Your Portfolio** option and follow the on-screen instructions to create a virtual portfolio. You will have to assign yourself a username and password.

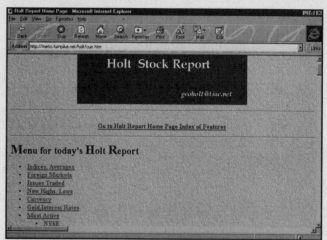

13 To check out the most recent closing report, scroll down and click the **Most Recent Closing Report** link. Then scroll down the page to find a menu of financial features like the one shown here. Explore whichever topics interest you.

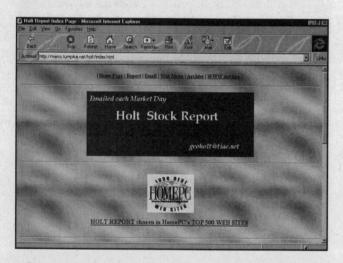

12 Another good place to check financial reports is the Holt Report Index site, which gives you access to market activity reports, financial news, archives of old reports, and links to other financial Web sites. The Holt Report Index is located at **http://metro.turnpike.net/holt/index.html**.

14 No financial tour would be complete without a visit to the Wall Street Journal site (**http://update.wsj.com/**). To take a tour of the site click the **TAKE A TOUR** link.

Do It Yourself Tour Financial Web Sites Using Netscape

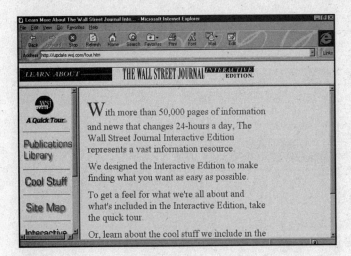

15 The Tour page provides you with links to previews of various Wall Street Journal resources as well as the short tour itself. Click the **A Quick Tour** icon, then click the **Main Sections** link.

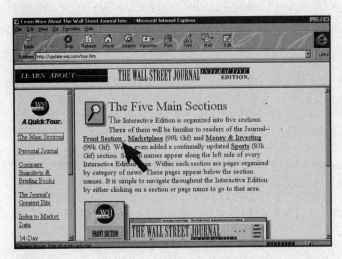

16 You are provided with information on the five parts of the Web version of the Journal. Click the **Front Section** link.

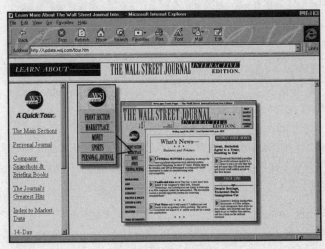

17 You're shown a diagram of the key features of the Journal's front page. You may find the tour interesting but not that informative.

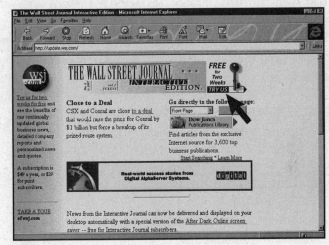

18 To sign up for a trial subscription return to the main page of the Journal and click the **FREE for Two Weeks Try Us** link.

19 To exit your browser at any time, click the **Close** button or select **File, Exit**.

Let Your Kids Color on a Web Coloring Book

The World Wide Web isn't just for adults, there are plenty of educational and entertaining Web sites that cater to children of all ages. Kids are just as interested in the Internet as adults and aren't as likely to be intimidated by the technology. In fact, many of today's kids know more about computers than their parents.

While you certainly don't want your children to explore the Internet without parental guidance and rules, you can help them find lots of fun things to do online. To track down kid-related sites, turn to Internet magazines that list Web sites, or use a search tool such as the Yahoo! Search site (**http://yahoo. com/search.html**). You'll quickly find numerous Web sites with kid appeal, such as Sports Illustrated for Kids Online (**http://www.pathfinder.com/SIFK/**) and The Big Busy House (**http://www.harpercollins. com/kids/**).

This project takes you to Carlos' Coloring Book so you can color a picture on your computer. Don't forget to let your kids have a try!

> For help using Internet search tools, turn to "Search for Information on the Web" on page 170.

A really neat place for younger kids to visit is the Carlos' Coloring Book site. It's incredibly simple to use and offers six pictures to color. Older kids and adults are bound to like it, too. It's an interactive Web page on which the user electronically colors pictures using techniques much like those of a paint program. When you finish coloring, you can save the picture as a GIF file and use your Web browser to download it onto your own computer.

> To find links to other great kid sites on the Web, use one of the Web search engines, such as WebCrawler. Lycos also supplies an alphabetical lists of kids sites at **http://a2z.lycos.com/ Just_For_Kids/**. I suggest you check out the Looney Tunes Home Page (**http://www-personal.usyd.edu.au/~swishart/looney.html**) or the Crayola Kids page (**http://www.crayola. com/crayola/crayolakids/home.html**) for even more fun.

Begin Do It Yourself   Color a Picture on a Web Page

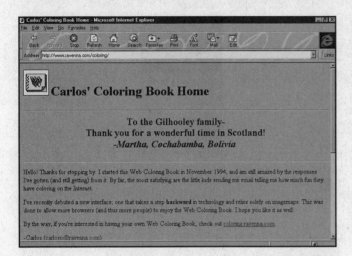

1 Connect to the Internet and start your Web browser. In the **Location** or **Go to** text box, type **http://www.ravenna.com/coloring/** and press **Enter**.

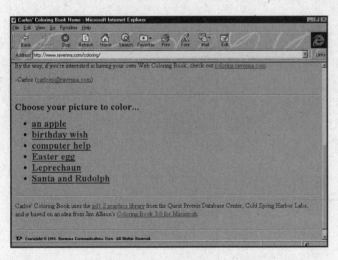

2 The Carlos' Coloring Book Home page appears. Scroll down the page until you reach a list of pictures.

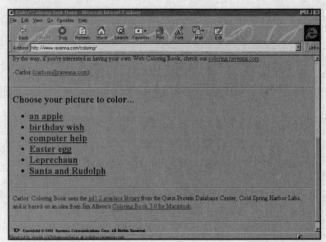

3 In the picture list, click the one you want to color.

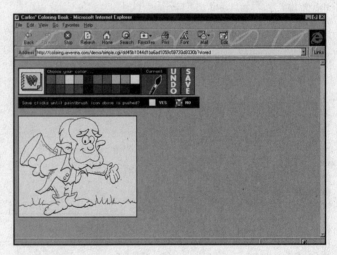

4 A color palette appears at the top of the page. Click the color you want to use, and it is displayed in the Current box (with the paintbrush icon).

(continues)

Do It Yourself   Color a Picture on a Web Page *(continued)*

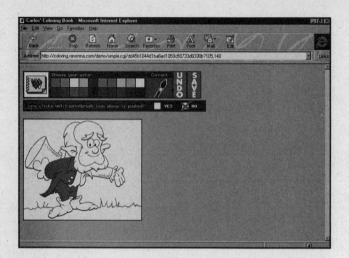

5 Move your mouse pointer to the area of the picture that you want to fill in with the selected color. You may have to scroll down the page to see the entire illustration. Click the area of the picture that you want to fill in, and it becomes the color you selected.

6 To change colors, select another color from the color palette. Repeat steps 4 and 5 until you finish the entire picture.

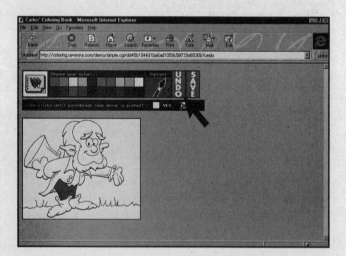

7 If you make a mistake at any time or change your mind about the color you filled in, click the **Undo** button.

8 To save the picture as a GIF file in a temporary directory on the server, click the **Save** button. Then click the **File** menu and select **Save As** to save the picture.

For more information about downloading files from the Internet, turn to "Find and Copy Files from the Internet" on page 179.

9 To color another picture, return to the Carlos' Coloring Book Home page by pressing the **Back** button. Choose another picture from the list.

Look Up the Latest Weather Report

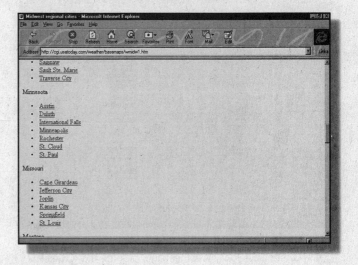

Want to find out what the weather's going to be like in your area of the country? Oh, sure, you can turn on the TV news or radio and find out—but it's just as easy to check the weather using your Internet connection. You can check any of dozens of Web sites for your local forecast, or you can pick up information about weather around the world.

Why check the weather with your computer? If you work in an office with no windows, you'll find it convenient: A quick visit to a weather Web site lets you know what's going on outside without ever leaving your office. Planning a business trip for the next few days? Take a peek at the extended forecast for that area so you know what to pack. Is it snowing at your favorite ski resort? That information is just a keystroke or two away. Online weather reports are constantly updated and easy to locate, as you'll learn in this project.

Not only do you have access to the latest forecasts around the world, but you can also tap into such weather information as satellite pictures, weather

history, rainfall tables, and even weather videos. Weather Web sites can be a great source of data for weather watchers everywhere and of all ages.

This project shows you several Weather-related Web sites. Feel free to deviate from the steps to follow links that may be of interest to you. There's a lot to explore when it comes to weather data.

Begin Do It Yourself Take a Tour of Weather-Related Web Sites

1 Connect to the Internet and start your Web browser. Go to the *USA Today* weather page by typing the URL **http:// web.usatoday.com/** and pressing **Enter**.

2 Click the **Weather** button.

(continues)

Do It Yourself Take a Tour of Weather-Related Web Sites

(continued)

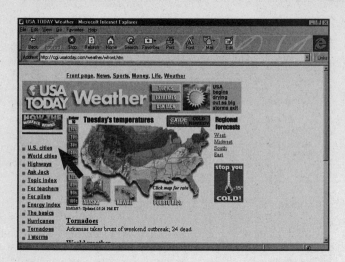

3 On the *USA Today* Weather page, click the **U.S. Cities** link.

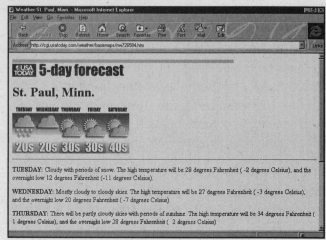

5 A five-day weather forecast for the selected city appears.

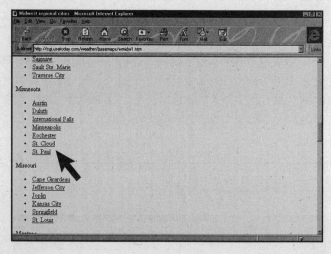

4 Scroll down and select the city nearest you. Click the city's link.

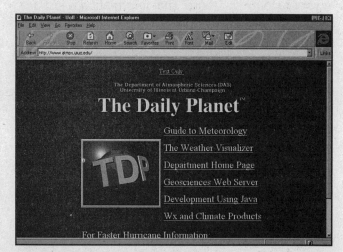

6 Let's jump to another Web site and look at a satellite photo. Type **http://www.atmos.uiuc.edu/** and press **Enter** to go to the University of Illinois Weather World site. Click the **Weather Visualizer** link.

Do It Yourself   Take a Tour of Weather-Related Web Sites

7 Click the **Satellite Imagery** button.

9 A satellite image corresponding to your imagery selections appears.

10 When you have completed your weather Web browsing click the **Close** button to close your Web browser.

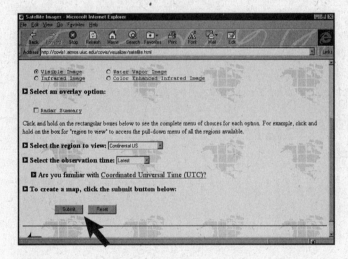

You can search for other weather sites on the Web using any of the search engines available. Another good site to check out for weather information is the National Weather Service site at **http://cominfo.nws.noaa.gov/**.

8 On the next page you can select the region to view and the time that the satellite image was taken. Once you make your selections, click **Submit**.

PART 3

Quick Fixes

This is the part of the book that no one really wants to read because if you have to turn to this part, you must be having a problem. But don't despair! This part contains 101 of the most common Internet-related problems, as well as their solutions. You won't have to fumble through the whole book saying to yourself, "I know I've seen the solution in here somewhere." The solutions are all right here for easy reference.

To use this section, look for your problem in the Quick-Finder table. The problems are grouped into such categories as connection problems, e-mail problems, problems with the Web, and problems with FTP. When you find your problem in the Quick-Finder table, turn to the listed page number to find the solution.

What You Will Find in This Part

Connection Frustrations

My modem is not receiving a dial tone.

The dial tone signals that the modem is properly attached to the actual phone line. On occasion, you may not hear a dial tone through the modem speaker, or you may receive an error message, such as "No dial tone" from your communications software. There are two common causes for this problem: a bad connection or a wrong configuration.

Checking to see if the phone line is improperly or incompletely connected to the modem is easy. Check the back of the modem, and be sure that the phone line from the wall is plugged into the modem jack labeled "line" or "in." If you want a telephone or answering machine unit on the same line, it should be connected to the modem jack labeled "phone" or "out."

Checking the configuration is slightly more difficult. To make sure you've configured your software to use the correct COM port, in Windows 95, open **My Computer**, select **Control Panel**, and click **Modems**. You should see the name of your modem. Click the **Properties** button. The dialog box shown in the next figure appears. If there is no way to select a COM port and one is already listed, Windows 95 installed your modem as a Plug and Play device and determined the correct COM port on its own. If, on the other hand, you have the option to select a COM port, you may have the wrong one selected. The thick gray cable that connects your modem to your PC plugs into your PC's serial port. Your PC's manufacturer assigned each serial port a COM number between 1 and 4. Most PCs use COM 2 for the serial port; some use 3. If you aren't sure which is correct, try each one, or contact the manufacturer.

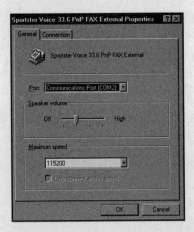

Although internal modems are not connected by cable to an external serial port, they are preconfigured to use a particular COM port, such as COM1 or COM2. Windows 95 should be able to automatically detect which COM port the internal modem is on. If it doesn't seem to be right, check the documentation or try each possibility.

If neither of those things seems to fix the problem, make sure the phone line from the wall is functioning properly. Plug a regular phone directly into the wall and check for a dial tone. Maybe you didn't pay your bill! (It happens—as I well know.)

I can't hear the modem dialing.

Most modems have a built-in speaker through which you can hear the dial and connect tones (that series of screeching sounds that would scare away even the most territorial of cats). Whether you listen to the modem's tones is usually a matter of personal preference; however, with some modems, those tones can let you know what is going on. For example, if you have an internal modem that has no other display, you may have to listen for the dial tones to make sure it is actually working.

In Windows 95, you can configure the modem speaker through the Modem Properties settings. Open **My Computer**, select **Control Panel**, and click **Modems**. You should then see the name of your modem. Click the **Properties** button. In the dialog box is a volume slider that controls the modem speaker (see the following figure). Drag the slider to any position you want, from low to medium to full blast.

Volume slider ——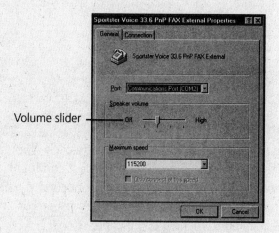

If you're not using Windows 95, configuring the modem speaker is a bit trickier. Most common modems share a command set, called AT commands. This tells the modem that it should pay attention to the next command. So to disable the modem's internal speaker, for example, you would type the command **AT M0** directly into the terminal program and press **Enter**. The next figure shows an example of using an AT command in HyperTerminal (the terminal program included with Windows 95).

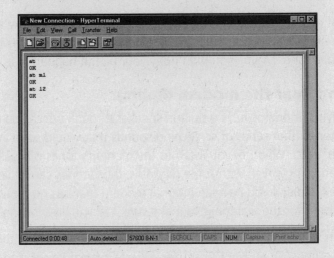

In response to your command, the modem returns **OK** to let you know that it under-stood the command. Other speaker-related AT commands include the following:

AT M1   Enable internal speaker

AT L1   Set speaker volume to low

AT L2   Set speaker volume to medium

AT L3   Set speaker volume to high

The line is busy. Can I auto-redial?

Some phone numbers are constantly busy, especially if you attempt to connect at peak hours (such as prime time on weeknights). Most communications software has a feature you can use to redial automatically until a connection is made—which gives you the freedom to make popcorn or eat Ben & Jerry's instead of sitting in front of the modem for 20 minutes trying to make a connection.

Each communications package is different, so it is impossible to describe exactly how each redial feature works; however, it is usually a very basic feature. If you use Windows 95's built-in Dial-Up Networking to connect to the Internet, you may find that you need to configure it to support redialing. To do that, follow these steps.

1. In Windows 95, open **My Computer** and select **Dial-Up Networking**.

2. From the Dial-Up Networking window, select **Connections** and select the **Settings** command.

3. In the configuration window that appears, check the **Redial** option (if it's not already selected). Then enter settings for how many times you want the modem to redial before giving up, and for how much time the modem should wait between attempts.

4. When you finish, click **OK** to save your settings for auto redialing.

For users of Trumpet Winsock with Windows 3.1, the redialing capability is built into the default login script that comes with the software. You'll encounter Trumpet login scripting in a bit more detail later in this section.

The line simply rings and rings.

If the line is ringing—that is, if you hear the traditional dialing sound coming from your modem's speaker—you know that the line is functioning. Actually, when the line just rings and rings, the problem is not on your end, but on the end you are trying to connect to.

A somewhat common problem for Internet Service Providers (ISP) is called *ringthrough*. Your ISP (the people you dial to access the Internet) has a series of modems. Although you dial only one phone number, you're supposed to be connected to the first available modem in the series. Sometimes a modem goes bad, and you're connected to one of these dud modems that doesn't answer the line. It simply rings and rings and rings. That is a ringthrough, and you should certainly notify your provider if this sort of thing is happening. Sometimes they don't realize that a modem is bad; it's tough for them to know because they don't dial in to their own modems. Other than that, the only thing you can do is hang up and dial again—and hope that you won't be connected to a dud modem.

The modem is connecting at the wrong speed.

Modem speeds often cause major confusion. All communications software enables you to select a baud rate for your modem connection. The general recommendation is that people with 14.4Kbps modems should select a baud rate of 57,600Kbps, and people with 28.8Kbps modems should select a baud rate of 115,200Kbps. But why?

The 14.4 and 28.8 numbers indicate the speed at which your modem can communicate with the other modem (assuming they both support the same speed). The 57.6 and 115.2 numbers indicate the speeds at which your modem and your own computer communicate. When you see communications software reporting the speed of a connection, it's important that you know which number it is telling you.

Users of Windows 95's Dial-Up Networking should note that once you're connected, a little window pops up saying **Connected at *some speed***. This is the modem-to-modem speed. If you have a 28.8Kbps modem and are connecting to another 28.8Kbps modem, you should see a number close to 28,800.

Now, you do want to pay attention if a reported connection speed is lower than the speed of your modem. For example, if you have a 14.4Kbps modem but receive connection speeds of only, say, 9,600 or 12,000, that is something to take note of. What might be the cause of that trouble? It's most likely a result of difficulties between the two modems attempting to connect. The trouble may lie in modem configuration settings on your end or on the other end.

On your end, the easiest solution is to try resetting the modem to factory defaults—just in case you somehow messed with certain connect speed settings. You usually do this using the **AT &F0** or **AT &F1** modem command in a terminal program; however, you should check your modem manual to be sure. If the problem is a modem on the other end, there's little you can do except notify the person who maintains that system. Then you might try dialing in again to see if you get another modem.

Lastly, two modems can connect only at the maximum speed of the slower modem. So a 14.4Kbps modem can only connect at 14.4 if the other modem supports at least 14.4. Similarly, a 28.8Kbps modem can only achieve that speed with another 28.8Kbps modem. When a 28.8Kbps modem connects with a 14.4Kbps modem, however, the fastest possible connection speed is 14.4Kbps. So it's good to know the speed of the modem you are calling (your provider will be able to tell you). If you connect to a modem slower than your own, you'll wind up with a connection at the slower speed.

I never connect at 28.8 even though I paid handsomely for a 28.8 modem.

Because so many variables can prevent a proper 28.8Kbps connection, it's surprising that they occur at all. Analog phone lines (the kind that connect your house and the local phone company) are the remains of older technology: they were not designed for high-speed digital communications. Communication at the speed of 28,800Kbps truly pushes these lines further than they can often handle. To achieve these speeds, the lines need to be of perfect quality and have no noise or interference along the way.

Many factors can cause interference. Poor-quality in-home wiring, the distance of a call, and the quality of phone lines in a general region all affect the amount of interference. In addition, the quality of the modems plays a part. A cheaper 28.8 modem is not likely to achieve 28.8Kbps connections under imperfect conditions; a more expensive one may be better able to maximize your connection speed on lines with minor imperfections.

Real-world results seem to indicate that many people can achieve 28.8Kbps connections on local calls between themselves and a provider who is only a few miles away. Many who can't reach 28.8 can usually reach 26.4, which is fairly close in terms of speed. However, if you are attempting to make long-distance connections, your chances of such speeds drop considerably.

I get garbage characters coming over the line.

Some people, when they are connected to their Internet account via modem, will see some garbage characters on the screen. By garbage characters, I simply mean nonsensical groups of symbols and characters, such as D##$@!~~+ . Garbage characters basically signal errors in data transmission coming over the line. These errors are often caused by noisy phone lines.

Most modern high-speed modems have built in error correction and should be able to detect such errors in transmission *before* you see the results. After they have found an error, these modems request retransmission of the data from the other end. Of course, this error correction only works to a point: If the lines are of absolutely atrocious quality, the modem will not be able to succeed in correcting errors and will probably just disconnect. However, that's a rare exception. Most people's lines are of decent but not perfect quality, in which case, some errors will arise.

Except for some of the cheapest 14.4 and 28.8 models, most modems include built-in error correction features that can handle regular, random errors. Therefore, a properly functioning error-correcting modem should not yield garbage characters. If—as a last resort—you need to disable error-correction, try resetting the modem to its factory settings. You can usually do this with the **AT &F0** or **AT &F1** command, but check the manual for certain. Some modems use DIP switches to determine factory settings.

Slow modems, especially those as slow as 2,400 baud, may not have any built-in error correction. Some do, but many do not. The ones that do not are definitely prone to spewing out garbage characters.

Letters are missing from the words when I use my account.

The problem of missing letters is called *dropping characters*, and it's as simple as it sounds: some of the data is lost on the way. Most often, this happens when you have the connection speed between your modem and the PC set higher than your PC can handle. While it is generally recommended, for example, that you configure your software to 57,600 baud for a 14.4 modem, slower CPUs may not be able to keep up.

The solution is to try lowering the speed of the computer's baud rate. If you have a 14.4Kbps modem, try lowering your baud rate to 38,400. You can lower the baud rate as much as necessary until it quits dropping characters—as long as the baud rate doesn't drop lower than the speed of the modem. Although lowering the baud rate limits the maximum speed at which you can transfer data, it's better than losing characters.

To change the computer's baud rate in Windows 95, open **My Computer**, select **Control Panel**, and click **Modems**. You should then see the name of your modem. Click the **Properties** button. At the bottom of the window pictured here, notice the setting labeled Maximum speed.

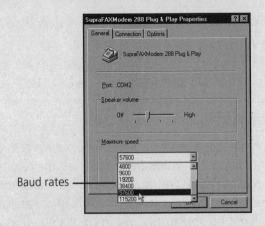

Baud rates

You can select the baud rate at which you want the modem to *attempt* a connection. I don't advise that you check the box just above the ok button marked **Only connect at this speed**. If you do enable it and the modem cannot connect at the selected baud rate, it will abort the connection attempt entirely.

Although Windows 3.1 offers a similar configuration in its Control Panel, virtually all communications software written for 3.1 ignores this setting. Instead, they provide their own configurations. So Windows 3.1 users will set the desired baud rate when setting the options of the communications software itself (such as their terminal programs).

Download speed is slower than I expected.

The first way to approach this question is to consider what you're expecting. Although modems' advertisements put a lot of emphasis on a speed (such as 28.8Kbps), it's not immediately obvious just how this number boils down into actual data transfer speeds.

Ultimately, data transfer speed depends on two main factors: the method of transfer (what protocols are used), and the data being transferred (how compressible is it). Making a few assumptions about these two factors, one can provide relatively accurate expectations.

Many large downloads consist of precompressed files (such as .ZIP files, .JPG files, and .GIF files). Thus, these files will not benefit much from the modem's built-in compression routines. For these sorts of files (and they are the most commonly transferred types), you can expect the following rough estimates.

Protocol	Modem Speed	Reasonable Expectation
Zmodem	14.4Kbps	1600–1650 cps
Zmodem	28.8Kbps	1.2–1.4 K/sec
FTP/WWW	14.4Kbps	3200–3300 cps
FTP/WWW	28.8Kbps	2.8–3.2 K/sec

Note that in the expected speed column, I've used two different forms to express the same information. Most programs using Zmodem report transfer speeds in the form of cps, while most FTP/WWW programs report transfer speeds in the form of K/sec. As a means of comparison, cps divided by 1,024 equals K/sec.

More compressible files (such as plain text files) will yield higher speeds than those listed above. So if you're pulling in speeds higher than these estimates (some text files can transfer up to four times faster), you don't need to worry at all. However, if you're pulling in speeds slower than these, you have a problem. Read on.

If you are using Zmodem, the most common causes of slow transfers are CRC errors. Skip ahead to the next problem to learn what to do. If you are using FTP or WWW, you face a potentially more confusing scenario. There are three major causes of slow transfers via FTP/WWW.

- **CRC errors.** As with Zmodem, CRC errors can be the problem with FTP/WWW transfers. Again, skip down to the next problem to learn how to banish CRC errors.

- **Poorly tuned MTU/RWIN settings in your TCP/IP software.** These settings essentially fine-tune the flow of data in and out of your computer. These are somewhat complicated settings to explain in a Quick Fix, and what's worse is that Microsoft's Dial-Up Networking makes them difficult to access. First, ask your service provider what MTU setting to use with their system. Then, if you use Trumpet Winsock, read the Trumpet Winsock documentation or the Trumpet Winsock coverage in this book to learn how to adjust these settings. If you use Windows 95, go to the Web site **http://www.windows95.com** and follow the links to information on how to modify the settings. You can also find discussions and help on these matters in the Usenet newsgroups at **alt.winsock**, **alt.winsock.trumpet**, and **comp.os.ms-windows.networking.tcp-ip**.

- **Heavy network traffic on the Internet.** The Internet is a place of varying busyness, and everyone has to share the same pathways. Thus, it is vulnerable to traffic jams. Even if you have the correct configurations, if you attempt to transfer large files—especially from far-away machines—across the Internet during high usage hours (business hours), you're likely to run into slowdowns. The only solution is to try finding information on geographically closer servers or servers that are less heavily used, or to wait until off-peak hours.

My communications software is reporting many "overrun" or "CRC" errors.

This error occurs when the data flows into your PC too quickly for your PC to process it. It is, in essence, a flood. This data overrun causes the PC to have to request repeat transmission of the lost data. Repeating transmission wastes time. And because you're transferring the same data multiple times, many repeated transmissions result in a slower overall transfer speed for the data.

Overruns (which are called *CRC errors* by some software) are the result of problems unrelated to your software configurations or what protocol you are using. They represent a more fundamental problem in which your computer cannot keep up with the incoming flow of data. Although many factors influence whether your computer is able to keep up, a few specific things cause the majority of all overruns.

- **The UART**   This only applies if you use an external modem. Your serial port (which is probably part of your I/O card) has a buffer on it that is intended to prevent data overruns. This buffer is called a UART chip. Old serial cards have a UART model 8250 or 16450. These older UARTs are generally not sufficient for today's high-speed modems of 14.4Kbps and higher. Current I/O cards have model numbers of 16550A or higher (16550AFN, for example), which are capable of higher speed buffering. Thus, the first and foremost recommendation if you experience many overruns is to check your UART.

  Checking your UART is simple. Whether you use Windows 3.1 or Windows 95, you must first exit to DOS; you *cannot* just open a DOS window. In Windows 3.1, then, open the **File** menu and select **Exit**; in Windows 95, click **Start**, select **Shutdown**, and click **Restart the Computer in MS-DOS Mode**. At the DOS prompt, type **msd** and press **Enter**. In that program, select **COM ports**, and it tells you what UART model you have. If it's not 16550A or higher, the simplest solution is to buy a new I/O card. (They cost around $30.) Most new PCs already have proper UARTs, but older ones may not.

The UART on this modem's COM port →

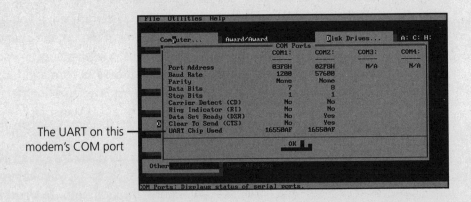

In addition, if you use Windows 3.1, you must tell it to use the UART by adding the line **COMxFIFO=1** in the [386enh] section of your windows\system.ini file. Replace **x** with the number of the COM port to which your modem is installed. Thus, if your modem is on COM 2 (which is common), the line should read **COM2FIFO=1**.

If you use Windows 95, verify that the UART (also called a FIFO) is functioning by opening **My Computer** and selecting **Control Panel**, **Modems**, **Properties**, **Connection**, and **Port Settings**. Check the **Use FIFO buffers** option if it's not already enabled.

- **Old hardware drivers** Drivers for some video cards and some hard drives use nasty tricks to increase their own performance, and in doing so, they cause Windows to be susceptible to data overruns. If you are still receiving many overrun errors and you've ruled out the UART as the source of the problem, contact the manufacturers of your video card and hard drive (or ask around on the Net) for updated, current drivers. Many manufacturers now offer drivers that will behave themselves.

The modem seems to hang up randomly while connected.

Sometimes you'll be merrily Netting along, when the modem will just hang up—apparently out of the blue. Why? One common cause is call waiting, which is discussed in detail in the problem "I want to disable or enable call waiting" (page 390). Aside from that, you need to try to determine whether the culprit is on your end of the connection or at the other end. Let's do a little detective work.

Do you only connect to one phone number? Try calling other modems in the area—local Bulletin Board Services, other service providers, and so forth—and see if it happens with them. This kind of experimentation helps you get an idea of whether the cause is you or your provider.

Next, ask other subscribers to your provider if they have the same problem. More often than not, random disconnects are problems on the provider's end, sometimes due to differing brands of modems. Most modems are supposed to be able to talk to one another regardless of manufacturer, but there are some exceptions. (One particular modem model may have trouble communicating with another particular model, for example.)

Finally, although random disconnects probably are not the result of a configuration problem on your end, if you aren't sure, try the factory reset command. You may have twiddled some esoteric setting that set it off. (Modern modems have hundreds of esoteric settings.)

My #!?@ roommates keep lifting the phone extension and ruining my connection.

This is not an uncommon problem in households or apartments in which multiple devices use the same phone line. Often, both a phone in the kitchen and the modem in the bedroom are on the same line. When someone in the kitchen lifts up the phone and hears the horrible screech of the modem, they have succeeded in ruining the connection. A solution? There are three possibilities.

Obviously, multiple phone lines are a solution, but not everyone can afford that. If it's not an option for you, try talking to the other people in the house to work out some system of knowing who is on the line.

If diplomacy doesn't work, try a technological solution. Most modems have a jack in the back for a phone. Some modems, if they are online, disable the phone hooked to this jack. Thus, although it's a wiring nightmare, if you can connect the aforementioned kitchen phone to the back of the modem, the phone will be disabled when the modem is in use. However, this only works with a modem that does, in fact, disable its phone jack when online.

The only other answer lies at that ubiquitous of gadget stores: Radio Shack. They sell a little doohickey that you can place on the phone line that disables one extension when the other is in use. That doohickey is called a "Teleprotector" (Radio Shack catalog #43-107), and it sells for approximately $10.

I want to disable or enable call waiting.

To many, the bane of telephone conversations is also the bane of modem communications. If you are using the modem when a call waiting beep comes down the lines, your connection will probably be broken. You may or may not appreciate this. Some people who are online frequently but cannot afford a second line may prefer being knocked off the line to having their callers get busy signals all day long. However, most people prefer not to be interrupted while online.

If you don't want those interruptions, you can usually disable call waiting on a per-call basis by inserting ***70** into the dial string of your communications software. For example, if you normally dial **555-1515** to access your service provider, change it so your software dials ***70,555-1515**. The *70 prefix works in most telephone regions. If it does not seem to work for you, contact the local phone company to find out how to disable call waiting. Note that this disables call waiting only during the current call; as soon as you disconnect the modem, call waiting is automatically enabled again.

When I quit my connection, the modem doesn't hang up the line.

Most communications software has some feature to "hang up." This isn't always the same as exiting. With some software, if you quit the software but do not choose to hang up the line, the modem won't disconnect.

The obvious rule is to hang up before you exit the software. However, if you forget to hang up first and the modem doesn't hang up automatically, try running the communications software again. It may hang up the line when it starts in order to clear it for use. If that doesn't work, try to run your terminal program and select **hang up**. The terminal program should pass the hang up command to the modem.

If you have an external modem, you can flip the power switch (turn it off and back on). Another possibility is to unplug the phone wire from the telephone jack and then plug it back in. Finally, as a last resort, reboot Windows, but only if all else fails.

E-Mail Troubles

The e-mail I sent came back to me undelivered.

This is known as *bounced* mail. It means that the mail could not be delivered to the specified recipient. A couple of things cause mail to bounce.

- **There's no such user.** The recipient you specified doesn't exist. Either you have the wrong e-mail address, or you typed it wrong.

- **The mailbox is full.** There isn't enough room in the recipient's mailbox to hold your e-mail.

When you receive a bounced e-mail, you get your original message back along with a brief explanation of the problem. For example, you might see a message like this at the top of the bounced message:

```
----- The following addresses had delivery problems -----
<markymark@interlog.com>  (unrecoverable error)
    ----- Transcript of session follows -----
... while talking to gold.interlog.com.:
>>> RCPT To:<markymark@interlog.com>
<<< 550 <markymark@interlog.com>... User unknown
550 <markymark@interlog.com>... User unknown
```

As you can see, in this example, the error is described as **User unknown**. In such a case, check your spelling to see if you made a typo in the address. Note that capitalization does not matter in an e-mail address, so that would not be the cause of a User unknown error.

My e-mail was never delivered to the other party, but it didn't bounce.

An e-mail message travels through several computers on the way to its ultimate destination. Sometimes one of these computers may be down temporarily. Or the destination computer itself might be down. In these cases, there will obviously be a delay in delivery.

There are procedures in place on the Internet that try to overcome obstacles. If the destination computer is down, delivery will often be attempted periodically (automatically—without your assistance or knowledge) until it's successful. Sometimes, however, it does not succeed after several attempts, usually because of network problems with the destination computer or another computer near that end of the line. In some such cases, after several days you will receive a warning e-mail saying that your message could not be successfully delivered. This is not a bounce, it's a notification. The system will continue to attempt delivery for a specified period of time.

Suppose you have a persistent problem with your e-mail not reaching recipients in various locations. If your e-mail seems to have truly vanished, you need to check two possible suspects: your e-mail software and your outgoing mail server (provided by your service provider).

- Make sure your e-mail software is, in fact, sending the e-mail and not queuing it. Mail applications such as Eudora and Pegasus Mail offer you the option whether to "queue" outgoing mail or send it immediately. If you choose to queue your mail, all of your composed messages are stored on your hard drive to be sent out in one batch when you instruct the program to "send all queued mail." Of course, if you never tell it to send the queued mail, that mail will never leave your PC. Queuing is generally only useful for users who compose mail offline and then dial in to their provider when they're ready to send all their e-mail in one batch. For users who remain online while they write e-mail, it's more sensible to have the mailer actually send it out when you complete the composition.

- Your service provider's outgoing server may not be working properly or reliably. You have two options: to speak to your provider or to use a different outgoing server. The outgoing server is known as the SMTP server, and you can configure it via options in your e-mail application. Often, you can use any SMTP server—not just the one your provider offers. Check around and see if you can find another provider locally, such as at a nearby university. If so, find out the name of their server (often, they are named in the form *mail.providername.com* or something very similar). If you find another SMTP server that's more reliable, stick with it. However, considering you are paying your ISP, it is worth talking to them about their server.

I need to send the same message to multiple people.

This is an easy one! There are two ways you can do this, depending on your needs.

- You can often include multiple e-mail addresses in the To: header, separated by commas. Perhaps more commonly, you can use the CC: header line provided by most e-mail programs to enter one or more addresses. This sends "carbon copies" of the one message to all cc recipients. Thus, you can address your message in either of the following ways:

**To: person1@isp.com,person2@otherisp.com,
person3@yetanotherisp.com**

or

**To: person1@isp.com
Subject: Hello
CC: person2@otherisp.com,person3@yetanotherisp.com**

- You can use distribution lists. Some e-mail applications enable you to create a distribution list. A distribution list contains multiple e-mail addresses that you can refer to with one label—very useful if you frequently send memos out to the same group of people. For example, you could create a list of all the people in your immediate department and name the whole group "Co-workers." Then when you compose a message in that e-mail program, you can simply address it **To: Co-workers**, and the message is sent to all the people on the list. Check to see if your e-mail program has this capability.

When I retrieve my e-mail, I keep receiving old messages along with the new.

Many users nowadays have SLIP/PPP accounts. You dial in to your provider and check e-mail with a program such as Eudora or Pegasus Mail. These programs retrieve your e-mail from a machine known as a POP server. The POP server holds all the e-mail that is sent to you.

Most e-mail programs allow you to configure at least two options related to retrieving this mail: a "delete mail from server" option and a "download only unread/new mail" option. If you choose to enable mail deletion, the program deletes each message after it is downloaded to your PC. Of course, the only copies of those messages are on your PC, and if you delete or lose them, they're gone for good. On the other hand, deleting from the server might be better, because you probably have a mailbox size limit and don't want all the mail you've ever received to keep piling up on the server.

If you turn on the mail deletion option, the "download only..." option is irrelevant. But if you prefer to leave your mail on the server instead of deleting it after retrieval, you will probably want to enable the download only unread/new mail option. If you don't enable this option, every time you check mail, *all* of your messages will be downloaded, including those you have downloaded in the past. If you do enable this option, only new messages will be downloaded; the rest remain on the server.

Although each e-mail application is different, these options are usually among the Network configurations settings. For Pegasus Mail users, for example, use the **File**, **Network Configuration** command to access these options.

How can I have e-mail checked automatically?

Almost all e-mail applications allow for *background polling*. This means that your program can automatically, periodically check your POP server for new e-mail. In many programs, you can configure how often the program polls, setting it to check mail every 10 minutes or—if you're like me—every 45 seconds!

Some mail programs prevent you from doing other tasks while they poll, others do not. If you intend to use the background polling feature, you should consider this when deciding which e-mail program to use. When they perform the background poll, most programs will notify you of new mail by way of either a pop-up window or a sound. This quickly leads to Pavlovian conditioning; you may soon find yourself anxiously awaiting the next "You have new mail" bell to sound.

Sometimes when I check e-mail, I get an error such as "POP server timed out."

This indicates that the e-mail program could not connect to the POP server. In most cases, the POP server is temporarily inaccessible, maybe because that machine (owned by your Internet service provider) has crashed or been taken down for some reason (usually only for a short time). In addition, POP servers usually have a limit of how many people can connect and check for e-mail at one time. So if you happen to attempt a connection when the machine is at its limit, it might refuse you. That could generate this error message or a similar one.

It is possible that you have a problem with your TCP/IP software, but if this were the case, you would always get the above message. If you only get timeout errors some of the time, it's basically not your fault. Just wait a few minutes and check again. If you find that your ISP's POP server times out a lot, complain to them. If there is a problem on your end, you're likely to have problems connecting to virtually anywhere else (FTP, the Web, and so on). In this case, verify your TCP/IP software settings as described in Quick Fixes under "Networking Niggles."

I have a slow connection, and it takes forever to retrieve very large e-mail messages.

Many people check their e-mail from several locations—perhaps from work or school during the day and from home at night. Generally, Internet connections from home are often slower than those at workplaces or school computer centers. Suppose you ask someone to e-mail you a one-megabyte file. You may not really want to download it from home, but if you check e-mail from home and the file is waiting for you, it's going to be downloaded. That is, unless you can configure your e-mail program *not* to download files that are particularly large.

Often, you can set such an option. Some e-mail programs may have a predetermined file size limit; others will let you specify with an option such as "Don't download messages over ___ K." In Pegasus Mail, for example, choose **File**, **Network Configuration** and set the **leave mail larger than** option to whatever size you want to be the maximum. Messages larger than that will not be deleted from the server when the rest of your e-mail is delivered and deleted. You can retrieve them at a later time—perhaps from work or school.

How can I have e-mail to my old account forwarded to my new one?

Just as people move from one home to another, they sometimes move from one Internet service provider to another. And that usually means a new e-mail account. Of course, the problem is that everyone knows your old address.

First, you should tell everyone you know about your new account. In addition, check with your service provider to see if they offer some form of forwarding. If you are still paying both providers, you definitely should be able to have mail forwarded from one account to another. The exact method varies; ask the provider that you want to forward your messages from what method to use. However, if you've stopped paying one service provider and signed up with a new one, you may not be able to cajole the old provider into forwarding mail. After all, you're no longer a paying customer to them. If they won't let you forward mail after leaving them, and it's important that you not miss messages, you might have to pay for both accounts until everyone you know catches up with your new address.

One solution to all of this is to use an e-mail forwarding service. The most popular by far is called Pobox (**http://pobox.com**). Although this is a for-pay service, the fees are low. When you use a forwarding service, you give out the address the forwarding service assigns you as if it were your true e-mail address. All e-mail sent to that address is then forwarded to your "real" address, which you give to the forwarding service. The nice thing about this arrangement is that if you change your "real" e-mail address, you simply reconfigure your account with the forwarding service and give them your new address. And no matter how many times you change accounts or service providers, people can always send your messages to the same address.

Help! I accidentally deleted a message.

The first question is, where did you delete it from? In most cases, deleting a message by accident is not a good thing. If you deleted it from your PC (your mailbox in your e-mail program), it may still be on the POP server if you are not configured to delete messages from the POP server upon download.

Some e-mail packages, such as Microsoft Internet Mail, maintain a "deleted" folder of messages. These e-mail messages are not truly deleted until you clean out this folder. Check to see if your e-mail package has a place where it keeps deleted items. You may be able to find your message.

If you really did, in fact, delete the message and it's no longer on the POP server, it's basically gone. One last resort is to contact the original sender. Many e-mail programs store copies of outgoing mail, and if the sender has a copy of the message saved, he could just resend it. You might also try asking your ISP if they keep backups of the POP server. It is highly unlikely that such a backup could help you, though, because chances would be slim that the backup was made in the time span between when the message was received and when you deleted it from the server.

People keep telling me that my e-mail has "long lines."

Not everyone uses the same size screen, fonts, and so on. You can't assume that text that fits on your screen will fit the same way on someone else's. It is generally considered proper practice to use no more than 75 characters per line in an e-mail message. This ensures that everyone will be able to read it properly, without strange line-wrapping that makes the message more difficult to read.

Some e-mail programs let you set the width of a message. If yours does, set it to 75 characters per line, and you won't have to worry about taking note yourself. If you're stuck with a program that doesn't have such an option, try to keep the 75-character limit in mind and hit Enter to break to each new line…or get a new e-mail program. If you cannot keep your line lengths to 75 characters, you may continue to hear about it from people who have a hard time reading your messages.

How can I make an e-mail signature?

A signature is a little blurb that appears at the bottom of every message. Some people use it as an opportunity to impart some clever witticism or express some personality trait. Others use it for more utilitarian purposes, such as to give their name, address, and contact information.

You do not have to have a signature at all, but if you want one, you can specify it in your e-mail program. For PC-based programs, either you can create a signature from an option directly in the program, or you can configure the program to use a pre-existing signature. Because a signature is just a text file, you can create one in any basic text editor such as WordPad or Notepad (in Windows 95). If your e-mail program doesn't enable you to create a signature, then, at the very least, your e-mail program should let you specify which file to use as the signature.

You should follow one basic rule when creating your signature: don't let the size get out of hand. As you know, you shouldn't use more than 75 characters per line. On top of that, you should keep your signature to no more than 4 lines. A very large signature is considered obnoxious; short and tasteful is recommended.

Can I filter incoming e-mail into separate mailboxes?

Would you believe—maybe? It depends entirely on your e-mail program. First, consider what mail filtering is all about. Suppose you frequently receive messages from a few sources: a mailing list about ferrets, a mailing list about chocolate, and a best friend. Normally, upon retrieval, all these messages would appear in one new-mail folder. Some people move the messages into specific folders, such as "ferrets," "chocolate," and "bestfriend." Filtering allows for the retrieved message to be automatically sorted into their appropriate folders.

Mail filtering is a feature (or lack thereof) of each particular e-mail application. Some do not provide any mail filtering capabilities at all. Some provide moderate capabilities (defined as how complexly you can define the filtering rules), while others provide advanced filtering capabilities (the ability to create detailed filtering rules). Both popular Windows programs Eudora Pro and Pegasus Mail offer mail filtering, although Pegasus Mail is generally considered the most capable in this area.

How do I handle/create messages with attached files?

As e-mail programs' capabilities to deal with attached files have improved, the popularity of attaching files to messages has grown accordingly. An attached file is a file that is sent with an e-mail message. Perhaps you want to send someone a .JPG format graphic file. You might write them a message which says "Here is that picture of my new puppy." Then, you would attach the file (perhaps puppy.jpg) to the message.

"Attach" refers to an e-mail program feature usually called **attach**. All modern e-mail programs allow you to select one or more files to attach to a given message. This is normally relatively straightforward. In Eudora, there is an Attachments header line where you can click to select files to attach. In Pegasus Mail, when in the message editor, you can select an **Attach** button and choose the files to attach.

When you receive an e-mail message with an attachment, your e-mail program may handle it in a number of ways. Some programs such as Pegasus Mail will show you that the e-mail contains one message and one attachment. You then have the opportunity to select the attachment and then save it to a file. Other programs such as Eudora will automatically save the attached file(s) upon receipt. From there, you can use them in whatever application they were intended. Some programs such as Eudora allow you to configure an "attachments directory" to where all received attachments are automatically saved.

E-mail packages like Microsoft Internet Mail and Microsoft Exchange actually show the attached file as an icon in your mail message. By double-clicking the attached file, you can open it in the application that it was created in. Then you can save the file to a new directory or with a new name.

The e-mail program won't open a file mailed to me.

Sometimes, you receive an attachment, but it doesn't seem to work properly. Perhaps the e-mail program complains that it cannot read the attachment.

Attached files must be "encoded" before being sent via e-mail. This encoding, to be brief, is used to convert a binary file (such as a document, graphic, sound, or executable program) to a text file suitable for e-mail transmission. There are several encoding schemes, and it's necessary that the encoding scheme used by the originating e-mail program be comprehensible to the receiving e-mail program.

The two major encoding schemes are UUENCODE and MIME. MIME is probably the more common scheme for attached files in e-mail. Some e-mail programs will allow you to select which scheme to use for encoding (sending) a file. Others do not allow a choice and automatically use one (probably MIME). Fortunately, most of this is done automatically: upon receipt of an encoded file, your mail program will attempt to determine what encoding scheme was used, and then automatically decode the file and save it to disk (or offer you the option of saving it to disk). Of course, if a scheme was used that your e-mail application cannot handle, you'll run into a problem.

The safest bet for all sides is to stick with MIME encoding, if you are offered such configurations. If you receive a file that your e-mail program cannot seem to decode, you have two options:

- Attempt to determine what encoding scheme was used. If you view the attached file as a text file somehow (perhaps by loading the message into Notepad), it might say what encoding scheme was used. There are auxiliary utilities for Windows that can decode most encoding schemes. However, doing this is a pain. Having an e-mail program that can decode on its own is certainly much better.

- Notify the original sender that his attachment is in the wrong format; tell him to use MIME.

I want off this mailing list!

Mailing lists can be great sources of information or discussion within a particular interest area. However, they can also generate a lot of e-mail, and you may eventually decide that you can't deal with it anymore. Or perhaps you simply have lost interest in the discussion.

To remove yourself from a mailing list, you have to *unsubscribe*. The confusing part is that many mailing lists have their own method of unsubscribing. It usually entails sending a message to a particular address—but often a different address than one uses to send messages to the list. This message might have various syntaxes depending on the list; usually, you need to at least write **unsubscribe**, sometimes followed by the list name and/or your e-mail address. It really varies, so you have to find out the specific procedure for your own mailing list.

If at all possible, find information on how to unsubscribe to your list before asking anyone in the list. Often the list has unsubscribe information posted in its signature file and makes it available via online information as well. Asking the list members how to unsubscribe is the most common "annoying question" that pops up in mailing lists. Of course, if the list has not made the information readily available elsewhere, then you have little other choice but to bug the list (in which case, they're asking for it anyway).

Somebody keeps sending me abusive or harassing messages.

Unfortunately, this is not an uncommon problem. Granted, it's not a technical problem, per se, but it's frequent enough to warrant addressing. Regardless of the technologies at their disposal, people aren't always very good at behaving themselves. Especially if you get into an online argument with someone, it is possible (not likely, but possible) to start receiving abusive e-mail from them.

You can simply ignore it, but if you would prefer to take other action, there are some options at your disposal. First and foremost, save all the abusive messages, as well as copies of what you wrote to them. No matter how offensive, if you delete them, you'll be destroying your own evidence.

It's always a move in your favor to keep a cool head and not to sink to the other person's level. Let him know that you plan to contact his system administrator. If that does not stop him, then go through with it; send a polite but detailed message to his system administrator. To do this, you need to figure out what provider he uses—in many cases, this is relatively easy. It is indicated in the portion of the e-mail address following the @ sign. The right-most two domains of the address are the best bet, for example:

> bobjerk@horribleguy.isp.com

In this example, isp.com is a good bet to be the provider. Every ISP has an account named *postmaster*. Thus, address your complaint to **postmaster@isp.com**, in this example. You needn't provide all your collected evidence in the first message to the postmaster, but let him know you have it. If he asks for the evidence, provide it. Although the postmaster of an ISP has no obligation to do anything to help you, most—for the sake of their own business—will reprimand or cut off service to users on their system who are being abusive to others.

I think someone is forging messages under my name.

A forged e-mail message occurs when someone fakes the From: address, so that it looks as if it originated from someone other than the actual source. This is very devious, although it's not terribly difficult to do. A "bad forgery" is easily traced, because even though the From: address may have been faked, the rest of the e-mail headers give away the actual source of the message. Good forgers cover their tracks.

In any case, sometimes—perhaps as a twisted form of abuse, or perhaps simply to hide his own identity—someone will attack others on the Net with messages forged as if they were from you. The most probable way in which you'll learn of this abuse is through complaint letters sent to you or your postmaster about you. Being totally innocent (presumably!), you will be bewildered as to why these accusations are being laid against you.

If messages are being forged under your name, and you protest against this accusation, you shouldn't have too difficult a case. The forged messages will almost always be traceable to some origin other than you. Note that forging is different than someone breaking into your account and sending abusive e-mails from it. That's not forging, since he is, in fact, e-mailing from your account. This is a different matter, in which case, you'd need to provide evidence that your account was broken into. Still, this is often traceable, as well, if your service provider is interested enough in doing so.

How can I find the someone's e-mail address?

There is no central directory of all Internet users. The easiest way to find someone's e-mail address is to ask him, if at all possible. Obviously, this is not applicable to many cases, such as searching for an old friend or some other person with whom you have no other pre-existing contact.

Many, if not most, colleges and universities provide online directories for their students, and sometimes staff and faculty. The Web pages of a university is a good place to start a search, if you know the person to be so affiliated. Many businesses and commercial Internet service providers do not provide directories of their users. In these cases, there really is no surefire way to locate someone's address.

There are a number of services that attempt to provide directories. A good place to browse is the Yahoo! catalog (**http://www.yahoo.com**) in the subject area Reference: White Pages. Some of these directories simply solicit users to enter their name and address, thus creating something of a volunteer phone book. Other directories pull names and addresses from UseNet postings. These can be a very good way to find someone, as long as they have ever participated in UseNet. Most directory services are a combination of these two strategies.

Another excellent resource for finding e-mail addresses is the Four11 Directory at **http://www.four11.com/**. Four11 is basically the equivalent of the Internet white pages. To use the service you must register, but it's free. Every time a new user joins Four11 adds another person and their e-mail address to their database.

World Wide Web Worries

Problem	Page
Applets not playing in Java	406
Audio links in Web pages not playing	405

Can I change the startup page for my browser?

Yes. Most browsers come preconfigured to access their own home page upon startup. If you like that, fine. However, many people prefer to choose a different startup page, or in some cases, no startup page. One way to speed startup is to choose a startup page that is saved on your own PC. This way, the browser doesn't immediately have to connect to a remote site to retrieve the startup page. Saves a little time.

In Netscape, choose **Options**, **General Preferences**, and **Appearance**. There is an entry that allows you to select either a blank startup page or a specified location. Enter the location of your choosing. If you have saved a page to a local .htm file on your PC, you may start up with a local page with the URL **file:///Cl/*yourpath*/*filename*.htm**.

In Internet Explorer, choose **View**, **Options**, **Start and Search Pages**. Here, you can select the current page loaded as the search page by clicking the **Use Current** button. This is a slightly awkward way to select a start page, because it means you have to go to that page before coming to this options setting.

Netscape keeps crashing!

No surprise, it does that to everyone. Netscape is somewhat notorious for crashing, even though it is a very nice browser otherwise. Netscape can be a little finicky, because it's a very complex program, but here are some things to watch for in case of crashes.

- Be sure to use the proper flavor of Netscape for your version of Windows. Navigator comes in two "flavors"—one for 16-bit operating systems (Windows 3.1), and one for 32-bit operating systems (Windows 95). So, be sure to get the one (16- or 32-bit) appropriate for your operating system. Also make sure that you are using the most up-to-date version of the software. Version 3.0 is now available and Version 4.0 will be available soon.

- I recommend that before you install a new version of Netscape, you uninstall the previous version. Doing this may prevent mysterious crashes. However, it also wipes out your Netscape preferences, including helper application definitions.

- If you do not choose to uninstall before upgrading, try deleting a file called **netscape.hs** from the Netscape directory. It seems to be the cause of crashes when upgrading to a newer version.

- Are you using a Beta version of Netscape? The Netscape Corporation likes to release Beta version of their product for users to play with, and they are labeled as Betas (a Beta is a version that is not fully tested or finished). But remember that a Beta version is known to have bugs and, therefore, will most likely crash in certain circumstances. Use Beta software at your own risk, but report crashes to Netscape so that they can investigate. To find out whether your copy of Netscape is a Beta or final version, open the **Help** menu and choose **About Netscape**. You'll see the Netscape logo and the words **Netscape Navigator Version x.x**; Beta versions will say **beta** in this message.

The graphics or colors appear all wrong.

The most common cause of messed-up graphic appearance in the Web browser is video card driver incompatibilities. Because browsers and Windows 95 are newer than many video card drivers, problems arise. One solution, then—and this applies to more than simply Web browsing—is to have the latest video card drivers for your video card. These are often made available by the manufacturers via the Web or online services.

If colors appear strange, also consider double-checking that you have set your Windows to 256 colors or higher (all new cards have these capabilities). Many images in Web pages have more than 16 colors, and if your Windows is set to only 16 colors, the images will look freaky on-screen. In Windows 95, you can check you screen preferences by right-clicking anywhere on the desktop background. A little menu will pop up, from which you choose **Properties** and **Settings**. There you will find a selector named **Color Palette** that allows you to choose between the varying numbers of colors your video card supports.

My browser redownloads images that have already been retrieved.

Some browsers have what are known as *caches*. The cache stores the files and graphics you retrieve from the Web on your hard drive so that if you return to one of those pages, your computer can quickly load the graphics from your local storage instead of having to download them from the Net again. However, several factors can cause the ideal principle behind a cache to fall short of reality.

The first major factor is size: be sure your cache is set large enough. You should usually configure your browser's cache to 4–5 M (4096–5000K). If the cache is too small, it won't have the room to store many graphics. If the cache is very large, it takes up a great deal of hard drive space.

Second, take note of how the browser is configured to operate with the cache. All three major browsers offer options similar to those listed below to increase cache-reliance. The following figure shows these typical cache settings in Netscape Navigator.

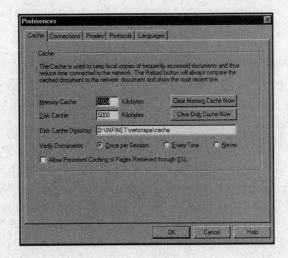

- Once per session: If you attempt to load a page you've already been to, the browser will check to see if the page has changed at all since last time. If so, it will reload the page anew. If not, it will use the files from the cache. With this option, it will only check for page updates one time during this session; subsequent returns to that page will be assumed to draw from the cache.

- Every time: The browser will always check the server to see if the page has been changed at all before drawing from cache.

- Never: If you've been to this page before, the browser will not even check to see if it has changed and will draw the files from the cache.

Understanding these options should help you to understand the logic behind the browser's cache behavior. To access these options in Netscape, use the **Options**, **Network Preferences**, **Cache** command sequence. In Internet Explorer, choose **View**, **Options**, **Advanced**.

Lastly, at the risk of really confusing matters, some browsers' cache management just doesn't work properly. Needless to say, if that's what you're up against, there's no good solution except to switch to a new browser. The browsers discussed here should work properly (although Beta versions of each release may not).

All of the letters look like Greek or something.

Probably because you somehow managed to change the browser font to Greek. This seems to happen to people periodically, although it's not clear if the user is doing something wrong or there are some goblins haunting the browsers. In any case, check your font settings.

Each browser allows you to configure which fonts to use to show the Web page contents. You can find the settings in Netscape by selecting **Options, General Preferences**, and **Fonts**; in Mosaic, select **Options, Preferences**, and **Fonts**. For Internet Explorer, select **View, Options**, and **Appearance**. In any case, simply be sure that the selected fonts are, in fact, legible fonts such as Times New Roman and Courier (popular choices). Choosing to change the font will allow you to see what the current fonts look like and help you make a proper selection.

Some Web pages never finish loading.

Isn't this frustrating? You attempt to connect to a Web page, it starts downloading, as indicated by the spinning progress icon or the shooting stars in Netscape, but never seems to finish. You may be left staring at a blank screen waiting for this endless page to complete.

Several factors could be at fault here, although this problem has been recognized as a particular bugaboo for Netscape users who also use Windows 95 Dial-Up Networking. In some cases, the delay may simply be justifiable network traffic. One simple solution is to hit the **STOP** button in the toolbar of the browser. This will cause it to give up and will probably show the contents that it has retrieved (which may be virtually all of the page minus a picture or three).

Links to sounds are not playing.

That's probably because you don't have an appropriate audio player configured as a helper application. When the Web browser encounters a link to a file that is a sound, it attempts to send that sound to whichever audio player you've chosen—if you've chosen one. Upon installation, some browsers may automatically default to a certain player; others may not.

The key here is to check your viewer or *helper app's* (same thing) configurations. Netscape carries these around in **General Preferences** (shown in the following figure) and **Helpers**, while Mosaic tucks them away in **Options**, **Preferences**, and **Viewers**. Internet Explorer bases its helpers on the file associations defined in Windows 95; select **View**, **Options**, **Filetypes** to get there.

File types   Actions   File name
                to take   extensions

Although you may encounter several types of sound files, WAV and AU files are the most common. Be sure you've configured a player for both. (You'll find entries for both in the viewer configurations previously mentioned.) You can certainly use the same player if it can play both types of files. Netscape comes with an AU player but not a WAV player. Windows 95 includes the program mplayer, which can play both types of sound files, so it is a common pick for a sound viewer.

If you want to check out others, you can find a cornucopia of helper apps at Stroud's Consummate Winsock Apps List or Shareware.com. Stroud's is on the Web at **http://cws.iworld.com/**. Shareware.com is at **http://shareware.com**.

Followed links are not remembered.

When you click a link to follow it, the browser may or may not "remember" that you've visited that link before. In some browsers, the link becomes a different color after you select it so you can keep track of which links you've followed in the past and which ones you have not. The following figure shows two different links in Netscape Navigator.

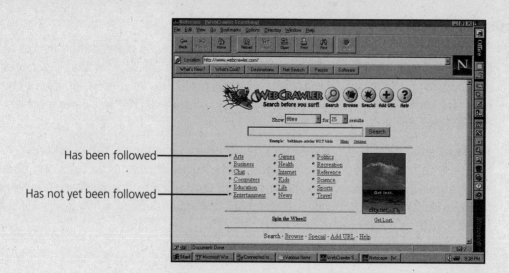

Has been followed

Has not yet been followed

This behavior is determined completely by the browser settings. Every browser that marks followed links allows you to determine how long it remembers the followed links. If you want, you can set this history to "expire" after some number of days (that is, you tell the browser when to forget the followed links).

In Netscape, you change this behavior by selecting **Options**, **General Preferences**, **Appearance**. In Mosaic, select **Options**, **Preferences**, **Anchors**. Internet Explorer offers a slightly more limited version of these settings in **View**, **Options**, **Appearance**.

Keeping track of followed links is only to help you know where you've been. It doesn't affect the browser's functionality.

Java applets are not playing.

Java applets are little programs that can add all manner of useful and nifty enhancements to a Web page, such as animated text or images. An increasing number of Web pages now feature Java applets. If you find that professed Java applets are not playing on your system, consider the following factors.

- This may sound obvious, but does your browser support Java? Netscape Navigator, Internet Explorer, and HotJava support Java applets. Check to make sure that your browser does as well; the easiest way to check is to go to the Sun Microsystem home page, **www.sun.com**, and see if the Java applets on this page will play. You can also check your Web browser's documentation or help files to see if it is Java compatible.

- If you are using a Java-compatible browser in Windows 95 but still do not see Java applets, check to be sure Java has not been disabled in your browser. Choose **Options** and **Security Preferences**, where you will find a disable Java check box. Of course, it should be deselected to enable Java.

- Lastly, some TCP/IP software has had trouble when run with Netscape, in playing Java applets. At the time of this writing, there are beta versions of Trumpet Winsock 32-bit in release that do not support Java applets. Windows 95's Dial-Up Networking does work with Java.

Sending e-mail from my browser doesn't work.

Most importantly, be sure you have configured a viable SMTP server in your browser's mail preferences. Use the same one that you've configured to use in your e-mail application, if you use one. Often, this will be an address provided by your provider with a name such as **mail.yourisp.com** or **smtp.yourisp.com**.

Check your Netscape mail settings by selecting **Options**, **Mail and News Preferences**, and **Servers**. Be sure the **Outgoing Mail (SMTP) Server** text box contains the name of a working server. You needn't fill in the **Incoming Mail (POP) Server** text box unless you want to use Netscape to retrieve e-mail as well. Also be sure you choose **Options**, **Mail and News Preferences**, and **Identity** and enter your name and e-mail address.

In Mosaic, you can find this information by choosing **Options**, **Preferences**, **Services**. Internet Explorer does not have a built-in e-mail capability; instead, it uses Microsoft Exchange, which is part of Windows 95.

I cannot convince audio- or video-on-demand programs (such as RealAudio) to work.

There are several new breeds of Web applications that provide audio and video in realtime; that is, they are played while they download, rather than having to be fully downloaded first. Some popular examples include RealAudio, Internet Wave, VDO Live, and XingStreamWorks.

As part of the normal installation, the browser needs to be configured to use these helper apps. Often, this is done automatically by the on-demand installation programs. However, if, for example, you select a RealAudio link and are presented with a query from the browser as to what to do with this type of file, then your helper app is not properly configured. In this case, go into the helper apps configuration of your browser, find the listing for the file type in question, and set the play program appropriately.

For some users, however, the helper app is configured properly; the on demand application simply doesn't work. The most common reason for this is that users are not using "real" SLIP/PPP connections. Many users nowadays use "pseudo-SLIP" connections, provided by such programs as The Internet Adaptor (TIA) and SLiRP. These programs allow users with only dial-up UNIX account to gain much SLIP/PPP functionality. While most Web browsing works fine with these sorts of connection, the multimedia on-demand programs often do not.

To be technical for a moment, the only way to get these programs to possibly work, if you use TIA or SLiRP instead of a "real" SLIP/PPP account, is to use a feature called *port redirection*. Current releases of TIA do not even support port redirection, so the point is moot there. SLiRP does, but it's too complicated to explain here; if you do use SLiRP for your Net connection and want to use one of these programs, check into the newsgroup **alt.dcom.slip-emulators**. There you can find or initiate discussion on exact port redirection settings for each on-demand application.

This page says "wait to continue" but nothing more ever happens.

Some Web servers use something called "push"ing and "pull"ing to automatically cause events to occur on your end, such as moving to a new Web page. Only problem is, not all browsers support the servers' pushy demands. In those cases, nothing will happen; the page will simply sit there.

Wise Web authors provide an alternative for those browsers that don't push or pull. Such an alternative might be a link to click to take you where they want you to go. Those who don't offer this alternative may simply leave you hanging without the proper browser. The three main browsers should all handle the pushy-pullies properly. If your browser does not support push-pull, and no alternative traditional link has been provided, then you've no choice but to abandon the page.

I'd like to maximize the usable space in my browser window.

With all window options enabled, a fair amount of desktop space is covered up by the browser's screen elements (see the following figure). Many users—especially those who use smaller-sized desktops such as 640x480—want all the browser space they can get. Although all those button bars and navigation icons are pretty, they take up screen space.

Each browser's configurations allow you to alter the appearance of the window. If you use the options right, you can maximize the window space. Here are some tips for doing so in each of our three browsers:

- In Netscape, uncheck **Options** and **Show Directory Buttons**. Select **Options**, **General Preference**, **Appearance**, and choose **Show Toolbar as Text**. You can even remove the entire toolbar (but you'll have to use the menus to navigate) and the window that shows your current location by deselecting **Options**, **Show Toolbar** and **Options**, **Show Location**. As you can see in the next figure, such judicious disabling of extra features gives you much more browser window real estate.

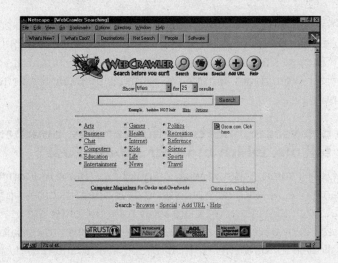

- Internet Explorer also lets you hide the toolbar, status bar, and location bar by deselecting those options in the **View** menu.

Lastly, you can fiddle with font sizes in the font configurations discussed previously. Obviously, making fonts smaller allows more text to fit in the window. But making them too small can mean many more visits to the optometrist. Find a healthy balance.

That's a neat picture. How can I save Web page images for my own use?

Many Web pages contain lots of *inline graphics* (images that are part of the page). Sometimes they are pictures or designs, and other times there are buttons, lines, and so on. You just want a picture because you like it, or you may want to capture a design element for your own use. Each browser provides a relatively easy way to grab these images from the page and save them to individual graphic files on your hard drive.

In Netscape, simply click the right mouse button on top of the image you want to save. In the menu that pops up (see the following figure), select **Save this image as**. Then you can select a location on your hard drive to which you want the image saved for your future pillaging.

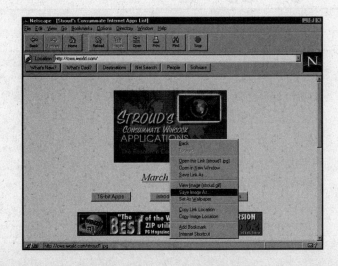

You use the same right-click technique in Internet Explorer. When you do, a slightly different menu pops up, giving you the option of saving the image in its original format ("Remote site format") or in a Windows .BMP format. If you plan to use the image in future Web pages, remote site format is probably the better choice for compatibility purposes.

One browser supports some features, another supports others. Just tell me, which browser should I use?

Okay, I admit, this isn't really a "quick fix." But it is a common question, and a reasonable one. As each new browser is developed, it comes up with new nifty features in an attempt to win market share away from the other browsers. Netscape took the early lead in by developing a number of "extensions" to traditional Web page design which allowed for new effects. Thus, people who wanted to design even "cooler" pages started adopting Netscape's extensions. In doing so, this meant Netscape's browser had to be used to view the page, thereby increasing Netscape's market share. At the time of this writing, Netscape is far and away the most popular browser with some 70% of the browser market.

Microsoft leapt out of the woodwork to play catch-up when it introduced Internet Explorer, which is probably the closest rival to Netscape. Explorer, in turn, offered its own *extensions*. Now there are pages that are designed for Netscape and some that are designed for Explorer. Most pages can be viewed on either browser, but special features may not be, and certain design elements may appear strange or distorted in the "wrong" browser. Microsoft's release of ActiveX technology has muddied the Web waters further. Now Navigator plays special content via plug-ins and Explorer plays them using ActiveX controls.

While Internet Explorer has increased its market share, Netscape Navigator is still the most-used browser. Many people choose to use both since Internet Explorer and Netscape Navigator are free. So, if you have the inclination, it's not unusual or unreasonable to have more than one browser on your computer.

Networking Niggles

Windows 95 includes the necessary software for connecting to the Internet, called Dial-Up Networking (or DUN). Most home users (and readers of this book) will want to connect to the Net via SLIP or PPP accounts, which are offered by most Internet service providers. And although they achieve essentially the same functionality and performance, PPP connections are slightly easier to set up in Windows 95. Having said that, Microsoft designed DUN setup and configuration are less-than-obvious to a novice user.

Windows 3.1 does not include software for SLIP or PPP connections. One very popular package, previously discussed in this book, which provides such access for Windows 3.1 users is Trumpet Winsock, a shareware product. Trumpet comes with very helpful documentation and is less subject to configuration difficulties.

How do I create a SLIP or PPP connection?

It's not quite obvious upon first glance just how one connects Windows 95 to the Internet. The key is to create a Dial-Up Networking connection (a.k.a. "DUN") by opening **My Computer**, opening the **Dial-Up Networking** window, and choosing **Make New Connection** from the **Connections** menu. The details for this are somewhat lengthy and are fully explained in "Configure Your TCP/IP Software" on page 81.

Again, Windows 3.1 users with Trumpet Winsock face a less confusing situation. After Trumpet Winsock has been installed, one must launch the software, which is represented by the TCPMAN icon. Once launched, simply choose **Setup** from the **File** menu. Although you still need to enter several strange-looking numbers, this procedure is documented clearly both in this book (see "Configure Your TCP/IP Software" on page 81) and in the Trumpet Winsock help file.

Why is there no SLIP option in Windows 95 DUN?

If you have access to only a SLIP account from your service provider, setting up Windows 95 DUN is bit trickier. While configuring the new DUN connection, you may have noticed that there is no SLIP option for the dial-up server type. You'll first need to install the following bit of software, which will provide the option of a SLIP-style DUN connection. Once you install this software, you can then choose a SLIP connection via the **Server Type** settings available in the **Properties** of your Dial-Up Networking connection.

If you do not have the CD versions of Windows 95 or the Plus! Pack, you must first download the SLIP software from Microsoft's Web page at **http://www. microsoft.com**. Follow the links for Windows 95 free software. (If you cannot access this site because you don't have any way to connect to the Internet yet, then you'll have to find a connected friend—a classic catch-22).

No matter how you go about it, the file you ultimately need is called Rnaplus.inf. Use **File Find** (available by clicking the Windows 95 **Start** button, selecting **Find**, and clicking **Files or Folders**) to locate it on your CD if necessary. Once you find this file, right-click it and select **Install** from the shortcut menu. The SLIP support will then be installed.

DUN claims to be establishing a connection, but never succeeds.

After DUN connects to your provider's modem, it then tries to negotiate the connection and log you in. In some cases, it will claim to be **Establishing connection** but never gets past that, and eventually the modem hangs up.

This may be caused by a variety of problems. Your modem may have difficulties negotiating a speed with your provider's modem. Be sure that your baud rate is set properly for this particular DUN connection. To check or change it, right-click the connection icon in the Dial-Up Networking window, and then select **Properties** from the pop-up menu. Once in the properties window, select **Configure**, wherein you'll find the baud rate selector.

Also, it may be that you are dialing the wrong phone number. Double-check that. Some providers offer multiple phone numbers for different modem speeds; consider that possibility, and be sure you are connecting to the correct one.

Finally, the most common cause of this problem is an improper login sequence on your end. Read the next question for the gory details.

How do I log in to my ISP with my user name and password?

For users of Trumpet Winsock, this is relatively straightforward: if you're not using an automatic login script, simply select **Manual Login** from the **Dialer** menu after launching Trumpet. This enables you to manually enter the commands to connect to your provider. You would use standard modem AT commands to dial up your provider (for example, **atdt 555-5555** or whatever phone number you must call). Once connected, you can log in by manually typing your user name and password at the respective prompts.

Unfortunately, as the result of a strange interface design on Microsoft's part, there is a common misunderstanding about how to log in to your provider using Windows 95's Dial-Up Networking. When you launch your DUN connection, a Connect To window appears (see the following figure).

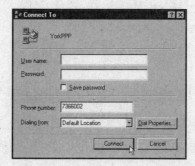

Although this window provides a place to enter your user name and password, these are misleading entries. Most Internet providers use a system in which you must manually type your user name and password to log in upon connection. If you've been filling in these entries expecting them to work, it's no wonder you've been confused when your connection was never established. Your provider's computer was waiting for you to manually enter your login information.

DUN won't allow you this opportunity unless you've properly configured the dial-up connection. Right-click the connection icon and choose **Properties** from the shortcut menu. In the Properties window, select the **Configure** button and the **Options** tab to access the dialog box shown in the next figure. Make sure the **Bring up terminal window after dialing** check box is enabled (contains a check mark). Then click **OK**.

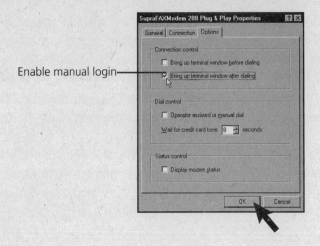

Enable manual login

From now on when you attempt to establish your connection, a window will appear after the connection is made, asking you to manually log in.

Clicking the Dial button is tedious.

It seems a repetitive task to be required to click **Dial** every time you attempt to launch a connection with DUN. While Microsoft provides no way around this, several Internauts have taken it upon themselves to circumvent this redundancy.

Three mini utilities worth recommending are RTRevco, Dunce, and Keep going. You can find these at any Windows 95 shareware site, such as **http://www.windows95.com**. Each of these will, among other features, allow you to automate the pressing of the Dial button, thus saving your finger muscles that many more clicks over a lifetime.

Can I create login scripts with Dial-Up Networking?

Manually logging in to your provider at every connection can become tedious. Fortunately, Microsoft provides a bit of add-on software that allows you to construct a *login script*. A login script is a simple mini program you can write to manually log in for you. Follow these steps to construct your own login script:

1. First, you need to obtain and install the Dial-Up Scripting Tool software. You can get it from one of three places:

   The Windows 95 installation CD. Access it using the path Admin/Apptools/Dscript/ scripter.exe.

   The Microsoft Plus! Pack. To get it from here, you must install the Internet Jumpstart component of the Plus! Pack.

   Microsoft's Web site.

   For now, open the Web page at **http://www.microsoft.com/windows/ software/admintools.htm**. Then click the **Dial-Up SLIP and Scripting Support** link, and the file dscrpt.exe is downloaded to your computer. When the download is complete, run the program by clicking the **Start** button, selecting **Run**, and clicking **dscrpt.exe**.

2. Once the scripting software is installed, you can access it by clicking the **Start** button, selecting **Programs**, selecting **Accessories**, and clicking **Dial-Up Scripting Tool**. You'll see the dialog box shown in the following figure.

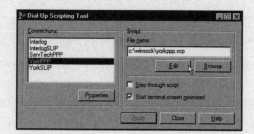

3. To automate your login, you must select which connection to script, and then assign a script file to it using the interface as pictured here.

Learning to write the script file is too involved for this Quick Fix, but the Help button in the Scripting Tool dialog box gives you access to everything you need to know. It is mostly a matter of describing which messages from the server to watch for, and what answers to supply in return. The exact format of these scripting commands is explained clearly in the associated Help topic.

My Trumpet Winsock login script isn't working.

The upside of a login script is that it allows you to automate the repetitive process of dialing and logging in to your service provider. The downside is that it opens up a whole new area for things to go wrong—getting the script to work!

Trumpet's scripting language is different from Windows 95's, although they aim for the same goal. Trumpet's built-in scripting is essentially a mini programming language. Overall, it is too detailed to go into fully here, but it was covered in detail in "Configure Your TCP/IP Software" (page 81).

If the login script is not working—that is, if it's not logging you in—consider these two questions.

1. Is it dialing your provider?

If the modem isn't even dialing or connecting to your provider, make sure that you're at least running the script. In Trumpet, you run the script one of two ways:

- Open the **Dialer** menu and choose **Other**. In the file dialog box, select the script file you want to run. Scripts in Trumpet usually end with the file name extension .cmd.

- Open the **Dialer** menu and choose **Login** or set up Trumpet to automatically log in upon launch (using **Dialer**, **Options**). Either way, your script *must* be named login.cmd.

2. Are your login entries followed by a carriage return?

This is another common problem in a Trumpet script. An appropriate script will, for example, wait for the provider to send the text **login:** (or something similar). When it receives the login command, the script sends your login name. However, the script must also send a carriage return after your login name. When the script doesn't send a carriage return, it's like you just typed your login name but didn't press Enter.

When you use Trumpet's **output** command to send text such as your user name back to the provider, the text must be followed by **\13**, which is the code for a carriage return. For example, say a portion of your login script looks like this:

```
input "Login:"
output "myusername"
```

This tells the program to wait for the provider to send the text Login: and then to reply with the text *myusername*. Without a carriage return code, you would never advance past this portion. (The provider would eventually give up on you, and the modem would disconnect.)

In reality, that section of script *should* look like this:

```
input "Login:"
output "myusername"\13
```

This is important to remember for all uses of the **output** command in your Trumpet scripts and when sending login info to the provider.

I need to use TIA or SLiRP, but how?

We'll start with an initial question: but what? TIA and SLiRP are two different software packages that perform similar functions. They are designed to give SLIP or PPP access to users who have only dial-up, text-based UNIX accounts. Because these connections are not *exactly* the same as a "true" SLIP/PPP connection, they are called "SLIP emulators" or "pseudo-SLIP." In any case, they both work quite well (TIA is a commercial product, available from **http://marketplace.com**, while SLiRP is freeware and available from **http://blitzen.canberra.edu.au/slirp/**).

Using either of these with Windows 95 DUN is only slightly more difficult. You still need to create a SLIP or PPP connection (both TIA and SLiRP support PPP emulation, so it makes the most sense to go with that) as previously explained. The documentation to TIA and SLiRP explain how to determine what your IP address and DNS server will be.

Most importantly, be sure that you have selected **Bring up terminal window after connection** in your connection properties (right-click your DUN connection icon, select **Properties**, select **Configure**, and click the Options tab). This way, when DUN connects to your UNIX host, you can log in to your shell account. From your UNIX prompt, you can then launch your TIA or SLiRP program (as described in their respective documentation), and then exit the terminal window (F7) to complete establishing the connection. You may also create a Dial-Up Script, which is only slightly trickier, because there may be more interaction to program as compared to a straightforward SLIP/PPP login.

For users of Trumpet Winsock and Windows 3.1, using TIA or SLiRP is no different, except that your login procedure has more steps because you first must log in to the UNIX account, and then run TIA or SLiRP. This can easily be done either by going through the motions manually (with Trumpet's **Dialer**, **Manual Login** command) or by coding the appropriate interaction into a Trumpet login script.

The reported connect speed seems wrong in DUN.

Keep in mind that Windows 95 DUN reports your connect speed as the *actual* modem speed of the connection, not the baud rate. Thus, if you have a 28.8Kbps modem, and your baud rate is configured (via the Modem Properties) to 57600, DUN will report the speed of the connection between the two modems. This might be 28,800 or lower, depending on the quality of your connection.

No need to worry in this scenario—everything is fine. Of course, if DUN is reporting a connection speed markedly lower than the maximum speed of your modem (for example, a 9,600 connection when you're using a 14.4Kbps modem), you may be experiencing some other problems, such as those addressed in the section "Connection Frustrations."

I frequently get DNS errors when using network applications.

Most commonly, this problem occurs when you're trying to use 32-bit network applications, such as Netscape Navigator 32-bit, with Windows 95 Dial-Up Networking. The common cause of the problem is quite esoteric: Windows 95 is failing to find the wsock32.dll file.

Normally, this file should be located in your windows\system folder, on whichever hard disk Win 95 is installed (usually C). The first thing to check is your windows\system folder for the wsock32.dll file. In the current release of Windows 95, this file should have the size 66,560 bytes.

The second potential culprit lies within the messy Windows Registry. The Registry is a large database of settings that control a huge variety of Windows' characteristics. The Registry is not something to play with unknowingly, as the system could become quite damaged. To browse or edit the Registry, choose **Run** from the **Start** menu, and enter **regedit**. The Registry Editor shown in this figure appears.

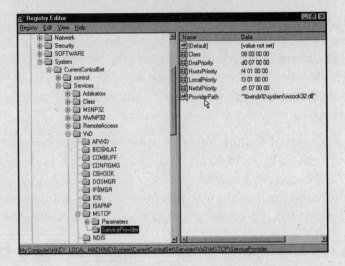

First, save a backup of the current Registry using the **Registry**, **Export Registry File** command. This way, if anything becomes damaged, you can simply rerun **regedit** and **Import** the backup file to restore everything to its predamaged state. Following these instructions should not yield any damage. But don't play around haphazardly.

To navigate the Registry, you click the folders (as specified) to open them into sublevels, just like you navigate files in the Windows Explorer. To check the DNS problem, first open the **Hkey_local_machine** folder. From there, open the following sequence of folders: **system**, **currentcontrolset**, **services vxd**, **mstcp**, and **serviceprovider**. Once there, you will notice in the right-hand window a Registry key called ProviderPath. A *Registry key* is simply one entry in the Registry, which is basically a value assigned to some label name. Be sure that the path specified is **%windir%\system\wsock32.dll**. If yours does not say that, right-click **ProviderPath** and choose **Modify** from the shortcut menu. Modify the path and exit the Registry Editor to preserve the changes.

The easiest way to find things in the Registry is to use the Find command. The Registry is large and can be hard to navigate. You can find a file related to a particular program by searching for it using a Search string and the Find command.

In this example, you verified a pair of problems that may or may not both exist on your system: That wsock32.dll does reside in windows\system, and that your relevant Registry key points to this location.

Running an Internet application *should* automatically run DUN, but it doesn't.

In theory, DUN features a *dial on demand* capability. This means that if you try to launch an Internet application before you've connected, the connection procedure will automatically be initiated first. Then, when you quit your Internet applications, the connection will be dropped. Again, *in theory*, all you need to do to use this feature is launch an Internet application without first having launched the Dial-Up Networking connection.

The problem: This only works with 32-bit applications. 16-bit Internet applications cannot dial on demand with Windows 95 DUN. Thus, the most likely cause of your problem is attempting to launch a 16-bit application. This is not entirely uncommon, as several high-quality Internet applications for Windows still only exist in 16-bit form—they still run fine, but won't dial on demand (Pegasus Mail is a good example).

Trumpet Winsock is not automatically running when I launch an Internet application.

Trumpet Winsock sports *dial on demand* capability. If you launch an Internet application such as Eudora before having run Trumpet, Trumpet should automatically run and connect (assuming your login script is named login.cmd). If this is not working, check two likely culprits.

First, be sure that you are launching a 16-bit Internet application. Many Internet programs now come in two "flavors"—16-bit and 32-bit. As a Windows 3.1 user, you should be using 16-bit software anyway. Because Trumpet Winsock for Windows 3.1 is a 16-bit program, only 16-bit Internet applications can take advantage of the dial on demand feature.

Second, be sure that Trumpet's main program, tcpman.exe, is in your Windows path. In fact, the entire Trumpet directory should be in your Windows path. The path is a list of directories on your hard drive that Windows searches for commands. This path is specified in your autoexec.bat file, probably located on the C: drive.

Open your autoexec.bat file in a text editor such as Windows Notepad. It should contain at least one line that looks something like this:

```
path C:\WINDOWS;C:\DOS
```

There may be many more directories listed in your particular autoexec.bat file. Notice that each directory is separated from the next with a semicolon (;). Be sure that the directory that includes Trumpet is listed on this line, preferably first. So after it's modified, the previous line should look like this:

```
path C:\TRUMPET;C:\WINDOWS;C:\DOS
```

Of course, that's assuming that Trumpet was installed to the directory c:\trumpet. Alter as necessary to conform with your particular setup.

Are there any alternatives to the DUN included with Windows 95? To Trumpet Winsock for Windows 3.1?

Dial-Up Networking is really just a name for Microsoft's stab at a 32-bit TCP/IP stack with dialer. In practice, any TCP/IP stack software for Windows will work fine. Others may have the advantage of less twisted configurations and speedier operation (Microsoft's implementation turns out to be rather slow compared to other manufacturers'). The main advantage of DUN is that it is a 32-bit stack, thus allowing you to run all the 32-bit network applications.

Older TCP/IP stacks, such as Trumpet Winsock, only support 16-bit applications. They will work fine but lose some of the efficiency of running 32-bit applications. The ultimate alternative, then, is third-party 32-bit TCP/IP stacks. Are there any? The pickings are slim at this point in time.

Without endorsing either of these, Core Systems offers their own DUN replacement called Internet Connect (**http://www.win.net/~core/**) and FTP Software offers their alternative called OnNet32 (**http://www.ftp.com/**). Finally, the ever-popular Trumpet Winsock is slowly working toward a 32-bit version but isn't quite there yet (there is a beta 32-bit, which means that a 32-bit version is available for public use, but it is unfinished and unstable). Keep track of their progress at **http://www.trumpet. com.au**.

There are a number of alternative Winsock TCP/IP stacks available for Windows 3.1 besides Trumpet Winsock. Trumpet is by far the most popular, as it is widely available and relatively low-cost shareware. Trumpet's competitors are generally bundled with other off-the-shelf software, such as Spry's Internet-in-a-Box, FTP software's OnNet, Netcom's Netcruiser, and yet others. All will work rather equally in Windows 3.1, as far as functionality goes.

UseNet News Jams

My news server says, "You have no permission to talk. Goodbye."

Most UseNet news servers are configured only to allow certain sites to connect to them. This prevents anyone in the world from connecting and draining the resources of the server. Some servers, as just explained, accept only certain domains to connect, while others require a user name and password.

First, be sure that you are connecting from a valid domain. For example, let's say that you go to school at Kazoo University and want to connect to their news server **news.kazoo.edu**. If you have a SLIP/PPP account provided by Kazoo, there should be no problem. However, let's say you are using another SLIP/PPP account, perhaps that of a local commercial Internet provider. In that case, Kazoo will not know that you have rights to their machine; thus, be sure you are connecting to the server from an account within its acceptable domain.

Secondly, although less common, if the server requires a user ID and password, be sure you've filled one into your UseNet application's configuration settings.

I'd like to post anonymously.

There are a variety of "noncriminal" reasons why someone would want to submit an anonymous post to a UseNet newsgroup. In any case, doing so simply requires that you submit your post via an anonymous-posting service.

This is done by contacting any one of several anonymous remailers and following their particular instructions, submitting your post. They will then send your post to the UseNet newsgroup(s) you request. Private e-mail replies to your post will come back to you, but the replier will not know who you are (and, often, nor will you know who they are).

Because there are many remailers to choose from, I cannot provide step-by-step instructions here. Most remailers are designed by default to send anonymous private e-mail, and thus they take special commands in the body of the message to make a UseNet post. You can read the help instructions for the popular remailers at the Web site **http://electron.rutgers.edu/~gambino/anon_servers/anon.html**.

Several Web sites offer easy interfaces via which you can compose a message and select a remailer; two worth trying are the Community **ConneXion (http://www.c2.org/remail/by-www.html)** and Noah's Place (**http://www.lookup.com/Homepages/64499/anon.html**).

I want to change my posted name and organization.

Although a non-anonymous UseNet post will always contain your e-mail address, it need not contain your real name. Some prefer to change their listed name, either for personal reasons or cosmetic. If you are using a PC newsreader, such as Agent, Free Agent, News Xpress, and so forth, changing these settings is quite easy.

For example, in Agent (rapidly becoming the most popular newsreader for the PC), simply choose **Options, Preferences** and click the **User** folder tab. You can enter any personal name and organization name that you want. Each of the newsreader applications have a similar capability, including the Netscape Navigator built-in newsreader (accessed via **Options, Mail and News Preferences, Identity**).

After I post, I receive "Post failed" errors.

A post can fail for several reasons. One common cause of a post failing is known as *throttling*, and the error message may indicate this if it's the problem. In short, throttling is a result of your provider's news server being filled to capacity. There is nothing you can do, except complain. If a provider is suffering from many throttling errors, they seriously need to upgrade their storage capacity.

Another cause of post failing errors is a server timeout. Your newsreader will attempt to contact the news server, to send it your post, but the news server may not answer. This may be because the news server machine is down or overloaded with users. The odd server timeout does occur, and you should simply wait a few minutes and then resubmit your post. Again, though, if this problem happens with some regularity, your provider is likely at fault.

Although it is possible that your TCP/IP settings are misconfigured, thus preventing connection to the server, if this were the case, none of your Internet applications would be connecting to anywhere.

Lastly, some newsreaders will attempt to enforce two UseNet customs:

- Signature files longer than four lines are considered a violation of netiquette (waste of network traffic), and although many newsreaders won't object if you break this custom, a few will.

- In another attempt to conserve traffic and improve content, some newsreaders disallow you from submitting a follow-up post, in which you include less new text than you quote from the previous message. This is a dubious "rule," intended to prevent someone from reposting an entire message and only adding "Yes I agree." Again, most newsreaders do not enforce this rule, although the custom is something to keep in mind when composing follow-up posts.

What is a moderated newsgroup? How can I post to one?

Although all UseNet newsgroups are publicly accessible, some are more democratic than others. The vast majority of newsgroups are *unmoderated*. This means that anyone can post anything to that newsgroup. Although this invites the widest possible array of discussion, it also draws a lot of garbage. Some newsgroups are *moderated*, which means that posts are submitted to a moderator, who then may accept or reject the post for the newsgroup.

Nobody is forcing anyone to use moderated newsgroups. In almost every instance, there are unmoderated alternatives in which to discuss the same subject matter. But, there are advantages to participating in moderated newsgroups; specifically, a high discussion content-to-noise ratio. Usually, a moderated newsgroup will be indicated as such in the newsgroup description, although some PC newsreaders don't display the newsgroup description. In other cases, you will usually find a FAQ posted regularly within the newsgroup that explains how to submit posts to the moderator. Besides being a tip-off that this is a moderated newsgroup, it'll also provide the instructions you need. The basic mechanism is that you'll e-mail your post to the moderator, per his guidelines as outlined in the FAQ, and he will take it from there.

Attempting to post directly to a moderated newsgroup will likely result in a rejected post.

Why are there messages missing from this newsgroup?

Nothing can be more frustrating than discovering that desired posts are missing from the newsgroup. You may be reading an ongoing discussion and find that reference is made to a post that you don't see. Or perhaps you are attempting to decode a binary file that is posted in multiple parts, and one or more of the parts are missing. Argh!

This isn't your fault and may only indirectly be your service provider's fault. The problem partially lies in the design of UseNet. In brief, UseNet is like a large network of rivers and streams, each feeding into one another at various nodes. In theory, the water from each stream should eventually feed into every other stream, except this doesn't always happen. There are blockages and dams, and sometimes, only partial feeds reach your local server. Ultimately, your service provider subscribes to a feed from another source; if that incoming feed is incomplete, yours will be, too. The only "fix" to this is to complain to your service provider and pressure them to add a new newsfeed from another source (for example, newsfeeds provided to service providers from MCI are known for being quite complete, whereas those from Sprint are notoriously incomplete).

Why does this group have few or no posts anymore?

If a well-trafficked group that you've been reading suddenly starts to plummet in activity, I'd suspect a news feed problem to your provider. Perhaps, the service feeding your provider decided to cut that newsgroup from their feed, for instance.

Other newsgroups are simply low-traffic by nature; there are quite a few newsgroups, especially in the alt.* hierarchy that are either "joke" creations or simply appeal to an extremely limited audience.

What is the best way to practice posting?

Given how many people read UseNet, if you've never made a post before, you might want to be sure that you know how before attempting it. Not only do you risk quite the public faux pas otherwise, but you also want to be sure that your message reaches the intended audience. In other cases, you may have plenty of UseNet experience but want to test new newsreading software to be sure you know how to post with it.

Although it is not uncommon to see messages posted in newsgroups with subject lines such as "TEST – ignore" or "Please ignore," this is the incorrect way to test your posting capabilities. There are several global groups in which you can post test messages; for example, try **alt.test** and **misc.test**. Note that if you post to one of these newsgroups, you may receive a flood of e-mail messages from automated news servers, notifying you that your message was successfully received.

You can also test to a local or university test newsgroup, such as **ny.test**, **tor.test**, or **cornell.test**. By doing this, you won't receive a flood of e-mail from servers around the world, but if you reread the newsgroup a few minutes later, you should see whether your post appeared.

When I reply by e-mail, it is never received by the other party.

To successfully reply to a poster via e-mail, your newsreader has to be properly configured for e-mail sending. Normally, this is done by at least choosing an e-mail server, known in technospeak as an SMTP server—the sort of machine which can send e-mail.

For example, in Agent or Free Agent for the PC, you would configure this setting via **Options, Preferences** and then the **System** folder tab. Which machine should you choose as your e-mail server? Your best bet is the same one you've chosen in your e-mail program. Your Internet provider should have supplied you with the name of your SMTP server; it is often something such as **mail.yourprovider.com**, but not necessarily.

Assuming you've set the e-mail server properly, don't forget to fill in your name and return e-mail address in the newsreader's other settings. This was covered briefly in an earlier question about changing your personal name in UseNet posts.

People tell me to read some group "such.and.such" but it doesn't seem to exist.

Again, this is most likely a newsfeed-related problem. Besides the fact that not all newsfeeds provide all the available posts, many do not provide all available newsgroups. If you are interested in a newsgroup that doesn't seem to be carried by your provider, ask them to add it. Often, they will do this upon request.

Note, though, that if your provider adds a new newsgroup, it may take several days to fill up with traffic.

How do I view posted pictures, sounds, and movies?

This question opens up quite the can of worms—creepy, crawly, slimy. UseNet was not originally designed to exchange binary data, which by its nature is 8-bit. Plain text data, such as messages from one human to another, are 7-bit, and thus so is the nature of UseNet. Nonetheless, people tried to devise ways to exchange binary data over this medium, because it is a convenient way of exchanging files publicly.

The most common method of posting binary files to UseNet is known as UUENCODING. UUENCODE is essentially a program that converts 8-bit data into 7-bit data for transport purposes. Once you retrieve this 7-bit data, it must be converted back to 8-bit data before it will be usable for whatever its purpose (video, sound, and so on).

Furthermore, because binary files tend to be of large size, they are often split into several smaller sections before posting. That is why you will often see binary files posted with subject lines such as these:

```
homer.wav (1/3)
homer.wav (2/3)
homer.wav (3/3)
```

Thus another step is added into the decoding process; each of the parts must be retrieved, combined, and then decoded back to 8-bit data. Whew! Over the years, newsreaders have grown increasingly intelligent about automating this entire process. The newest newsreaders such as Free Agent and Agent make life easy as pie; you simply select one of the sections of the posted file, and it finds all of them, retrieves them in order, and then decodes them. You need only select **File**, **Decode Binary Attachment** after highlighting the binary messages you want to download.

Other popular newsreaders have similar capabilities, and thus it is recommended that you use the latest versions of your newsreading software, such as the Agent siblings, News Xpress, and so forth. Netscape Navigator 2.0 includes a built-in newsreader that automatically decodes single-part binary files. However, it doesn't do such a good job with multipart binary postings, and so the above-named newsreaders are recommended if you plan on working with many binary posts in UseNet.

How do I post my own binary files?

Of course, the concepts described in the previous Quick Fix hold true in this scenario, too—they're just reversed. The same newsreaders are also capable of taking a specified binary file, chopping it into slices, encoding it, and then posting it. For example, you can configure how Agent manages this task by choosing the **Options**, **Preferences** command and clicking the **Attachments** folder tab. The Preferences dialog box shown here contains options with which Agent can convert a binary file suitable for posting.

In the first half of the window, you select whether Agent should post the whole file in one large piece or chop it up into several pieces. Because some news servers will reject files larger than a certain size, you should slice files into 900-line segments. To do so, enable the **Send attachment as multiple messages** option and enter **900** in the **Lines per Message** box.

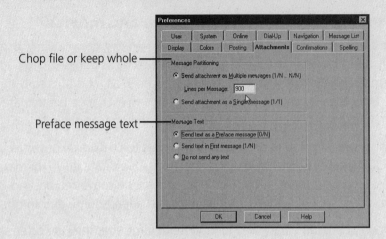

Chop file or keep whole

Preface message text

The bottom half of the settings window deals with any text you may want to include as a preface to the file (such as "This file is an MPG format video of my dog Scrappy in a compromising position"). If you select the option labeled Send text as a preface message (0/N), Agent will post a message numbered part 0 (which contains only the text) before the post(s) containing the UUENCODED binary file. If you choose the second option, Agent will include the text at the beginning of the first part of the binary file post. The second option is inconvenient because the user must download at least one whole chunk of the file just to read your description. The third option here tells Agent not to include any preface text at all.

Again, other newsreaders will have similar configuration capabilities. When you choose to compose a new UseNet post, there will be an Attach file option, which lets you select the particular file to post.

Someone is flaming me; what should I do?

A flame in UseNet is much like a flame in e-mail: a rude, often coarse, derogatory message directed at someone, either for his statements or beliefs. The best strategies for handling flames are those same strategies that work best in the playground: Ignore them.

If you cannot, or feel that the flames are damaging to you in a public sphere, publicly ask the flamer to stop. If he does not, privately ask him to stop flaming you. Remember to keep copies of all messages you send to him and those that he sends to you, in case future evidence is needed. Finally, if none of this quiets the storm, write e-mail to their postmaster, in the same manner recommended earlier in this chapter.

The recourse you never want to take is to flame back and become involved in a flame-war. Besides wasting your time, it is also a waste of network traffic, and extremely tedious for everyone else to sift through.

Basic UNIX Account Snarls

The text on my screen is totally misaligned/jumbled.

This is because of a terminal emulation problem. For the purpose of formatting text on the screen and mapping the keyboard, UNIX relies on a *terminal*. There are many possible terminals UNIX can use, and they have names such as Heath-19, VT100, VT200, and many more. Once upon a time, these were all actual hardware devices—keyboards with screens—that people used to connect to mainframe computers. Nowadays, your PC acts as the terminal, and the software you use to connect to and use your UNIX account (a terminal program) has the capability to emulate some of these terminals.

Your terminal program software must be set to emulate the same terminal that your UNIX account thinks it is running on. In the great majority of cases, the preferred terminal is VT100. Your UNIX account probably assumes this by default. You can check what terminal your UNIX account is assuming by entering the following command at your UNIX account prompt:

```
echo $term
```

Most likely, it will report `vt100`. Your next step is to check your terminal software, which varies, for which emulation it is using. Be sure to set it to the same emulation that the above echo command reports, such as `vt100`. You may then need to exit your account and reconnect for the changes to take effect.

I want to use the arrow keys to see a command history.

In some UNIX command lines (a.k.a. *shells*), you can use the up and down arrow keys to scroll through a history of commands you've already entered. This makes life easier, especially if you recently typed a long command and need to run it again.

A shell is the command line in which you enter commands. In fact, there are a variety of shells that a UNIX account might use, and each sports its own special conveniences. Shells often have names such as csh, tcsh, ksh, and bash. All of those except csh support command histories as described here. Unfortunately, many UNIX accounts are created by default to use the csh shell—which does not support the arrow keys. To see which shell you are using, enter the following command at your UNIX prompt:

```
echo $SHELL
```

It might report the shell as a pathname, such as /bin/csh. All you care about is the rightmost part, which is the shell name—in this case, csh. On most systems, you can change your login shell by entering the command **chsh** and selecting a new shell. On a few systems, the chsh command has been disabled for security reasons. If you run into that, e-mail your system administrator and request a different login shell such as tcsh. Make sure you get one that allows you to use command histories with the arrow keys.

I changed my password, and now it doesn't seem to work.

Changing your password is certainly a vital matter—and not being able to log back in would certainly be frightening! Your password may no longer work for one of two reasons.

- You're not entering the new password correctly. This sounds silly and obvious, but be sure that you are, in fact, entering the password exactly as you just changed it to.

- The password database has not been updated yet. Sometimes, a password change does not take effect immediately. Some systems may take several minutes to distribute the new password information within the system. In these cases, you may still be able to use your old password (before you changed it), or even better, simply wait 5–10 minutes and all should be well.

How much disk space am I eating up?

Many service providers allow you a quota of disk space that your account can use. If you hog up space beyond that, they may charge you extra fees. There are a variety of quota-tracking systems implemented, some of which keep a close eye on you, such as preventing you from surpassing the quota. Other systems only check your account periodically, and tally up how far you've exceeded your quota.

To determine how corpulent your account has grown, first try the **quota** command, at the UNIX shell prompt. On some systems, this will reveal how much space you are taking, and how much space you are allowed left. If that command does not work on your system, this one will:

```
du -s ~userid
```

Of course, replace *userid* with your actual login ID, but don't overlook the tilde (~) mark, which is necessary. This command will report the size of your account in kilobytes, such as 2150. 2,150K is about 2M (there are 1,024K in 1M). If your provider has told you that your limit is 5M, you have about 3M of space left.

I've suspended a program and can't get back into it.

UNIX can run multiple programs simultaneously, but you have only one window in your account. If you are, say, running TIN to read news, but would like to check your e-mail, you needn't quit TIN outright. You can simply "suspend" it in the background, run your e-mail program, and then return to TIN. You suspend a program in UNIX by pressing Ctrl+Z. Other times, you may have hit Ctrl+Z by accident.

To return to a suspended program, simply type the **fg** command at your UNIX shell prompt (as in "foreground"). That will bring the suspended application back to your screen.

I cannot figure out how to quit this program I've run.

You've found yourself in a strange UNIX program and cannot quit. The typical keys such as "Q" don't seem to help. You're trapped! Maybe. But one of these three recommendations might work.

- Try **Ctrl+D**, which can be used to quit some UNIX programs.

- Attempt to find some online help for the program, perhaps by pressing **H** or **Shift+H**. There may be a clue there.

- A more brutal solution is to suspend the program in question, and then once you're back at the shell prompt, kill the program. To do this, first suspend the program with **Ctrl+Z**. Then, at the shell prompt, type **ps**. This will produce a list of current "processes" that you are running, each with its own ID, such as:

```
PID    TT STAT    TIME COMMAND
21535  p1 S       0:00 -tcsh (tcsh)
21545  p1 T       0:03 tin
21547  p1 R       0:00 ps
```

In this example, we suspended the program TIN, and as you can see, it has a process ID ("PID") of 21545. Thus, the semibrutal way to quit TIN is to kill its process, to wit:

```
kill -9 21545
```

which will shortly thereafter produce the message

```
[1]    Killed              tin
```

Finally, if none of these methods manages to exterminate your problem program, you can just abruptly disconnect from your account, such as by manually powering off your modem, or choosing the hang up option from your terminal program software. Then, wait a few minutes before reconnecting; your UNIX account will likely figure out that you were wiped out, and it'll kill your leftover processes. Even if it fails to kill them, when you log back in, you'll then be at a shell prompt, and you can use the **ps** command to kill them.

My witty .plan file is not being seen by people who finger me.

If you have a UNIX account, people around the world may be able to *finger* you to learn more about you. Many users create what is known as a "plan" file: a text file that contains information about you that you want others to see when they finger your UNIX account.

Creating a plan file is simple. You create a file named **.plan** (note the preceeding decimal point) and include any text information you want. The problem many people run into, though, is that when people finger them they don't get the plan file.

When you create the .plan file, it is viewable by you only—not the outside world. Why? Every file in UNIX has *permissions* that define who can access it. If you're facing this problem, you need to change the permission for your file to make it "readable" to others. So, after you've created your .plan file, type this command:

```
chmod 775 .plan
```

That enables anyone who fingers you to see your plan—and after all, isn't that the whole point?

I want my own signature for e-mail and UseNet news.

Creating a signature—a bit of text that appears at the end of every e-mail message or Usenet post you send—is quite simple. Just as with the plan, simply create a file named **.signature** and enter whatever text you like.

Creating a new text file in UNIX is also relatively easy. There are many text editors in UNIX, but one of the most common and popular is called Pico. So, to create a .signature file, type this (be sure to use lowercase, as pictured):

```
pico .signature
```

Then, type out your text. Pico sports a small guide to its functions at the bottom of the screen (see the following figure). As you can see there, you can press **Ctrl+X** to exit and save the file.

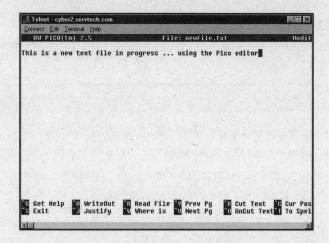

The files that I ftp to my UNIX account wind up corrupted.

There are two common FTP programs available in many UNIX accounts: standard ftp, and NcFTP. The latter is preferable, because it is quite easy for a new user to use, and it automatically takes care of little details that might be overlooked otherwise. To see if your UNIX account has NcFTP available, simply type **ncftp** at the UNIX shell prompt.

If that doesn't yield anything, you'll have to use the standard UNIX FTP program, simply called FTP, which is what you type to launch it. The major cause of corrupted ftp'd files is making an ASCII mode text transfer when you needed to make a binary mode transfer.

After you connect to the FTP site, but before you begin a transfer, typing the FTP command **asc** will put you into ASCII mode, and the command **bin** will put you into binary mode. The majority of file types you will be transferring are binary, including all graphics, sounds, and compressed archives (such as .ZIP files). Thus, remember to use the bin command in the FTP program before beginning most transfers. Note that NcFTP defaults to bin mode when launched, thus saving you from needing to remember this step. The standard FTP program defaults to ASCII transfer mode, unfortunately.

Some user keeps causing messages to pop up onto my screen.

There are two invasive ways for another user to attempt to grab your attention. One is to send you a talk request, with the command **talk you@your.provider.com**. Another is the write command, which allows a user on your same service provider to pop messages onto your screen.

If you'd like to be left alone from such intrusions, enter the following command at your shell prompt:

```
mesg n
```

You may want to add this command at the bottom of the file named .cshrc in your account, which contains all the commands to execute automatically upon login. Note, though, that refusing messages (which is what **mesg n** does) refuses both talk requests and write messages. To re-enable message accepting, use **mesg y**.

FTP Hangups

How do I log in using anonymous FTP?

Anonymous FTP is a phrase that pops up repeatedly in Internet circles (and books, and articles, and posts). FTP, or File Transfer Protocol, is a common method for transferring files from one computer on the Internet to any other. For authorization purposes, passwords are implemented to control who can access the files on what computer.

Anonymous FTP is used for public archives: file storage that may be accessed by anyone in the public, hence anonymous. To access such archives, you connect to the site and log in with the user ID **anonymous**, and at the password prompt, enter your e-mail address. Thus, if someone told you to ftp some files from **ftp.site.com** via anonymous FTP, you would do the following (the parts in bold text are what you would type):

```
ftp> open ftp.gated.cornell.edu
Connected to GATED.CORNELL.EDU.
220 comet.cit.cornell.edu FTP server Wed Jun 7 17:22:02
995) ready.
Name: anonymous
331 Guest login ok, send your complete e-mail address
Password: dog@woof.woof.com
230-Please read the file README
230-  it was last modified on Fri Jan 26 09:52:01 1996
230 Guest login ok, access restrictions apply.
```

The estimated time of transfer is inaccurate.

Some FTP programs, such as NcFTP, attempt to estimate how long the transfer will take. Simply keep in mind one rule of thumb for any file transfer time estimates, be they FTP or anywhere else. Take them with several grains of salt. An estimated time of transfer necessarily assumes consistent transfer speed. This rarely happens, especially when using

FTP. Network traffic and bottlenecks anywhere between you and the remote computer can alter the speed of the transfer. Thus, these time estimates are quite like their brethren in the auto repair world: *estimates*.

Can I salvage an interrupted transfer?

Recall that in the UNIX account scenario, downloading a file from the Internet to your PC is a two-step process. First, you must retrieve the file into your UNIX account, such as via FTP. Then, you must download the file from UNIX to your PC, as with Zmodem. For this question, we are considering the first step only: retrieving the file from the Internet to your UNIX account.

Whether you retrieve files to your account with FTP, Gopher, or the World Wide Web (with the program Lynx, for instance), none of these commonly support *resumed transfers*. Resuming transfer is the capability to start a transfer at some mid-way point, picking up where a previously interrupted transfer left off. This is quite a convenient feature, but not yet implemented widely enough to be feasible.

Thus, the short answer is "no," you basically cannot salvage an interrupted transfer from the Internet to your UNIX account. The only real solution is to simply retransfer the file again from scratch.

But my FTP program has a "resume transfer" option; why doesn't it work?

The truth is that FTP *can* support resuming transfers. Some FTP programs have implemented support for the reget command, which is the FTP command that can be used to resume a transfer. However, both the FTP program *and* FTP server must support reget, and very few FTP servers do.

So, you have a situation where few FTP servers support reget, and few FTP programs support it. Therefore, it is not a very commonly available feature. So, if your FTP program does support resume transfer, it'll still only work if you've connected to one of the few FTP servers that support it in kind.

I'm trying to access my UNIX account at ftp.myprovider.com but it denies me access.

This is a common error users make. Let's say that your UNIX account is on the provider.com machine. You want to FTP some files from your UNIX account to some other machine. So, naturally, you attempt to connect to **ftp.provider.com**, but when you log in with your account user ID and password, access is denied. Why?

Because ftp.provider.com is probably not the machine you need to be connecting to. That is their "public" FTP server, meant to serve files for public availability. Your UNIX account resides on provider.com, and so you, in fact, want to open your FTP connection to provider.com. Then, your user id and password will work, and you'll have access to the contents of your account.

Downloading Difficulties

My download was interrupted partway through!

Recall above the doom and gloom about resume transfer. Now, though, you are considering the second step of the UNIX two-step: transferring the file from your UNIX account to your PC. In this case, you have the benefit of the magical Zmodem.

Zmodem fully supports resuming transfers, although it prefers to term it *crash recovery*—different words, same meaning. Be sure that you have Zmodem crash recovery enabled; check the Zmodem settings in your particular terminal program.

Assuming that it is enabled, if a Zmodem download dies partway through, you can simply begin the download again. Zmodem will automatically recognize that a portion of the file has already been downloaded, and it will pick up from where it left off. Nice!

I try to download the file, but nothing seems to happen.

Now you run into some of Zmodem's other settings. Not all terminal programs allow you to configure all possible Zmodem settings, but assume that yours does.

In many terminal programs, you can determine exactly how crash recovery will behave. For instance, if you attempt to download a file that already exists on your PC, Zmodem can compare them against each other. Suppose that both have the same time and date—which they would if you were attempting to resume a file previously interrupted. Zmodem, upon realizing this, can either crash recover, start over from scratch for that file, or skip transferring that file altogether. Your terminal may allow you to select these behaviors from its Zmodem configuration screen, but this varies from product to product.

If you attempt to Zmodem download a file and nothing happens, a common cause of this is that you already have a file with the same name in your download path on your PC. Your terminal program is probably configured to skip transfers, rather than resume or overwrite them. This is why the settings explained previously are important—this is one of those "easily forgotten" settings.

Strange text started spewing all over my screen.

Ugh! The transfer seemed to be motoring along just fine, and then suddenly the progress window disappeared and illegible goop starting being output to the screen. This is a Zmodem transfer problem that happens from time to time when the connection between you and your provider burps.

There isn't any notable way to prevent this from occurring. Once it has occurred, the file is no longer being properly transferred, so simply hang up the modem. Wait a few minutes, reconnect to your UNIX account, and then you should be able to resume the transfer with Zmodem.

Why do some files download much faster than others?

Your terminal program probably displays a progress window while a transfer is in progress. This figure shows a transfer progress meter from HyperTerminal, the terminal program included with Windows 95.

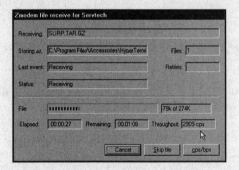

Speed of transfer is often measured in "characters per second" (cps) or "bytes per second" (bps), although they mean the same thing. If you, for example, have a 14.4K modem, you may have noticed that many files download at around 1600–1650cps, or thereabouts. Owners of 28.8K will generally see twice that speed.

However, some files seem to transfer much faster—perhaps 3000 cps on a 14.4 or 5000 on a 28.8. What's going on? Compression. Your modem always attempts to compress the data that is being transferred. Doing so results in less data to transfer, and thus a shorter transfer time, and thus a faster perceived transfer rate.

Many binary file types, though, such as .ZIP files, are already compressed. Thus, your modem can do no more to help them, and you see the typical speeds of 1650cps. Other files, which are not compressed (such as ASCII text files) gain great benefit from your modem's built-in compression, and thus they appear to transfer much faster.

In the end, it makes little difference where the compression took place. If you compressed the text file in UNIX before transferring it, the cps rate would drop back to 1650, but the file would be a smaller size. After the smoke is cleared, the total amount of time it takes to download the file is no different whether it was compressed before transfer or during.

I downloaded a text file to my PC, and it looks messed up.

Once again, the ASCII versus binary mix-up claims another victim. Don't be a statistic!

The reason the file appears all screwy is that it has improper "end-of-line" markers (EOL). These are special characters that tell the computer where the end of a line of text is. The classic problem is that UNIX uses a different EOL than does MS-DOS/Windows. There are two feasible solutions to this:

- When downloading a file from UNIX to your PC, you are most likely using Zmodem, with the UNIX sz command. In this case, if you are going to transfer a plain text (ASCII) file, use the sz -a command instead; that will automatically convert the UNIX EOLs into PC-compatible ones.

- If you've already downloaded the file with improper EOLs, all is not lost. There are many tiny utilities available for the PC that can convert the file into correct form for you. All are available at a major PC archive site, such as **http://www.winsite. com**. One I especially recommend is the shareware product UltraEdit, also available at any major site for Windows software. UltraEdit is a versatile text editor that includes a built-in option for converting EOLs from UNIX to PC and vice versa.

The program I downloaded to my PC claims to be corrupted.

What if you have ftp'd a file to your UNIX account, and it was not corrupted, but then downloaded the file to your PC only to find that it now is corrupted? Where is the culprit in this scenario?

First, we have to consider whether this is, in fact, true. If you mistakenly ftp'd a binary file in ASCII mode, for instance, it has been corrupted already. Assuming, though, that you did not make this error, what might corrupt a perfectly good file on its way from your UNIX account to your PC?

In my experience, the most common answer to this question, strangely enough, is "nothing." That is, I almost bet that if you investigate, you will find that the file was, in fact, corrupted in its original location. That is, the file you ftp'd was *already* in a corrupt state of affairs before you even came around. Of course, this means there is nothing you can do about it, except perhaps notify the administrator of the site from which you ftp'd the file.

Were the above not the case, though, do be sure that you are using a robust transfer protocol between your UNIX account and your PC. By far, the recommended choice is Zmodem, which any good terminal program supports. The sz *filenames* command is used in UNIX to initiate a Zmodem download. A protocol such as Zmodem will not corrupt your files, but do remember to use **sz -a *filenames*** if you're downloading an ASCII text file.

Miscellaneous Lukewarm Leftover Grumbles

My ISP does not offer an IRC server; how can I connect?

The many available public IRC servers should more than fulfill your global chatting needs. However, because they change often, listing particular servers here would be fruitless. Instead, I can recommend some reliable sources for current information on public IRC servers:

- On UseNet, check the newsgroup alt.irc. There are periodic posts of public servers, or you can post a request.

- On the World Wide Web, go to the Yahoo! catalog (**http://www.yahoo.com**). Enter **IRC** in the search box, and it will bring up a list of IRC-related Web sites, some of which contain lists of public servers. Even these Web sites change, which is why they are not listed here. This method, though, will lead you to a list.

When choosing a public IRC server, try your best to use one as geographically close to you as possible. Not only will it reduce network traffic for everyone, but you will see speedier response times as well.

While on IRC, somebody asked me to DCC a file; what is that?

DCC is a form of file transfer for use within the IRC public chat system. Using DCC, users can exchange files with one another. It is quite simple to use; recall that all IRC commands begin with a slash (/).

In your IRC program, to send a file to someone via DCC enter

```
/dcc send theirnick fullfilename
```

Suppose you want to send the file beagle.jpg to the IRC user whose nickname is harry. You would type the following:

```
/dcc send harry c:\pix\beagle.jpg
```

If someone attempts to DCC send a file to you, your IRC program will notify you. Some IRC programs will automatically accept the file and begin receiving it. If yours does not, simply use the command **/dcc get *theirnick***. Enter the command /dcc without any other parameters to see the current progress of the transfer.

Do those "Internet telephone" programs really work?

Admittedly, this is not a Quick Fix, but it *is* a common curiosity. Internet telephony has become a hot market in the past year, as several products are competing for your voice (for instance, Internet Phone, WebPhone, DigiPhone). The main attraction of these products is that you can speak to anyone on the Internet, anywhere in the world, without needing to use a traditional long-distance phone call.

But are they as good as a real phone call? Not really, is the answer at this point in time. It takes a great deal of compression technology to push your voice through a typical 14.4 or 28.8K modem. Beyond that obstacle, the Internet is a vast network of shared pathways, wherein data cannot travel at a consistent speed from point A to point B. The result of these factors are that Internet telephone programs tend to produce speech that is slightly fuzzy and noticeably choppy.

Certainly, the closer the two speaking parties are to one another on the Internet, the more fluidly these programs will work (that is, if both users are on the same service provider, speech will work far better than if one is in New York and the other in Melbourne, or even Los Angeles). All is not lost forever, though. As home connections speed up and the Internet itself becomes more robust, these sorts of "telephones" will become much more feasible to use.

Other software packages such as CU-SeeMe and Microsoft Netmeeting offer the possibility of video conferencing on the Internet. As modem speeds increase, this type of software will become more popular. The efficiency of this product at the present time is related to band-width. The hardware and software available will do the job; hopefully Internet through-put will catch up with the possibilities.

This is costing me; how can I keep track of my time online?

This is an important consideration for many Internet users who are charged by the hour. Most terminal programs have built-in online time displays, which are often located on a status line like the one shown here.

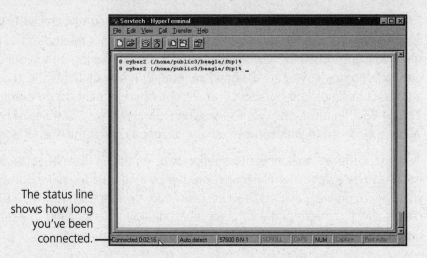

The status line shows how long you've been connected. ——

However, this is of no help to SLIP/PPP users, who don't use a terminal program. Fortunately, Windows 95 provided a built-in solution for those who use its Dial-Up Networking. After your connection is established, a small window (shown in the next figure) displays the connection speed and online duration. This window remains on the screen unless you choose to minimize it to the taskbar.

My connection disconnects if I am idle for too long.

To prevent users from leaving their modems connected and hogging up the modem resources, some service providers institute an idle-time rule. If you remain connected but don't engage in any activity for longer than, say, 30 minutes, you are automatically disconnected. While this is a reasonable practice, it may be a problem under certain circumstances, such as if you are awaiting an important e-mail message or chat request. As you might expect, there are ways around it.

One little utility program written to work around this idle time disconnect is called Keep Alive. You can find Keep Alive at many major software sites, such as Winsite (**http://www.winsite.com**) or Stroud's Consummate Winsock Apps (**http://cws.iworld.com/**). Keep Alive simply sends a bit of data (known as a *ping*) every so often to keep your connection from being completely idle.

I get a *GetHostName()* error message, when I try to connect to a reflector using CU-SeeMe.

Setting up the software and hardware for video conferencing on your PC is really quite easy. Both the Cornell and White Pine versions of CU-SeeMe (the most commonly used video conferencing software) provide you with automatic installations. Make sure that you install your camera hardware and the software drivers for the camera before you install the CU-SeeMe software. CU-SeeMe automatically detects the camera drivers that are installed on your PC and sets them up as the default for video conferencing.

One of the most commonly experienced problems related to CU-SeeMe video conferencing is the GetHostName error message, which is related to the IP address that you are assigned by your service provider. When you log on to your service provider's computer you are assigned an internet protocol (IP for short) address. This IP address consists of four numbers that are separated by periods; an example would be 228.74.88.2. In most cases your service provider will "own" a series of IP addresses. When you log on to your service, you are assigned one of the IP addresses randomly.

When you attempt to connect to a reflector using the CU-SeeMe software, the reflector expects to be able to identify your computer by a name and an IP address. However, if your service provider assigns IP addresses randomly, there is not an IP address that relates directly to your and your computer. Unable to identify you, the reflector returns the GetHostName() error and does not connect you to reflector.

A fairly easy-to-apply fix has been developed to get around the fact that you are not assigned a permanent IP number. By creating a text file called HOSTS. (the file name must end with the period delimiter) you can fool the reflector into thinking that you have an IP number all your own. The HOSTS. file, which will actually contain a range of possible IP addresses (the range is based on the IP addresses used by your service provider), is placed in your Windows directory.

To generate the HOSTS file all you have to do is connect to your service provider and check what IP address you've been assigned. You can do this by starting the CU-SeeMe software. Your IP address will appear in the CU-SeeMe command window. Once you know your current IP address use your Web browser to go to the Cornell CU-SeeMe page on the Web at **http://cu-seeme.cornell.edu/~WCW/.** On this page are directions to download a program called MAKEHOST.COM. This freeware software can be used to generate your own HOSTS. file using the IP address that you are currently assigned. Once the GetHostName()error is overcome using the HOSTS. file, you should be able to connect to any of the reflectors listed in the CU-SeeMe software phone book.

I have a color video camera but it doesn't seem to work with CU-SeeMe.

The first thing that you should check is which CU-SeeMe software version you are using. The White Pine version of CU-SeeMe (Enhanced CU-SeeMe version 2.1) supports color. If you are getting a grayscale image in your video box when you start the Enhanced CU-SeeMe software, you may only need to select the appropriate video compression codec (the video protocol for the software) to send color video. To check the current codec select the Edit menu and then select **Preferences**. A drop down box in the Video tab of the Preferences dialog box allows you to select the grayscale codec or the enhanced color codec.

Unfortunately, users of the Cornell freeware version of CU-SeeMe will not be able to see your video. If you get a message from another user that your video window is blank, it may be due to their choice of CU-SeeMe version.

PART 4

Handy References

I n this final part of the book, you'll find a handy reference section of items to help you use the Internet. For example, if you need help looking for an IRC chat server to access Internet chat, turn to "IRC Chat Servers" on page 444. You'll also find other tables in this part of the book that include lists of Internet service providers and their phone numbers, the top World Wide Web pages to view, famous Internet addresses, and more.

You can use this reference section when you need to look up a particular item, or when you need to find out what a specific Internet emoticon means.

What You Will Find in This Part

List of Service Providers

The first step to accessing the Internet is finding a connection. Unless you're directly connected, you'll need to use a service provider for Internet access. There are thousands of companies across the country that sell access to the information superhighway using their own Internet connections. Look in computer magazines and your local yellow pages for a service provider near you.

To help you begin, the following list displays the names of a few vendors you can contact for more information about Internet accounts. Many of them also offer local access numbers you can use to connect to the Internet so you won't have to incur long distance charges.

Service Provider	Voice Phone Number
aaaa.net	800-611-6044
All West Communications	888-292-6381
AT&T WorldNet Service	800-worldnet
Camelot Internet Access Services	800-442-7120
Circle Net, Inc.	800-321-2237
Delphi	800-695-4005
EarthLink Network	800-395-8425
Hypercon	800-652-2590
InfiNet Company	800-849-7214
Imagine Communications Corp.	800-542-4499
InternetMCI	800-550-0927
NETCOM	800-NETCOM1
NovaLink Interactive Networks	800-274-2814
NTC's Earthlink.Net	800-359-8425
Questar Microsystems, Inc.	800-925-2140
I-2000	800-464-3820

IRC Chat Servers

In order to use IRC chat, you must first log on to an IRC chat server. IRC servers are connected to a network that allows various users from all over the world to log on and carry on conversations. There are several different IRC networks you can connect to, as well as a variety of servers. The following list includes chat servers from different IRC networks. Keep in mind that not all servers will accept everyone who tries to log on. Sometimes there are restrictions, such as the number of users or the specific domains that are allowed to connect. Servers also come and go, even though many of them are at educational institutions. For the most up-to-date list of IRC servers go to **http://www.irchelp.org/**—the EFnet #IRChelp help archive on the World Wide Web. This site keeps an updated list of IRC servers.

IRC Chat Servers in the U.S.

irc.escape.com	irc-2.mit.edu
irc.texas.net	anarchy.tamu.edu
irc-2.texas.net	eff.org
irc.colorado.edu	irc.cerf.net
irc.ilstu.edu	irc.gate.net
irc.iastate.edu	irc.catt.ncsu.edu
irc.harvard.edu	irc.eskimo.com
droopy.colorado.edu	nitro.decade.net
cs-pub.bu.edu	azure.acsu.buffalo.edu
backer1.u.washington.edu	dewey.cc.utexas.edu
irc.ime.net	irc.digex.net
irc.cs.rpi.edu	irc.caltech.edu
irc.bridge.net	irc.apk.net
irc.indiana.edu	irc.ksu.edu
copper.ucs.indiana.edu	irc.uiuc.edu
irc.ecn.bgu.edu	t8.mscf.uky.edu
world.std.com	pegasus.ccs.itd.umich.edu
irc.ucsd.edu	irc.ucdavis.edu
w6yx.stanford.edu	harp.aix.calpoly.edu
irc.netcom.com	irc.primenet.com
irc.HACKS.Arizona.EDU	merlin.acf-lab.alaska.edu

IRC Chat Servers in the U.S.	
irc.tc.umn.edu	sluaxa.slu.edu
hertz.njit.edu	irc.rutgers.edu
organ.ctr.columbia.edu	alfred1.u.washington.edu
irc02.irc.aol.com	irc.math.byu.edu
acme.etsu.edu	irc.pitt.edu
chestnut.chem.upenn.edu	mcnet02.med.nyu.edu
norman.ok.us.undernet.org	austin.tx.us.undernet.org
davis.ca.us.undernet.org	boston.ma.us.undernet.org
manhattan.ks.us.undernet.org	washington.dc.us.undernet.org
sanjose.ca.us.undernet.org	stgeorge.ut.us.undernet.org
rochester.mi.us.undernet.org	tampa.fl.us.undernet.org
irc.ucdavis.edu	groucho.sonoma.edu
blackstone-36.rh.uchicago.edu	moe.bu.edu
unccsun.uncc.edu	ca.us.iao.net
de.eu.iao.net	tn.us.iao.net
fl.us.iao.net	mi.us.iao.net
ny.us.iao.net	va.sura.ideal.net
tx.sprint.ideal.net	nd.nw.ideal.net
il.ans.ideal.net	ca.barr.ideal.net
ny.sprint.ideal.net	ca2.barr.ideal.net
ny2.sprint.ideal.net	tn.surs.ideal.net
nasa.ideal.net	tn2.sura.ideal.net

Internet Emoticons and Acronyms

Emoticons, or smileys, are symbols used in Internet communications to express emotions or convey facial expressions. Emoticons are often used on the IRC chat channels, among newsgroup messages, and in Internet e-mail. Emoticons are created using symbols on your keyboard keys. For example, a simple smiley :) consists of a colon and a right parenthesis. You read emoticons by tilting your head to the left.

The following table lists the various types of emoticons you can use in your own Internet messages.

Emoticons

Emoticon Symbol	What It Means	Emoticon Symbol	What It Means
:)	a smile, happy	:-)	a smiley with a nose (nose dash is optional for any smiley symbol)
;)	a wink	:(	a frown
:-<	really sad	:->	devious smile
>:-(	someone mad or annoyed	:-c	bummed out, pouting
:-l	grim	:-/	skeptical
:-o	shouting	:-O	shouting loudly
:-D	laughing	:-p	sticking out tongue
:-&	tongue-tied	:-*	puckering for a kiss
:-x	my lips are sealed	l-o	yawning
l^o	snoring	l-l	asleep
X-(	dead	:*)	drunk
#-(	hung over	:-()	big mouth
:-)~~~	drooling	:~(	crying
8-)	wearing glasses	B-)	wearing cool shades
%-)	I've been staring at this screen too long	:-{)	I have a mustache
{(:-)	wearing a toupee	=l:-)	wearing a top hat
*<:-()	I'm Santa Claus	C=:-)	I'm a chef
0:-)	an angel	xxooxxoo	love, or hugs and kisses
@>--,--'--	a rose	<g>	grin

Aside from emoticons, Internet communications also include acronyms and abbreviations that work like online shorthand. They're used to speed up typing, and you'll find them sprinkled among Internet e-mail, newsgroups, and chat channels. They can be used with all capital letters, or all lowercase letters.

Acronyms

Acronym	Meaning	Acronym	Meaning
AAMOF	as a matter of fact	AFAIK	as far as I know
AKA	also known as	AOL	America Online
AFK	away from keyboard	BAK	back at keyboard
BBS	bulletin board system	BBL	be back later
BIF	basis in fact	BRB	be right back
BTW	by the way	CIS	CompuServe Information Service
CU	see you	CUL	see you later
DIIK	darned if I know	DL	download
FAQ	frequently asked question	FOAF	friend of a friend
FOTCL	falling off the chair laughing	FWIW	for what it's worth
FTF	face to face	FYA	for your amusement
FYI	for your information	GMTA	great minds think alike
GR&D	grinning, running, and ducking	HHOJ	ha ha, only joking
HHOK	ha ha, only kidding	HHOS	ha ha, only serious
IAC	in any case	IAE	in any event
IANAL	I am not a lawyer	IMO	in my opinion
IMHO	in my humble opinion	IMNSHO	in my not-so-humble opinion
IMAO	in my arrogant opinion	IOW	in other words
LOL	laughing out loud	LOLSCOK	laughing out loud, spitting coffee on keyboard
LTNS	long time no see	LTNT	long time no type
L8R	later	MEGO	my eyes glaze over

(continues)

(continued)

Acronym	Meaning	Acronym	Meaning
MOTAS	member of the appropriate sex	MOTD	message of the day
MOTOS	member of the opposite sex	MOTSS	member of the same sex
NBIF	no basis in fact	NBD	no big deal
NRN	no response necessary	OIC	oh, I see
OTB	off to bed	OTOH	on the other hand
OTW	on the way	PITA	pain in the a**
PMJI	pardon my jumping in	PC	politically correct, or personal computer
PI or PIC	politically incorrect	POV	point of view
RL	real life	ROFL	rolling on the floor, laughing
ROFLOLPIMP	rolling on the floor, laughing out loud, peeing in my pants	RSN	real soon now
RTM	read the manual	RTFM	read the #*@!#@* manual
SIFOTCN	sitting in front of the computer naked	SITD	still in the dark
SO	significant other	SOS	same old stuff
SYSOP	system operator		
TANSTAAFL	there ain't no such thing as a free lunch	TIA	thanks in advance
TIC	tongue in cheek	TM	trademark
TPTB	the powers that be	TTFN	ta-ta for now
TTYL	talk to you later	UL	upload
WB	welcome back	WTG	way to go
WTH	what the heck (or h***)	YMMV	your mileage may vary
unPC	politically incorrect		

Interesting Internet E-Mail Addresses

With the potential to e-mail messages all over the globe, it's sometimes fun to target specific people and places. The following table lists some or the more interesting ways you can use e-mail on the Internet, as well as very important people you can contact electronically.

Service/Person	Address/Details
President of United States of America	**president@whitehouse.gov**, and then fill in your e-mail message
Vice President of the United States of America	**vice.president@whitehouse.gov** and fill in your e-mail message
To find your congressman's e-mail address, use this address to receive a list of all congressional e-mail addresses	**congress@hr.house.gov**, then leave the subject line and message body blank
To find White House-related documents, use this address	**publications@whitehouse.gov**, leave the subject line blank, type **help** in the message body
To have a WWW page sent to your electronic mailbox, try this address procedure	**listproc@www0.cern.ch**, leave the subject line blank, but specify the page's URL in the message body (for example, send **http://www.netwave.net/wave_reviews/**)
To have David Letterman's latest Top Ten list e-mailed to you, use this address	**infobot@infomania.com**, then type **topten** in the subject line
To look up word definitions, use this address	**infobot@infomania.com**, then type **webster** and the word you're looking up, and leave the message body blank
E-mail yourself a word puzzle from the WordSmith wordserver at Case Western Reserve University	**wsmith@wordsmith.org**, type **rhyme-n-reason** in the subject line, and leave the message body blank
To subscribe to the WordSmith's A.Word.A.Day mailing list, use this address	**wsmith@wordsmith.org**, type **subscribe yourname**, leave the message body blank
For a quick quote from a famous person, contact the Almanac Information Server	**almanac@oes.orst.edu**, leave the subject line blank, type **send quote** in the message body

(continues)

(continued)

Service/Person	Address/Details
OLYMPUCK is an e-mail list service dedicated to olympic hockey	**listserv@maine.maine.edu**, type **subscribe** in the message body
E-mail yourself recent stock quotes from QuoteCom	**services@quote.com**, type **help** in the subject line, leave the message body blank
The OnVideo E-Mail Newsletter provides you with lists and reviews of the latest theatrical films out on video	**onvideo@cyberpod.com**, type **subscribe** in the body of the e-mail
For a list of electronic magazines on the Net, use this address to get a copy of The Internet Press	**ipress-request@northcoast.com**, type **send ipress** in the message body
If you like astronomy try this e-mail address	**majordomo@mindspring.com**, type **subscribe astro** in the message body
Business entrepreneurs can get a free trial copy of *Innovation*, a publication about business innovations, trends, and other strategies	**innovation-request@NewsScan.com** leave the subject line blank, type **subscribe** in the message body
For a list of wacky weekly news stories, contact Randy Cassingham's weekly newsletter	**listserv@netcom.com**, leave the subject line blank, type **subscribe this-just-in** in the message body

FTP Servers

When searching for information and files on the Internet, you'll need to know some popular FTP servers to start out with. The table below lists 14 popular FTP sites that you can try. For each site listed, log on as an anonymous user, and use your own e-mail address.

Site	FTP
University of Michigan's Electronic Texts Archive	etext.archive.umich.edu
Washington University's Archives	wuarchive.wustl.edu
Rutgers University's FTP Archives	quartz.rutgers.edu
The Bloom-Picayune FTP Server at MIT	rtfm.mit.edu
Library of Congress Archives	seq1.loc.gov

Site	FTP
UUNET Archives	ftp.uu.net
Princeton University's FTP Server	princeton.edu
University of Michigan's Software Archives	archive.umich.edu
The Typhoon FTP Server at Berkeley	ocf.berkeley.edu
Sunsite's FTP Server	sunsite.unc.edu
Netcom FTP Server	ftp.netcom.com
Mississippi State Archives	ra.msstate.edu
The Gatekeeper Archives	gatekeeper.dec.com
The Oak Software Repository	oak.oakland.edu
Netscape	ftp1.netscape.com (Netscape has eight ftp servers, change the # after ftp to connect)
Microsoft	ftp1.microsoft.com (microsoft offers three servers, change the # after ftp to connect)

101 Best Places to Visit on the Net

The Internet is chock-full of interesting places to visit, and the following list describes a few that you might try. They range in interest and in seriousness, so have some fun, too.

Description	Site
Microsoft junkies will find lots to appease them at Microsoft's WWW site, including technical support, product information, freeware, and even Bill Gates' keynote speeches.	http://www.microsoft.com
To keep on top of the latest Internet browser programs, tap into the BrowserWatch site for an up-to-date look at the major browsers, sites where you can get the programs, and news about up-and-coming browsers.	http://www.browserwatch.com/

(continues)

(continued)

Description	Site
The Netscape home page is full of information, including the latest versions of Netscape Navigator, lists of other cool sites, and Internet directories.	http://home.netscape.com
If you're interested in all things Web-related, then you should definitely check out the Silicon Graphics page. It has dazzling art, along with Web authoring and serving software, including freeware.	http://www.sgi.com
You'll find some interesting photography on Quang-Tuan Luong's Web page, plus photo tips for photography enthusiasts.	http://www.cs.berkeley.edu/ ~qtluong/photography/
To find your favorite music CD or the latest music industry gossip, turn to CDNow. It offers over 165,000 CD titles you can purchase, plus music news.	http://cdnow.com
Post free classified ads on the Web at Fun City Classifieds. If you're looking to buy or looking to sell, you'll find plenty of ads for all kinds of items. It's tons of fun for bargain and treasure hunters.	http://www.funcity.com/ads/
"Shop-aholics" will find all kinds of thrills with the Internet Shopping Network. Like the home shopping shows on cable TV, the Internet Shopping Network lets you buy everything from flowers and jewelry to computer software and hardware.	http://www.internet.net
If you're at all curious about the CIA, check out the Central Intelligence Agency site, which includes a virtual tour of the facility in Washington D.C., collections of maps, and CIA publications.	http://www.odci.gov/cia
NASA fans can find the latest information about shuttle flights, video and sound files, and even a real-time Mercator tracking map to view the mission.	http://shuttle.nasa.gov

Description	Site
If you like *MTV's Real World* soap opera show, you'll love The Spot on the Internet. It's an episodic virtual soap opera following the lives of six inhabitants of a Santa Monica beach house.	http://www.thespot.com/
If you don't like The Spot, then visit its evil twin, The Squat. It's a parody of the MTV-like phenomena, except it takes place in a trailer park instead of a hip California beac4¡ñouse.	http://theory.physics. missouri.edu/~georges/Josh/squat/
Have an Internet hangover that has you craving Java? This site will link you to some of the best Java pages on the Web.	http://.gamelan.com
If you're trying to figure out what Web sites to visit, you might want to stop at Point Communication's Top Sites page. It lists ratings of Web sites, based on content, presentation, and number of visits (popularity).	http://www.pointcom.com/gifs/topsites/
If you subscribe to cable TV's Discovery Channel, you already know what a great source it is for nature and science programs, among others. Tune in to the Discovery site for the same great information.	http://www.discovery.com
Another great TV-related Web page is the Sci-Fi Channel's Dominion page. You'll find video and sound clips, information about programming, and even interactive polling.	http://www.scifi.com/
Not sure about where you came from or where you're going? This site, Family TreeMaker, will at least help you put together a family tree. Hopefully you won't have to go out on a limb to get it done.	http://www.familytreemaker.com

(continues)

(continued)

Description	Site
Kids going to college soon? Visit the Financial Aid Information page for some tips and links to useful information about college loans, scholarships, and more.	http://www.finaid.org/
For the hippest fashions, surf over to the Product page. You'll find a collection of wild New York and L.A. fashion items, ranging from python leather to Mongolian faux fur.	http://www.ProductNet.com
If you need the complete works of Shakespeare, this Web page should be your first stop. It includes a hypertext glossary for looking up those old-fashioned Elizabethan words.	http://the-tech.mit.edu/Shakespeare/works.html
The renowned Old Sturbridge Village Museum in Massachusetts now offers a virtual tour of the facility, including a gift shop.	http://www.osv.org
Ever wonder what's in a Hostess Twinkie? You're not alone, and you can find out the latest test results on the T.W.I.N.K.I.E.S. Project page, including how the cream-filled snacks hold up to radiation tests.	http://www.owlnet.rice.edu/~gouge/twinkies.html
Learn how to prepare for emergencies on the Epicenter: Emergency Preparedness Information Center page. It includes tips for dealing with emergencies such as earthquakes and bombings, plus dozens of links to related sites.	http://nwlink.com/epicenter/links.html
Wired magazine has a great Web site to explore, called HotWired. You'll find back issues of the magazine and all kinds of hip computer information.	http://www.hotwired.com/
Another great electronic 'zine (magazine) to check out is Urban Desires, a collection of metropolitan passions such as book reviews, art, and interviews with celebrities.	http://desires.com/issues.html

Description	Site
Learn everything you want to know about wolves on the Wolf Haven Web site. You can even "adopt" a wolf on the preserve.	http://www.teleport.com/~wnorton/wolf.html
You don't have to be a kid to enjoy The Looney Tunes Home Page. It has all your favorite Looney Tunes characters and more.	http://www-personal.usyd.edu.au/~swishart/looney.html
The world's most famous art museum is now accessible through the Internet. Stop and stroll through the galleries of The Louvre in Paris, France. The site offers pictures of the greatest works of art, museum history, and a floor plan of the museum.	http://www.paris.org/Musees/Louvre
If it's heavy sarcasm you're looking for, you'll find it in the electronic magazine, Suck. It's devoted to Web sarcasm and the online phenomena.	http://www.suck.com
For American art, visit The National Museum of American Art site. It has over 1,000 pieces of art to view, plus video tours of the museum.	http://www.nmaa.si.edu:80
For help guiding your children on the Internet, turn to Berit's Best Sites for Children. It has a list of fun and entertaining Net sites for kids, as well as educational stops.	http://www.cochran.com/theodore/noframe/ksites.html
Beatles fans will rejoice at the detailed Beatlemania information on The Internet Beatles Album. It includes a photo gallery of the Fab Four and a screen-saver you can download.	http://www.primenet.com/~dhaber/beatles.html
The Dilbert cartoon strip, a long-time favorite of Internet users, can be found on The Dilbert Zone Web page. It offers a daily dose of Dilbert, plus other Dilbert and Dogbert fun.	http://www.unitedmedia.com/comics/dilbert

(continues)

(continued)

Description	Site
Here's an online version of the ESPN Sports Network, in the form of the ESPNet Sportzone site. It's a great source of sports-related information, team schedules, game recaps, and more.	http://espnet.sportszone.com/
USA Today has a Web page that equals this daily newspaper publication, complete with colorful graphics and zippy photographs.	http://www.usatoday.com
If you're looking for newspapers and news sites around the nation, then stop by the NewsLink site for directions. You'll find over 2,000 links to news sites ranging from national newspapers to college campus papers.	http://www.newslink.org
You can find London's renowned *The Telegraph* newspaper on the Electronic Telegraph Web page. You'll find the standard news, weather, and sports, plus international stories, too.	http://www.telegraph.co.uk/
Pick up your electronic copy of *Time* magazine at the Time Magazine site. You'll find the latest editions, plus late-breaking news.	http://www.pathfinder.com/time
If it's documents you want, then the Library of Congress site is the place to be. With over 70 million documents, you can spend hours wading through text on American history and politics.	http://www.loc.gov
Tour the U.N. building without leaving your chair. Access The United Nations site to learn about U.N. activities and events.	http://www.un.org
If you're shopping for something a little different, try out the Speak To Me! site. It's full of products that use audio, such as talking clocks or teddy bears. You can even sample the sounds before buying anything.	http://clickshop.com

Description	Site
If you're really into news, then you won't want to miss a daily visit to CNN Interactive. The site lets you view the latest stories, search for archived stories, and view videos from the video vault.	http://www.cnn.com
Looking for the latest stock market news? Check out The Wall Street Journal Money and Investing Update site: It has corporate and market news, including information about mutual funds.	http://update.wsj.com/
Good consumers can find information on a variety of topics using the Web site Consumer Information Catalog. You can download all kinds of brochures, and many are free.	http://www.gsa.gov/staff/pa/cic/ cic.htm
If you need to e-mail the FBI, you can do so on The United States Department of Justice site. Here you'll find information about law enforcement agencies and organizations, and a list of the 10 most wanted criminals.	http://www.usdoj.gov/
If you're looking for a city map, try the City Net page. It includes detailed maps and information about cities all over the world. It's a great place for vacation planning.	http://www.city.net
To find a good quote, there's no better place to look than Bartlett's Familiar Quotations. You can use keywords or search for quotes from specific authors.	http://www.cc.columbia.edu/acis/bartleby/ bartlett
Look at the online magazine, Hype, for amazing graphics. You'll also find sound files, links to other graphical sites, and more.	http://www.phantom.com/~giant/ hype.html
Computer-art lovers should stop by Joseph Squier's Web site and browse the electronic art gallery. The art here has been created just for the Web.	http://gertrude.art.uiuc.edu/ludgate/the/ place/place2.html

(continues)

(continued)

Description	Site
For even more culture, stop by Salvador Dali's Home Page. It's worth the visit.	http://wildsau.idv.uni-linz.ac.at/~chris/Dali/
If fine art isn't for you, perhaps, you'll be interested in something less serious, such as Big Dave's Cow Page. You'll find a tribute to cows of all sorts.	http://www.gl.umbc.edu/~dschmi1/links/cow.html
Crayola Kids magazine has a Web page that's tons of fun. It also sponsors contests, so drop in and see what you can win.	http://www.crayola.com/crayola/crayolakids/home.html
Kids interested in kids' books and the people who author them will find The Big Busy House site very educational. Created by HarperCollins Children's Books, children can log on and meet illustrators and authors, plus learn how books are published.	http://www.harpercollins.com/kids/
Nickelodeon fans of the *Rugrats* cartoon will find lots to interest them on The Rugrats Home Page.	http://www.gti.net/azog/rugrats/
If you want to fall in love, you might try posting an ad on the Web Personals. It has worked for some people, and they've even gone on to marry.	http://www.webpersonals.com/date/
If it's games you want, then check out the Fun and Games at VirtuMall, an online game room for people who like crossword puzzles, Concentration, and other games.	http://virtumall.com/fast/fun_games.html
Open the Crossword Crossroads Web page and print out a crossword puzzle to do, and if it's a tough one, the Web site has links to help you find the answer.	http://www.polar7.com/cc/default.html
If live-action, role-playing games are more your style, then try the Nero Ashbury LARP site. Its role-playing game combines King Arthur-like legends with a Tolkien's *Lord of the Rings* environment.	http://members.aol.com/nerony

Description	Site
The Digital Nostalgia Web site has over 30 vintage video games you can play (IBM format).	http://www.umich.edu/~sloane/games.html
Kids will enjoy Sports Illustrated for Kids Online page. It's an electronic version of the magazine.	http://www.pathfinder.com/SIFK/
The Bible Gateway site lets you view several translations of the *Bible*, in seven languages. The Web page lets you search for words and verses much like an electronic concordance.	http://www.gospelcom.net/bible
For a real taste of global sights and sounds, turn to the RootsWorld page and explore "Real Music for the Real World," which includes everything from bagpipes to drums from India.	http://www.rootsworld.com/rw/
Did you know you can visit the Rock and Roll Hall of Fame on the Internet? You can, and it lets you access information about each inductee, plus sound files, too.	http://www.rockhall.com
For a variety of online items, stop by The Gigaplex page. This site has a Filmplex, Bookplex, Artplex, and many other "plexes" you can enjoy. Each plex has all kinds of information about the topic, plus video and sound clips.	http://www.directnet.com/wow
For the latest scoop about the entertainment business, visit the Mr. Showbiz page. You'll find juicy gossip, news, and reviews about your favorite stars. It's also a good place for celebrity photos.	http://Web3.starwave.com/showbiz
S.P.Q.R.: The Virtual Rome offers visitors something a little unusual—an interactive Web game that taps into ancient Rome, complete with famous Roman architecture. It takes a while to get used to playing, but it's well worth the effort.	http://www.pathfinder.com/@@PhaM2uHPFgAAQJ18/twep/rome/

(continues)

(continued)

Description	Site
There are over 130 government-related electronic bulletin boards you can tap into with the FedWorld Information Network, including boards focusing on space, health care, natural resources, and more.	http://www.fedworld.gov/
For the latest stats on U.S. populations in cities and towns across the country, open The U.S. Census Bureau Web page. You'll also find all kinds of demographics on such topics as leading economic indicators.	http://www.census.gov
There's a digital version of *Roget's Thesaurus*, and you'll find it at the ARTFL Project: ROGET'S Form site. You can look up words and find out what they mean before you use them.	http://humanities.uchicago.edu/forms_unrest/ROGET.html
If you're looking for literature, start with a search of the Internet Public Library Web site. You'll find reference materials, children's books, and even reading rooms.	http://ipl.sils.umich.edu/
If you're a hypochondriac or a medical student, you'll find The Global Health Network has a wonderful collection of health-related sites to explore.	http://www.pitt.edu/HOME/GHNet/GHNet.html
Need to look up a translation of Homer's *Odyssey*? The Tech Classics Archive can help. With over 375 translations of Italian, Greek, and Roman classics, it's a great place to search for ancient works.	http://the-tech.mit.edu/Classics
One of the best Web search tools you can use is the Yahoo! Search site. Simply type in the topic you're looking for, and it compiles a list of related Web sites.	http://yahoo.com/search.html
The World Wide Web Worm is another search engine you can use to find Web pages of interest. It lets you look for specific hypertext links, and it's easy to use.	http://www.cs.colorado.edu/home/mcbryan/WWWW.html

Description	Site
To quickly track down businesses utilizing Web pages, let the Web NetSearch site help you.	http://www.netmail.com/
Want to learn to speak Italian? There's a Web site that can help you, sponsored by Ragu.	http://www.eat.com/learn-italian.html
Having trouble with your grammar? English teacher Jack Lynch has a Web site for all manner of grammar and style notes.	http://www.english.upenn.edu/~jlynch/grammar.html
Music fans can find a compendium of music information, bibliographies, and more at The MIT Music Library. There's also an index of over 17,000 musical recordings.	http://web.mit.edu/afs/athena/dept/libdata/applications/www/depts/music/music-top.html
Memorabilia collectors will find plenty to interest them at the collectible.com site, including old movie posters and celebrity photos.	http://www.collectible.com/
L.L. Bean has a great online catalog to browse, complete with color photos and even a Park Search tool to help you look up information about 900 national parks and forests.	http://www.llbean.com/
Mystery book lovers will enjoy book reviews and author interviews on The Mystery Zone page.	http://www.mindspring.com/~walter/mystzone.html
If you're looking for recipes, subscribe to the alt.food.recipes newsgroup and swap proven recipes with your fellow Internet travelers.	Usenet: alt.food.recipes
If seafood's your passion, then you'll want to sample the catch on The Alaska Seafood Cookbook site. It includes recipes, tips, and more.	http://www.state.ak.us/local/akpages/COMMERCE/ascmain.htm
Chocolate lovers will find the scoop on chocolate facts and fiction on the I Need My Chocolate page. It even includes mouth-watering recipes.	http://www.qrc.com/~sholubek/choco/start.htm

(continues)

(continued)

Description	Site
For even more chocolate focus, stop by the Chocolate Town U.S.A. page for a visit to Hershey's chocolate company. It's packed with chocolate recipes the entire family will drool over.	http://www.hersheys.com/~hershey/
Geologists and map lovers will enjoy the U.S. Geological Survey National Mapping Information site, complete with earth science information, educational information, and many maps.	http://www-nmd.usgs.gov/
Do you watch the popular television show, *Friends*? If you do, then you'll definitely want to visit The Friends Official Web Page. If you ever miss an episode, you can catch up here.	http://www.nbc.com/entertainment/shows/friends/index.html
World famous secret agent 007 has a hit Web site that you must see at least once. It contains great photos, sound files, and even James Bond trivia.	http://www.mcs.net/~klast/www/bond.html
If you're ready to explore the realm of classical music, Classical Net is the place to start. Here, you'll find information about all the world's great classical composers, plus links to other musical sites.	http://www.classical.net/music/
Here's a dazzling page for sports fans; the NBA.com page is not only a clever promotional tool, but full of videos and sound files of basketball's finest players and games.	http://www.nba.com/
Create your own hometown newspaper on the CRAYON page. It's fun and easy.	http://crayon.net/
If you're interested in travel, don't pack your bags until you check out the Travel Channel on the Internet. It's a great source of travel information, as well as pictures from vacation sites around the world.	http://www.travelchannel.com/

Description	Site
If it's e-mail you want, then it's e-mail you shall have, if you search the LISTSERV Archives. You can look for topics alphabetically and learn how to launch your own listserv database.	Internet: gopher sjuvm.stjohns.edu select **disabled, listserv**
America's Job Bank site offers the employment-challenged access to thousands of jobs across the country. If you're serious about a new job or career change, this is the place to start looking.	http://www.ajb.dni.us/index.html
CareerWEB offers another database source for job opportunities, allowing you to search by job type, company, or location.	http://www.cweb.com/
Crashsite is one of those odd but interesting Web sites you just have to stop and see for yourself. It has Quick-Time movies, animation, and more.	http://www.crashsite.com/Crash
WebMonkey is a great place to get Netscape plug-ins and learn about HTML. It's also a good place to see the latest and greatest in "geekdom."	http://www.webmonkey.com/webmonkey/
Worried that you just don't have anything to wear to that special event? Check out what Mr. Blackwell has to say about the fashion sense of your favorite celebrities.	http://www.mrblackwell.com/

Index

G

U

Complete and Return this Card
for a *FREE* Computer Book Catalog

Thank you for purchasing this book! You have purchased a superior computer book written expressly for your needs. To continue to provide the kind of up-to-date, pertinent coverage you've come to expect from us, we need to hear from you. Please take a minute to complete and return this self-addressed, postage-paid form. In return, we'll send you a free catalog of all our computer books on topics ranging from word processing to programming and the internet.

Mr. ☐   Mrs. ☐   Ms. ☐   Dr. ☐

Name (first) ☐☐☐☐☐☐☐☐☐☐☐☐   (M.I.) ☐   (last) ☐☐☐☐☐☐☐☐☐☐☐☐☐☐☐☐☐

Address ☐☐☐☐☐☐☐☐☐☐☐☐☐☐☐☐☐☐☐☐☐☐☐☐☐☐☐☐☐☐☐☐☐☐

☐☐☐☐☐☐☐☐☐☐☐☐☐☐☐☐☐☐☐☐☐☐☐☐☐☐☐☐☐☐☐☐☐☐

City ☐☐☐☐☐☐☐☐☐☐☐☐☐☐☐☐☐   State ☐☐   Zip ☐☐☐☐☐ ☐☐☐☐

Phone ☐☐☐ ☐☐☐ ☐☐☐☐   Fax ☐☐☐ ☐☐☐ ☐☐☐☐

Company Name ☐☐☐☐☐☐☐☐☐☐☐☐☐☐☐☐☐☐☐☐☐☐☐☐☐☐☐☐☐☐☐☐☐

E-mail address ☐☐☐☐☐☐☐☐☐☐☐☐☐☐☐☐☐☐☐☐☐☐☐☐☐☐☐☐☐☐☐☐☐

1. Please check at least (3) influencing factors for purchasing this book.

Front or back cover information on book .... ☐
Special approach to the content .... ☐
Completeness of content.. ☐
Author's reputation .... ☐
Publisher's reputation .... ☐
Book cover design or layout .... ☐
Index or table of contents of book .... ☐
Price of book.. ☐
Special effects, graphics, illustrations .... ☐
Other (Please specify): _____ ☐

2. How did you first learn about this book?

Saw in Macmillan Computer Publishing catalog .... ☐
Recommended by store personnel .... ☐
Saw the book on bookshelf at store .... ☐
Recommended by a friend... ☐
Received advertisement in the mail .... ☐
Saw an advertisement in: _____ ☐
Read book review in: _____ ☐
Other (Please specify): _____ ☐

3. How many computer books have you purchased in the last six months?

This book only .... ☐   3 to 5 books .... ☐
2 books.................. ☐   More than 5 .... ☐

4. Where did you purchase this book?

Bookstore .... ☐
Computer Store .... ☐
Consumer Electronics Store .... ☐
Department Store .... ☐
Office Club .... ☐
Warehouse Club .... ☐
Mail Order .... ☐
Direct from Publisher .... ☐
Internet site .... ☐
Other (Please specify): _____ ☐

5. How long have you been using a computer?

☐ Less than 6 months   ☐ 6 months to a year
☐ 1 to 3 years   ☐ More than 3 years

6. What is your level of experience with personal computers and with the subject of this book?

	With PCs	With subject of book
New	☐	☐
Casual	☐	☐
Accomplished	☐	☐
Expert	☐	☐

7. Which of the following best describes your job title?

Administrative Assistant .... ☐
Coordinator .... ☐
Manager/Supervisor .... ☐
Director .... ☐
Vice President .... ☐
President/CEO/COO .... ☐
Lawyer/Doctor/Medical Professional .... ☐
Teacher/Educator/Trainer .... ☐
Engineer/Technician .... ☐
Consultant .... ☐
Not employed/Student/Retired .... ☐
Other (Please specify): _____ ☐

8. Which of the following best describes the area of the company your job title falls under?

Accounting .... ☐
Engineering .... ☐
Manufacturing .... ☐
Operations .... ☐
Marketing .... ☐
Sales .... ☐
Other (Please specify): _____ ☐

9. What is your age?

Under 20 .... ☐
21-29 .... ☐
30-39 .... ☐
40-49 .... ☐
50-59 .... ☐
60-over .... ☐

10. Are you:

Male .... ☐
Female .... ☐

11. Which computer publications do you read regularly? (Please list)

_____
_____
_____
_____
_____
_____
_____
_____
_____

Comments: _____
_____
_____

Fold here and scotch-tape to mail.

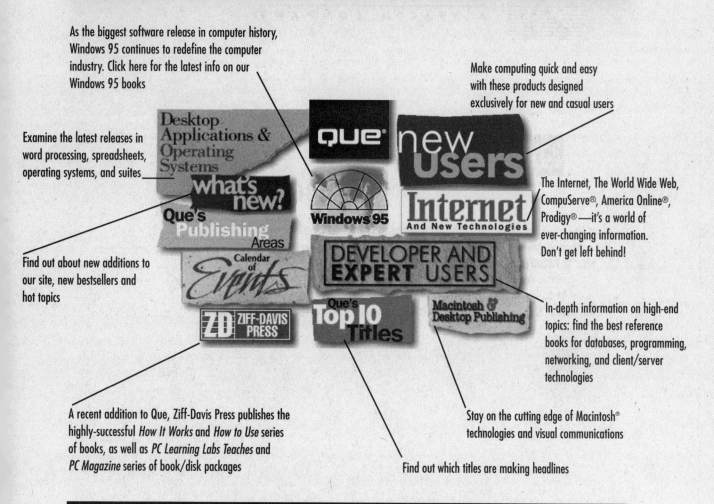
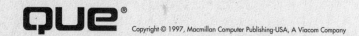

MACMILLAN COMPUTER PUBLISHING USA

A VIACOM COMPANY

Technical Support:

If you need assistance with the information in this book or with a CD/Disk accompanying the book, please access the Knowledge Base on our Web site at **http://www.superlibrary.com/general/support**. Our most Frequently Asked Questions are answered there. If you do not find the answer to your questions on our Web site, you may contact Macmillan Technical Support **(317) 581-3833** or e-mail us at **support@mcp.com**.